We, the Women of Hawaii

COOKBOOK

FAVORITE RECIPES OF PROMINENT WOMEN OF HAWAII

PRESS PACIFICA

Revised edition 1986

ISBN 0-916630-47-1

Published for We the Women of Hawaii by Press Pacifica.

Manufactured by Kingsport Press, Kingsport, Tennessee.

Available from:
 Pacific Trade Group, P.O. Box 668, Pearl City, HI, 96782.

To We, The Women of Hawaii —

May I wish you my congratulations and the very best of success with "WE, THE WOMEN OF HAWAII COOKBOOK". Your motto, "There is nothing a woman can not do, once she makes up her mind" is so aptly exemplified in this, your first cookbook effort. I hope this is the first of many.

Nino J. Martin
The International Chef

The Front Cover was designed by Artist Sunny Aigner Pauole. She has studied at the Art Center in California and The Honolulu Academy of Art. A resident of Oahu since 1975, Sunny has been greatly influenced by the islands in her paintings, prints and murals.

We,·the·Women·of·Hawaii

CHAPTER MEMBERS

July 26, 1946, a general utility strike was threatened in Honolulu. A spontaneous group of women "sparked" by Mrs. E. E. Black, held a series of mass meetings to protest the strike, saying, "There is nothing a woman can not do, once she makes up her mind." From resolution starting — "We, The Women of Hawaii" our name was born. In January 1947 we were organized as a "Club."

Black, Mrs, E.E. (Ruth) — deceased
Boyd, Mrs. Gladys K. — deceased
Buffet, Mrs, Helene (C.)
Carter, Mrs. Margaret E, (F.)
Clark, Mrs. Verna (G.W.)
Crossley, Mrs, Randolph
Darrow, Mrs. Esther (D.F. — deceased)
Harrison, Mrs, Thelma Akana — deceased
Robinson, Mrs. Mary K. (D.F.) — deceased
Schleif, Miss Rose Louise — deceased
Smith, Mrs. Clara — deceased
Smythe, Mrs, Oriet (R.)
Wills, Mrs. Jessie F. (C.M.) — deceased

IN CHRONOLOGICAL ORDER OF PRESIDENCY

1.	Clark, Mrs, Verna	1947–1949.
2.	Robinson, Mrs. Mary K. (M.A.) – deceased.	1949–1950.
3.	Black, Mrs. (E.E.) – deceased	1950–1953.
4.	Zinke, Mrs. Lou P. Shane	1953–1955.
5.	Birtley, Mrs. Pauline (T.B.)	1955–1957
6.	Tuttle, Mrs. Dorothy (W.W.)	1957–1961.
7.	Henderson, Mrs, Monica (M.)	1961–1963.
8.	Lyle, Mrs. Dorothy (W.G.)	1963–1965.
9.	Kim. Mrs. Vale (V.) – deceased	1965–1968.
10.	Weamer, Mrs. June (V.)	1968–1971.
11.	Steward, Mrs. Mary B. (4 months)	1971–
12.	Weamer, Mrs. June (V.)	1971–1972.
13.	Capellas, Mrs. Bonnie (D.) Resigned 9/2/74.	1972–1974.
14.	Kim. Mrs, Vale (S.) – deceased 9/2/74 – 6/17/75.	1974–1975.
15.	Capellas, Mrs. Bonnie (D.)	1975–1977.
16.	Guy, Mrs. Elizabeth D.	1977–1979.
17.	Tuttle, Mrs. Dorothy (W.W.)	1979–1981.
18.	Guy, Mrs. Elizabeth D.	1981–

CONTRIBUTORS

Ariyoshi, Jean

Akaka, Millie

Anderson, Eileen

Becker, Merle

Box Gladys

Burnett, Barol

Christoph, Ida

Dixon, Rebecca

Do, Charlene

Ebsen, Nancy

Goderre, Lucille

Hambley, Anna

Holmes, Col. Margaret

Howard, Liz

Katz, Iram

Krause, Bonnie

Loo, Marian

Lyle, Dorothy

Mesaku, Millie

Mink, Patsy

Nelson, Ruth

Pieklo, Judy

Quirk, Noreen

Riley, Linda

Spencer, Caroline

Stanley, Kate

Tungapalan, Eloise Yamashito

Alexander, Daisy

Barry, Betty

Bornhorst, Maryiln

Burger, Lorna

Chateauneuf, Roberta

Chunn, Connie

Do, Billie

Ebsen, Annie

George, Mary

Grimes, Lucille

Heftel, Joyce

Holland, Allison

Inouye, Maggie

Kobayashi, Ann

Lindquist, Freda

Lyle, Col. Jean

Matsuda, Fujia (Amy)

Meyers, Irma

Nelson, Ingrid

Occie, Aunt

Post, June

Richman, Nathalia

Sevey, Mrs. Bob

Stanley, Evelyn

Tufte, Ruth

Wright, Arlene

Wright, Francis

CONTRIBUTIONS OF OUR MEMBERS

Adams, Bessie

Awbrey, Faye

Bekken, Sylvia

Beyer, Dora

Carmody, Roma

Daughters, Maude

Doyle, Virginia

Gomes, Mae

Harmas, Velma

Hemings, Sarah

Keys, Jean

Luis, Zana

O'Brien, Nancy

Reiner, Rosella

Swope, Jean

Upchurch, Mary

Wilson, Valeria

Alvedo, Flora

Beasley, Georgia

Berg, Evelyn

Buchanan, Annette

Coscino, Rennee

Davis, Adele

Edmondson, Elinor

Guy, Elizabeth, (Betty)

Harper, Opal

Kann, Lillian

Kirschbaum, Ebba

Morrison, Dorothy

Pimental, Irene

Ryan, Madeline

Tuttle, Dorothy

Walters, Jean

Wong, Marie.

The collection of recipes for our Cookbook is the response from our Friends and Members. Submitted are "Family Favorites" and a great variety of recipes of our Ethnic Culture. In our Paradise, through the blending of our Nationalities, we are very fortunate to be able to obtain the proper ingredients for our recipes.

We especially want to thank our "Prominent Women of Hawaii," who have taken time from their busy schedules to present their contributions.

Mahalo.

We, the Woman of Hawaii.
Jean Keys — Adele Davis. Editors.

CHAPTERS

B·E·V·E·R·A·G·E·S

* MAUI ICED TEA *

2 Qts. med. strong tea
8 limes (juice)
5 oranges (juice)

1 c. pineapple juice
½ c. guava juice
Sugar to taste

Steep some mint in hot water 3—5 min. Combine all ingredients. Cool then chill.
Serve with pieces of pineapple in tall glasses.   Jean Keys.

* SPARKLING ICED TEA PUNCH *

8 tea bags
4 sprigs of mint
4 c. boiling water
½ c. sugar

½ c. lemon juice
1—28 oz. carbonated water
ice.

Steep tea bags and mint leaves in boiling water for 5 min. Discard bags and leaves.
Add sugar to tea; stir until dissolved. Stir in lemon juice. Chill. Pour into punch
bowl or 1 gal. pitcher. Slowly add carbonated water and ice.   Adele Davis.

* REAL LEMONADE *

Prepare syrup; In a 1 qt. jar with tight lid, shake 1-½ c. sugar with 1 Tbsp. grated
lemon peel and 1-½ c. very hot water. Be sure sugar is dissolved. Add 1½ c. lemon
juice. Refrigerate. Pour over ice cubes in 12 oz. glasses, pour in ¼ c. syrup. Stir
in ¾ c. cold water.   Jean Keys.

* RASPBERRY PUNCH *

1 pt. raspberry sherbet
2 c. apple juice
2 c. water
1 c. sugar

1 c. lemon juice
1—10 oz. pkg. frozen
    raspberries
1 qt. ginger ale

Spoon sherbet into punch bowl. Combine apple juice, water, sugar, and lemon
juice; stir until sugar dissolves. Add raspberries; stir until raspberries separate.
Stir into sherbet in bowl. Slowly add the ginger ale.   Adele Davis.

* LILIKOI BASE FOR DRINKS *

4 c. water
6 c. sugar

2 c. liliko juice

Heat to boiling to dissolve sugar.
Add 2 c. Lilikoi juice and refrigerate.
Pour into tall glasses (about 1/3 full) then add ice and water, cherry and mint.
                                                                   Jean Keys.

1

* PARTY PUNCH *

1 can each — frozen lime, orange and lemon concentrate. (12 oz.)
1 can Hawaiian punch. (12 oz.)
Dilute concentrate juices lightly. Add Hawaiian punch.
Add Ginger ale or seven-up to taste. Chill.
Freeze fresh mint leaves in ice cubes.
Serve in tall glasses with 1 semi-circle of pineapple (slip to impale on edge of glass or fresh strawberry with leaf on). Use plastic colored straws to accent the garnish.
Opal Harper.

* COFFEE PUNCH FOR A PARTY *

In a large bowl combine 2 qts. cold strong coffee with 2 c. milk, ½ c. sugar, 2 tsp. vanilla and stir until sugar is dissolved. Chill thoroughly. Just before serving pour the chilled mixture over 1 qt. vanilla ice cream in punch bowl. Top with 1 c. heavy cream (whipped) and sprinkle with nutmeg. Makes 15—18 servings.
Jean Keys.

* KAHLUA *

4 c. sugar and 4 c. water-Boil ten minutes to make simple syrup.
Add ¾ c. instant coffee mixed with ½ c. water.
Cool syrup and add one vanilla bean (cut in pieces).
Add a Fifth of Vodka or Brandy.
Put in a jug and shake daily for three weeks, then bottle.
Velma Harmas.

* MULLED WINE *

¾ c. water	1 tsp. whole cloves
¾ c. sugar	2 c. Burgundy wine
6 cinnamon sticks	1 qt. Cranberry juice
dash of salt	

Bring to boil the first five ingredients, simmer for 10 minute. Cool, then add wine and cranberry juice. Pour into jars or into a punch bowl, ice well.
This is a mild, tasty and delicious drink. I make it for Christmas gifts in fancy bottles.
Jean Keys.

* JEAN KEY'S MAI-TAI*

1—½ oz. Light Rum	1 oz. lemon juice
1—½ oz. Gold Rum	¼ oz. Orange Curacao
1 oz. Trader Vic's orgeat syrup.	Combine ingredients

Float 1 Tbsp. dark Rum on top, stir and pour into glasses, filled with crushed ice. Garnish with slice of pineapple and mint, cherry or orange slices.

* HOLIDAY EGGNOG *

2 eggs (separated)
1—4 serving pkg. instant vanilla
    pudding mix.
5-½ c. milk

¼ c. sugar
1 tso. vanilla
¼ tsp. ground cloves

Beat egg whites until stiff peaks form. Combine egg yolks and remaining ingredients, beat until smooth. Fold in egg whites. Chill. Pour into glasses, sprinkle with additional nutmeg. SPIKED EGGNOG; Prepare eggnog as above, except use 5 c. milk and add ½ c. Bourbon, Rum or Brandy. Adele Davis.

* LILIKOI SWIPE *

1 Gal. pure Lilikoi juice
10 pounds white sugar
2 pkgs. dry yeast

5 Gal. tap water
1 lg. container 7—7 gal.

Dissolve the yeast in a little water. Stir all ingredients in container. Stir once in AM. and PM. for 5 days. On 6th day strain, then pour into ½ gal. containers; Place caps on without tightening as the brew will still be working. Serve chilled. Makes about 5½ gallons. Jean Keys.

* PUNCH FOR PARTY *

8 lemon lift tea bags (Bigelow)
2 cinnamon tea bags
4 c. water
2-½ c. unsweetened pineapple juice.

3 c. orange soda
2 c. Club soda
1 can. Pineapple tidbits

Mix all together and chill. Georgia Bleasley.

* SOUTHERN CHRISTMAS EGG-NOGG *

½ doz. eggs (separated)
1 pt. *Real* whipping cream
12 Tbsp. sugar

12 Tbsp :- 4 Tbsp. Bourbon
           4 Tbsp. Rum
           4 Tbsp. Grand Marnier

Cream yolks with sugar, add liquors. Whip egg whites, whip cream. Blend all together (whites last). Refrigerate until cold. Grate nutmeg on top. Serve with a spoon. Allison Holland.

* IRISH CREAM *

3 eggs
1 can Eagle Brand milk
½ tsp. (scant) coconut flavoring

1 tsp. vanilla
12 oz. Blended whiskey
2 Tbsp. half and half

Blend. Store in refrigerator. Serve as liqueur. Lucille Goderre.

 **H·O·R·S D'O·U·V·R·E·S**

* CHRISTMAS DIP *

½ lb. ground beef
½ c. chopped onion
1—8 oz. tomato sauce
1-½ tsp. chili powder
½ c. grated cheese
Taco chips

½ tsp. salt
1—8 oz. can pork and beans
   (regular or ranch style)
   mashed
¼ c. chopped black olives

Lightly spray a heavy 10 in. skillet with vegetable cookware spray. or use a non-stick skillet.
Put beef and ¼ c. the onion in the skillet and cook 5 min. over moderately high heat, stirring frequently, until beef is lightly browned. Stir in tomato sauce, chili powder and salt and bring to a simmer. Stir in mashed beans and simmer for 3 to 4 min. to blend flavors.
Turn into a chafing dish and sprinkle with cheese, olives and remaining onions. (Can keep warm for hours.)

* EXOTIC CHEESE DIP *

1—8 oz. pkg. Philadelphia cream cheese
½ c. sour cream
1 pkg. Good Seasons Salad mix.

Blend thoroughly and chill.
Freezes well.   Dorothy Tuttle.

* DILL DIP FOR VEGETABLES *

1—8 oz. pkg. cream cheese
1—8 oz. tub sour cream
1 c. Mayonnaise
Few drops of Worcestershire sauce
2 Tbsp. chopped onion

1 Tbsp. chopped parsley
1 tsp. garlic salt mix
3 tsp. Beau Monde spice
3 tsp. dill weed
1 tsp. lemon juice

Blend cream cheese and sour cream, then mayonnaise, using electric blender. Add other ingredients and blend by hand. Chill overnight and serve with the following:
Bell pepper strips, celery sticks, carrot sticks, zucchini strips, mushroom slices, cherry tomatoes, green onions, broccoli and cauliflower pieces and cucumber slices.   Jean Keys.

* ONION CHEESE DIP *

½ c. dairy sour cream
½ c. Mayonnaise or salad dressing
½ c. Cheese-Wiz (I use a bit more)

1 Tbsp. Liptons onion soup mix
½ tsp. Worcestershire sauce

Beat all until smooth. Serve with vegetables or crackers. Especially good with diagonally cut zucchini.   Dorothy Tuttle.

* CHILI CON QUESO DIP *

1—8 oz. bottle of taco sauce
1—4 oz. can green chili peppers
    (rinsed, seeded and chopped)
1 garlic clove (minced)

2 cups Cheddar or Monterey
    cheese (shredded)
Celery sticks or tortilla chips

In saucepan heat taco sauce, chili peppers and garlic to boiling, reduce heat and simmer for 5 min. Stir in cheese until melted. Transfer to Fondue pot, keep warm. Serve with celery sticks or tortilla chips. (If you prefer your chili fiery, use hot sauce, more subtle use mild sauce.)   Adele Davis.

* GOOD DIP *

1 small can tuna
1 egg hard-boiled (chopped)
1 celery stick (minced)

1 small cream cheese
1 Tbsp. sweet pickle
Mayonnaise to spread

Use with assorted crackers.   Betty Barry.

* CRABMENT DIP FOR CHIPS *

1—8 oz. pkg. cream cheese
½ onion (chopped fine)
1 Tbsp. chives (chopped)

1 can crabmeat (in pieces)
salt to taste
milk to thin

Cream cheese, and milk to desired consistency. Add other ingredients and mix. Chill. Garnish with paprika and chopped chives.   Adele Davis.

* LAZY MANS DIP *

1—8 oz. pkg. cream cheese

1 can Cream of Mushroom soup

Green onion tops (all you feel like slicing into circles.)
Serve with Potato Chips.   Dorothy Tuttle.

* CLAM DIP *

1 garlic clove (crushed
2 cans minced clams (7-½ oz. each)
   drained
2 pkg. 8 oz. cream cheese.

1 tsp. salt
2 tsp. Worcestershire sauce
2 tsp. lemon juice

Combine and chill. Save clam juice to thin dip later when ready to serve.

Jean Keys.

* HOT LOBSTER DIP *

16 oz. cream cheese (softened)
½ c. mayonnaise
1 Tbsp. prepared mustard
1 Tbsp. onion (minced)

1 garlic clove (minced)
¼ c. pale dry Sherry
2 c. crabmeat (fresh or frozen)
   flaked

In a double boiler, heat the cream cheese and mayonnaise. Stir until the cream cheese is melted.

Add the mustard, onion, garlic, sherry and crabmeat. Stir until all ingredients are blended.

Serve hot in Chafing dish.

Adele Davis.

* MEXICAN PUPU DIP *

1 lb. ground round or chuck
1 lb. hot Italian sausage
   (chopped — skin removed)
1 sm. onion (minced)
1 sm. bottle Taco sauce

1 can green chili peppers
   (chopped)
1 can refried beans (med. size.)
Cheddar and Jack cheese
   (grated)

Saute ground meat, sausage and onions. Drain oil. Add chili peppers and Taco sauce. Lay this mixture in a pan or casserole. Spread the refried beans on top of mixture, then the Cheddar and Jack cheeses.

Bake in 350° oven for about 10 to 15 min. until cheese bubbles.

Serve hot as a dip for Tostitos or corn Tortilla chips. If desired, before serving garnish with sliced pitted olives or mashed avocado and lemon juice.

Eileen Anderson.

* POLYNESIAN GINGER DIP *

1 c. mayonnaise
1 c. sour cream
¼ c. chopped onion
¼ c. minced parsley

¼ c. chopped water chestnuts
2–3 Tbsp. chopped candied ginger
2 garlic cloves (minced)
1 Tbsp. shoyu

Mix all together and serve with raw vegetables or sesame wafers.   Ruth Nelson.

* CURRIED SOUR CREAM DIP *

1 c. sour cream
¾ tsp. curry powder

¼ tsp. salt
1 Tbsp. chopped green onion.

Combine ingredients and blend well.

Jean Ariyoshi.

* SPINACH DIP *

1 pkg. frozen spinach (thawed-mois-
    ture pressed out through a sieve)
½ c. sour cream
½ c. mayonnaise
¼ c. chopped
¼ c. chopped parsley

¼ tsp. dill weed
½ tsp. seasoned salt
1 Tbsp. lemon juice
½ clove garlic (minced)
salt—pepper to taste

Mix all ingredients and blend well.

Rebecca Dixon.

* MUSTARD STUFFED EGGS *

Peel and halve 6 hard-cooked eggs. Mash yolks with,
½ c. Bleu cheese
½ c. mayonnaise

¼ c. prepared mustard.

Mix all ingredients and stuff eggs and garnish with piminetos. Note; This is my daughter's recipe.

Dorothy Tuttle.

* FANCY EGG SCRAMBLE *

1 c. (4 oz.) diced ham, bacon, or
    Canadian bacon
¼ c. chopped green onions
3 Tbsp. butter or oleo
12 beaten eggs
1 can (3 oz.) mushrooms (drained)

2-¼ c. soft bread crumbs
    (3 slices of bread)
1/8 tsp. paprika
* 1 recipe for the Cheese Sauce.

In a large skillet cook bacon and onion in the butter or oleo. Until onion is tender but not browned. Add eggs and scramble until just set. Fold in mushrooms and cooked eggs into the cheese sauce. Turn into a 12 x 7 x 2 baking dish. Combine remaining butter, crumbs and paprika. Sprinkle on top of eggs. Cover and chill until 30 min. before serving. Bake uncovered for 30 min. at 350°. Cheese Sauce:

Melt 2 Tbsp. butter or oleo, blended in 2 Tbsp. flour, ½ tsp salt, 1/8 tsp. pepper. Add 2 c. milk. Cook and stir until bubbly. Stir in 1 c. (4 oz.) shredded processed American cheese till melted. Can also use Cracker Barrel sharp Cheddar cheese. Double everything to serve 12.

Georgia Bleasley.

* CHICKEN LIVER — BACON PATE *

1 lb. chicken livers	6—8 slices crisp bacon
1-½ c. chicken broth	1/3 c. soft butter or margarine
(or part white wine)	½ tsp. dry mustard
¼ c. chopped onion	¼ tsp. salt
1/8 tsp. rosemary	

Simmer livers in broth with onion and rosemary until tender. Cool in cooking broth that remains. Drain and reserve broth. Put livers and bacon through food chopper using fine blade. (or press through wire strainer). Blend with butter, mustard and salt. (Add a small amount of cooking liquid if a softer pate is desired).

Refrigerate at least 24 hours covered. To mold pack into lightly oiled ring mold. Place into serving dish to unmold and garnish with finely chopped green onions or parsley.   Mary George.

* OLIVE PATE *

2 cans (6—8 oz.) chopped mushrooms	2 cans (10 oz.) liver spread
1 can condensed beef consomme	¼ c. dairy sour cream
1 envelope unflavored gelatin	2 Tbsp. chopped parsley
8 pitted ripe olives	½ tsp. Worcestershire sauce

Combine liquid from mushrooms with consomme and gelatin in a pan, heat, stirring constantly until gelatin is dissolved. Pour ½ c. into a 4 cup mold; chill until as thick as unbeaten egg whites. Slice 2 of the olives and arrange in gelatin in mold to form a pretty pattern, chill again until sticky firm. Beat remaining gelatin mixture with all remaining ingredients until smooth in blender, spoon over layer in mold, chill until firm.

Unmold on a serving platter. Serve with rye bread if you wish.   Mary George.

* PARMESAN ROUNDS *

¾ c. grated Parmesan cheese	2 Tbsp. cold water
½ c. flour	2 Tbsp. sesame seeds
1/8 tsp. cayenne pepper	1 Tbsp. parsley flakes (crumbled)
¼ c. butter or margarine	

Stir together cheese, flour and cayenne. Cut in butter. Sprinkle with water. Shape into a 1-½ wide roll. Roll in sesame seeds and parsley. Refrigerate slightly. Slice ¼ in. thick. Place on ungreased cookie sheet. Bake at 375° for 12—15 min.
                                                    Ingrid Nelson.

* ARTFUL GUACAMOLE *

4 ripe avocados (peeled and mashed)
2 tomatoes (finely shopped)
1 onion (chopped)
2 hard cooked eggs (mashed)

juice of 1 lemon
pinch dry mint
salt and pepper
8 sm. tomatoes

Mix avocados, tomatoes, onion, eggs, lemon juice, salt and mint. Blend well. Slice off tops of tomatoes and carefully remove inside pulp. Place on paper towel upside down to drain. Fill with avocado mixture and garnish parsley.

Adele Davis.

* POOR MAN'S CAVIAR *

1 lg. eggplant
4 Tbsp. olive oil
1 garlic clove (chopped)
½ c. onions (chopped)
½ c. green pepper (chopped)
2 c. plum tomatoes (chopped)
3 Tbsp. garlic wine vinegar

2 tsp. capers
1 Tbsp. lemon juice
1/8 tsp. Tabasco sauce
1 tsp. salt
1/8 tsp. pepper
1 tsp. dried basil
Melba toast

Place unpeeled eggplant in shallow pan in preheated oven (350°) and bake for 1 hour. Remove from oven and cool. Heat olive oil in skillet and add garlic, onion and green pepper. Cook until onion is tender.
Cut eggplant lengthwise and scoop out the flesh, discarding skin. Mash pulp with a potato masher. Stir eggplant into onion mixture and add tomatoes, capers, lemon juice, tabasco, salt, pepper, vinegar and basil. Simmer over low heat, uncovered for 20 min. Remove from heat and place in a bowl and refrigerate for several hours.
Serve with Melba toast.

Adele Davis.

* INDIAN CURRY SPREAD *

1—8 oz. pkg. cream cheese
1 c. cooked chicken (chopped)
1 c. almonds (slivered)
½ c. coconut (grated)

2 Tbsp. mayonnaise
1 Tbsp. chutney
1 Tbsp curry powder
½ tsp. salt

Mix all together well.
Serve with crackers or raw vegetables.

Adele Davis

9

* SHRIMP PUPUS *

1—8 oz. cream cheese (softened)   1 can sm. shrimp (drained)
3 Tbsp. mayonnaise
1/3 to ½ tsp. curry powder

Blend all above and shape into ¾ inch patty (about the size of a salad plate.)
Place small shrimp on top of cheese mixture. Top with green onion (chopped),
hard boiled egg (chopped), salt, pepper, paprika and parsley. Serve with crackers.

Georgia Bleasley.

* ROQUEFORT CHEESE BALL *

4 oz. cream cheese (softened)   1 Tbsp. green onions (minced)
2 oz. Roquefort or Blue cheese   1 Tbsp. dry white wine or
  (crumbled)   dry Vermouth
2 oz. sharp cheddar (1-½ c.)   ¼ tsp mustard (dry)
  (finely shredded)   ½ c. walnuts (finely chopped)

In a small mixer bowl at low speed, beat cheeses for 2 min. Add green onions,
wine and mustard and beat for 3 min. at med. speed until fluffy. Cover and chill
for 2 hours.
With wet hands shape into a ball and roll in nuts. Place cheese on serving board
and garnish with parsley. Serve with crackers.   Irma Meyers.

* PIZZA APPETIZERS *

1—8 oz. cream cheese (softened). Spread on 13" round Pizza pan. Combine 1 sm.
can shrimp (drained), 1 c. catsup, 2 Tbsp. horseradish, and spread over cheese.
Sprinkle on in this order;
    1 c. chopped green pepper
    1 c. chopped tomatoes
    4 chopped green onions
    ½ c. chopped ripe olives
    2 Tbsp. Bacon Bits
    8 oz. shredded Mozarella cheese

Chill at least 2 hours or more. Serve with Doritos or Tostados.   Georgia Bleasley

* CHUTNEY PUPU *

Spread 1 c. hot pepper jelly or chutney over an 8 oz. block of cream cheese.
Serve with crackers.   Jean Keys.

* CHEESE SNOW MAN *

One layer Is cream cheese   One layer is blue cheese
One layer is smokey cheese
Make a round ball of each and roll in chopped nuts. Then put one on top of each other and add eyes, nose and buttons.
Use for eyes—black olives   Use for nose—carrots
Use for buttons—pimentos.   Jean Keys

* MARY'S FRUIT DIP *

1 c. mangoes (diced)   ¾ tsp. lime juice
1—3 oz. pkg. cream cheese   ½ tsp. grated orange rind
1 c. sour cream

Put mangoes in blender until smooth. Stir in remaining ingredients. Chill. Serve with pieces of fruit.   Jean Keys.

* PARMESAN ARTICHOKE PUPU'S *

1—14 oz. can artichoke hearts (drained and cut in quarters)
1 c. mayonnaise
¼ c. Parmesan cheese (grated)

Mix all ingredients together. Heat in oven-proof 8 x 8 shallow dish for 10 min., until bubbly or slightly browned on top, (350°). Serve as a dip with Melba toast.   Jean Walters.

* ARTICHOKE NIBBLES *

2 jars (6 oz. each) marinated   ½ tsp. salt
   artichoke hearts   1/8 tsp. pepper
1 sm. onion (chopped)   1/8 tsp. oregano
1 garlic clove (chopped)   1/8 tsp. hot pepper sauce
4 eggs (beaten)   2 c. sharp Cheddar cheese
¼ c. fine bread crumbs   (shredded)
2 Tbsp. parsley (minced)

Preheat oven to 325°. Drain marinade from one jar of artichoke hearts and pour into a skillet. Drain second jar and discard marinade (use for salads). Chop artichokes and set aside. Heat marinade oil and add onion, garlic and saute 5 min. Combine eggs, bread crumbs, salt, pepper, oregano and pepper sauce. Fold in cheese and parsley. Add artichoke and onion mixture and blend well. Pour into buttered baking dish (9 in. square) and bake for about 30 min. Allow to cool briefly before cutting into 1 in. squares. May be served hot or cold. Can be prepared a day or two in advance and reheat 10 to 12 min.   Adele Davis

* OLIVE CHEESE SNACKS *

1—5 oz. jar bacon-cheese spread
4 Tbsp. Margarine (beat until fluffy)
Add dash of hot sauce and dash of Worcestershire sauce
¾ c. flour.
Make into dough.
1 sm. jar of medium stuffed olives.

Shape dough around olives, roll to make a ball.
Bake on ungreased baking sheet (400°) for 12 to 14 minutes.
Freeze well before baking.   Dorothy Tuttle.

* HOT PARMESAN PUFFS *

3 oz. cream cheese   1 c. Parmesan cheese
1 c. mayonnaise   1/8 tsp. cayenne pepper
1-½ tsp. grated onion

Mix all ingredients well. Spread on half slices of bread and broil until bubbly.
Papricka sprinkled on lightly gives more color. Great for Pupu Party! Can be
made ahead and kept refrigerated for weeks.   Jean Keys.

* CHEESE — SAUSAGE BALLS *

3 c. Bisquick
1 lb. bulk sausage
10 oz. Cheddar cheese (grated)

Mix all by hand — if too dry add a few drops of water. Make into small balls.
Bake 350° for 25 minutes. These freeze well.   Dorothy Tuttle.

* CHEESE SQUARES *

Cut 1 inch squares of unsliced bread.
Melt together 3 oz. cream cheese, ¼ lb. butter and ¼ lb. sharp Cheddar cheese.
Cool.

Beat two egg whites until stiff and fold into batter.
Dip bread squares into batter and place on buttered cookie sheet. Bake at 400°
until bubbly and slightly brown. Can be frozen and then baked.   Lillian Kann

12

* CANAPE PIE *

1—9 in. frozen pie shell
   (thawed)
1—12 oz. pkg. cream cheese
1—2 oz. pkg. blue cheese

½ c. mayonnaise
½ tsp. onion salt

On a lg. baking sheet, pat pie shell into a 11 in. circle. Pierce with fork. Bake in (425°) oven until lightly browned. Cool. Place on serving platter.
Beat cream cheese, blue cheese, mayonnaise and onion salt until fluffy. Spread on pastry, cover and chill for at least 4 hours.
Garnish with cherry tomato halves, sliced mushrooms, parsley sprigs, chopped hard-cooked eggs, sliced ripe olives. Makes 12 wedges.   Adele Davis

* COCKTAIL MEAT BALLS — CURRY SAUCE *

1 lb. ground beef
¼ c. milk
1 egg—beaten
1 tsp. salt

½ c. soft grated crumbs
¼ c. Sherry
2 Tbsp. onion (grated)
¼ tsp. pepper

Shape into 64 balls (1 tsp. each.)
Melt two tsp. fat in heavy skillet. Brown meat balls (not too many at one time) about 10 minutes. Remove and keep hot.

CURRY SAUCE:

1 can cream of mushroom soup.
¼ c. Sherry — 1 tsp. curry powder. Heat. Pour over meat balls in Chating dish.
Serve with tooth-picks.   Dorothy Tuttle.

* TERIYAKI ROLLUPS *

¼ c. shoyu
1 Tbsp. onion (minced)
1 garlic clove (minced)
1 Tbsp. sugar
1 tsp. Worcestershire sauce
1 can water chestnuts (halved)

½ lb. round or sirloin steak
   (cut diagonally in
   thin strips.)
¼ tsp. ginger (ground)
¼ tsp. salt

Combine shoyu, garlic, onion, sugar, Worcestershire, ginger and salt in mixing bowl. Add meat and stir to coat strips evenly with the sauce. Marinate for 30 minutes at room temperature. Drain on paper towels.
Wrap each piece of meat around each water chestnut half and secure with tooth-pick. Place on oiled cookie sheet. Bake in preheated oven (375°) for 30 minutes. Turn and baste often. Serve hot or cold.   Adele Davis

* PINEAPPLE—BACON — WATER CHESTNUT ROLLUPS *

Cut bacon slices in thirds. Slice chestnuts in half. Drain pineapple chunks. Wrap a slice of bacon around the pineapple and chestnut and secure with a toothpick. Broil until bacon is crisp.
Drain on paper towel and serve warm.   Jean Keys

* CHUTNEY EGGS *

12 hard cooked eggs   ¼ c. chutney (finely chopped)
6 slices of bacon (cooked crisp)   3 Tbsp. mayonnaise

Cut eggs in half and remove yolks. Mash eggs with fork, add crumbled bacon along with chutney and mayonnaise.
With pastry bag or spoon, fill whites with mixture. Top with a dash of paprika.
                                                                   Jean Keys

* COCKTAIL MEAT BALLS—SWEET SOUR SAUCE *

¾ c. soy sauce   2 tsp. ground ginger
¾ c. water   3 lbs. ground chuck
2 sm. garlic cloves (minced)

Combine first 4 ingredients and mix well. Add beef and blend thoroughly. Lift out spoonfuls of meat and lightly form 1 in. balls.
Cook by putting on cookie sheet (with sides) in a 275° oven for 15 minutes. Turn meat balls and cook for another few minutes.
Serve hot with dip or plain. (makes 175 meatballs)

SWEET—SOUR SAUCE:

¾ c. sugar   1 c. vinegar
¼ c. soy   1 Tbsp. cornstarch

Mix together, then blend, let thicken in sauce pan slowly   Jean Keys.

* MASLINE FRECATE (RUMANIA)*
(Black Olive Pate)

1 can (lg.) black olives (pitted)
1 c. unsalted butter (softened)

Sweet peppers, chives, onions, parsley (finely chopped) to taste. Puree olives in blender with a little olive oil. Add softened butter and beat until smooth. Add other ingredients to your taste and serve at room temperature or shape into squares and chill to form a Pate. Serve with dark bread.   Adele Davis.

14

* CHICKEN LIVER PATE *

2-½ lbs. fresh chicken livers
2 qts. water
2 tsp. peppercorns
2 tsp. cloves
3 bay leaves
2 sprigs of parsley
2 c. softened butter

1 onion (chopped)
1 garlic clove (minced)
1 Tbsp. salt
2 tsp. dry mustard
½ tsp. nutmeg
dash of hot sauce
¼ c. Brandy

Combine chicken livers, water, peppercorns, cloves, bay leaves, and parsley in a sauce pan, bring to a boil and simmer for 10 minutes. Cook just enough to clear liquid and livers are tender. Drain livers and pass through meat grinder. Set aside.

Mix all the other ingredients (except Brandy), blend well and add chicken livers and stir until smooth. Stir in Brandy.

Line a 9 x 12 loaf pan with foil. Pack Pate into pan. Chill thoroughly before serving.

To serve, remove foil and place on plate and serve with crackers or small slices of rye bread.

Note: flavor will develop more fully if it is allowed to chill overnight.

Adele Davis.

* MUSHROOM LIVER PATE *

3 Tbsp. oil
1 med. onion (chopped)
1 lb. chicken livers
   (cut in sm. pieces)
½ lb. fresh mushrooms (sliced)

¼ c. Sherry
3 Tbsp. parsley (minced)
2 garlic cloves (minced)
2 Tbsp. cloves (pressed)
pinch of nutmeg

Heat oil in skillet and saute onions for 2 — 3 minutes. Add livers and mushrooms and cook until livers are no longer pink. Transfer to blender in small amounts and process into a paste. Add remaining ingredients and mix thoroughly.
Serve in bowl with small pieces of rye bread.

Adele Davis.

* CRAB PUFFS *

24 miniture cream puff shells (halved)

1 can—6 oz. crabmeat

¼ c. black olives (chopped)

2 Tbsp. onions (minced)

2 Tbsp. gr. onion (minced)

2 Tbsp. gr. pepper (minced)

2 Tbsp. celery (minced)

3 drops of pepper sauce

½ c. mayonnaise

Combine crab, olives, pepper, celery, and pepper sauce in mixing bowl. Blend in enough mayonnaise to moisten. Pile into bottom of puff shells and top with the lids. Place on greased cookie sheet and bake in preheated over (350°) for 20 minutes. Serve hot. May be made in advance and frozen. To serve, heat as above. Note: Shrimp or tuna can be substituted for crab. **Adele Davis**

* SHRIMP CAKE *

¾ c. flour

1 egg

1 tsp. sugar

¼ c. water

½ tsp. salt

1 fish cake (red) grated

6 shrimps (cooked—chopped)

4 gr. onions (chopped)

½ c. water chestnuts (chopped)

Mix flour, egg, sugar, water and salt. Add other ingredients and blend well. Drop by tsp. in hot oil. Serve with mustard, shoyu sauce. **Millie Mesaku**

* STUFFED LYCHEES *

2 cans Lychees (halved)

1 pkg.—8 oz. cream cheese

1/8 tsp. salt

1 Tbsp. Sherry wine

6 Tbsp. Macadamia nuts

(chopped)

Drain Lychees. In a small bowl, cream cheese with Sherry and salt till well blended. Stir in nuts. Stuff Lychee halves. Chill well and serve at the end of a pupu party. (I sometimes add a slice of maraschino cherry on top of each stuffed Lychee.) **Jean Keys.**

* CHOW MEIN SNACK *

½ c. butter or oleo

2 Tbsp. soy sauce

½ tsp. onion powder

½ tsp. lemon pepper

¼ tsp. garlic powder

2 c. chow mein noodles

2 c. bite size crispy corn
cereal squares

2 c. round oat cereal

1 c. unsalted peanuts

In a lg. skillet over low heat melt butter. Stir in soy sauce, onion powder, lemon powder and garlic powder until well blended. Add other ingredients and stir over low heat for another 2—3 min. or until moisture is absorbed. Cool on paper towels. Store in air-tight container in a cool place. **Irma Meyers**

* SPICED POPCORN *

6 Tbsp. butter (¼ stick)
3 Tbsp. gr. onion tops (minced)
2 Tbsp. sesame seeds

salt
½ c. popcorn

Combine all ingredients (except popcorn) in a skillet and set on low heat to melt. Keep warm. Pop corn and pour butter mixture on top. Serve warm.

Adele Davis.

* PUPU CHIPS (HAWAIIAN) *

Taro root
garlic salt
oil for frying

Wash and boil unpeeled Taro until barely tender. Cool and peel and chill thoroughly. Slice as thin as possible. Fry in deep fat until crisp and brown. Drain on paper towel. Sprinkly with garlic salt while still warm.

Adele Davis.

* PETITS CHOUX *
(Tiny Cream Puffs)

4 eggs
1 c. water
½ c. butter or oleo

1 c. all purpose flour

Preheat oven to 400°. Break eggs in a sm. bowl and set aside. In med. saucepan, bring water and butter to a rolling boil, reduce heat to low. Add flour all at once and stir vigorously with wire whisk or wooden spoon, for 1 minute or until mixture farms a ball. Add eggs all at once and continue beating until mixture is smooth.

Drop dough 1 tsp. at a time (about 1-½ in. apart) onto ungreased baking sheets. Bake for 22 to 25 minutes or until golden brown. Remove from baking sheet and cool on wire racks (away from drafts). Cut off top and fill with your favorite sandwich filling (chicken, ham, etc.).

Irma Meyers.

S·O·U·P·S

* SPAETZLE FOR SOUPS (GERMAN) *

½ c. sifted flour
½ tsp. salt
2 eggs
½ c. milk

½ c. water
¼ lb. butter
brown bread crumbs
boiling salted water

Beat eggs with milk and water, add flour and salt. Mix until smooth. Pour batter through a large-holed colander into boiling water. Boil 3 or 3 minutes until they rise. Rinse in colander with cold water, drain well.

Serve with soup or brown in foamy butter and pour over 2 beaten eggs and let set.   Adele Davis

* EINLAUF (GERMAN) *
(Egg drops for soup)

1 egg
¼ c. water
1 Tbsp. parsley (chopped)

1/8 tsp. salt
3 Tbsp. flour

Beat egg, and salt, flour and water. Stir until smooth. Pour slowly into boiling soup. Cook 2 or 3 minutes. Garnish with parsley.   Adele Davis.

* LEBERKNOEDEL (GERMAN) *
(Liver dumplings)

½ lb. liver (ground)
1 med. onion (minced)
2 Tbsp. butter
¼ lb. raw spinach

2 eggs (well beaten)
2 Tbsp. parsley (chopped)
1 Tbsp. flour

Mix all ingredients thoroughly. Shape into small balls. Drop into boiling soup and cook for 5 minutes.   Adele Davis.

KNAIDLACH (JEWISH) *
(Soup Dumplings)

2 eggs
4 Tbsp. chicken fat (melted)
1/3 c. cold water

1 tsp. salt
1 c. Matzo meal

Beat eggs, fat, water and salt together. Stir in Matzo meal. Add enough meal to make a stiff dough. Chill 1 m. Form into small balls and cook for 30 minutes in boiling soup.   Adele Davis.

* HOME MADE NOODLES

2 c. flour   1 Tbsp. water
2 eggs   ½ tsp. salt

Place flour on board and make well in center. Drop eggs, water and salt into it.
Work into flour and knead until smooth and elastic. Roll and stretch dough as
thin as possible. (the thinner the better the noodles).
Let dough stand until dry to the touch but not too dry. Cut into squares or
strips. Roll up like jelly roll and slice as thin as possible. Shake until they separate. Let dry thoroughly. Cook in boiling water or soup.   Adele Davis.

* MEAT BALL SOUP *

2 lbs. meat with bone   2 tsps. salt
2 qts. water   1 onion
4 stems celery (cut thick)   ½ c. parsley (minced)

Bring to boil and a simmer for 1½ hours.

MEAT BALLS

1 lb. lean ground beef   ½ tsp. pepper
1 c. flour   2 tsp. nutmeg

Add to soup and cook for 30 minutes.   Evelyn Staley.

* MEAT BALL VEGETABLE !SOUP *

MEAT BALLS:
1 lb. ground beef   ¼ tsp salt
¼ c. onions (chopped)   1/8 tsp. pepper
¼ tsp garlic powder   2 Tbsp. tomato sauce
2 tsp. Parmesan cheese   1 lg. egg

Mix all ingredients for meat balls, shape by using 2 Tbsp. for each one. Bring
broth to a boil, add meatballs, turn down heat and simmer for 45 minutes.

BROTH:

2—13 oz. cans beef broth   1 c. carrots (1 in. slices)
½ tsp. salt   1 c. onions (sliced)
1 c. celery (1 in. slices)   1 tsp. dried bay leaves

                                                   Jean Keys.

* MY PORTUGUESE BEAN SOUP *

Ham hocks or thick ham slices (diced)
Portuguese sausage (1 hot and 1 mild) casing removed and sausage fried and fat drained off.

1 can black bean soup—2 cans water
1 can stewed tomatoes
sm. can lima beans
lg. can sm. red beans
lg. can green beans
cabbage (cut up)
potatoes (optional)

lg. can garbanzos
lg. can diced or sliced
   carrots
sm. can corn
lg. can white onions
   (cut up)

Save the juice from the carrots and onions and add to soup. Simmer for several hours and serve. (several cans of water if needed)   Jean Keys.

* PORTUGUESE SOUP *

12 c. water
3 sm. smoked ham hocks (meaty)
1 Portuguese sausage
   (Gouveia — average size)
1 lb. shin meat
3 potatoes
1 sm. head cabbage
1 bunch watercress

1 Tbsp. parsley)chopped)
3 Tbsp. celery (diced)
1 1g. carrot (sliced)
3 cans lima beans or
   kidney beans

Peal and cut potatoes in 1" cubes. Cut sausage in ½" pieces. Trim ham hocks of excess fat and cut in pieces. Wash watercress and use tops. Cut stems into sm. pieces. Add ham hocks, meat and beans to water and cook until meat is tender. Add all the other prepared ingredients and cook until done. Season according to ones taste.
Grated cheese may be added after soup is done (just before serving). Serve soup with buttered French bread.   Mae Gomes.

* GERMAN BEAN SOUP *

½ lb. white beans (washed and soaked)
Salt and pepper to taste
finely chopped parsley
2 bay leaves
1 Tsp. oil
½ lb. German Bratwurst or
   frankfurts (cut in thick slices)

2 small carrots
4 pts. stock or water
1 large cabbage leaf
2 medium leaks (2" in. pieces)
pinch of nutmeg

20

Cover beans with cold water and bring to a boil. Season with salt and pepper, parsley and bay leaves. Simmer gently for 1 hour, until beans are tender. Drain. Heat oil in pan and add sliced carrots. Fry for 10 minutes. Add stock and cabbage. Correct seasoning and add nutmeg. Cook for 15 minutes, add sliced sausage and simmer gently for 15 minutes.   Jean Keys.

* LINSENSUPPE (GERMAN) *
(Lentil Soup)

1 c. lentils
3 pts. cold water
1-½ lbs. brisket of beef
   or ham bone
¼ c. celery (diced)

1 sm. onion
1 Tbsp. butter
1 Tbsp. flour
Croutons or sliced cooked
   frankfurters.

Soak lentils overnight. Drain. Place in soup pot with meat and simmer (covered) for 2 hours. Add celery.
Brown onions in fat and add flour. Gradually add 1 c. of the soup. Return to soup. Season to taste.
Garnish with Croutons or sliced frankfurters.   Adele Davis.

* BLACK BEAN SOUP (FLORIDA) *

½ lb. black beans
   (soaked overnight)
½ lb. boneless veal (cubed)
1 sm. veal knuckle bone
2 sm. onions (chopped)
½ lemon (halved)

2 whole cloves
½ tsp. allspice
1-½ tsp. salt
pepper to taste
1 hard-cooked egg (chopped)
slices of limes or lemons

Place 1½ qts. water in sauce pan, add veal, knuckle, beans, onions, lemon halves, cloves, allspice, salt and pepper. Bring to a boil, reduce heat and simmer for 5 hours, until beans are soft. Take out meat and bones and set aside. Discard lemon and cloves. Puree the soup in a blender, return to saucepan and add shredded veal. Simmer for 5 minutes (add sherry to taste).
Garnish with chopped egg and lemon slices.   Roberta Chateauneuf.

* LIMA BEAN CHOWDER *

3 lbs. frying chicken
   (cut up)
4 qts. water
1 onion (stuck with 4 cloves)

1 pkg. (10 oz.) frozen corn
2 pkgs. (10 oz. each) frozen
   lima beans
1 tsp. Worcestershire sauce

21

3 Tbsp. flour
1 can (16 oz.) tomatoes
2 med. potatoes (peeled-diced)

1 c. whipping cream
4 sprigs parsley (minced)

Bouquet Garni: 4 bay leaves, 6 peppercorns, 1 tsp. whole thyme. (tied in cheese cloth)

Place chicken in water in a lg. kettle with bouquet garni and onion. Bring to a boil, cover and simmer until chicken is tender. Remove chicken and cool. Bone and chop chicken into 1 in. pieces and set aside.
Strain broth, return to pot and bring to a boil.
Mix flour with 5 Tbsp. water to form a paste. Add to the boiling soup, stirring until thickened.
Add tomatoes and potatoes and simmer for 20 minutes. Add lima beans, corn, Worcestershire sauce and a little cayenne pepper. Simmer another 15 minutes.
Add chicken and whipping cream and just heat through. Season to taste.
Garnish with minced parsley.   Adele Davis.

* CHERRY COVE CLAM CHOWDER *

2 med. potatoes (peeled-cubed)
1 med. onion (chopped)
1 pt. minced clams (include nectar)
3 slices bacon (fried crisp and
   crumbled)

1 qt. milk
instant potato flakes
   (optional)
minced parsley
salt and pepper

Boil potatoes and onions in small amount of water until potatoes are done.
Add clams, nectar and bacon and simmer: Simmer for 15 to 20 minutes.
Add milk and reheat. *Do Not Boil*.
Add instant potatoes if you like, will make a thicker chowder.
Add parsley and salt to taste.   Dorothy Lyle.

* PENNY PINCHING CHOWDER *

4 slices of bacon
6 frankfurters (sliced)
   (can use turkey franks)
2 med. onions
4 med. potatoes (peeled-sliced)
1—1 lb. can kernel corn
   (undrained)

2 tsp. salt
1 tsp. thyme
1 can beef broth
½ tsp. pepper
½ tsp. caraway seed
1 beef bouillon cube
½ c. dry white wine
2 c. milk

22

In bottom of a heavy pot, brown bacon. When done remove and drain on paper towel.

Add to the bacon drippings the onions and frankfurters and brown slightly. Stir in the sliced potatoes, corn, bouillon cube, beef broth and water. Simmer covered for 30 minutes, after it has been brought to a boil. When potatoes start to break, add wine and milk and heat just to boiling. Serve with crumbled bacon on top.   Irma Meyers.

* CLAM VICHYSSOISE *

1 med. onion (chopped)	3 c. potatoes (diced)
4 leeks (white parts-sliced)	3 c. chicken broth
1 garlic clove (minced)	2 cans (7 oz. each) clams and juice
3 Tbsp. butter	2 c. milk
salt and pepper to taste	1 c. cream

Saute leeks, onion and garlic in butter until soft and transparent. Add potatoes and chicken broth. Cover and simmer until potatoes are done. Add clams and juice.

Puree the mixture in a blender. Add milk and cream and season to taste with salt and pepper. Chill.

Serve with sprinkle of chopped chives.   Adele Davis.

* TOMATO AND CLAM BISQUE *

1/3 c. butter	salt — pepper
1/3 c. flour	2 can (6 oz. each) chopped clams
2 c. whipping cream	(drained — reserve liquid)
2 cans (6 oz. each) peeled tomatoes	bottle of clam juice
(undrained-diced)	pinch of sugar
1 tsp. curry powder	1 bay leaf
½ tsp. thyme	

Place butter in a sauce pan, stir in flour and cook over very low heat for 2 to 3 minutes. Combine reserved clam juice and additional bottle clam juice to measure 1 c.

Slowly add to roux, increase heat to med. and cook, stirring until well blended. Add tomatoes, sugar and seasonings. Simmer uncovered over low heat for 30 minutes. Remove bay leaf. Add clams and adjust seasoning to taste. (do not cook too long as clams become tough.)   Nancy Ebsen

* HEARTY SUPPER SOUP *

3 Tbsp. butter or oleo
2 med. red or green peppers
   (thinly sliced)
1 med. carrot (thinly sliced)
1 can (28 oz.) tomatoes
1 gr. onion (thinly sliced)
¼ tsp. thyme leaves

1 pkg. (10 oz.) frozen whole
   kernel corn
1 cup lettuce (loosely packed shredded)
1-½ cups water
1 pkg. (16 oz.) frankfurters

In 5 qt. sauce pan over med. heat, melt butter and cook peppers, carrots and gr. onion until lightly browned and tender. Stir occasionally.
Add tomatoes with the liquid, corn, lettuce and water and thyme. Heat to boiling and stir to break up the tomatoes and separate corn. Reduce heat to simmer, cover and cook for 5 minutes or until corn is tender. Slice frankfurters diagonally, add to soup mixture.   Irma Meyers.

* KARTOFFELSUPPE (GERMAN) *
(Potato Soup)

2 lbs. potato (diced)
3 c. chicken or beef broth
1 stalk celery

1 leek
3 carrots
salt and pepper to taste

Cook all ingredients in stock until potatoes are tender. Place in blender until smooth. Serve hot or cold. Garnish with chives, parsley or browned chopped onions.   Adele Davis.

* CLAM CHOWDER *

4 Tbsp. bacon grease
1 med. onion (chopped fine)
1 med. carrot (shredded)
1 c. diced celery
1 Tbsp. chopped parsley

¼ tsp. thyme leaves
2 cans minced clams
1 can cream of potato soup
3 c. liquid (water—milk—half and half)

Combine first six ingredients in a 3 qt. saucepan and cook until limp. Add remaining ingredients and heat thoroughly. Season with salt and pepper to taste. For variation, add 1 can (16 oz.) stewed tomatoes.   Anna Hambley.

* CHICKEN FRUIT SOUP *

1/3 c. barley or minute rice
3 cans Swanson chicken broth
1 chicken cube
1 carrot (shredded)
1 med. onion (chopped)

1/8 tsp. anise seeds
¼ tsp. orange zest
1 can Manderine oranges
1 Tbsp. chopped parsley

Boil first seven items about 45 minutes. Add oranges to just heat, Sprinkle in parsley. For added flavor, when serving sprinkle with your favorite cheese.

Anna Hambley.

* MINESTRONE SOUP *

¼ lb. salt pork
3 garlic cloves (minced)
2 Tbsp. olive oil
2 carrots (diced)
1 lg. onion (diced)
2 c. celery (diced)
1 can tomato paste (6 oz.)
2 gr. peppers (seeded—diced)
2 zucchini (diced)
1 bunch spinach (chopped)
¾ c. elbow macaroni (cooked)

4 qts. water
3 beef bouillon cubes
½ tsp. white pepper
1 tsp. oregano
1 tsp. thyme
2 potatoes (peeled—diced)
¼ head cabbage (chopped)
1 can (12 oz.) tomatoes (chopped)
1 can (12 oz.) garbanzo beans
   (drained)
1 can (12 oz) kidney beans

In a lg. sauce pan, saute pork and garlic in very hot oil. Add carrots, onion and celery. Cook over med. heat for 10 minutes. Add the water and bring to a boil for 5 minutes.

Add beef bouillon cubes and seasonings, mix well. Add potatoes, cabbage and gr. peppers and cook for 5 minutes. Turn heat to med. low. Add zucchini and spinach and cook until all vegetables are tender. Add cooked macaroni, tomatoes and beans. Heat thoroughly.

(Reduce recipe if desired or can be frozen.)

Nancy Ebsen.

* ONION SOUP *

½ c. peanut oil
6 lg. brown onions
   (coarsely chopped)
1 tsp. thyme
3 bay leaves
10 c. beef consomme

1 bottle dry red wine
1-½ lb. Swiss cheese (grated)

8 slices stale French bread

Heat oil in lg. pot. Add onions and saute until cooked but not browned. Add thyme and bay leaves, stir in wine, bring to a boil and let soup reduce for a few minutes.

Add consomme and simmer (uncovered) for 20 minutes.

Pour soup in ovenproof bowls. Top with a slice of French bread and sprinkle with the cheese. Broil quickly until cheese is bubbly and golden.   Adele Davis

* MUSHROOM SOUP *

½ lb. mushrooms (sliced)   2 Tbsp. flour
¼ c. butter   1 qt. beef stock
½ c. croutons   2 eggs (beaten)

Saute mustrooms in butter, add flour and salt. Add stock and simmer for 10 minutes.

Place croutons in a pan. Add 2 Tbsp. white wine to beaten eggs. Pour over croutons, serve in hot soup.   Judy Pieklo

*SPINACH SOUP *

1 pkg. (10 oz.) chopped   1/8 tsp. nutmeg
   frozen spinach   dash of white pepper
2 Tbsp. onion (chopped)   1 tsp. lemon juice
1 garlic clove (chopped)   1 c. light cream
1 Tbsp. butter   salt to taste
2 c. chicken broth
1/3 tsp. tarragon

Saute onion and garlic in butter until transparent. Add 1 c. chicken broth, tarragon, nutmeg and pepper and bring to a boil. Add chopped spinach (thawed) and lemon juice and simmer for 2 minutes. Cover and set aside to cool. When lukewarm, puree in a blender until smooth.

Add cream and second cup of broth and salt to taste. Heat to simmer.
Garnish with sour cream with caviar or chopped crisp bacon.   Charlene Do.

* POLISH BARSHCH (POLAND) *
(Beet Soup)

1 No. 2 can diced beets   1 frankfurter (cooked)
1 No. 1 can consomme   ½ cucumber (sliced)

Drain juice from beets in saucepan, add consomme and beets and simmer for 1 hour. Season to taste.

Serve hot in cups with frankfurters and sliced cucumbers. (This is a clear Barshch, not like the Russian Bortsch.   Adele Davis.

*RUSSIAN BORTSCH *

1-½ lbs. stew beef
2-½ qts. beef stock
4 beets (matchstick strips)
1 med. cabbage (shredded)
2 carrots (matchstick strips)
1 parsnip (matchstick strips)
2 celery stalks (chopped)
1 Tbsp. lemon juice
1 Tbsp. parsley (chopped)
Sour cream

1 lg. onion (chopped)
½ lb. tomatoes
   (skinned—diced)
1 Tbsp. red wine vinegar
1 Tbsp. sugar
2 bay leaves
1-½ tsp. salt
½ tsp. black pepper
½ tsp. allspice

Trim surplus fat from meat and dice. Place stock in sauce pan and add meat and bring to a boil. Skim. Reduce heat and simmer for 45 minutes. Add all vegetables (except tomatoes). Simmer 20 minutes. Add tomatoes, vinegar, sugar, bay leaves, allspice, salt and pepper. Cook gently for 15 minutes. Check for seasoning, sharpen with lemon juice.

To serve: Sprinkle with dill and parsley. Serve sour cream separately, each person adds to his soup.   Evelyn Staley.

* MURGHI SHOORVA (INDIA) *
(Mulligatawny Soup)

2 qts. water
1 Tbsp. salt
6 peppercorns
2 tsp. coriander
1 tsp. tumeric
2 chickens (broilers or fryers 2 lbs.
   each — cut up)
½ tsp. ginger
¼ tsp. red pepper

1-½ tsp. vinegar
½ c. onions (sliced)
2 Tbsp. butter or oelo

Combine water, salt, peppercorns and chicken in soup pot. Heat to boiling, then reduce heat, cover loosely and a simmer until chicken is tender. Skim fat from broth.

Mix spices and vinegar into a paste. Saute onions in butter until tender (not brown). Stir spice paste into onions. simmer for 5 minutes. Stir onion mixture into soup.

Remove chicken from bones and cut into pieces (no skin). Return to soup. Garnish with parsley.   Roberta Chateauneuf.

* CHICKEN GUMBO *

1 lg. stewing chicken
1 slice ham (diced)
2 Tbsp. butter
1 sm. onion (diced)
1 gr. pepper (chopped)
1 sprig of parsley

1-½ c. canned tomatoes
4 okra pods (sliced)
3 qts. water
1 bay leaf
salt and pepper to taste.

Cut chicken as for stewing. Add salt and pepper. Heat butter in soup kettle, add chicken and ham, simmer for 10 minutes. Add onion and seasonings and brown. Add tomatoes, okra and boiling water. Simmer for 2 hours.
Serve in Tureen, accompany with bowls of steaming rice.   Francis Wright.

* MEXICAN CORN SOUP *

¼ c. butter
2 c. milk
1 garlic clove (minced)
1 tsp. oregano
1 Tbsp. canned chilies (rinsed—diced)
1 Chicken breast
   (cooked—boned—chopped)

1 c. chicken stock
½ c. fresh corn kernels
1 c. tomatoes (diced)
1 c. Monterey cheese (diced)
2 Tbsp. parsley (minced)
salt and pepper
Tortilla squares

Combine chicken stock and corn in a blender and puree. Combine corn and butter in a sauce pan and simmer slowly for 5 minutes, stirring to keep corn from sticking.
Add milk, garlic, oregano, salt and pepper and bring to a boil. Reduce heat and add chilies and simmer for 5 minutes. Keep hot. To serve: Divide chicken and tomatoes in soup bowls. Remove soup from heat, add cheese and stir until cheese is melted. Ladle into bowls, sprinkle with parsley and Tortilla chips. Tortilla squares; Stack 8 to 10 tortillas on a cutting board and slice into ½ in. squares. Heat some oil and drop by handfuls into oil. Stir with wooden spoon until golden. Drain on paper towels. (These are good with soups and salads and may be stored in a covered container in a dry place.)   Adele Davis.

* BEET MADRILENE *

1 onion (chopped)
¾ lb. sm. beets (peeled)
1 tsp. salt
¼ tsp. sugar
1-½ tsp. lemon juice

4 c. chicken broth
4 tsp. gelatin (unsweetened)
¼ c. water
chopped parsley (garnish)
lightly salted whipped cream (garnish)

Grate the beets and place in a sauce pan with onion, salt, sugar, lemon juice and chicken broth. Bring to a boil, then lower heat and simmer uncovered for 15 minutes.

Dissolve gelatin in cold water. Stir in a few Tbsp. of hot soup and then add to strained soup.

Refrigerate at least 2 hours until firm but not resistant to the fork.

When ready to serve, spoon madrilene into chilled glass bowls whose rims have been dipped in chopped parsley. Garnish with dollops of lightly salted whipped cream.

Judy Pieklo.

* AVOCADO SOUP *

1 onion (chopped)	1 tart apple (peeled—cored)
1 stalk celery (chopped)	4 c. chicken broth
2 Tbsp. butter	1 c. avocado (peeled—chopped)
1 Tbsp. flour	1 c. light cream
2 tsp. curry powder	Garnish; Avocado slices — toasted grated coconut

Saute onion and celery in butter until transparent. Stir in flour and curry powder, stirring constantly until blended. Add apple and 2 c. broth, stirring to blend and cook until apples are soft. Transfer to a blender, add avocado and whirl until smooth. Return to saucepan, add remaining broth and cream, stir thoroughly. Add salt to taste. Chill.

Serve garnished with thin slices of avocados and a dusting of toasted coconut.

Ingrid Nelson.

*ICY SPICY TOMATO SOUP *

1 can (12 oz.) plum tomatoes	¼ tsp. thyme
4 c. beef broth	¼ tsp. celery seed
1-½ c. celery root (grated)	½ tsp. sugar
2 Tbsp. parsley (minced)	1/8 tsp. red pepper (crushed)
½ tsp. fresh dill (chopped)	Garnish: Sour cream-finely chopped dill.

Place all ingredients in a sauce pan (except sour cream and dill). Bring to a boil, cover and simmer for 45 minutes, until celery root is tender. Transfer soup to a blender and puree.

Refrigerate. Serve with a tsp. of sour cream and a sprinkling of fresh chopped dill.

Charlene Do.

* GREEN ONION SOUP (KOREAN) *

½ c. dry shrimp
3-½ c. water
Shoyu
Ajinomoto

1 tsp. salad oil
2 tsp. sesame seeds
3 eggs (scrambled)
½ c. gr. onions (chopped)

Wash shrimp and add to water to make stock. Bring to a boil and simmer for 30 minutes. Add shoyu, Ajinomoto, sesame seeds and eggs. Just before serving, add chopped onions. (Do not over cook)   Charlene Do.

* WINTER MELON SOUP (CHINESE) *

1 lg. stewing chicken (cut up)
1 fresh pork hock
1 whole chicken breast
6 dried mushrooms (chopped)
2 oz. Virginia ham (cubed)
2 slices ginger
1 Tbsp. shoyu

1 c. water chestnuts (sliced)
1 c. bamboo shoots (sliced)
1 tsp. sugar
1 Winter melon (10 lbs.)
salt and pepper to taste

Cover chicken and pork with water, bring to a boil and simmer for 1 hour. Add chicken breast. Remove chicken breast from stewing chicken. Continue simmering for 2 hours. Strain. Reserve chicken and pork for other dishes.
Cut off top melon and reserve. Scoop out seeds and stringy portions. Place all ingredients in melon (except chicken breasts). Set melon in a bowl and make a twine harness. Lower into a cooking pan (steamer) with a rack on bottom. Pour chicken broth inside melon ¾ full. Put top on melon. Add enough water to pan to come to 2 in. up on bottom of the bowl. Cover pan and steam over low heat for ¾ hours.
Dice chicken breasts and add to broth just before serving. Lift melon (still sitting in bowl) and take to table. Ladle some of the flesh of the melon into each bowl as you serve. (very spectacular dish)   Adele Davis.

* DIET SOUP *

1 c. gr. beans (1 in. pieces)
1 c. celery (diced)
1 med. zucchini (sliced)

3 med. tomatoes (diced)
2 c. stock

Season to taste. Serve hot or cold.

S·A·L·A·D·S

* GARDEN SALAD DRESSING *

1/3 c. canned milk
½ tsp. salt
½ tsp. dry mustard
2 Tbsp. salad oil

2 Tbsp. catsup
1 tsp. Worcestershire sauce
2 Tbsp. vinegar

Place all in covered jar and shake well. Keep chilled until ready to use.

Francis Wright.

* POPPY SEED DRESSING *

1-½ c. sugar
2 tsp. dry mustard
2 tsp. salt
2/3 c. vinegar

3 Tbsp. onion juice
2 c. salad oil
3 Tbsp. poppy seeds

Mix sugar, mustard, salt and pepper in a blender. Whirl until blended. Add onion juice and blend again. While blender is running, add oil slowly and continue mixing until thick. Add poppy seeds and whirl for a few seconds. Store in covered jar in refrigerator.

Adele Davis.

* CHILI SAUCE DRESSING *

2 c. chili sauce
1 c. olive oil
1 c. red vinegar
1 c. celery (minced)
3 garlic cloves (minced)

1 Tbsp. oregano
1 Tbsp. black pepper
   (freshly ground)
1 Tbsp. salt
1/3 c. sugar

Mix ingredients thoroughly in a blender. Store in tightly covered jars in refrigerator.
Note: This is a large quantity; recipe may be cut in half.

Ida Christoph.

* SALAD DRESSING FOR FRUIT *

2 Tbsp. butter
½ c. orange juice
¼ c. lemon juice

2 Tbsp. flour
½ c. sugar

Cream butter, add flour, stir in sugar and add juices. Cook slowly until thick. Cool. Serve over fruit for salads.

Nancy Ebsen

* MAYONNAISE AU MENTHE *

½ c. water	1 Tbsp. salt
1/3 c. fresh mint (chopped)	¼ tsp. cayenne pepper
1 Tbsp. sugar	juice of 2 lemons
2 eggs	1 c. vegetable oil
2 egg yolks	¼ c. green creme de menthe

Combine water, mint and sugar in a small pan. Bring to a boil over med. heat and boil for 4 minutes, let cool.

Place eggs and egg yolks in a large bowl, season with salt and pepper. Mix with a hand electric beater on high speed, slowly add lemon juice, beating constantly. Add oil in a slow stream and beat until thick. Blend in cooled mint syrup and gradually add creme de menthe. Cover and chill.

Note: This is good with fruit salads and hot or cold lamb.   Judy Pieklo.

* CELERY SEED DRESSING *

½ c. sugar	2 tsp. grated onion
1 tsp. dry mustard	1/3 c. vinegar
1 tsp. salt	1 c. salad oil
2 tsp. celery seeds	2 tsp. creamed horseradish

Combine all ingredients (except oil and vinegar). Put in a blender and turn to high speed, pour in oil very slowly, add vinegar slowly. Chill. (Very good on head lettuce or tossed salad.)   Annie Ebsen.

* GREEN GODDESS DRESSING *

1 garlic clove (minced)	3 Tbsp. snipped chives
½ tsp. salt	1/3 c. snipped parsley
½ tsp. dry mustard	1 c. mayonnaise
1 tsp. Worcestershire sauce	½ c. sour cream
2 Tbsp. anchovy paste	1/8 tsp. pepper
3 Tbsp. tarragon wine vinegar	

Combine all, mix well. Refrigerate. Makes about 1-¾ cups.   Jean Keys

* CANARY COTTAGE DRESSING *

1 can tomato soup	1 tsp. salt
¾ c. oil	¾ c. vinegar
1 tsp. grated onion	¾ c. sugar
1 Tbsp. Worcestershire	

Mix all in blender. Afterwards, drop in 3 garlic cloves and leave them.

           Dorothy Tuttle

* TOMATO SOUP DRESSING *

1 can tomato soup
¾ c. vinegar
1 tsp. salt
½ tsp. paprika
1 tsp. dry mustard

½ c. sugar
1 sm. onion (chopped)
1 garlic clove (minced)
1-½ c. vegetable oil

Combine soup, vinegar, salt, paprika, mustard, garlic and onion in blender. Whirl until smooth. Set speed of blender to slow and add oil very slowly. Whirl a few seconds longer to blend.
Or put all ingredients in a large bowl and beat a rotary beater until blended.

Irma Meyers.

* TOMATO SOUP FRENCH DRESSING *

1 can tomato soup
½ c. sugar
¾ c. vinegar
½ tsp. pepper & 1 tsp. salt

½ tsp. paprika
2 tsp. prepared mustard
1 Tbsp. Worchestershire sauce
1-½ c. oil

Mix in a bowl, beat with egg beater or use electric on low. Add oil slowly and beat until blended. Refrigerate.

Jean Keys.

* LOW CALERIE SALAD DRESSING *

1 sm. can Sacramento tomato plus
½ tsp. dry mustard
½ tsp. celery seeds
½ tsp. dill weed
2 tsp. sugar (I use equivalent Sweet and low)

1 tsp. garlic powder
1 tsp. Heinz chili sauce
¼ c. vinegar (1/3 apple cider—1/3 tarragon—1/3 red wine, vinegar)

Mix all ingredients and place in a jar and refrigerate.

Arlene Wright

* BOILED SALAD DRESSING *

Cook and bring to a boil:

¼ c. vinegar
¼ c. water
¼ tsp. salt

¼ c. sugar
1 tsp. mustard
dash of pepper

Reduce heat, add 2 well beaten eggs. Cook until slightly thick, add 1 c. mayonnaise.

For potato salad:

4 c. new potatoes (diced)
2 hard-cooked eggs
½ c. cucumbers (chopped)

1 Tbsp. onions (minced)
1 Tbsp. green pepper (chopped)

Mix enough dressing to moist stage. Chill.

Freda Lindquist.

* PINEAPPLE MOLD SALAD *

2 c. crushed pineapple (drained)
juice of 1 lemon
1 c. white sugar
2 Tbsp. Knox gelatine (2 sm. pkgs.)
½ c. cold water

½ c. cheddar cheese (grated)
½ c. cottage cheese
½ pt. Avoset whipping
    cream — (whipped)
Maraschino cherries

Heat crushed pineapple, add lemon juice and sugar. Stir until sugar is dissolved. Soak gelatin in cold water, then melt over hot water (double-boiler). Add gelatin mixture to hot mixture and mix thoroughly. Refrigerate until mixture begins to set. Add cheeses and whipped cream. Pour into mold.
Either dice cherries and fold into mixture or place them on top of mold.

Merle Becker.

* CARROT — PINEAPPLE MOLDED SALAD *

Mixture 1:

3 oz . pkg. Philadelphia cream cheese
2 pkg. (3 oz. each) lemon Jello
2 c. hot water

Mixture 2:

1 c. grated carrots
1 sm. can crushed pineapple
½ c. mayonnaise

¼ c. nut meats (chopped)
¼ c. celery (chopped)

Dissolve Jello in hot water—add cream cheese. Cool slightly and mix. (put in blender)
Mix 1 and 2 mixtures, pour into Tupperware mold and let stand overnite.

Bessie Adams.

* PINEAPPLE SALAD FOR PARTIES *

1 "2 can crushed pineapple
    (save the juice)
1 (3 oz.) pkg. lime Jello
1 (3 oz.) pkg. lemon Jello

¼ tsp. salt
1 c. cottage cheese
1 c. mayonnaise

Combine juice and enough water to make two cups. Heat to boiling, pour over gelatins and stir to dissolve. Add salt. Cool in refrigerator and when slightly thickened fold in remaining ingredients. Chill till firm (overnight is best), then unmold on lettuce. Serve with dollop of mayonnaise.   Jean Keys.

* CARROT — PINEAPPLE APPLE RING *

1 pkg. orange Jello
1 pkg. lemon Jello
2-½ c. boiling water
2 stalks celery and leaves
   (chopped fine)
2 Tbsp. vinegar or lemon juice

1/8 tsp. salt
1 c. grated carrots
1 can (8-¼ oz.) crushed pineapple
   (syrup included)
1 pkg. Knox gelatin

Pour boiling water over lemon and orange Jello (in a lg. bowl). Pour cold water over Knox gelatin in a cup. Add knox gelatin to lg. bowl. Add lemon juice, salt, carrots, pineapple and celery. Mix well and pour int a (well oiled) mold. Place in refrigerator to chill. Serve with your favorite sauce. Dora L.R. Beyer

* SEAFOAM SALAD *

1 can (1 lb. 4 oz.) crushed pineapple
1 pkg. (6 oz.) lime gelatin
1 c. water
1 tsp. salt or seasoned salt

½ tsp dill weed
½ c. dry Vermouth
2 c. dairy sour cream
Crisp salad greens

Drain pineapple well, reserving liquid. Add pineapple syrup to gelatin in a saucepan. Stir in water, salt and dill weed. Heat to boiling, stirring to dissolve gelatin. Remove from heat and stir in Vermouth. Chill until mixture resembles unbeaten egg whites. Blend in sour cream. Fold in pineapple, pour into a 1-½ qt. mold. Chill firm. Unmold onto greens. (makes 6—8 servings) Jean Keys.

* CRANBERRY — PINEAPPLE SALAD *

1 c. chopped cranberries
2 c. crushed pineapple
1 tsp. powdered sugar.

½ c. salad dressing
   (cooked kind)

Combine cranberries and pineapple. Arrange on lettuce. Serve with salad dressing sweetened with sugar. Garnish with chopped mint. Adele Davis.

* RASPBERRY SALAD *

1 pkg. raspberry Jello
1 c. boiling water

1 c. apple sauce
1 pkg. frozen red raspberries

Dissolve Jello well, add apple sauce and pkg. of frozen raspberries. Pour into mold and chill. Unmold and serve with dressing.
Dressing:
1-½ c. sour cream
16 sm. marshmallows
Let stand over nite, Beat with rotary beater. Ammon Swope

* MELON SALAD *

Peel and remove seeds from whole honey dew melon.
Fill the cavity with your favorite Jello fruit mixture.
Place the bowl in the refrigerator (so Jello will not spill).
Before serving — spread melon with 2 parts cream cheese and 1 part mayonnaise.
To serve — place slice of melon on lettuce leaf and garnish.   Lillian Kann.

* 24 HOUR SALAD *

2 c. marshmallows (cut-up)
2 c. pineapple (cut-up)
2 c. orange sections (cut-up)

2 c. canned white cherries
  (pitted — cut-up)
2 c. whipping cream (whipped)

Dressing:

2 eggs
4 Tbsp. sugar

4 Tbsp. vinegar
2 Tbsp. butter

Beat eggs, add sugar and vinegar. Cook over slow heat until thick, and butter. Cool.
Place remaining ingredients in a salad bowl, mix in dressing. Cover and refrigerate for 24 hours or more.
Garnish with red and green marischino cherries.   Adele Davis.

* ORANGE — LYCHEE MOLDED SALAD *

1 can (11 oz.) Mandarin oranges
1 can (15 oz.) Lychees
1 pkg. orange gelatin

1 pkg. lemon gelatin
2 c. gingerale (chilled)

Drain fruits, reserving liquid. Add enough water to liquid to make 1-¾ c. Bring to a boil and add gelatin, stirring until gelatin is dissolved. Chill until mixture begins to thicken. Stir in fruits and gingerale. Pour into a 1-½ qt. mold. Chill until well set. Makes 6 servings.
(This is a delightful salad for lunch or dinner, especially for people who like fruit. Refreshing, cool and tangy.)   Jean Keys.

* COTTAGE CHEESE SALAD *

2 c. creamed cottage cheese (drained)
1. sm. can crushed pineapple
    (drained)

2 c. Cool Whip
1 pkg. (3 oz.) orange Jello

Mix together, creamed cheese, pineapple and Cool Whip. Add dry orange Jello and mix thoroughly. Let stand several hours or overnight.   Rosella Reiner.

36

* CUCUMBER AND PINEAPPLE SALAD *

1 pkg. (sm.) lime Jello
1 pkg. Knox gelatin
1-½ c. boiling water
½ c. pineapple juice
3 Tbsp. vinegar

½ tsp. salt
2 Tbsp. onion juice
1 c. cucumbers (diced)
1 c. canned pineapple (diced)
½ c. mayonnaise

Soak gelatin in ¼ c. cold water. Dissolve Jello in boiling water, add gelatin. Cool. Add remaining ingredients when slightly thickened. Pour into a mold (greased with mayonnaise). Chill. Unmold and garnish with mint sprigs.   Nancy Ebsen.

* CUCUMBER AND OLIVE SALAD *

1 sm pkg. lime Jello
3 c. water
1 (3 oz.) pkg. cream cheese
   (softened)
½ c. vinegar
1 Tbsp. horseradish
1 tsp. Tabasco

½ tsp. salt
1/3 c. chives (chopped)
½ c. parsley (chopped)
2 c. ripe olives (sliced)
1 lg. unpeeled cucumber (sliced)
Garnish; parsley, cucumber, olives.

Dissolve Jello and gelatin in hot water and stir until dissolved. Add cream cheese and beat until smooth. Mix in vinegar, horseradish, Tabasco and salt. Refrigerate until slightly thick. Stir in chives, parsley, olives and cucumber. Pour into a greased mold.   Adele Davis.

* CAULIFLOWER SALAD *

4 c. thinly sliced cauliflower
1 c. coarsely chopped pitted
   black olives
¾ c. chopped green pepper

½ c. coarsely chopped onions
½ c. chopped pimentos

Dressing:

½ c. salad oil
3 Tbsp. lemon juice
3 Tbsp. white vinegar

2 tsp. salt
¼ tsp. pepper
½ tsp. sugar

Mix salad ingredients well. Beat dressing ingredients with rotary beater, until well blended. Pour over vegetable mix. Refrigerate overnight or for at least 4 hours.   Lucille Grimes

* MANGO SALAD *

1 Tbsp. unflavored gelatin
2 c. cold water
1 pkg. (6 oz.) lemon Jello
2 c. boiling water

1 pkg. (3 oz.) cream cheese
1 c. sm. creamed cottage cheese
1-½ c. mangoes (finely sliced)

Dissolve gelatin in water, set aside. Dissolve lemon Jello in boiling water, combine gelatin and chill until it begins to thicken. Stir in remaining ingredients. Pour into 1-½ quart mold. Chill.   Jean Keys.

* ORANGE PICO SALAD (ITALY) *

4 oranges (peeled—sliced—seeded and
    drained—reserve juice)
1 med. cucumber (unpared—sliced thin)
6 c. fresh spinach (torn in pieces)
2 hds. bibbs lettuce (torn in pieces)

2 sm. red onion (sliced —separated
    in rings)
½ c. toasted walnuts
(coarsely chopped)

Arrange orange slices and cucumber alternately around sides of a glass bowl Arrange spinach, bibbs lettuce, remaining orange slices, onion rings, cucumber slices, onion rings and walnuts in center in layers.

Dressing:

Remaining orange juice
½ c. salad oil
1-½ tsp. sugar

¼ tsp. salt
1/8 tsp. fresh ground pepper

Place in jar with tight cover. Just before serving, shake dressing and pour over salad.   Evelyn Staley.

* AVOCADO MADRILENE *

¼ to ½ c. chilled Madrilene
    Consomme (depending on size
    of cavity)
1 tomato (peeled—seeded—diced).

2 Tbsp. sour cream
chopped chives or minced parsley

Cut avocado in half, do not peel. Twist gently to separate seed. Spoon the tomatoes in the avocados and place chilled consomme on top. Chill until ready to use.

To serve; top with a dollop of sour cream and garnish with chives or parsley.
Note: Save extra consomme for another night and serve with curry touched, salted whipped cream.   Roberta Chateauneuf.

* AVOCADO MOUSSE *

1 Tbsp. gelatin (dissolved in
  2 Tbsp. water)
1 pkg. Lime Jello
2 c. hot water
1 c. mashed avocados

½ c. mayonnaise
½ c. cream (whipped)

Dissolve gelatin and Jello in hot water. When partially congealed stir in remaining ingredients. Pour into a ring mold (greased with mayonnaise and chilled). To serve: Garnish with pineapple sticks, orange sections, cluster of grapes, bing cheeries and sprigs of mint. The center filled with mayonnaise combined with chopped pecans and grated orange peel.   Adele Davis

* AVOCADO RING *

1 pkg. lime Jello
1 c. hot water
3 Tbsp. minced parsley
½ tsp. salt

2 c. avocado (mashed)
¾ c. whipped cream
¼ c. mayonnaise
1 Tbsp. lemon juice

Dissolve Jello in hot water. Chill. Fold in all ingredients. Pour into mold and refrigerate. Garnish with lime slices.   Lillian Kann.

* ALLIGATOR PEAR RING *

2 c. alligator pear pulp
1 c. whipped cream
1 c. mayonnaise

1 pkg. gelatin
1 c. boiling water
salt—pepper—lemon juice to taste

Dissolve gelatin in hot water. Chill mix ingredients together and add to gelatin. Place in ring mold. Cut one alligator pear into strips and fold in mixture carefully. Serve on lettuce with thousand island dressing.   Nancy Ebsen.

* CUCUMBER SOUFFLE SALAD *

1 pkg. (3 oz.) lime or lemon Jello
1 c. hot water
½ c. mayonnaise

½ c. cold water
2 Tbst. lemon juice
½ tsp salt

Dissolve Jello in hot water, add cold water and other ingredients, pour into an ice-cube tray, freeze for 20 minutes (no longer). Put in bowl and beat until fluffy. Mix following ingredients and fold into gelatin mixture.

1 c. cottage cheese
¾ c. finely chopped cucumbers
1 Tbsp. finely chopped scallions
Pour into 8 individual molds.   Dorothy Tuttle.

* TOMATO ASPIC *

2 pkg. Knox gelatin
¼ c. water
1 sm. pkg. lemon Jello
1 c. boiling water
4 bouillon cubes
2 cans. (10 oz.) tomato soup
2 cans. (8 oz. each tomato sauce)

3 Tbsp. Worcestershire sauce
juice of 1 lemon
2 dashes of pepper sauce
½ c. celery (chopped)
½ c. green onion (minced)
salt—pepper

Generously grease a ring mold and set aside. Sprinkle gelatin over ¼ c. cold water and let stand to soften. Dissolve lemon Jello in 1 c. boiling water. Blend both gelatin mixtures together. Set aside.

Bring 2-½ c. water to a boil in lg. saucepan, add bouillon cubes and stir until dissolved. Reduce heat. Blend in soup and tomato sauce and bring to a boil over low heat. Add Worcestershire lemon and pepper sauce. Remove from heat and add gelatin mixture. Refrigerate until slightly thick (about 1 hour). Add vegetables and season to taste.

Pour into mold and refrigerate for several hours or overnight. Unmold on lettuce lined platter.

Adele Davis.

* TOMATO SALAD IN PAPAYA SAMPANS *

1 papaya
1 tsp. lemon juice
1 tomato (peeled—seeded diced)
1 celery stalk (diced)

1 green onion (chopped)
¼ c. bean sprouts
2 Tbsp. walnuts (chopped
lettuce.

Halve papaya lengthwise, remove seeds, sprinkle with lemon juice. Combine tomato, celery, green onion and bean sprouts. Add dressing and toss lightly. Fill papaya and place on lettuce leaf and top with walnuts.

Dressing:

3 Tbsp. oil
1 Tbsp. lemon juice
Combine all ingredients and mix well.

1/8 tsp. basil
½ tsp. sugar

Judy Pieklo.

* VEGETABLE SALAD *

1-½ c. cooked beets (diced)
½ c. cooked peas (drained)
½ c. cooked carrots (diced)

½ c. sour cream
¼ tsp. coriander (ground)

Use canned, frozen or fresh vegetables. Lightly mix and serve as salad on lettuce or on appetizer plates.

Francis Wright

* PICKLED BEET SALAD *

1 can sliced pickled beets
  (cubed drain)
2 c. cranberry juice

¾ c. water
2 Tbsp. lemon juice
¼ tsp. salt
1 bay leaf

Bring ingredients to a boil. Add 6 oz. pkg. lemon Jello. Chill until syrupy. Add 2 Tbsp. minced onion. 3 Tbsp. chopped celery and diced beets. Pour into mold and chill until firm.

Dressing:

1 pkg. Imo or sour cream
2 Tbsp. milk
1 Tbsp. prepared horseradish

1 tsp. sugar.
¼ tsp. salt

Mix all — Chill. Remove from refrigerator 30 minutes before serving.

Dorothy Tuttle.

* MARINATED VEGETABLE BOUQUET *

1 can Garbanzos
1 can cut green beans
1 can pitted riped olives
1 can whole or sliced mushrooms
1 can artichoke hearts

1-½ c. sliced celery
1 med. onion (sliced thin)
1 can sm. red beans
(lima and wax beans may be added)

Drain all cans. Blend carefully. Combine all ingredients for dressing, Pour over salad and toss well. Chill in refrigerator overnite, tossing well twice. (This is best made a day or two ahead.)

Dressing:

¼ c. tarragon vinegar
1-½ tsp. Accent (optional)
1-1/3 tsp. salt
1 tsp. sugar

1 Tbsp. herbs or salad herbs
¼ tsp. Tabasco
½ c. salad oil
Parsley (minced)

Jean Keys.

* CUCUMBERS AND YOGURT *

5 lg. cucumbers (peeled—seeded—
  cubed)
1 carton (32 oz.) plain yogurt
mint leaves for garnish.

½ c. fresh mint (finely—chopped)

1-½ tsp. salt

Place cucumbers in a bowl, add remaining ingredients (except garnish). Mix well and refrigerate for several hours or overnight. Garnish with mint leaves.

Nancy Ebsen.

41

* BEAN SALAD *

1 No. 2 can kidney beans
1 No. 2 can wax beans
1 No. 2 can green beans

Dressing:

¾ c. sugar
2 tsp. salt
1 lg. tsp. pepper

1 green pepper (sliced thin)
2 onions (sliced thin)

1/3 c. oil
2/3 c. vinegar

Mix dressing and pour over drained vegetables. Refrigerate overnight. Garnish with chopped parsley.

Ida Christoph.

* GREEN BEAN WITH BACON SALAD *

1 pkg. (9 oz.) frozen French cut
   green beans
¼ c. mayonnaise
1 Tbsp. onion (grated)

salt — pepper
1 tsp. Dijon mustard
¼ c. crisped bacon (crumbled)

Partially thaw and chop French cut beans and blanch for 1 minute in boiling water with 1 tsp. lemon juice. Drain well and chill. Mix mayonnaise, onion, mustard and remaining lemon juice. Fold into cooled beans and crumbled bacon. Season to taste with salt and pepper. Chill thoroughly. Serve on bed of greens. (note: This makes a delicious sandwich filling.)

Evelyn Staley.

* CHEESE AND SWEET RED PEPPER SALAD *

4 lg. sweet red peppers
1 head lettuce (bite size pieces)
1 sm. bunch green onions
   (finely chopped)

½ c. celery (diced)
4 anchovy strips (diced)
4 oz. Fontina cheese (cubed)
Vinaigrette dressing

Roast peppers by placing over a flame until blackened and blistered on all sides. (Note: if you do not have a burner with flame, preheat over to 350°. Place peppers on a baking sheet and bake for approximately 35 to 40 minutes. Remove from oven and place in a damp towel for 15 to 20 minutes. Peel skins and continue with recipe.) Peel peppers under cold running water, discard seeds and white membranes. Cut into ¼ in. strips. In a lg. bowl, toss lettuce with onion, celery and anchovies.

Arrange cheese cubes and pepper slices on top. Just before serving, toss with your favorite dressing.

Charlene Do.

* EASY SOUR BEAN SALAD *

1 can cut yellow beans
1 can cut green beans
1 can red kidney beans
Dressing:
½ c. oil
2/3 c. vinegar
½ c. sugar

1 sm. green pepper (chopped)
1 sm. onion (chopped fine)

1 tsp. salt
½ tsp. pepper

Drain beans and put in lg. bowl. Add the chopped vegetables. In separate bowl mix all remaining ingredients, then pour over veggies. Refrigerate overnight.
Jean Keys.

* EGGPLANT SALAD (SPAIN) *

2 med. eggplants
1 tsp. lemon juice
1 tsp. minced onion

1 c. celery (diced)
½ c. nuts (chopped)
¼ c. dressing

Peel and cube eggplants and cook until tender in salted water with lemon juice. Drain and cool. Add remaining ingredients. Chill. Serve on romaine lettuce with sliced hard-cooked eggs and black olives. Dot with mayonnaise.   Adele Davis.

* COLE SLAW *

1 med. head cabbage
2 med. onions (sliced)
¾ c. sugar
Shred cabbage — stir in sugar, add sliced onion rings. Mix well.
Dressing:
1 tsp. celery seed
1 tsp. sugar
1-½ tsp salt
1 tsp. dry mustard

1 c. vinegar
¾ c. oil

Combine all ingredients (except oil) and bring to a boil—add oil. Pour over cabbage and refrigerate overnite covered. Note: The older it gets the better it gets—up to 10 days.   Valerie Wilson

* MUSHROOM SALAD *

1-¼ lb. mushrooms (chopped)
8 oz. cream cheese
1/3 c. mayonnaise

½ tsp. salt
¼ tsp. pepper
1-½ Tbsp. onion (grated)

Beat until cream cheese is softened, add all the other ingredients, fold in the mushrooms. Chill. Serve on bed of lettuce or use as a sandwich filling with watercress.   Ida Christoph.

* SPINACH — RED CABBAGE AND MUSHROOM SALAD *

1 lb. spinach (washed—drained—
   torn into pieces)
½ lb. bean sprouts (rinsed—drained)
½ lb. red cabbage (cut in wedges—
   sliced thin)

½ c. parsley (minced)
10—12 mushrooms (sliced)
Vinaigrette dressing

Place spinach, bean sprouts and red cabbage in a bowl and toss. Add Vinaigrette dressing and toss again. Garnish top with mushroom slices and parsley. Chill
Judy Pieklo.

* CHEESE—CAPPED ICEBURG LETTUCE *

1 med. head iceburg lettuce
1 pkg. (8 oz.) cream cheese
¼ c. mayonnaise
½ c. pimiento olives (chopped)
dash of hot sauce

2 Tbsp. green onions (chopped)
¼ c. catsup
2 tsp. vinegar
¾ tsp. chili powder

Beat cream cheese until fluffy. Stir in ¼ c. mayonnaise, olive and onion. Core lettuce, remove the center leaving 1 in. shell. — Fill shell with cheese mixture. Wrap in heavy foil. Mix ½ c. mayonnaise with the remaining ingredients, cover. Chill lettuce and dressing overnite.
To serve: Cut lettuce into wedges and serve with dressing in a bowl.
Adele Davis.

* SPINACH SALAD FLAMBE *

6 bunches (12 oz. each) spinach
6 hard-cooked eggs (sliced)
12 fried bacon strips (chopped)
¾ c. bacon drippings
salt—pepper

½ c. vinegar
¼ c. lemon juice
4 tsp. sugar
1 tsp. Worcestershire sauce
2 oz. brandy (100 proof)

Tear spinach into bite size pieces and place in salad bowl. Add egg slices, salt and pepper.
Mix remaining ingredients (except Brandy) in a sm. saucepan and heat until very hot. Heat Brandy briefly, add to saucepan and ignite. Pour flaming dressing over spinach and toss gently. Serve on warm salad plates.
Nathalia Richman.

44

* WATERCRESS AND CHESTNUT SALAD *

3 bunches watercress (stems
   removed)
½ c. walnut oil
1 tsp. Dijon mustard
1 Tbsp. lemon juice

2 lbs. chestnuts (roasted—skinned—
   quartered)
3 Tbsp. wine vinegar
salt—pepper

Arrange watercress in center of each plate. Mix oil, lemon juice, vinegar, salt and pepper to taste, in a sm. jar. Cover and refrigerate. A serving time, shake jar, pour over watercress. Surround with garland of chestnuts.   **Evelyn Staley.**

* BEAN SPROUT SALAD *

1-½ lbs. fresh crisp bean sprouts
¾ c. oil
1/3 c. red wine vinegar
¼ tsp. oregano
1 garlic clove (minced)
¼ c. celery (finely chopped)

1-½ tsp. aromat (a sweet spice)
2 med. red peppers (seeded—diced)
2 med. green peppers
   (seeded—diced)

Wash beans in colander under cold water, drain, dry and chill. Mix oil, vinegar, oregano, garlic and aromat. Place in a blender and whirl 1 minute. Pour over prepared vegetables. Chill. Toss with cold bean sprouts.   **Millie Mesaku**

* MACARONI SALAD *

1 c. uncooked macaroni (cook it)
Dressing:
1/3 c. mayonnaise
1 Tbsp. prepared mustard
1 Tbsp. lemon juice
1-½ c. sliced celery
2 Tbsp. parsley (cut fine)

2 hard-cooked eggs (chopped)

1/3 c. pickle relish (drained)
1/3 c. chopped onion
2 Tbsp. pimiento (chopped)

Mix dressing with macaroni and chill. (This is super).   **Dorothy Tuttle.**

* CORNED BEEF SALAD *

1 sm pkg. lemon Jello
1 c. hot water
1 c. beef consomme
1 Tbsp. green pepper (chopped)
1 Tbsp. parsley (chopped)

1 c. mayonnaise
1 sm. onion (diced)
1 c. celery (diced)
1 can cornbeef
1 (12 oz.) can corn

Dissolve Jello in hot water and add consomme, chill slightly. Add all ingredients and refrigerate. Unmold and serve with half of canned peach filled with mince meat.   **Francis Wright.**

* CHINESE SALAD *

Won Bok — head lettuce
Equal amounts — shredded.
Dressing:

1 c. salad oil	2 tsp. salt
½ c. sesame oil	½ tsp. pepper
¼ c. sesame seeds (toasted)	½ c. white vinegar
½ c. sugar	¼ c. lemon juice
1 med. onion (diced)	1 tsp. dry mustard
1 lg. garlic clove (minced)	¼ c. mayonnaise (to thicken)

At serving time, mix dressing with the greens and add crushed Won Ton chips.
Add chicken pieces to make a luncheon salad.   Dorothy Tuttle.

* TOSTADA SALAD *

2 lbs. ground beef	1 can (8 oz.) chili hot sauce
2 cans (1 lb. each) red kidney	4 c. cheddar cheese (shredded)
beans (drained)	2 avocados (chopped)
1 head lettuce (shredded)	2 c. corn chips
4 tomatoes (chopped)	2 c. Thousand island dressing.
2 onions (finely chopped)	

Saute beef in skillet until brown. Mix in kidney beans, cover and simmer for 10
minutes.
Arrange lettuce in a lg. salad bowl. Arrange mounds of tomatoes, onion, cheese,
avocado, chips and the cooled meat mixture. Just before serving, toss with
dressing and hot sauce to taste.   June Post.

* TACO SALAD *

1 to 1-½ lbs. ground beef	1 med. head lettuce
¼ c. minced onions	3 tomatoes
¼ tsp. garlic powder	1 c. Miracle whip or Thousand
1 pkg. Taco seasoning mix	Island dressing
1 can red kidney beans (drained)	1 pkg. Taco flavored Dorito chips
1 lb. sharp cheddar cheese or Colby cheese	

Brown beef, onion, and garlic—drain off all fat. Add Taco seasoning and ¼ to
½ c. water. Simmer. Add beans. (add more water, if it sticks). Slice or chop
lettuce and cut tomatoes into sm. pieces. Crush Doritos (puncture bag with sm.
pointed object before opening.) Combine with all but ¼ of the chips in a lg.
bowl. Mix in Miracle whip. Combine meat mixture and toss lightly. Top with
remaining Taco chips and cheese.   Rebecca Dixon.

* CRISP SHOESTRING SALAD *

2 c. chopped chicken or 1 can tuna
1 c. chopped celery
1 c. grated carrots

1 sm. onion (chopped)
2 Tbsp. salad dressing
1 med. can shoestring potatoes

Mix first 5 ingredients and refrigerate. Just before serving, add shoestrings, save some for the top.   Madeline Ryan.

* SUMMER CHICKEN SALAD *

¾ c. mayonnaise
¾ c. frozen whipped topping
   (thawed)
3 cans (5 oz. each) chunk chicken
   (drained)
1-½ c. sliced celery

¾ c. seedless grapes (halved)
¾ c. slivered almonds (toasted)
½ c. black olives (sliced)

Combine mayonnaise and whipped topping. Add chicken, celery, grapes, almonds and olives, toss mixture well. Chill. Serve salad on lettuce leaves.
                                              Millie Akaka.

* RICERONI SALAD *

1 pkg. Almond Riceroni prepared
   as directed and cooled.
1/3 c. mayonnaise
1 jar marinated artichoke hearts
   (chopped—use oil also)
¼ c. green pepper (chopped—optional)
1 c. water chestnuts (chopped

1 c. whole black olives (chopped)
3 green onions (thin sliced to
   the tips of green tops)
¼ c. slivered almonds

Mix well. Cover tightly and refrigerate.
Note: Keeps very well for several days.   Eileen Weberg.

* TACO SALAD *

1 lb. ground beef
1 pkg. (1-1/8 oz.) taco seasoning mix.
¼ c. water

Brown ground beef, add seasonings and water. Cook until water cooks out. Cool completely.

½ to 1 head of lettuce (shredded)
A few green onions (chopped—tops
   and all)
2—3 tomatoes (diced)

1 can garbanzo beans (optional)
1 can kidney beans (drained)
1 c. Cheddar cheese (grated)
Doritos, (crushed into bite-size pieces)

Toss all ingredients together with Taco sauce to taste.

Note: This is my recipe for Taco Salad. Can add black olives, green beans, etc. or substitute Fritos for Doritos and Monterey Jack cheese in place of the Cheddar.

Millie Akaka.

* THREE BEAN SALAD *

1 tall can whole green beans	¼ c. pimento
1 tall can yellow wax beans	½ c. green pepper (chopped)
1 tall can kidney beans	1 small onion (sliced)
Dressing:	
¾ c. sugar	2/3 tsp. celery seed
2/3 c. vinegar	1 tsp. salt
2/3 c. salad oil	¼ tsp. pepper

Drain beans, pimento and add pepper and onions. Mix well and pour dressing over mixture. Refrigerate.

Ann Kobayashi.

* KARTOFFEL SALAT (GERMAN) *
(Hot Potato Salad)

2 lbs. potatoes	½ tsp. dry mustard
4 slices of bacon	1 Tbsp. capers
1 onion (sliced)	4 Tbsp. beef bouillon
4 Tbsp. olive oil	2 tsp. salt
2 Tbsp. wine vinegar	1 c. pitted ripe olives
2 hard-cooked eggs	

Boil potatoes until tender. Peel and slice. Saute bacon (cut in sm. pieces) until crisp (not brown). Remove bacon, saute onions and add olive oil, vinegar, seasonings and boulllon. Bring to a boil and pour over warm potatoes. Garnish with sliced eggs and olives.

Adele Davis

* HOT CHICKEN SALAD *

2 c. cubed cooked chicken	2 Tbsp. lemon juice
2 c. sliced celery	½ tsp. grated lemon rind
½ c. slivered almonds	½ c. mayonnaise
¼ c. minced onions	½ c. sour cream
½ tsp. salt	½ c. Parmesan cheese
1 Tbsp. chopped parsley.	2 whole pimentos (chopped)

Mix all and put in a casserole (9 in. round or rectangular). Put into a 450° oven sprinkle crushed potato chips on top and bake for 25 — 30 minutes. (Smells like chop suey and will it ever taste good.)

Jean Keys.

* RICE SALAD *

4 c. cooked rice
½ c. green pepper (diced)
2 Tbsp. green onion (finely chopped)
3 Tbsp. radishes (finely chopped)
½ c. celery (finely chopped)
¼ c. mayonnaise
½ c. sweet pickle relish
1 garlic clove (minced)
¼ tsp. nutmeg
1 Tbsp. curry powder
½ tsp. cloves
salt to taste

Combine all ingredients in a salad bowl, cover and chill for 3 to 4 hours. Garnish with chopped parsley.   Francis Wright.

* BIRD'S NEST SALAD (SWEDEN) *

1 Tbsp. capers (rinsed—drained)
1 med. onion (chopped)
¼ c. anchovy fillets (chopped)
3 Tbsp. parsley (chopped)
½ c. cooked beets (diced canned or
    fresh)
1 egg yolk.

Starting at center of serving plate, arrange ingredients in rings in the following order. Capers, onion, anchovies, parsley, then the beets. Place egg yolk in it's shell in an egg cup at the side of plate. Custom is for the guest of honor to pour the yolk into the nest and mix all ingredients together. Serve with Swedish flat bread.   Adele Davis

* HAM AND TATER LOAF *

4 c. cooked ham (chopped)
¾ c. mayonnaise
½ c. celery (diced)
½ c. sweet pickle (diced)
3 Tbsp. pickle juice
2 tsp. prepared mustard
1 tsp. salt
1½ lbs. potatoes (cooked—diced)

Line 9 in. loaf pan with wax paper. Mix ham with ½ c. mayonnaise into bottom of pan. Mix celery, sweet pickle, pickle juice and salt and remaining mayonnaise. Add potatoes and toss. Press lightly over ham layer. Cover and chill at least 4 hr. Unmold on salad plates and garnish with lettuce leaves.   Nathalia Richman.

* MEXICAN SALAD BOWL *

½ c. mayonnaise
¼ c. green onions (minced)
2 tsp. cider vinegar
1 tsp. onion salt
½ tsp. chili powder
2 c. lettuce (shredded)
4 drops of hot pepper sauce
1 can (8 oz.) whole kernel corn
1 can (8 oz.) red kidney beans
1 can (7 oz.) pitted black olives

Mix mayonnaise, green onions, vinegar, chili powder, salt, and hot sauce, Chill. Drain and combine corn, beans and olives. Spoon into lettuce—lined bowls and serve with the dressing.   Linda Riley.

*SHRIMP AND RICE SALAD *

½ c. cooked and chilled rice
½ lb. cooked—shrimp
  (cut into two pieces)

¼ c. raw cauliflower (flowerlets
  cut into sm. pieces)
½ c. mayonnaise

Note: Use water chestnuts in place of cauliflower. Mix together and serve on lettuce leaves. Garnish with hard-cooked eggs (quartered), ripe olives, watercress, cucumber slices or green or red peppers (chopped).　　　　　　Jean Walters.

* SHRIMP SALAD *

2 lbs. lg. cooked shrimp
  (shelled—deveined)
2 papayas (peeled—sliced—seeded)
2 mangoes (peeled—sliced)
2 avocados (peeled—sliced)

½ c. fresh pineapple
  (cut in spears)
1 kiwifruit (sliced)

Arrange shrimp and fruit attractively on lettuce on a lg. platter or individual salad and garnish with toasted coconut, macadamia nuts, grapes and fresh chopped mint.

Dressing:

1 c. mayonnaise
½ c. whipped cream
2 Tbsp. coconut (grated)
3 Tbsp. lime juice

1 Tbsp. lime rind (grated)
2 tsp. honey
1 tsp. fresh ginger (grated)

Combine all ingredients (except mayonnaise) in a blender and whirl until fluffy. Fold mixture into mayonnaise. Chill. Note: Slices of cooked chicken breasts may be used in place of shrimp.　　　　　　Adele Davis.

* SHRIMP MOUSSE *

Heat until creamy:

8 oz. cream cheese
2 pkg. Knox gelatin

1 can cream of mushroom soup
6 Tbsp. water

Add:

1 c. mayonnaise
½ c. celery (chopped)
½ c. green onions (chopped)

1 can. pimentos (chopped)
2 cans. tiny shrimp

Mix all together, place in mold or serve as a spread with Triscuits.

Annie Ebsen.

V·E·G·E·T·A·B·L·E·S

* GREEN BEANS PARMESAN *

2 pkg. frozen green beans (French style) — cooked barely tender. Cool.
1 sm. onion (finely chopped)

½ c. salad oil
¼ c. wine vinegar
1 tsp. salt

¼ tsp. pepper
½ c. Parmesan cheese (grated)
2 Tbsp. anchovy fillets (chopped)

Mix all ingredients together. Chill thoroughly.   Dorothy Tuttle.

* BEANS (FINLAND) *

4 cans. red kidney beans
1 bunch green onions (cut-up)
¾ lb. bacon (diced and fried —
    drain off fat)

1 c. chili sauce
dash of Tabasco sauce.

Mix in casserole. Top with brown sugar and bake at 350° for about 2 hours.
                                                            Rosella Reines.

* STRING BEANS IN EGG SAUCE *

1 can (16 oz.) string beans
2 Tbsp. butter or oleo
½ c. milk
½ c. bean liquid
buttered crumbs

1/8 tsp. celery seed
¼ tsp. salt
dash of pepper
3 hard-cooked eggs (sliced)

Drain beans. Reserve ½ c. liquid. Make white sauce of the 6 other ingredients. Add sliced eggs. Put hot beans in buttered casserole. Pour sauce over beans, top with crumbs. Bake in 350° oven until hot. (about 20 minutes).   Dorothy Lyle.

* SAME KI BHAJ (INDIA) *
(Green beans in coconut)

2 c. coconut (flaked)
2 c. water
2 c. onions (chopped)
½ tsp. salad oil
2 tsp. tumeric (ground)

1 garlic clove (chopped)
4 lbs. fresh green beans
    (cut in 2 in. pieces)
2 tsp. coriander seeds (crushed)
3 tsp. salt

Place coconut in blender (med. speed) for 3 minutes. Saute onions, mustard seed and garlic in oil in a 1g. skillet for 5 minutes. Mix in remaining ingredients (reserve coconut mixture). Heat to boiling, lower heat and simmer for 15 min. Stir occasionally. Add coconut mixture and toss gently. Garnish with lemon slices.   Adele Davis.

* GREEN BEANS *

2 lbs. green beens (cut in 5 in. lengths)
3 sm. sweet red peppers (sliced in rings)

Use pepper rings to circle bunches of beans. Fasten with toothpicks if necessary.
Steam for 15 minutes. Garlic butter may be poured on top if desired

Nancy Ebsen.

* BAKED ASPARAGUS *

2 cans. (15 oz. each) white or green asparagus or 1 pkg. frozen asparagus —
(cooked)
½ c. mayonnaise   ½ tsp. paprika
½ c. Parmesan cheese (grated)   butter

Preheat oven to 350°. Butter bottom and sides of a small baking dish. Place
asparagus in one layer in baking dish. Spread mayonnaise over top and sprinkle
Cheese and paprika generously. Head in oven for 20 minutes. Just before serving.
place under broiler to brown lightly.   Nathalia Richman.

* ASPARAGUS WITH ANCHOVY — SAUCE *

2¼ lbs. fresh asparagus   6 anchovies (chopped)
1 tsp. salt   3 Tbsp. parsley (chopped)
2 Tbsp. green onions (chopped)   2 tsp. lemon juice
1 stick butter

Trim off ends of asparagus. Bring to a boil in salted water. Cook over med. heat
for 7 minutes or until tender. Drain. Melt butter, add onions, anchovies, parsley
and lemon juice. Pour over asparagus. Garnish with pimientos.

Francis Wright.

*ASPARAGUS WITH PEANUT DRESSING *

2¼ lbs. fresh asparagus or 3 pkgs. (10 oz. each) frozen asparagus
3 Tbsp. peanut butter   2 Tbsp. Sherry
¼ c. sugar   1 sm. piece ginger (grated)
¼ c. shoyu sauce

If using frozen asparagus, cook as directed on pkg. For fresh asparagus, cut into
2 in. pieces. Cook simmering until tender. Drain and rinse in cold water. Mix
peanut butter and sugar, add other ingredients slowly. Pour over chilled asparagus, stir to coat.   Evelyn Staley.

* ARTICHOKES WITH CAULIFLOWER *

4 artichokes (tough leaves removed)
1 med. head cauliflower
  (chop in lg, pieces)
2 tsp. salt
6 Tbsp. butter (melted)

white pepper to taste
3 Tbsp. chives (chopped)
1½ c. heavy cream
dash of nutmeg

Steam artichokes for 30 to 40 minutes until tender. Remove from heat drain and keep warm. Drop 1/3 of the cauliflower into a blender, add 2 Tbsp. butter, 1 tsp. chives and ½ c. cream and blend into a rich texture. Remove to a sauce—pan. Repeat once more, using 1/3 of the ingredients each time. Stir in nutmeg, salt and pepper. Five minutes before serving. Heat cauliflower mixture (add more butter if needed). Split artichoke down the middle, fill cavity with cauli-flower (remove the choke if larger cavity is wanted). To keep warm until served, wrap in foil and place in a 200° oven. Should be served very hot.

Adele Davis.

* SOUFFLED AVOCADOS *

1½ lb. salmon, halibut or turbot
  (poached-diced)
1½ c. clam juice.
4 Tbsp. butter
3 Tbsp. flour
2 shallots (minced)
2 c. dry white wine
3 egg yolks
2 Tbsp. Gruyere cheese (grated)

4 egg whites (stiffly beaten)
1/8 tsp. salt
1/8 tsp. cream of tartar
1 tsp. fresh dill (minced)
¼ tsp. curry powder
salt-pepper
4 avocados (unpeeled-coated with
  lemon juice)
2 Tbsp. Parmesan (grated)

In a lg. saucepan melt butter and add flour, then stir in clam juice until thic-kened, set aside. Saute shallots in a little butter in a lg. skillet, add wine. Cook until wine is reduced by half. Add seafood and mix. Stir in half of clam sauce and the cream. Add seasonings. Preheat over to 400°. Place avocados on a baking sheet and fill with the seasoned mixture.
Beat egg yolks with the remaining clam juice. Beat egg whites with cream of tartar until stiff but not dry. Fold into egg mixture. Add grated cheeses. Put 2 Tbsp. of mixture on top of each avocado and bake for 10 minutes.

Roberta Chateauneuf.

* BROCCOLI SUPREME *

1 egg (slightly beaten)
1 pkg. frozen broccoli
  (partially thawed)
1 can (8 oz.) creamed corn
1 c. stuffing mix toss with 3 Tsp. melted butter or oleo.

1 Tbsp. onion (grated)
¼ tsp. salt
dash of pepper
¾ c. stuffing mix

Mix first seven ingredients and put in a 1 qt. casserole, top with buttered stuffing mix. Bake (uncovered) for 30 to 40 minutes   Dorothy Tuttle.

*BROCCOLI NEUFCHATEL *

2 lb. fresh broccoli
¼ c. onion (minced)
3 Tbsp. flour
2 tsp. chicken bouillon
  instant powder
4 oz. Neufchatel cheese (whipped)

1½ c. milk
½ c. plain yogurt
¼ c. butter
6 tomato wedges (garnish)

Melt butter in saucepan, add onion and simmer until light brown. Blend in flour and bouillon powder. Add milk gradually. Stirring constantly with a whisk. Cook stirring over med. heat until thick and bubbly.
Remove from heat, cover and keep warm until broccoli is cooked. Remove lg. leaves from broccoli, cook covered in small amount of water until tender but not soft. Drain. Blend whipped cheese into sauce and heat through, gently blend in yogurt. Pour over broccoli in serving dish and garnish with tomato wedges.
                    Adele Davis.

* SESAME BROCCOLI *

2 lbs. fresh broccoli
  (cut in 2 in. pieces)
2½ Tbsp. sugar
2 Tbsp. sesame seeds (toasted)

2 Tbsp. oil
2 Tbsp. vinegar
2 Tbsp. shoyu

Cook broccoli in salted water until tender (do not overcook). Drain and keep warm. Combine remaining ingredients in saucepan and bring to a boil over med. heat. Pour over broccoli, turning spears to coat well.
Garnish with chopped parsley.   Nancy Ebsen.

* BOHEMIAN CABBAGE *

1½ lbs. cabbage
1 c. water
1 med. onion (chopped)
2 Tbsp. bacon grease
½ tsp. caraway seed
2 Tbsp. flour

pinch of salt
1 to 2 tsp. sugar (add sprinkle
 of Sweet—10).
1 tsp. vinegar
½ tsp. lemon juice

Simmer cabbage in water—drain. Add onion (browned in bacon fat). Salt and saute for 10—15 minutes. Add sugar, lemon juice and vinegar. Add caraway seed and simmer for 5 minutes. Serve hot. Georgia Beasley.

* CHINESE CABBAGE (OR CELERY MILKYWAY) *

1½ lbs. Chinese cabbage
3 Tbsp. peanut or vegetable oil
1½ c. cream
2 tsp. corn starch
¾ tsp. salt

½ tsp. fresh ground pepper
1 tsp. paprika
6 strips bacon (cooked-crumbled)
¼ c. Chinese parsley
 (chopped fine — no stems)

Cut Chinese cabbage lengthwise in half. in a lg, saucepan cook cabbage in boiling salted water for 3 or 4 minutes. Remove from pan, drain, let cool. Cut in 2 in. by 4 in. strips. Heat oil in Wok or lg. heavy skillet and stir fry for 2 to 3 minutes. In sm. bowl blend cream, cornstarch, salt and pepper. Add milk mixture to pan and cook, stirring over med. heat until thickened. Place cabbage and sauce on heated platter, sprinkle with paprika and crumbled bacon and decorate with Chinese parsley. Faye Awbrey.

* UMINTAS (BOLIVIA) *
(Baked Corn)

5 ears fresh corn or 2 cans
 corn kernels
2 eggs
½ tsp. chili powder

1/8 tsp. anise seed
1 tsp. flour
¼ lb. Swiss or Cheddar cheese

Scrape kernels from uncooked corn cobs. Beat eggs and add to corn. Heat butter and add chili powder, anise seed and flour and simmer 1 minute.
Combine corn and flour mixture. Pour mixture into buttered casserole (½ of the mixture) and cover with thin slices of cheese. Top with remaining mixture. Bake at 350° for 1 hour. Judy Pieklo.

* HERBED GRILLED CORN *

½ c. butter (softened)   ½ tsp. salt
2 Tbsp. parsley (chopped)   dash of pepper
2 Tbsp. chives (chopped   8 ears of corn (husks and silks removed)

Blend butter with parsley, chives, salt and pepper. Spread 1 Tbsp. over each ear, wrap individually in heavy foil.
Grill over glowing coals for 15 to 20 minutes. Turn occasionally. May also be baked in over (preheated at 350°) for 30 minutes or until tender.

Evelyn Staley.

* BEETS AND MANDARIN ORANGES *

1 can (3 c.) sliced beets   1/3 c. vinegar
1 c. beet juice and water (combined)   1 tsp. salt
1½ Tbsp. cornstarch   dash of pepper
2 Tbsp. sugar

Heat beets and beet juice. Mix remaining ingredients, add to beets, stirring constantly until blended. Add 1 can drained mandarin oranges and simmer for a few minutes.

Colonel Jean Lyle.

* GERMAN SLAW *

8 slices bacon (cut in sm. pcs.)   1/8 tsp. Beau Monde seasoning
3 Tbsp. sugar   ¼ c. water
1 tsp. salt   1 med. head cabbage (chopped)
½ tsp white pepper   ¼ c. minced onion
¼ c. vinegar   ½ c. red or green peppers
                                          (cut in thin strips)

Fry bacon slowly until crisp. Remove from drippings with a slotted spoon and drain on paper towels. Add sugar, salt, pepper Beau Monda to the bacon drippings and stir until dissolved. Add vinegar and water and cook slowly until dressing is slightly reduced. Pour dressing over cabbage and onion, while still hot. Top with the bacon and pepper strips. Note: White or red cabbage may be used for the recipe.

Adele Davis.

* NEW YEARS DAY BLACK EYED PEAS *

2 c. chopped onions
1 c. chopped celery
2 c. chopped green pepper

Saute in bacon grease and 2 Tbsp. butter. Add 2 cans of black eyed peas (or 2 c. dried and drained). Add 2—3 fresh tomatoes (chopped). Cook over low heat, stirring often.

To reduce the liquid. Take off heat when vegetables are done, but still crunchy, add spices to taste, cumin, oregano, thyme and salt and pepper. Use crumbled crisp bacon on top. *"Tis good luck!"*   Allison Holland.

* VEGETARIAN LOAF *

1 c. finely chopped onion	½ tsp. salt
1 c. finely chopped celery	½ tsp. lemon pepper
1 c. finely chopped walnuts	¼ tsp. celery seeds
1 c. shredded carrots	2 eggs (slightly beaten)
1 c. fine—dry whole wheat bread crumbs	½ c. mayonnaise

Line 8½ in. by 2½ in. loaf pan with foil (unless glass pan is used—grease same). In a lg. bowl, stir together the 8 listed ingredients. in small bowl stir eggs and mayonnaise, then stir all together. Pour into prepared pan. Bake at 350° for 50 minutes. Note: Loaf will keep—use cold or in sandwiches.   Virginia Doyle.

* CORN BAKE CASSEROLE *

3 eggs (slightly beaten)	1 c. sour cream
1 pkg. (8 oz.) corn muffin	½ c. butter (melted)
1 can (8 oz.) creamed corn	1 c. grated cheese
2 cans (16 oz.) whole corn (drained)	1 can (4 oz.) green chili (chopped)

Combine all but cheese. Mix all ingredients in casserole and bake for 1 hour at 350°. Top with cheese and bake for 15 minutes more.   Dorothy Tuttle.

* HERRING STUFFED BEETS *

24 sm. whole beets (cooked)	¼ c. sour cream
1 jar (6 oz.) pickled herring bits	dill sprigs.

With sm. melon scoop hollow out the top of each beet. Drain herring and coarsely chop and fill each beet with ½ tsp. Dot with sour cream and garnish with dill sprigs. Serve cold.   Adele Davis.

* MOCK OYSTERS *
(Eggplant)

3 c. brown rice flakes
1 med. eggplant
1 c. milk
½ lb Cheddar cheese (grated)

3 Tbsp. butter
1 Tbsp. bread crumbs
salt-pepper to taste

Cover whole eggplant with boiling water, add a pinch of soda. Cook 15 minutes. Wash in cold water. Butter casserole, chop eggplant.
Layer eggplant and flakes, dot with butter and cheese. Top with bread crumbs and add milk. Bake in preheated over (375°) for 30 minutes.

Roberta Chateauneuf.

* EGGPLANT FINGERS *

2 eggplants (1 lb. each.)
2 c. milk
2 c. bread crumbs

powdered sugar
oil for frying
2 c. flour

Peel eggplant and cut into ½ in. strips. Heat oil in deep fat fryer to 375°. Dip eggplant strips into milk, then in flour, into milk again, and finally into bread crumbs.
Place about 12 strips into the fryer at a time and fry until golden brown (about 4 minutes). Drain on paper towels. Continue until all strips are fried. Sprinkle with powdered sugar and serve hot or cold.

Annie Ebsen

* SUMMER HARVEST VEGETABLES *

1 bunch broccoli
1 sm. cauliflower
2 c. mushrooms (diced)
juice of ½ lemon
2 Tbsp. peanut oil
1 sm. ginger root (sliced)
½ lb. Cheddar cheese (grated)

1 gr. pepper (sliced lengthwise)
2 c. celery (sliced diagonally)
1 garlic clove (minced)
1 tsp. salt
1 tsp. onion salt
1 tsp. pepper
2 Tbsp. shoyu

Trim stems from broccoli and cauliflower. Divide into florets. Pour lemon juice over the mushrooms and set aside.
Heat oil in Wok to high heat. Arrange broccoli and cauliflower on bottom and sides of Wok. Distribute mushrooms., pepper, celery, ginger, and garlic in layers. Add all seasonings (except shoyu). Stir fry until vegetables are just crispy. Add shoyu and grated cheese and stir fry until cheese is melted.

Millie Mesaku.

* FAR EAST CELERY *

4 c. celery slice (1 in.)—cooked in sm. amount of water. Drain.
1 can water chestnuts (sliced)   ½ c. soft bread crumbs
¼ c. pimentos (diced)   ¼ c. slivered almonds
1 can chicken soup   2 Tbsp. butter

Mix celery and water chestnuts in a casserole. Add pimentos and chicken soup.
Toss bread crumbs with the almonds and sprinkle over top.
Bake in 350° oven until hot and browned.   Lillian Kann.

* SAVORY LEMON VEGETABLES *

½ lb. bacon (cooked-crumbled)   1 med. cauliflower
   (reserve ¼ c. drippings)   1 tsp. salt
1 c. onion (finely chopped)   1 tsp. thyme leaves
½ c. lemon juice   1 lbs. carrots (pared-diced)
½ c. water
4 tsp. sugar

Place bacon drippings into a skillet and add onion, water, lemon juice sugar, salt,
and thyme and bring to a boil. keep warm.
Place carrots and cauliflower in saucepan, just enough water to cover and cook
until tender. Drain.
Arrange on serving dish and pour sauce over vegetables. Serve warm. Note: Left-
overs may be refrigerated and served cold as salad.   Nathalia Richman.

* GARDEN SCRAMBLE *

2 Tbsp. oil   3 Tbsp. water
1 garlic clove (crushed)   salt-pepper
1 c. broccoli florets   ½ c. carrots (cut diagonally
   (1 in. slices)   in ½ in. slices)
whole cashews (toasted)   ½ red pepper (½ in. slices)

Place Wok over high heat add 1 Tbsp. oil. Add garlic and stir-fry 1 minute. Add
broccoli and carrots. Add 2 Tbsp. water and stir-fry for 3 minutes. Remove and
keep warm.
Add remaining oil to Wok and stir fry red peppers for 1 minute. Add remaining
water and vegetables. Salt and pepper to taste.
Serve hot and garnish with cashew nuts.   Norene Quirk.

* CRUSTLESS VEGETABLE PIE *

1 med. eggplant (peeled-cubed)	¾ c. Parmesan cheese (grated)
2 med. zucchinis (cubed)	1 Tbsp. parsley (minced)
1 lg. onion (chopped)	½ tsp. basil
¼ c. olive oil	salt — pepper
4 med. tomatoes (peeled—chopped)	¼ lb. Mozzarella cheese
3 eggs	(thinly sliced)

Saute eggplant, zucchini and onion in the oil until vegetables are softened about 10 minutes. Add tomatoes, cover and simmer for 25 to 30 minutes until mixture is soft. Transfer to mixing bowl and let cool.

Preheat over to 350° Beat eggs with ¼ c. Parmesan cheese, parsley, basil. Add to the vegetables with salt and pepper to taste.

Pour half of mixture into greased 9 in. pie pan and top with ¼ c. Parmesan cheese. Layer with remaining ingredients, top with Mozzarella cheese and bake 40 to 45 min. or until pie is set and cheese is golden brown.   Adele Davis

* VEGETABLE TAMALE *

1½ c. whole kernel corn	2 c. grated cheese
¾ c. canned tomatoes	1 med. onion (grated)
1/3 c. corn meal	2 oz. can pimentos

Mix all and let stand for 30 minutes.
Add:
2 beaten eggs
¾ c. mllk
salt and pepper to taste.

Place in 9 x 12" casserole. Bake at 350° for 1½ hours or until firm.

Dorothy Tuttle.

* COCONUT SPINACH *

3 pkgs. (10 oz. each) frozen spinach	1-1/3 c. fresh coconut milk or 1 can
(chopped type)	(12 oz.) frozen coconut milk
salt—pepper	(thawed)

Cook spinach according to pkg. directions. Drain well, squeeze out all moisture with paper towel. Place spinach and coconut milk in a saucepan. Season to taste with salt and pepper and heat to just boiling. (do not overcook).
Serve in bowl with some grated coconut and a dash of nutmeg.

Charlene Do.

* SPINACH PIE *

1 bunch spinach (10 to 12 oz.)
   (trimmed-chopped)
¼ c. parsley (minced)
1 c. cottage cheese
1 c. flour
1 c. water

4 eggs
1 c. Feta cheese
½ tsp. dill weed
2 bunches green onions (chopped)

Preheat over to 350°. Squeeze all moisture from spinach. Heat 2 Tbsp. oil in lg. skillet over med. heat, add green onions and parsley and saute until onions are soft. Mix in spinach, cheese, 2 lightly beat-eggs and dill weed, add pepper and salt to taste. Remove from heat. Combine 2 eggs, flour and water in bowl and mix well to make a thin batter. Coat 8" x 12" baking pan with oil and pour in half of the batter, spreading evenly. Top with spinach mix and pour in remaining batter. Bake 45 to 50 minutes or until set.

Cut into sm. squares or into larger squares for lunch or dinner. Serve hot. (Note: Swiss chard or beet greens may be substituted)   **Bonnie Krause.**

* SPINACH CASSEROLE *

2 pkgs. (10 oz.) spinach
   (cooked and squeeze dry)
4 slices bacon (cooked crisp and crumbled)
1 garlic clove
2 tsp. seasoned salt

½ tsp. seasoned pepper
4 Tbsp. flour

Cook onion and garlic in bacon fat until onions are limp. Add seasoned salt and pepper, flour and milk. Cook slowly until thick. Stir in spinach and mix well. Place in casserole and bake (350°) topped with buttered crumbs. Bake until brown.   **Dorothy Tuttle**

* BAKED TOMATOES AND SPINACH *

8 lg. tomatoes
2 pkg.(10 oz. each) frozen spinach
   (thawed—squeezed dry)

1 c. Parmesan cheese (grated)
½ c. bread crumbs
butter topping

Preheat over to 350°. Halve tomatoes and remove core and some seeds, leaving all pulp. Sprinkle with salt. Fill with spinach. Spread butter topping on thickly and top with Parmesan cheese and bread crumbs. Bake about 15 minutes or until soft. Place under broiler to brown slightly.

Butter topping:

1 c. butter
2 garlic cloves (crushed)
2 Tbsp. shallots
Mix all ingredients together.

2 Tbsp. parsley (minced)
½ tsp salt
fresh ground pepper

     Judy Pieklo.

* CREAMY CHERRY TOMATOES *

2 pts. cherry tomatoes
¼ c. butter
½ tsp. salt
freshly ground pepper

½ pt. whipping cream
2 Tbsp. fresh herbs (chives—basil or
tarragon)

Wash tomatoes and remove the stems. Heat butter in a lg. skillet over med. heat, add tomatoes, salt and pepper to taste. Cook for a few minutes, stirring constantly. Add cream and herbs and stir a few minutes longer. Carefully remove tomatoes to a heated platter. Cook sauce until thickened and pour over tomatoes.

Adele Davis.

* POMODORI ALLA SICILIANA (ITALIAN) *
(Baked Stuffed Tomatoes)

4 firm tomatoes
2 Tbsp. olive oil
¼ onion (chopped)
1 garlic clove (crushed)
4 anchovy fillets (chopped)
1 can (7 oz.) tuna (drained)

3 Tbsp. parsley (chopped)
2 Tbsp. capers
6 black olives (chopped)
1 Tbsp. Parmesan cheese (grated)
1 c. bread crumbs

Slice ¼ in. off top of tomatoes. Scoop out all pulp and seeds, leave shells ¼ in. thick. Salt inside and turn upside down to drain. Heat oil in skillet and saute onions and garlic until brown. Stir in bread crumbs, anchovies and pieces of tuna. Saute for 2 minutes. Remove from heat, add parsley, capers and chives. (if mixture is too dry- add 1 tsp. olive oil).

Spoon mixture into tomato shells, sprinkle with the Parmesan cheese. Arrange in lightly oiled baking dish and bake in preheated over (375°) for 20 to 30 minutes until tender but not limp.

Serve hot or cold.

Evelyn Staley.

* SHREDDED ZUCCHINI AND TOMATOES *

1 Tbsp. vegetable oil
1 garlic clove (minced)
1 med. zucchini per serving (shredded)

½ tomato per serving (chopped)
salt—pepper

Heat oil to bubbling and saute garlic lightly. Add zucchini and saute quickly. Add tomatoes, Season with salt and pepper.

Note: Recipe is for per serving. Increase the recipe as needed. Serve with meats.

Nancy Ebsen

* BAKED TOMATO CRISPS *

Allow 1 med. tomato per serving—tomatoes must be green or just ripe.
¼ c. butter (melted)
1 c. cornmeal
salt—pepper

Cut tomatoes into ¾ in. slices. Dip slices in melted butter and dredge with cornmeal. Salt and pepper to taste.
Arrange slices on foil-lined baking sheet. Bake in preheated oven (500°) until brown. (about 20 minutes) Remove from oven, if slices stick to foil, cool slightly. Garnish with dry or fresh dill. Roberta Chateauneuf.

* BROILED TOMATOES *

6 med. tomatoes
½ c. freshly made bread crumbs
3 Tbsp. parsley (finely chopped)
2 Tbsp. chives (chopped)
1 tsp. basil
1 tsp. salt
freshly ground pepper
6 Tbsp. butter

Cut each tomato in half and place on cookie sheet.
Combine crumbs with all remaining ingredients (except butter). Press a small mound of the mixture on top of each tomato half and dot with a tsp. butter. Bake in a 350° oven for 15 minutes. Then place under the broiler for 3 minutes until crumbs are lightly browned. Jean Keys.

* RED CABBAGE YASEEN *

3 med. heads red cabbage
(finely shredded)
½ c. red wine vinegar
½ c. currant Jelly

Place cabbage in a lg. pot with vinegar and jelly. Cover and cook over low heat until cabbage begins to create its own juice. (about 10 minutes) Raise heat to med. and cook, covered for 45 minutes until cabbage is tender but still crisp. Season to taste. Nancy Ebsen.

* ROTKOHL (GERMAN) *
(Red Cabbage)

1 head red cabbage
1 tsp. vinegar
2 Tbsp. butter
1 Tbsp. onion (chopped)
1 Tbsp. red wine
2 Tbsp. vinegar
1 Tbsp. sugar

Wash cabbage, remove outer leaves and shred. Cook covered in boiling water with 1 tsp. vinegar. Do not overcook. Drain. Reheat with other ingredients.
Adele Davis

* RED CABBAGE AND APPLES (AUSTRIAN) *

1 med. head red cabbage
  (finely chopped)
5 tart cooking apples (finely sliced)
3 Tbsp. butter
2½ Tsp. flour
1 c. red wine vinegar

½ c. brown sugar
1/3 c. dry red wine
2 Tbsp. lemon juice
2 Tsp. salt
fresh ground pepper

Steam cabbage until tender but still crispy. Drain well. Combine with apples and set aside.

Melt butter in saucepan, add flour and stir constantly until smooth and well blended. Bring to a simmer and add next 6 ingredients. Simmer until sauce begins to thicken slightly. Add cabbage and apples and toss until evenly coated. Reduce heat to low and cook for 10 minutes, stirring constantly. Taste and adjust the seasonings. Serve warm or cold. Charlene Do.

* HOT SLAW *

2 c. red or white cabbage (Shredded)
3 Tbsp. butter
1/3 c. red wine vinegar
salt

fresh ground pepper
1½ Tsp. caraway seeds
1 Tbsp. sugar

Place cabbage in med. size saucepan with enough water to cover. Cook over med. heat for 6 to 7 minutes or until crispy tender. Drain. Melt butter in skillet over low heat. Add cabbage and toss to coat. Season with salt and pepper. Stir in vinegar, caraway seeds and sugar. Toss gently and continue cooking over low heat for 4 to 5 minutes.

An unusual accompaniment to your favorite meat dishes. Rebecca Dixon.

* KELKAPOSZTA FASIRT (HUNGARIAN) *
(White Cabbage Pancake)

1 bread roll
3 Tbsp. milk
2 lbs. head of cabbage (shredded)
1 garlic clove (chopped)
¼ c. butter

2 eggs (well beaten)
2 Tbsp. dry bread crumbs
salt—pepper
oil for frying

Soak roll in milk until soft. Place cabbage and garlic in skillet, add enough water to cover. Simmer until tender. Remove from skillet. Squeeze roll dry and mash until smooth. Mix with eggs, bread roll, salt and pepper. Add cabbage and mix well. Heat oil in skillet (just enough to cover the bottom). Pour cabbage mixture on oil and fry pancake until brown underneath. Put pan under broiler and brown (crispy) on top. Serve cut into wedges. Annie Ebsen.

* CREAMED ONIONS AND CARROTS *

¼ c. sliced celery
2 Tbsp. butter or oleo
1 c. cream of chicken soup
½ c. sour cream
1 lb. sm. whole onion (cooked—
   about 16)

¼ c. dry white wine
2 Tbsp. parsley (chopped)
1 lb. med. carrots (cooked—cut
   in half lengthwise)

Carrots: I have often used sm. French carrots or baby carrots.
Onions: I use those in a jar or can or fresh.
In saucepan, cook celery in butter until tender. Blend in soup and sour cream.
Cut carrot halves into 2 in. pieces, add carrots and onions to soup mix. Heat,
stirring occasionally.   Georgia Beasley.

* GLASIERTE ZWIEBELN (GERMAN) *
(Glazed Onions)

1½ lbs. white boiling onions
4 Tbsp. butter
1 c. chicken stock

2 Tbsp. sugar
½ tsp. salt

Peel onions. Place in saucepan with butter, stock, sugar and salt. Simmer until
tender and liquid is gone.   Adele Davis.

* STUFFED ONION CUPS *

8 lg. Spanish or Maui onions (peeled)
1 pkg. melba toast dressing
1 c. chicken stock

1 lb. bulk sausage (cooked—drained)
salt—pepper

Parboil onions for about 20 minutes. Cool. Scoop out a lg. hollow in center of
each onion. Combine dressing, sausage, salt and pepper.
Spoon dressing into onions, mounding slightly on top. Tent with foil. Bake in
preheated oven (325°) for 45 minutes.
Garnish with chopped parsley.   Colonel Jean Lyle.

* LAUCH MIT WEISWEIN (GERMAN) *
(Leeks in White Wine)

1 lb. leeks (uniform size)
2 Tbsp. butter

½ c. Sauterne wine
salt—pepper

Wash leeks. Saute leeks in butter for 3 minutes. Cover with the wine and simmer
until tender. Season with the salt and pepper   Adele Davis.

* BRAISED LEEKS *

1 lb. leeks
¼ c. chicken broth
1 tomato (peeled—chopped)
¼ c. pitted black olives
salt—pepper

1 tsp. lemon juice
1 tsp. lemon rind (grated)
1 garlic clove (grated)
½ tsp. olive oil
minced parsley for garnish

Wash leeks carefully to remove all sand. Cut into ½ in rounds. Heat chicken broth in med. skillet and add leeks. Cover and simmer for 10 to 15 minutes until leeks are just tender.

Drain off chicken broth and add remaining ingredients and simmer uncovered for 5 minutes. Serve while hot and garnish with the parsley.

Note: Increase the recipe for more servings.   Nancy Ebsen.

* BUTTERED PARSNIPS WITH ONIONS *

4 parsnips (pared—cubed)
½ onion (chopped)

2 Tbsp. butter
salt—pepper

Cook onions and parsnips in sm. amount of water for 10 to 15 minutes or until tender, but not soft. Drain well. Toss parsnips and onion with the butter, salt and pepper and serve warm.   Ida Christoph.

* SAUTEED PARSNIPS *

1 pkg. fresh parsnips (about 6—7)
¼ c. butter

salt—pepper
dash of nutmeg

Peel parsnips and cut lengthwise into quarters. Place butter and 1 c. water in a skillet, add parsnips and simmer covered. When tender, remove cover and let brown. Turn with spatula. Salt and pepper to taste. Add a dash of nutmeg. (Note: Parsnips are also delicious served raw. Peel and slice or cut into strips and serve with other vegetables with a dip.   Francis Wright.

* SAUTEED FLUTED MUSHROOMS *

2 lbs. fresh mushrooms
½ c. butter
2 Tbsp. lemon juice

1 tsp. salt
½ tsp. fresh ground
   pepper

Wipe mushrooms, clean with a paper towel. Cut off stems (do not twist stems off or caps will collapse). With a sm. curved knife cut grooves that spiral out from center of each cap to edges. Melt butter in a skillet until hot and foaming. Add mushrooms fluted side down. Mix in lemon juice and sprinkle with salt and pepper. Toss lightly over high heat for about 3 minutes or until mushrooms are evenly browned.   Evelyn Staley.

* ALMOND FILLED MUSHROOMS *

8 lg. mushroom caps
½ lb. mushrooms
2 Tbsp. butter
½ c. blanched almonds
(finely chopped)

½ c. whipping cream
1 Tbsp. parsley (chopped)
½ c. white wine
salt—pepper

Preheat over to 250°. Wipe lg. mushrooms and remove stems. Reserve stems. Grind remaining stems and mushrooms in a blender. Saute mushrooms in the butter. Add almonds and cream and cook for a few minutes until mixture looks like whipped potatoes. Spoon mixture into mushroom caps. Sprinkle with parsley, salt and pepper. Place in a baking pan and pour white wine in the pan. Bake for 15 minutes. After baking may be placed under broiler for a few minutes.

Roberta Chateauneuf

* GLORIFIED ZUCCHINI *

4—5 med. zucchinis
1 lg. onion (chopped)
2 Tbsp. butter
2 Tbsp. flour

¾ c. Sauterne
1 can. cream of mushroom soup
½ lb. Cheddar cheese (grated)

Parboil zucchini in salted water. Drain. Place in buttered baking dish. Saute onion in butter, add flour, soup and wine. Mix well. Sprinkle with cheese. Bake, uncovered (350°) for 30 minutes.   Billie Do.

* SCALLOPED SQUASH CASSEROLE *

3 lbs. yellow (summer) squash
3 slices of onion
1 bay leaf
1/8 tsp. thyme
1 c. water
2 tsp. salt
3 Tbsp. dry bread crumbs

4 Tbsp. butter
3 Tbsp. flour
1/8 tsp. white pepper
1½ c. light cream
3 egg yolks
¾ c. Swiss cheese (grated)

Lightly scrape the squash and slice paper thin. In a saucepan, combine squash, onion, bay leaf, thyme, water and 1 tsp. salt. Bring to a boil, cover and cook over low heat of 10 minutes. Drain, discarding the onion and bay leaf.

Melt the butter in a saucepan, blend in flour, pepper and remaining salt. Add the cream gradually, stirring steadily to the boiling point; cook over low heat 5 min. Beat egg yolks in a bowl; gradually add the hot sauce, stirring steadily to prevent curdling. Mix in half of the cheese, then the squash. Turn into a buttered baking dish; sprinkle with a mixture of the bread crumbs and remaining cheese. Bake in a 325° oven for 30 minutes.   Rebecca Dixon.

* ZUCCHINI AND YELLOW SQUASH *

1 lb. sm.zucchini
1 lb. sm. yellow squash
salt—pepper

1 Tbsp. butter
1/3 c. Parmesan cheese (grated)

Steam zucchini and squash (about 15 minutes.) Remove zucchini first as squash takes a little longer to cook. Rinse in cold water.

Slice in 1/8 in. widths. Grease a shallow baking dish, arrange slices of zucchini and squash in rows. Sprinkle with salt and pepper. Dot with butter and cover with cheese. When ready to serve, place in preheated oven (450°) for about 10 minutes until cheese is bubbly.   Francis Wright.

* PARSLIED BUTTERNUT SQUASH *

4 lbs. butternut squash
1 Tbsp. butter

1 Tbsp. parsley (chopped)

Remove seeds from squash. Pare and cut into ¾ in. cubes. Cook, covered in a sm. amount of water about 15 minutes until tender. Add butter and parsley and toss.   Annie Ebsen.

* STUFFED PARTY—PAN SQUASH *
(The little flat scalloped ones)

Cut thin slice off of bottom. Make slight hollow in the top. Par-boil until tender, fill with creamed peas. Sprinkle heavily with grated Parmesan cheese.

Just before serving, broil until hot and brown. Servings: one to each person. Note: All can be done day before, except the broiling. Have at room temperature before broiling.   Dorothy Tuttle.

* OKRA RATATOUILLE (NEW ORLEANS) *

½ lb. fresh okra pods
   (coarsley chopped)
1 med. onion (sliced)
2 Tbsp. butter

1 can (1 lb.) tomatoes in
   tomato puree
1 tsp. sugar

Place all ingredients in a skillet, add 2 Tbsp. water. Cover and simmer until okra is soft and the sauce is thickened. Season to taste.

Note: Additional vegetables may be added in cooking—sliced mushrooms, kernel corn, green beans, whatever you fancy.

Serve as a vegetable dish or cold as a menu relish or as an hors d'oeuvre.
                                    Rebecca Dixon.

* FRIED GREEN PEPPER STRIPS *

3 green peppers (seeded)   ½ tsp. oregano
2 Tbsp. olive oil   salt—pepper

Slice peppers into strips about ¾ in. wide. Heat oil in lg. skillet, add pepper strips and cook over low heat, turning frequently, until tender—crisp, about 15 to 20 minutes. Season with salt, pepper and oregano.   Adele Davis.

* CHEESY SHOE STRING POTATOES *

1 can shoestring potatoes (4 oz.) — 1/3 c. Parmesan cheese (grated). Spread potatoes evenly and close on cookie sheet, Sprinkle with the Parmesan cheese. Bake in 450° oven about 4 minutes. Serve hot.   Dorothy Tuttle.

* PITTSBURG POTATOES *

3 c. raw potatoes (diced)   1 pimiento, cut up
1 sm. onion (diced fine)
Boil for 10 minutes.

Mix with: 1 c. white sauce and 1 c. grated cheese. Bake at 350° for 45 minutes.   Dorothy Tuttle.

* SWEET POTATO MALLOW *

1 lb. sweet potatoes or yams   ½ tsp. salt
   (3 med.) (cooked)   ¼ tsp. mace
½ c. dairy sour cream   ½ c. miniature marshmallows
1 egg.

Preheat oven to 350°. In mixer bowl combine potatoes, sour cream, egg, salt and mace. (med. speed). Top with the marshmallows and bake for 30 minutes.   Virginia Doyle.

* ORANGE HONEY YAMS *

3 or 4 lg. yams (cooked)   butter
1 (4 oz.) jar orange honey   nutmeg

Slice yams into a baking dish. Dot with butter and sprinkle with honey, nutmeg, bake 300° over for 30 to 40 minutes.   Elizabeth Betty Guy.

* APPLE YAMS *

3 med. yams or sweet potatoes or
   1 can (2½ lb.) yams—drained
4 tart apples (peeled—sliced)

¾ c. brown sugar
1 stick butter (melted)
cinnamon

Peel and quarter yams. Butter a shallow baking dish, and place alternate layers of sweet potatoes and apples. Sprinkle layers with cinnamon, sugar and butter. Bake covered in oven (350°) for 30 minutes. Uncover and bake an additional 40 minutes.

Adele Davis

* SWEET POTATOES HAWAIIAN *

6 sweet potatoes (peeled—cut
   in quarters)
¼ c. butter

1 c. brown sugar
1½ c. crushed pineapple
   (undrained)

Melt butter in skillet. Brown potatoes, add brown sugar and pineapple. Cook over low heat for 45 minutes, until tender. Turn frequently.
Garnish with chopped fresh mint.

Lorna Burger.

* CAVIAR STUFFED POTATOES *

12 sm. new potatoes (boiled)
   (do not over cook)
½ c. sour cream

1 jar (2 oz.) caviar
2 eggs (hard cooked)

Using a small spoon or melon scoop, hollow out the top of each potato. Fill each hollow with the sour cream. Push egg yolks through a sieve and sprinkle on the sour cream. Top with a dab of caviar. Serve cold.

Judy Pieklo.

* PAPAYA AS A VEGETABLE *

4 green papayas (peeled—diced)
5 Tbsp. margarine
1 Maui onion (chopped)
4 tomatoes (peeled—seeded—
   chopped)

1 chicken bouillon cube
¼ c. Macadamia nuts (chopped)
¼ c. freshly grated Parmesan cheese.
salt and pepper to taste

Combine first five ingredients in a large saucepan and cook until papaya is soft. Add cheese and nuts, mix and serve. Some chopped parsley can be sprinkled on top for color.

Anna Hambley.

* THE "BIG MAC" *

½ c. soaked garbanzo beans
½ c. water
1 c. rolled oats (uncooked)
1 c. chopped walnuts
1 Tbsp. shoyu

1 med. onion (chopped)
4 Tbsp. rich milk
1 tsp. salt
1 tsp. sage

Whiz in blender the water and the beans. Remove to a bowl. Add the remaining ingredients and mix with a spoon.

Drop from spoon or ice-cream scoop to form patties in oiled skillet. Brown on both sides over med. heat.

Serve in hamburger buns with all the trimmings or in a casserole with gravy on top, baking ½ hour at 350°.

Makes 6 patties.   Adele Davis.

* BROWN RICE BURGERS *

1 lg. onion (chopped)
1 c. celery (chopped)
½ c. parsley (minced)
3 garlic cloves (minced)
3 Tbsp. oil
½ c. whole wheat flour

oil for frying
lemon wedges
4 c. cooked brown rice
2 c. carrots (grated)
2 lg. eggs (beaten)
salt—pepper

In a lg. skillet over med. heat, saute onions, celery, parsley and garlic in 3 Tbsp. oil for 10 minutes. Mix in rice, carrots, eggs, salt and pepper to taste.

Form into patties (I make about 19). Add more flour if patties are too soft. Fry in additional oil over med. heat until golden brown on both sides.

Serve with lemon wedges, hot or cold and a cheese sauce may be added.

Adele Davis.

C·A·S·S·E·R·O·L·E·S

* SUPER – DUPER BAKED BEANS *

Drain and put together cans of baked beans, kidney beans and lima beans.

3 Tbsp. vinegar	1 med. onion (sliced)
2 Tbsp. brown sugar	½ c. catsup
1 garlic clove (minced)	1 Tbsp. prepared mustard.

Cook garlic and onion in a little bacon grease until limp. Mix all well. Pour into a 9" x 13" casserole. Bake for 45 minutes in a 350° oven.   Dorothy Tuttle.

* MALTY BAKED BEANS *

2 c. navy beans	½ tsp. onion powder
½ lb. salt pork	1½ tsp. salt
3 c. beer	
1 tsp. dry mustard	

Cook beans until tender. On bottom of baking dish, arrange half of the salt pork. Add beans and remaining ingredients. Top with salt pork. Add enough bean water to just cover. Bake at 275° for 2 hours.   Roberta Chateauneuf

* CALICO BEAN BAKE *

½ lb. lamb (cubed)	1 tsp. dry mustard
½ lb. bacon (cut-up)	¾ c. brown sugar
1 c. onions (chopped)	2 tsp. vinegar
½ c. catsup	
1 tsp. salt	

1 No. 2 can (each) pork and beans, butter beans, lima beans, pinto beans and kidney beans (drained).

Mix all ingredients and place in a baking dish, bake at 350° for 40 minutes.
Adele Davis

* SWEET SOUR BAKED BEANS *

8 slices bacon (crisp—drained—crumbled)	1 tsp. dry mustard
	1 tsp. salt
4 lg. onions (chopped)	½ c. cider vinegar
½ to 1 c. brown sugar	
½ tsp. garlic powder	

Combine all above ingredients and simmer (covered) for 20 minutes. Use No. 1 size cans of:

2 cans lima beans	1 can red kidney beans
1 can green lima beens	1 can New England style baked beans.

Mix all, add bacon. Bake in 3 qt. casserole at 350° for 1 hour.   Dorothy Tuttle.

* PICNIC BAKED BEANS *

4 slices bacon
2 onions (sliced)
1/3 c. brown sugar
1 Tsp. dry mustard
½ tsp. garlic powder
1 tsp. salt

½ c. cider vinegar
1 (1 lb.) can green lima beans
1 (1 lb.) can red kidney beans
1 (1 lb.) can baked beans
2 (15 oz.) cans butter beans

Fry bacon in a skillet until crisp. Remove from pan, drain on paper towels, then crumble and set aside.

Separate onion slices into rings and saute in bacon fat, until tender but not browned. Stir in sugar, mustard, garlic powder, salt and vinegar. Cover and simmer for 20 minutes.

Drain butter beans, lima beans and kidney beans and combine with baked beans, onion mixture and bacon in a 3 qt. casserole. Bake at 350° for 1 hour.

Charlene Do.

* TEXAS TAMALE PIE *

2 cans chili with beans
   (homemade is better)
1 pkg. Fritos (large size)

1 lg. onion (chopped)
1 pkg. Cheddar sharp cheese
   (grated)

Layer ingredients in a casserole dish and bake at 350° until bubbly and smells divine.
Allison Holland.

* BAKED BEANS FOR PICNICS *

Brown 1 lb. ground beef with 1 lg. chopped onion and ½ lb. bacon, cut up, drain off fat.

Add:

1 can pork and beans
1 can lima beans (drained)

1 can kidney beans (drained)
1 can butter beans (drained)

Heat:

1 c. catsup
1 c. brown sugar

2 Tbsp. vinegar
2 Tbsp. prepared mustard

Mix and pour over beans. Heat for 1 hour at 300°.
Virginia Doyle.

* SAUSAGE — BEAN CASSEROLE *

2 c. lg. dry lima beans.
1½ qts. water
2 lbs. bulk pork sausage
1 c. onion (chopped)
1 c. celery (chopped)
½ tsp. dry mustard

½ c. green pepper (chopped)
1 Tbsp. salt
½ tsp. pepper
1 lg. can tomatoes (cut-up)

Combine beans and water in a large pot and bring to a boil and boil for 2 min. Remove from heat, cover and let stand 1 hour (or soak beans overnight) Drain. Cook sausage, onion, celery and green pepper in lg. skillet until sausage is browned and vegetables are tender. Drain off fat. Combine beans, sausage mix, salt. pepper and tomatoes. Turn into a 3 qt. casserole. Bake in oven (350°) for 1 hour or until beans are tender.

Note: If beans become too dry, add some tomato sauce.   Francis Wright.

* GREEN BEAN CASSEROLE *

1 can green beans or 1 pkg. frozen
1 sm. onion (sauted)
1 c. mushroom soup
1 c. water chestnuts (sliced)

½ lb. sharp Cheddar cheese
10 slices bacon (fried crisp)
salt—pepper

Place sauteed onions in a skillet, add soup and other ingredients and mix well. Place in casserole and bake (350°) for ½ hour.   Elinor Edmondson.

* MY GREEN BEAN CASSEROLE *

2 pkgs. frozen green beans
   (cooked—drained)
1 can cream of mushroom soup

1 can water chestnuts
1 can french fried onion rings

Place beans in a 1 qt. casserole. Dilute mushroom soup to med. thickness. Add onion and water chesnuts, pour over beans. Bake at 400° for 20 minutes. Place onion rings on top and bake another 10 minutes   Jean Keys.

* CALIFLOWER ALMONDINE *

1 pkg. frozen cauliflower
¼ c. boiling salted water
1 c. cream of mushroom soup
   (undiluted)

¼ c. blanched almonds (slivered)
1 Tbsp. butter (melted)
2 Tbsp. corn flake crumbs

Cook cauliflower in the water until barely tender, drain, and arrange in a sm. casserole. Heat the soup and stir in the almonds. Pour over cauliflower. Top with butter and corn flake crumbs. Preheat oven to 325°. Bake casserole for 10 to 15 minutes. Serve hot.   Adele Davis

74

* RUTABAGA CASSEROLE *

2 lbs. rutabagas (peeled and cubed)
1 Tbsp. flour
2 Tbsp. butter
½ to 1 c. milk

4 Tbsp. dry bread crumbs
grated nutmeg
salt — pepper — sugar
2 eggs (lightly beaten)

Cover rutabagas with salted water and simmer until tender. Drain and mash. Add the flour and half of the butter, mix until smooth. Slowly beat in milk, add eggs, salt, pepper, nutmeg and sugar to taste. Pour into buttered casserole, top with the bread crumbs, dot with butter. Bake in preheated oven (350°) for 1 hour. Note. This is my Mother's recipe and we always had this dish for Thanksgiving and Christmas.

Adele Davis.

* MAMIES SPINACH CASSEROLE *

2 pkgs. frozen spinach
  (cooked — drained)
4 slices bacon (crisp—crumbled)
1 c. onions (diced)
1 lg. garlic clove

4 Tbsp. flour
2 c. milk
2 tsp. Lowry seasoning salt
½ tsp. Lowry seasoning pepper

Saute onion and garlic in the bacon grease. Add flour, milk and seasonings and simmer until thick. Stir in spinach and bacon, mix well.
Pour into a 9" x 13" casserole, sprinkle top with the bread crumbs. Bake until browned. Note: This is excellent made with coconut milk.   Dorothy Tuttle.

* VEGETABLE GHIVETCHI (RUMANIAN) *

10 baby carrots (sliced)
2 potatoes (diced)
½ eggplant (diced—unpeeled)
1 can (8 oz.) sm. onions
½ c. each, lima beans, peas, and
  cut green beans
½ green pepper (in strips)
½ sm. cabbage (shredded)
1 sm. cauliflower (florets)
½ c. olive oil

1 Tbsp. salt
fresh ground pepper
½ summer squash (diced)
½ celery root (diced)
5 sm. tomatoes (quartered)
2 onions (sliced thin)
2 garlic cloves (mashed)
¼ c. butter
1 c. chicken stock

Arrange all vegetables (except the onions) in a lg. casserole in the order given. Saute the onions and garlic in the butter until golden. Add the stock and bring to a boil. Stir in the oil, salt and pepper and pour over the vegetables. Bake in preheated oven (325°) for 30 to 40 minutes until tender but crisp. Note: This is a good casserole for Buffet party. Best of all it can be made in advance and placed in the refrigerator. Take out 2 hours before Baking.   Evelyn Staley.

* BAKED ZUCCHINI *

3 Tbsp. olive oil
1 med. onion (minced)
6 med. zucchinis (unpeeled—
   chopped)
2 c. cooked rice
½ c. Swiss cheese (grated)

½ c. parsley (chopped)
2 lg. eggs (beaten)
salt — pepper
2 Tbsp. bread crumbs
1 Tbsp. olive oil (top)

Preheat oven to 375°. Heat oil in skillet and saute onions until soft. Add zucchini and simmer over low heat for 10 minutes (stir occasionally). Remove from heat and allow to cool slightly. Combine rice, cheese, parsley, eggs, salt and pepper. Add zucchini and mix well. Place in buttered casserole and sprinkle with bread crumbs and olive oil. Bake uncovered for 20 minutes.   Judy Pieklo.

* SAUERKRAUT CASSEROLE (GERMAN) *

1 lb. sauerkraut
1 Tbsp. butter
2 c. chicken stock
1 onion (chopped)
3 tart apples

½ Tbsp. sugar
1 raw potato (grated)
½ tsp. caraway seeds
1 Tbsp. flour
salt — pepper

Peel and slice apples. Saute sauerkraut in butter for 3 minutes. Add stock, apples, onion, sugar, potatoes, flour, caraway seeds, salt and pepper. Bake in buttered casserole 1 hour at 350°.   Adele Davis.

* "TIAN" *
(Cold Vegetable Casserole)

1 lb. spinach (chopped)
1 lb. Swiss chard (chopped)
3 sm. zucchini (diced—unpeeled)
1 med. onion (chopped)
2 garlic cloves (mashed
olive oil

1 Tbsp. basil
¾ tsp. salt
¼ tsp. pepper
4 eggs (beaten)
¾ c. Parmesan cheese (grated)
corn flake crumbs

Heat enough oil to cover the bottom of a skillet. Cook spinach and Swiss chard in it until barely wilted. Remove and drain well. Add more oil to skillet and simmer the zucchini, onion and garlic, until onion is transparent. Mix all the vegetables and stir in the basil, salt and pepper. Arrange in a buttered casserole. Pour eggs on top and sprinkle with cheese and bread crumbs.
Bake in preheated over (350°) for 25 to 30 minutes until eggs are set.
Serve very chilled.   Francis Wright.

* SWEET POTATO CASSEROLE (HAITI) *

1 c. mashed sweet potatoes
2 sm. bananas (mashed)
1 c. milk
2 Tbsp. sugar

½ tsp. salt
2 egg yolks (beaten)
3 Tbsp. raisins (cut fine)

Combine sweet potatoes and bananas. Add milk and blend. Add sugar, salt, egg yolks and raisins. Mix well. Pour into buttered casserole (shallow). Bake slow in oven (300°) for 45 minutes or until firm.

To serve — cut into pie shape pieces.   Francis Wright.

* COTTAGE CHEESE LOAF *

1 onion (chopped)
1 block butter
½ c. pecans or walnuts (chopped)
1 lb. cottage cheese

3 eggs
4 c. Special K. cereal
1 pkg. G. Washington broth

Saute onion in block of butter. Add nuts. Saute. Add mixture to all other ingredients and mix thoroughly.

Place in greased casserole and bake at 350° for 45 to 60 minutes. Let stand before slicing.

Note: May be served with mushroom sauce.   Lynne Waihee.

* STUFFED BELL PEPPER CASSEROLE *

6 med. green peppers
1 lb. ground beef
1/3 c. chopped onions
¾ c. catsup

¾ c. Minute Rice
2 Tbsp. Worcestershire sauce
salt — pepper
1 c. Cheddar cheese (shredded)

Cut off tops of the green peppers — remove seeds and membrane. Precook peppers in boiling salted water about 5 minutes. Drain.

Brown meat and onion, add catsup, rice. Worcestershire and salt and pepper to taste.

Cover and simmer until rice is almost tender (about 5 minutes). Stir in cheese. Stuff peppers and stand upright in baking dish. Bake uncovered in 350° oven for 25 minutes, or until hot. Sprinkle with more cheese.

Note: May be made ahead and refrigerated, but allow extra time for baking.
                                                          Rosalie Sevey.

* BRUNCH CASSEROLE *

A 9" x 13" pan. Sprinkle in 1 box of seasoned croutons. Cover with cooked ham, bacon or sausage. Next put in a layer of canned mushroom soup., and ½ c. shredded Cheddar cheese.

Mix 4 eggs with 1¾ c. milk. 1 tsp. prepared mustard. Spread on top. Refrigerate overnight. Next day combine 1 can mushroom soup and ½ c. milk and spoon on top. Sprinkle with ½ c. shredded Cheddar cheese (I use about 1 c.). Bake at 250° for 1½ hours uncovered. Let stand 5 minutes and then cut into squares.

Note: This recipe is easily doubled for a large group.   Rosalie Sevey.

* EGGPLANT CASSEROLE *

1 lg. eggplant, (cubed) — 1 garlic clove, boiled for 10 minutes.

Mix in bowl:

½ c. milk   ½ onion (diced)
2 eggs (beaten)   ½ green pepper (diced)
¼ c. bread crumbs   ¼ c. Macadamia nuts (minced)
salt and pepper
* 1 c. grated cheese

Alternate layers of eggplant, cheese and bowl mixture. Topping with layer of cheese. Bake 25 to 30 minutes at 350°.   Dorothy Morrison.

* POKER FLAT POTATO CASSEROLE *

2 lbs. frozen hash brown potatoes   1 pt. sour cream
   (completely thawed)   1 c. cream of chicken soup (as is)
½ c. margarine (melted)   2 c. Cheddar cheese (grated)
1 Tsp. salt
½ tsp. pepper
1 sm. onion (cut fine)

Mix all together and put in a 9" x 13" casserole.

Topping:

2 c. corn flakes (crushed)   ¼ c. melted margarine
   (do not buy corn flake crumbs)

Bake for 60 minutes at 350°.
Freezes beautifully.   Dorothy Tuttle.

* POTATO CASSEROLE *

6 med. potatoes
1 can cream of chicken soup
3 green onions (chopped with tops)
1½ c. sour cream

½ tsp. salt
¼ tsp. pepper
¼ c. margarine (melted)
2 c. sharp Cheddar cheese (grated)

Boil potatoes until almost done (not more than 15 minutes.) Peel and grate on large grater. Melt margarine in lg. skillet. Take off stove and add soup, sour cream, salt, pepper and onions. Stir. Add grated cheese and stir again.
Put potatoes in 9" x 13" baking pan. Pour the mixture over the potatoes. Sprinkle with remaining cheese.
Bake 350° for 30 minutes. (Everyone likes this recipe)   Valerie Wilson.

* COUNTRY SAUSAGE AND POTATO CASSEROLE *

1 lb. smoked sausage
  (cut in ½ in. length)

1 lg. onion (chopped)
1 Tbsp. oil

Saute both until onions are soft. (5 minutes).

Stir in:

1 box Au Gratin potatoes and sauce   2½ c. hot water. Simmer, covered for 10 minutes. Stir occasionally.
Add 4 med. carrots (cut in julliene strips),
1 pkg. (10 oz.) frozen broccoli (chopped).

Cook 10 minutes. Place in casserole and top with 1 c. grated cheese.
Bake in oven 350° for 30 minutes.   Dorothy Tuttle.

* GOLDEN SHRIMP CASSEROLE *

5 slices buttered bread
2 c. cooked shrimp
2 c. Cheddar cheese (grated)

3 eggs
1 can cream of celery soup.

Cut bread into ½ in. cubes. Line bottom of buttered casserole with bread. Cut shrimp lengthwise, place layer of shrimp on the bread. Cover with layer of cheese. Repeat layers. Add enough milk to soup to make 2 c. liquid, add eggs and beat. Pour over mixture. Place casserole in pan filled with warm water up to 1 in. of top of casserole. Bake in warmed over (375°) for 1 hour.
Garnish with chopped dill and paprika.   Adele Davis.

* TUNA—CASHEW CASSEROLE *

1 can tuna
1 c. cream of mushroom soup
1 c. celery (diced)
1 can (4 oz.) Chinese noodles

1 sm. pkg. cashew nuts
¼ c. onions (diced)
¼ c. water
salt — pepper

In buttered casserole. Place layer of tuna, onions, soup, celery and nuts. Repeat. Pour in the water. Top with the Chinese noodles. Bake in preheated oven (350°) for 30 minutes.   Roberta Chateauneuf.

* CLAM — CHICKEN CASSEROLE (SCOTTISH) *

2 doz. clams (chopped) or
   2 cans clams (chopped)
1 c. cooked chicken (diced)
12 sm. white onions or canned
   onions
2 Tbsp. butter
2 hard-cooked eggs (diced)

1 c. cooked potatoes (diced)
½ c. celery (diced)
¼ c. dry Sherry
1 Tbsp. flour
½ c. cream
pastry for 1 crust pie

Saute the onions in hot butter in a skillet until they are somewhat soft (if canned are used, just warm). Stir in clams, chicken, eggs, potatoes, celery and Sherry. Season to taste. Simmer for 5 minutes over low heat.
Make a paste of flour and cream and blend well. Pour into clam mixture and simmer for 5 minutes. Pour into sm. casserole that will be filled within ¼ in. from the top. Roll out the pastry, about 1/8 in. thick and lay on top of the mixture. Slash several times for steam to escape. Bake in a preheated oven (400°) for 15 minutes, reduce the heat to 350° and bake an additional 20 minutes.
                                                    Judy Pieklo.

* CHOP STICK CASSEROLE *

1 can (3 oz.) Chow Mein noodles
   (reserve ½ c.)
1 can cream of mushroom soup
¼ c. water
1 can chunk tuna

½ c. cashew nuts
1 c, celery (diced)
¼ c. onion (chopped)
dash of pepper

Mix all together and put in shallow casserole. Top with the noodles. Bake (uncovered) in 350° oven for 45 minutes.   Dorothy Tuttle.

80

* TWELVE CAN CASSEROLE *

3 cans tuna
1 can cream of mushroom soup
1 can cream of chicken soup
1 sm. can Pet milk
1 sm. can water chestnuts
2 cans Chinese noodles

8 stalks celery (chopped)
1 lg. green pepper (chopped)
2 sm. cans french cut green beans
1 sm. can mushrooms
2 cans onion rings (1 for mixing 1
    for topping)

Mix all ingredients and place in a shallow casserole, cover with second can of onion rings. Bake at 350° for half hour or until top is crusty.   Jean Keys.

* CRAB BAKE *

8 slices bread (4 in bottom of buttered shallow baking pan.)
Mix and pour over the bread.

2 cans crab
½ c. mayonnaise
1 onion (chopped)

1 c. chopped green onions
1 c. chopped celery
1 c. chopped green pepper

Top with the other 4 slices of bread.

Mix together 4 beaten eggs and 2½ c. milk. Pour over top slices of bread.
Refrigerate over night. Bake at 350° for 15 minutes. Then spoon over 1 can mushroom soup, grated cheese and paprika. Bake 1 hour longer at 300°.

                  Rosella Reiner.

* SHRIMP CHINESE *

3 c. chopped celery and 1 c. chopped onion-cook until almost tender in 1 c. water. Drain.

2 can. cream of shrimp soup
1 can milk
1 can (4 oz.) sliced mushrooms
   (drained)
6 oz. cashews
½ c. dry sherry

4 oz. pimientos (diced)
5 oz. water chestnuts (sliced)
2 cans shrimp (rinsed-drained)
Chow Mein noodles

In bottom of 9" x 13" casserole, put in 1 can (3 oz.) noodles. Mix other ingredients and warm. Pour over the noodles. Top with 1 can (3 oz.) noodles
Bake at 350° for 50 minutes.
Note: the mixture can be made the day before — refrigerated, then reheated lightly and assembled and baked.   Dorothy Tuttls.

* LEMON CHICKEN CASSEROLE *

4 whole chicken breasts
(skinned — boned — halved)
½ c. flour
1½ tsp. salt
fresh ground pepper
paprika
¼ c. parsley (chopped)

¼ c. butter
1 Tbsp. olive oil
4 Tbsp. Madeira wine
3 Tbsp. lemon juice
4 Tbsp. capers
lemon slices

Place chicken breasts between 2 sheets of waxed paper and pound until thin (about ¼ in.) Combine flour, salt, pepper and paprika in a bag, add chicken breasts and shake well. Shake off excess. Heat butter and olive oil in a skillet until bubbling, saute chicken breasts, a few at a time. (do not overcook).
Drain off all but 2 Tbsp. butter and oil. Stir in the Madeira wine and scrape bottom of skillet to loosen any browned parts. Add lemon juice and heat briefly. Return chicken to skillet and warm through.
Place chicken breasts in a casserole. Interspersing lemon slices and place in a pre-heated oven (350°) for 20 minutes. Add capers and parsley the last 10 minutes of baking.   Adele Davis.

* PEPPERIDGE FARM CASSEROLE *

1 pkg. Pepperidge Farm poultry
dressing
1 can green beans (drained)
2 small cans chicken or turkey

1 can cream of mushroom soup
¼ c. milk

Mix all ingredients and place in shallow casserole, top with buttered bread crumbs. Bake 350° for 30 minutes   Dorothy Tuttle.

* GREEN BEAN CASSEROLE *

1 can green beans or 1 pkg. frozen beans
1 sm. onion
1 c. mushroom soup
salt and pepper to taste

1 c. water chestnuts (sliced)
½ lb. sharp Cheddar cheese (grated)
10 slices bacon (fried crisp)

Saute onion, and add soup. Mix in other ingredients. Place in casserole and bake in preheated oven (350°) for 30 minutes   Elinor Edmondson.

* CHICKEN MUSHROOM CASSEROLE *

8—10 pcs. chicken breasts or thighs
1 Tbsp. butter (cut in pieces)
1/3 c. slivered almonds
salt and pepper
freshly grated Parmesan cheese

1 can (10 oz.) cream of chicken soup
2/3 c. white wine
1 can (4 oz.) whole or sliced mushrooms

Preheat oven to 350°. Place chicken in lg. baking pan and dot with the butter.
Sprinkle with almonds, pepper and salt. Mix together soup, wine and mushrooms
in a sm. bowl and pour over chicken.
Bake uncovered in oven for 45 to 60 minutes.   Jean Keys.

* CORNED BEEF CASSEROLE *

Crumble 12 oz. can corned beef

Combine with: 1 c. American cheese, 1 can (10½ oz.) cream of chicken soup
(mixed with 1 c. milk) and ½ c. chopped onions.
Cook and drain an 8 oz. pkg. noodles.
Alternate layers of corned beef mixture, with a layer of noodles, in a greased
baking dish. Top with buttered crumbs.
Bake for 45 minutes at 350°.   Georgia Beasley.

* BEEF CASSEROLE WITH POTATO TOPPING *

2 c. cooked beef (cubed)
2 cans green pea soup (condensed)
½ c. sauteed mushrooms (sliced)
½ c. milk
1 tsp. parsley (chopped)

½ tsp. basil
1 sm. onion (chopped)
2 c. fresh mashed potatoes
1 c. cooked peas
1 egg (beaten)
2 Tbsp. melted butter
salt — pepper

In a 2 qt. casserole place beef, soup, mushrooms, herbs and onion. Season to
taste. (This will blend better if you warm the soup first and stir in the milk. Bake
covered in a preheated oven (350°) for 25 minutes.
Make fresh mashed potatoes or instant will serve as well. Stir in the peas and egg
and spread evenly over casserole and drizzle butter on top. Increase heat to 450°
and bake 10 minutes longer. Serve with cole slaw.   Nancy Ebsen.

* BEEF — OLIVE CASSEROLE *

3 lbs. chuck (cubed)
1 c. pitted green olives.
½ c. flour
salt — pepper
2 Tbsp. salad oil
12 sm. onions (peeled)
1 garlic clove (mashed)

½ tsp. thyme
1½ c. condensed consomme
¼ c. parsley (chopped)
2 Tbsp. butter
2 Tbsp. flour

Put the ½ c. flour, salt and pepper in a bag and dredge the beef cubes. Brown in hot oil and place in a lg. casserole. In the oil, lightly saute the onions and garlic. Add thyme and the consomme and pour over the meat. Cover and bake in oven (300°) for 1 hour. Stir in the olives and parsley, cover again and bake for 45 minutes longer, until meat is tender.

Mix the 2 Tbsp. butter and flour to thicken the sauce just before serving. Serve with buttered wide noodles. Adele Davis.

* MEAT BALLS BAKED IN CREAM OF MUSHROOM SOUP *

2 lbs. ground chuck
1 egg (beaten)
1 sm. can tomato sauce (optional)

½ c. milk
1 c. wheat germ or crumbs or oatmeal
1 sm. onion (chopped)

Mix ground beef, egg, milk, onion and wheat germ and make into balls. Place meat balls in a rectangular baking dish.

To one can of cream of mushroom soup add 1 can water or milk. Mix well. Pour over meat balls and cover. Bake 1 hour at 350°. Dora Beyer.

* DINNER IN A DISH *

2 slices of bacon
1 lb. ground beef
1 sm. onion (sliced thin)
1 Tbsp. flour
1 can (14½ oz.) stewing tomatoes
salt and pepper

1 c. carrot cubes (cooked)
1 c. green beans (cooked)
1 c. lima beans (cooked)
1 stalk celery + leaves (chopped)

Cut bacon into small pieces and fry in iron skillet. Add beef, stir, add onion and brown well. Add flour and stir. Place on low heat and add tomatoes. Stir well. Then add all your vegetables and seasonings. When the mixture is well heated, place in casserole and keep warm.

Serve with rice, buttered toasted bread or noodles. Note: You may leave out a vegetable or add if you wish. Garlic also gives a good flavor. Dora Beyer.

* NOODLES NAPOLI *

1 med. onion (chopped)
1 garlic clove (chopped)
1 Tbsp. salad oil
1 lb. or more ground beef
1 can mushrooms (or more)
1 can (8 oz.) tomato sauce
1/3 c. Parmesan cheese (grated)
Sliced cheese for topping.

1 can (6 oz.) tomato paste
2 tsp. salt
½ to ¾ tsp. oregano
1 pkg. Lasagne noodles (cooked)
1 pkg. frozen chopped spinach
    (thawed but not cooked-drain)
1 c. creamed cottage cheese
2 eggs

Brown onion and garlic in 1 Tbsp. oil, add beef and cook and stir until browned. Stir in mushrooms and liquid, tomato sauce, tomato paste, 1 tsp. salt and oregano. Simmer for 15 minutes. Beat one egg lightly and pour over the noodles. Mix well. Beat second egg, add spinach, 1 Tbsp. oil, cottage cheese, Parmesan cheese and 1 tsp. salt. Mix well.

Pour ½ of the tomato mixture in the bottom of a shallow baking dish (9" x 12"), layer ½ of the noodles on top. Spread with all the spinach mixture. Repeat noodle layer, top with remaining tomato mixture. Cover with foil.

Bake in moderate oven at 350° for 45 minutes. Remove foil. Arrange cheese strips on top and bake for 5 minutes longer.   Georgia Beasley.

* MACARONI AND SAUSAGE CASSEROLE *

1½ c. uncooked macaroni
    (cooked — drained)
1 lb. bulk sausage (cut in pieces)
    (sauteed until slightly brown)
1 c. sliced onions (sauteed until limp)

1 c. mushrooms sauce (not soup)
1 c. canned tomatoes
    (to make 2 cups)

Mix all together and bake in a 9" x 13" casserole for 50 minutes at 350°.
                                                    Dorothy Tuttle

* NOODLE RING *

1 pkg. fine noodles
4 eggs
4 c. milk

1 tsp. salt
nutmeg

Cook noodles in salted water. (eldente). Rinse in cold water and drain. Pour into buttered ring mold. Mix eggs until lemon colored, add salt, milk and a pinch of nutmeg. Pour over noodles. Bake at 375° in pan of hot water until set, about 30 minutes. Serve with buttered carrots on outside of ring and buttered peas on the inside.   Francis Wright.

* CHINESE NOODLES *

1 pkg. Chinese bean threads
   (long rice)
1 Tbsp. fat
2 c. onion (chopped)
½ c. chopped green pepper

1 c.an (4 oz.) sliced mushrooms
1 Tbsp. honey
2 Tbsp. soy sauce
2 c. sliced water chestnuts

Saute onion and pepper in fat until just glazed. Add chestnuts, soy sauce and honey. Cut noodles in pieces and boil for 5 minutes. Drain well.
Combine with the other ingredients and place in casserole and steam until hot.

Lillian Kann.

* COMPANY RICE *

½ c. butter or margarine
1 lg. onion (minced)
1½ c. Cheddar cheese (shredded)
1¾ c. uncooked rice.

1 can (4 oz.) mushrooms (drained)
2 cans. (10½ oz.) consomme
1 c. almonds (sliced)

Melt butter in skillet. Add onion and saute until tender, but no browned. Combine onion, cheese, rice, mushrooms, consomme and almonds in a 4 — 5 qt. casserole. Mix well.
Cover and bake at 325° for 1 hour. Remove the cover and bake for 15 minutes longer.

Millie Mesaku.

* TIMBALE OF RICE *

1 med. onion (minced)
2 Tbsp. butter
2 Tbsp. olive oil
2 c. precooked pkg. rice
1 tsp. salt
¼ tsp. pepper
¼ c. Parmesan cheese (grated)

¼ c. sauted mushrooms (chopped)
2 cups chicken broth
¼ c. dry white wine or Vermouth
Strips of Proscuitto or any
   flavored ham.
Saffron (optional)

Saute the onion in the butter and olive oil until glossy. Add 2 cups of the precooked rice. Stir until coated. Add salt, saffron, pepper, chicken broth and wine. Bring to a full boil. Cover. Remove from heat and allow to stand in a warm place for 5 minutes.
Butter generously a qt. size oven proof bowl or mold of Le Cruset ware and line with paper thin stripes of the cooked ham. Stir the rice, grated cheese and the mushrooms. Pack it in the mold. Cover with foil and bake in moderate oven 8 to 10 minutes.
Unmold and serve with wedges of tomatoes, and tomato sauce.   Adele Davis.

86

TOMATO SAUCE:

An excellent tomato sauce can be achieved by starting with an 8 oz. can of tomato sauce with cheese. Add ¼ tsp. each of garlic salt, oregano, dried basil, dash of salt and a few grains of cayenne pepper. Mae Gomes.

* MAUNA LOA RICE RING *

2 Tbsp. butter
½ lb. mushrooms (sliced)
½ c. green onions (sliced)
3 c. hot cooked rice
salt — pepper to taste

1 jar (2 oz.) pimentos (drained—sliced)
1 jar (3½ oz.) bits of Macadamia nuts

Melt butter and saute the onions and mushrooms. In a large bowl combine hot rice, mushrooms, green onions, pimentos, Macadamia nuts, salt and pepper, toss lightly. Moisten a 9 inch ring mold with water, press rice mixture firmly. May also be put in a small casserole. Unmold onto platter. Charlene Do.

* RICE PILAF *

1 c. uncooked rice
2 cans bouillon

½ cube butter or oleo
1 tsp. oregano

Melt butter — fry rice for 7—10 minutes until golden brown. Add bouillion and oregano. Pour into casserole and bake covered for 30 minutes at 350°.

Valerie Wilson.

* FRIED RICE WITH ALMONDS *

8 Tbsp. salad oil
3 sm. onions (chopped)
2 sm. green peppers (chopped)
8 c. cold boiled rice

2 tsp. garlic salt
1 tsp. pepper
8 Tbsp. soy sauce
2 c. blanched almonds

Cook the onion, pepper, garlic salt and pepper in the oil for 5 minutes. Add the rice, soy sauce and almonds and mix well. Place all in buttered casserole and place in oven until well heated. Velma Harmas.

* ORIENTAL RICE *

Prepare: 6 oz. pkg. white and wild rice mix according to directions. (Use a little less water)

1 c. onions (chopped)
1 c. celery (chopped)
2 Tbsp. soy sauce
1/3 c. toasted almonds (slivered)

1 can (3 oz.) mushrooms (stems — pieces — drained)
1 can (5 oz.) water chestnuts (drained — sliced)

Mix all ingredients and bake in casserole for 30 minutes in preheated oven.

Dorothy Tuttle.

* WILD RICE AND MUSHROOMS *

1 c. wild rice
1 med. can mushrooms
½ c. butter
2/3 c. milk

½ tsp salt
2 Tbsp. flour
pepper to taste

Cover rice with boiling water. Let stand 20 minutes. Drain. Brown mushrooms in butter, add liquid and flour to make sauce. Add rice and seasonings. Place in buttered casserole. Top with bread crumbs. Bake in preheated oven (350°) for 30 minutes.
Judy Pieklo.

* RICE AND CHEESE CASSEROLE *

2 c. cooked rice
6 med. onions
2 tsp. butter or oleo
2 Tbsp. flour

1 c. milk
¾ c. Cheddar cheese (grated)
1 tsp. salt
½ tsp. cayenne pepper

Parboil onions until tender. Make sauce of butter, flour, salt and cayenne pepper. Let cool and add cheese. Place in casserole, alternating rice and onion (pulled apart). Pour on cheese sauce. Bake at 350° for 20 minutes. Garnish with hard-cooked egg slices.
Roberta Chateauneuf.

* RICE CASSEROLE *

1 lb. ground sausage
1 lb. mushrooms
2 chopped onions
2 pkg. brown and wild rice

1 tsp. salt
2 cans cream of chicken soup
½ tsp. black pepper
pinch of thyme oregano

Cook rice as directed on pkg. Fry sausage meat and crumble. Saute mushrooms and onions in the sausage fat. Mix all ingredients and bake in a casserole at 350° for 1 hour.
Note: This is delicious and quite rich. Goes well with Party Chicken for a special luncheon.
Gladys Box.

* CHEESE PUFF CASSEROLE *

½ stick of butter
8 slices bread (firm texture)
½ lb. Cheddar cheese
4 eggs
2 c. milk

1 tsp. Worcestershire sauce
¾ tsp. salt
cayenne pepper

Place butter in casserole or baking dish (7" x 9") and set in a warm oven until butter melts. Trim crusts from bread and cut into 1 in. cubes. Toss the cubes in melted butter with slotted spoon, remove to a bowl. Spread remaining butter on sides of casserole. Cut cheese into slices and place half in bottom of casserole. Repeat using the bread with the cheese. Beat eggs with milk, Worcestershire, salt and cayenne. Pour over bread and cheese. Refrigerate overnight. Preheat oven to 325°. Remove casserole from refrigerator and return to room temperature. Bake about 1 hour or until puffed and set.   Adele Davis.

* AUSTRALIAN BACON AND EGG PIE *

1½ lb. short pastry
5 eggs
4 slices of bacon (cut in 2" lengths)

1 dessert spoon chopped parsley
1 tsp. salt

Line bottom and sides of a 8" x 2" deep round cake pan with the pastry. Line bottom and sides with 2/3 of the bacon. Slightly beat eggs and pour into crust lined cake pan. Sprinkle with salt and parsley. Cover with the pastry — glaze — slit top slightly. Bake at 450° for 10 minutes, then reduce the heat to 350° for another 20 to 30 minutes.   Nancy O'Brien.

* ENCHILADA CASSEROLE *

1½ dz. flour tortillas (lg.)
6 lbs. ground beef
½ lb. chopped bacon
2 c. chopped onion
2 c. chopped celery

¼ c. bell pepper (chopped)
5 sm. cans sliced black olives
2 blocks Monterey cheese (grated)
5 pkgs. Lawrys Enchilada sauce mix
2 cans. tomato paste.

Note: I use tomato sauce with tibits if available instead of the plain tomato sauce. Saute bacon, add onion, celery and bell pepper. Put aside. Saute ground meat, then drain off all fat, add bacon, olives, mixture and Monterey cheese. Set aside. Make sauce with the Enchilada pkgs. according to directions, let simmer for 15 minutes. Pour about ¼ in. of sauce in bottom of the pan. Take a tortilla and dip it in some of the sauce. Add hamburger mixture on the tortilla, roll and place seam side down in baking pan. Repeat the process. When pan is filled, pour remaining sauce over all. Keep warm in oven and serve with garlic bread.

Flora Azevedo.

* MUFFIN PIZZAS *

Spread muffins with tomato paste or ketchup. Top with cheese slices. Dice salami, crushed pineapple (drained), sprinkle with oregano. Bake for 15 minutes at 450°.   Lillian Kann

89

* ENCHILADAS DE CREME *

12 tortillas
1 lb. jack cheese
1 onion (minced)
2 cans (4 oz. each) green chilies
  (peeled)
1 garlic clove (minced)

1 can (8 0z. each) tomato sauce
1 tsp. salt
1 tsp. oregano
1 pt. dairy sour cream
oil for frying

Fry tortillas lightly in small amount of oil. Fill with cheese and chilies (that have been cut in strips (discard the seeds). Roll and place in casserole.

Fry onion and garlic in 1 Tbsp. oil until lightly browned, add tomato sauce, salt and oregano. Cover and simmer for 15 minutes. (Add a little water if sauce gets too thick). Remove from heat, stir in the sour cream and pour over the tortillas. Cover and bake at 350° for 30 minutes or until bubbling hot.

Serve with green salad and refried beans.
Rosella Reiner.

* ENCHILADAS CASSEROLE *

1 lb. beef (ground)
1 Tbsp. margarine
1 onion (minced)
1 can (15 oz.) tomato sauce
2 tsp. chili powder

Garlic powder, salt, pepper
1 pkg. tortillas (6–8 dia.)
1½ c. Cheddar cheese (grated)
tub of sour cream
cut up tomatoes and lettuce

Fry beef in margarine, add onions till soft, drain off fat. Add chili powder, garlic, salt and pepper. Heat through.

Line a 9½ in. pan (pie pan) with tortillas, overlapping the sides, 1 in. Place ½ of the mixture, ½ of the cheese, cover with 1–2 tortillas, leaving the sides open. Add remaining beef, then cheese. Bake at 325° for 25 to 30 minutes, ONO.
Jean Keys.

* CHILI RELLENOS IN CUSTARD *

3 sm. cans (4 oz. each) whole
  green chilies (not hot)
½ lb. Cheddar cheese

2 eggs
2 c. milk
1 tsp. salt

Remove seed from chilies. Place a slice of cheese in each. Mix eggs, milk, salt and pour over chilies in butter baking dish.

Bake at 350° for 50 to 60 minutes. Let stand for 5 minutes then serve.
Jean Keys

* CHILIES RELLENOS CASSEROLE *

Trim crusts off 4—6 slices of white bread. Butter one side of each and place buttered side down in baking dish. Sprinkle 2 c. grated sharp Cheddar cheese over this. Then 2 c. shredded Monterey cheese over it.

Seed and mince 2 cans (4—6 oz. each) of green chilies, sprinkle over the cheese Beat 6 eggs and 2 c. milk with 2 tsp. paprika, 1 tsp. salt, ½ tsp. oregano, ½ tsp. pepper and ¼tsp. dry mustard. Pour over cheese. Cover and chill 4 hours, then bake uncovered at 325° for 50 minutes. Let stand for 10 minutes. Then cut and serve.

Jean Keys.

* VEGETABLE RAVIOLE CASSEROLE *

1 c. onions (sliced)	1 tsp. sweet basil
2 Tbsp oleo	dash of nutmeg
2 pkgs. mixed frozen vegetables	3 cans Raviole

Saute onions in the oleo until soft. Add vegetables and seasoning. Layer Raviole and vegetable mixture and top with ¼ c. Parmesan cheese,. Bake (covered) in 350° oven for 30 minutes.

Dorothy Tuttle

* CHEESE AND BACON FRITTATA *

6 eggs	1/8 tsp. pepper
1 c. milk	½ tsp. salt
1 green onion (chopped)	1 4 oz. pkg. shredded Cheddar cheese
2 Tbsp. butter or oleo (melted)	½ of a 3 oz. can real crumbled bacon

Preheat oven to 400°. Grease a 10—11 in. round au gratin or fry pan. In medium bowl with beaters, beat thoroughly the eggs, milk, green and cheese evenly over the mixture.

Bake at 400° for 20 minutes. It will puff up and turn slightly golden.

Jean Keys.

* SOUR CREAM TORTILLA CASSEROLE *

½ c. onions (chopped)	12 corn tortillas
2 Tbsp. cooking oil	¼ c. onion (chopped)
1 lg. can tomatoes	1 lb. Monterey cheese (grated)
1 pkg. Spanish rice seasoning mix	2 c. sour cream
2 Tbsp. salsa Jalapena	1 tsp. seasoned salt pepper

Saute onion in oil until tender. Add tomatoes, Spanish rice mix, and salsa jalapena and simmer for 20 minutes. Set aside to cool.

Fry tortillas in oil for 10 to 15 minutes on each side but do not allow to become crisp.

Pour ½ c. of sauce in bottom of a 9" x 13" baking dish. Arrange layers of tortillas over the sauce. (They can overlap). Top with 1/3 sauce, 1/3 onion and 1/3 cheese. Repeat, making 3 layers of tortillas.

Combine sour cream with seasoned salt, spread over the cheese to the edge of dish. Sprinkle with fresh ground pepper.

Bake in preheated oven 325° for 25—30 minutes.

To serve cut into squares.   Adele Davis

* CURRIED FRUIT CASSEROLE BAKE *

1 can No. 303 peach halves	1 can No. 303 pear halves
1 can No. 2 — sliced pineapple	Maraschino cherries with stems.

Drain all for 6—8 hours. Dry with paper towel.

½ c. butter (melted)	4 tsp. curry powder
¾ c. light brown sugar (packed)	

Place fruit in a baking dish. Mix all other ingredients and spoon over the fruit. Bake 60 minutes uncovered at 325°. Refrigerate over night.

Before serving — reheat—30 minutes at 350°.

Serve warm. Excellent with ham, lamb or chicken.   Dorothy Tuttle.

 **QUICHES · SOUFFLES**

* CALIFORNIA VEGETABLE QUICHE *

1 lb. summer squash
(green or yellow)
4 eggs (well beaten)
2 c. Swiss or Monterey cheese (grated)

1 tsp. dill
1½ tsp. salt
¼ c. Parmesan cheese (grated)

Grate squash coarsely in a bowl. Sprinkle lightly with salt and let stand 10 min. Squeeze out all liquid.

Combine squash, eggs, cheese (except Parmesan) and seasonings. Pour into an 8 in. square baking dish and top with the Parmesan cheese. Bake in preheated oven (350°) for 30 to 40 minutes or until quiche is set in center and edges are slightly browned.. Serve with sliced tomatoes on the side

Note:2½ to 3 c. steamed chopped greens (spinach, mustard, etc.) may be substitued for squash.   Francis Wright.

* CRUSTLESS SPINACH QUICHE *

1 pkg. (10 oz.) frozen spinach
(chopped kind)
8 oz. Gruyere cheese (grated)
2 slices day old bread
(crusts removed)
sour cream (optional)

6 eggs (beaten)
4 tsp. onion (grated)
salt — pepper
¼ tsp. nutmeg.

Preheat oven to 350°. Place spinach in a colander to thaw. Press out all moisture. Mix spinach with cheese and bread, torn into small pieces. Add nutmeg, eggs, onion, salt and pepper. Transfer to an 8 in. pie plate and bake 30 minutes or until center is set.

Serve hot or cold with, or without sour cream.   Ida Christoph.

* CREAMY ZUCCHINI QUICHE *

1 unbaked pie shell (9 or 10 in.)
2 Tbsp. Dijon mustard
3 c. zucchini (grated)
8 lg. mushrooms (sliced)
2 c. Monterey cheese (grated)

½ c. whipping cream
3 egg yolks
1 whole egg
salt — pepper
1 c. cream cheese

Preheat oven to 450°. Spread bottom of pastry with mustard and bake for 10 minutes. Cool. Reduce oven heat to 350°.

Place zucchini in a colander, sprinkle with salt and drain after 5 minutes.

Saute mushrooms in butter. Sprinkle the grated cheese into bottom of pastry shell, separating and fluffing with the fingers. Spoon mushrooms on top. Squeeze zucchini to remove all moisture and put in shell.

Beat together cream, cream cheese, egg yolks, and whole egg. Season with salt and pepper.

Set pastry shell on a baking sheet and carefully pour in cream mixture. Sprinkle remaining cheese on top. Bake 35 minutes until top is puffed and golden and center is set.

Let stand 5 minutes before serving. Adele Davis.

* INDIVIDUAL QUICHES *

Pastry for 2 crust pie
¾ c. cooked shrimp (chopped)
¼ c. green onion (chopped)
1 c. Swiss cheese (grated)
½ c. mayonnaise

1/3 c. milk
2 eggs
¼ tsp. salt
¼ tsp. dry dill weed

On floured board, roll out half of pastry into 12 in. circle. Cut six 4 in. circles. Repeat with remaining pastry. Fit into 2½ in. muffin pan cups. Fill each cup with some onion, shrimp and cheese. Beat remaining ingredients and pour into cups. Bake in preheated oven (400°) for 15 to 20 minutes or until browned.

Charlene Do.

* QUICHE LORRAINE *

6 bacon slices
½ lb. Gruyere cheese
4 eggs
2 c. light cream

2 Tbsp. butter
salt to taste
rich pastry for quiche pan.

Cut bacon strips in half and saute until golden brown. Drain on paper towel. Cut 12 thin slices of cheese (size of bacon strips.) Cover pastry in layers of cheese and bacon.

Beat eggs with the cream, add a pinch of salt. Pour over bacon strips. Dot with butter. Bake in a preheated oven (375°) until custard is set and top is browned. Serve warm. Daisy Alexander.

* TOMATO CHICKEN QUICHE *

1 unbaked pie shell
2 Tbsp. butter
3 med. leeks or onions (sliced)
1 c. cooked chicken (diced)
½ lb. fried bacon (crumbled)
1 egg white
1/4 tsp. nutmeg
1/8 tsp. steak sauce

4 oz. Gruyere or Swiss cheese (sliced)
4 eggs
1 egg yolk
1 c. milk or buttermilk
1 tsp. sugar
3 med. tomatoes (thinly sliced)

94

Garnish — minced parsley

Preheat oven to 450°. Fit pastry into a quiche dish and bake for 5 minutes and set aside.

Melt butter over med. heat in a lg. skillet, add leeks and saute until very soft. Stir in chicken and bacon. Remove from heat and set aside.

Beat eggs whites slightly and spread over pie shell. Spread leek mixture evenly over the bottom and cover with the cheese.

Combine eggs, yolk, cream, sugar nutmeg, steak sauce and salt and pepper to taste, Whisk thoroughly. Carefully pour into pie shell. Arrange tomatoes over top. Bake 12 minutes and then reduce heat to 350° and bake an additional 45 to 60 minutes until center is set. Sprinkle with the parsley.   Rebecca Dixon.

* HOT CRAB MEAT QUICHE *

1 pkg. cream cheese (8 oz.) (softened) 1/3 c. toasted almonds (sliced)
1 can (6 oz.) flaked crab meat   ½ tsp. (creamy type) horseradish
1 Tbsp. onion (chopped)   salt — pepper
1 Tbsp. milk   Dash of Worcestershire sauce.

Preheat oven to 375°. Combine all ingredients (except almonds) and mix until well blended. Pour into pie shell or any other shallow oven pan. Top with the almonds and bake for 15 to 20 minutes.

Serve hot with crisp raw vegetables or crackers.   Adele Davis.

* NEW ENGLAND CLAM QUICHE *

1 unbaked pie shell (10 in.)   ½ c. onions (chopped)
½ lb. cooked bacon (crumbled)   ½ c. sour cream
1 can (15 oz.) clam chowder   2 Tbsp. parsley (chopped)
   (condensed)   ¼ tsp. pepper
4 eggs (slightly beaten)
4 slices Cheddar cheese

Preheat over to 400°. Bake shell 8 minutes. Remove from oven. Reduce heat to 325°.

Combine bacon, chowder, eggs, onion, sour cream, parsley and pepper. Pour about 1/3 of the mixture in shell, arrange cheese slices on top. Top with the remaining mixture. Bake to 55 minutes or until set. Let stand before cutting.
                                                          Nancy Ebsen.

* MADE IN ADVANCE SOUFFLE *

½ c. butter   2 c. milk
½ c. flour (sifted)   ½ lb. Cheddar cheese
½ tsp. paprika   8 lg. eggs (separated)

Melt butter in top of double boiler over hot water (not boiling). Add flour, salt and paprika, mix well and gradually add the flour, stirring constantly until sauce is thick.

Dice cheese and stir into cream sauce until cheese is melted. Beat egg yolks until light and pour into cheese mixture. Cool slightly. Beat egg whites until stiff but not dry. Fold cheese mixture into the egg whites and pour into a prepared souffle dish.

Bake in a preheated oven 475° for 10 minutes. Reduce the heat to 400° and bake 25 minutes longer. (Souffle dish must be put in pan of hot water before placing in the oven.)

Note: You can mix this souffle as much as 3 hours. before baking time, if you like and set in refrigerator. Remove it about 20 minutes before placing in preheated oven. Serve with tossed green salad or orange and grapefruit salad.

Adele Davis.

* BASIC SOUFFLE *

4 Tbsp. butter   ¼ tsp. salt
3 Tbsp. flour   ¼ tsp. cream of tartar
1¼ c. milk   1½ c. main ingredients
5 lg. eggs (separated)

Main ingredients may consist of meat, fowl, cheese, seafood, or vegetables. (finely chopped)

Melt butter in saucepan, stir in flour and blend. Cook over med. heat until mixture simmers for 1 minute. Remove from heat and add milk and stir constantly. Mix in main ingredients, beat in egg yolks and place on low heat and stir for 1 minute re-pour into lg. mixing bowl.

Beat egg whites with salt and cream of tartar until stiff but not dry. Fold into yolk mixture.

Spoon into buttered, crumbed and collared souffle dish. Place souffle in lower third of oven. Bake in preheated oven (375°) for 25 to 35 minutes. Test for doneness.

Francis Wright.

* CHEESE SOUFFLE *

4 Tbsp. butter
3 Tbsp. flour
½ tsp. salt
cayenne pepper
1¼ c. light cream
1 tsp. Dijon mustard
½ tsp. dry mustard
¼ tsp. salt
2 Tbsp. Parmesan cheese (grated) for topping.

½ c. Gruyere cheese (grated)
3 oz. Camembert cheese
   (pressed through strainer)
¼ c. Parmesan cheese (grated)
2 Tbsp. sour cream
2 Tbsp. dry sherry
6 lg. eggs (separated)
¼ tsp. cream of tartar

Melt butter in saucepan and add flour and stir until smooth, add ½ tsp. salt, cayenne and cream and stir over low heat until thickened. Add mustards, cheese, sour cream and sherry. Add egg yolks (that have been beaten) and stir until thick. Pour into a lg. mixing bowl. Beat egg whites with salt and cream of tartar and fold into cheese mixture. Spoon mixture into buttered, crumbed and collared 1½ qt. souffle dish. Sprinkle top with the Parmesan cheese.

Place souffle dish in lower third of preheated oven (400°) for 10 minutes. Reduce heat to 375° and bake for 30 to 40 minutes. Test for doneness.

Daisy Alexander

* CHEESE AND RICE SOUFFLE *

1½ c. cooked rice
1½ c. white sauce
2 eggs (separated)

1¼ c. Cheddar cheese (grated)
1/8 tsp. baking powder
salt — paprika

Season sauce highly with salt and paprika. Add cheese and heat slowly until cheese is melted. Add rice and beaten egg yolks. Cool slightly. Fold in stiffly beaten egg whites. Add baking powder. Pour into well buttered souffle pan — set in pan of hot water. Bake in preheated oven (350°) for 30 minutes

Margaret Holmes

* EGGPLANT SOUFFLE *

2 med. eggplants
1 c. soft bread crumbs
3 lg. eggs (separated)
2 Tbsp. butter
½ c. nut meats (chopped)

½ c. Cheddar cheese (grated)
2 Tbsp. milk
1 Tbsp. flour
1 c. corn flakes (crumbled)

Cut eggplant into halves and scoop out pulp. Place shells in cold water with a little lemon juice added. (to keep from discoloring). Drop pulp in a small amount of water and cook until tender. Drain well and mash.

Combine in mashed eggplant, bread crumbs, butter, 3 eggs (beaten), nut meats, cheese, milk, and flour. Heat over very low heat until cheese is just melted. (if mixture seems a little thick, add a bit of milk).

Beat egg whites until just stiff, and fold in eggplant mixture. Drain eggplants shells very well and spoon in mixture. Place shells in a baking pan with a little water and bake in preheated oven (350°) for 30 to 35 minutes. Sprinkle corn flakes on top the last 10 minutes of baking. Serve hot.   Ida Christoph.

* SURPRISE SOUFFLE *

Most everyone likes surprises, poached egg is hidden in each serving.

4 Tbsp. butter	6 med. eggs (poached 3 minutes)
3 Tbsp. flour	6 lg. eggs (separated)
1¼ c. milk	¼ tsp. salt
1½ tsp. salt	¼ tsp. cream of tartar
½ c. Cheddar cheese (grated)	1 c. cooked spinach (pureed)
½ c. Cottage cheese (sm. curd)	pinch of nutmeg
½ c. Parmesan cheese (grated)	1½ Tbsp. shallots (sliced – sauted)

Melt butter in a saucepan, add flour and stir. Add milk and salt and simmer until sauce is thickened. Add cheeses and beaten egg yolks and stir very slowly over very low heat until slightly thick. Cool. Beat egg whites until stiff with the salt and cream of tartar, and fold into one half of cheese mixture.

Combine spinach, shallots and nutmeg and fold into other half of cheese mixture. Place spinach mixture in bottom of 1—12 qt. souffle dish that has been buttered, crumbed abd collared.

Place well drained eggs on spinach. Spoon remaining cheese mixture over eggs. Place souffle in lower half of oven in preheated oven (400°) and bake for 30 to 40 minutes. Test souffle for doneness. Cut souffle so that each serving contains a poached egg. Note: Egg mixture without the spinach and poached egg makes an excellent cheese souffle.   Adele Davis.

* FRESH FRUIT SOUFFLE *

Prepare souffle dish as in chocolate souffle recipe.
Prepare by peeling and mashing ripe fruit to make:

1 c. sweetened fruit pulp. (fresh apricots, peaches, plums or raspberries)

1½ Tbsp. lemon juice	1/8 tsp. salt
4 lg. eggs (separated)	1 Tbsp. orange rind (grated)

Beat egg yolks until light, add fruit pulp, orange rind, lemon juice and salt. Beat egg whites until stiff but not dry and fold into egg yolk mixture. Pour into prepared souffle dish. Place dish in pan of hot water and bake in preheated oven (350°) for 30 to 40 minutes until set.

Serve hot with whipped cream or custard sauce.   Charlene Do.

* CHOCOLATE SOUFFLE *

Prepare souffle dish by oiling inside and dust lightly with powdered sugar. Cut piece of waxed paper or foil enough to encircle dish with ½ in. overlap and fold in half lengthwise. Grease upper half and sprinkle with sugar. Wrap around outside of dish allowing paper to extend 2 in. above the rim and secure with string.

2 Tbsp. butter	1/3 c. sugar
1 Tbsp. flour	3 lg. eggs (separated)
1 c. milk	1 tsp. vanilla
1 oz. chocolate (cut in pieces)	

Melt butter and stir in flour. Heat chocolate in the milk and sugar over low heat until chocolate is melted and add butter to the mixture stirring until well blended. Beat egg yolks until light and add to chocolate mixture and stir the custard over low heat to thicken. Cool. When cooled add vanilla. Whip egg whites until stiff but not dry and fold into the custard. Spoon into prepared souffle dish and set in a pan of hot water and bake in a preheated oven (350°) for 30 to 35 minutes. Serve at once.   Adele Davis.

* CREAM CHEESE SOUFFLE *

6 oz. cream cheese	4 eggs (separated)
¾ c. sour cream	pinch of salt
2 Tbsp. honey	

Soften cream cheese, add sour cream and beat until smooth. Stir in honey, salt and beaten egg yolks. Fold in stiffly beaten egg whites.
Pour into buttered souffle dish.
Bake in preheated oven (350°) for 35 minutes.
Serve with whipped cream and strawberries or raspberries.   Ida Christoph.

* LEMON CUSTARD SOUFFLE *

1½ Tbsp. butter
½ c. sugar
2 lg. eggs (separated)
2 Tbsp. lemon juice
1 Tbsp. lemon rind (grated)

¼ tsp. vanilla
½ c.milk
mint sprigs for garnish

Cream butter and sugar well. Add egg yolks and beat until light and fluffy. Mix in flour, lemon juice, lemon rind and vanilla. Add milk and stir until well blended. Beat egg whites until stiff, gently fold into the egg mixture. Spoon into ungreased 1 qt. souffle dish. Place dish in pan of hot water and bake in preheated oven (400°) for 20 minutes until set and slightly brown.

Note: This is a small recipe, may be increased.   Nancy Ebsen.

* BLINTZ SOUFFLE *

1 pkg. (8) cheese blintzes
½ c. butter (melted)
2 c. sour cream
6 eggs (beaten)

¼ c. orange juice
¼ c. sugar
2 tsp. vanilla
2 tsp. salt.

Garnish: Sour cream, frozen starwberries (thawed).

Preheat oven to 350°. Place blintzes in a 2 qt. souffle dish and cover with melted butter.

Combine eggs, sour cream, orange juice, sugar, vanilla and salt and pour over blintzes. Bake for 1 hour until puffed and browned. Serve with sour cream and strawberries.   Irma Katz.

* PINEAPPLE SOUFFLE *

Prepare souffle dish as in chocolate souffle recipe.

3 Tbsp. butter
3 Tbsp. flour
1 c. crushed pineapple (drained)
4 lg. eggs (separated)

2 Tbsp. sugar
½ tsp. vanilla
2/3 c. Macaroons (crushed)

Melt butter in sauce pan and add flour and stir, add macaroons and let thicken slightly. Cool. When cool add vanilla.

Beat egg whites until stiff but not dry, gradually add the sugar. Fold into the pineapple mixture and pour into prepared souffle dish. Bake in preheated oven (325°) for 30 to 35 minutes until formed.

Serve warm or cold.   Millie Mesaku.

* COFFEE NUT SOUFFLE *

1 pkg. gelatin
¼ c. water
3 Tbsp. instant coffee
2/3 c. walnut pieces

4 lg. eggs (separated)
½ c. sugar
3 Tbsp. Rum or Cognac
1½ c. whipping cream

Cut piece of foil large enough to encircle a 1 qt. souffle dish. Fold in half and lightly grease one side. Place folded side in, wrap foil around dish, allowing to extend 2 in. above the rim, tie or tape in place.

Combine gelatin, water and coffee and let stand until water is absorbed. Place in a pan of hot water over low heat and simmer for 2 minutes. Cool.

Mince walnuts in a blender, add egg yolks and sugar and process until thick. Place egg mix and gelatin in a saucepan over med. heat whisking constantly until thickened. Allow to cool slightly. Add Rum. Beat egg whites until stiff but not dry and fold into coffee mixture. Whip cream until stiff and fold in gently. Spoon into prepared dish and cover with plastic wrap and refrigerate for at least 6 hours or overnight. Just before serving, use a flexible knife and separate collar from the souffle.

Serve with additional whipped cream, if desired.   Adele Davis.

 # ITALIAN · CUISINE

* PASTA SAUCES *

SAUCE BOLOGNESE

2 Tbsp. olive oil
½ c. bacon (diced)
½ c. prosciutto (diced)
1 onion (minced)
1 celery rib (minced)
1 carrot (minced)
salt — pepper
2 Tbsp. tomato sauce
¼ tsp. rosemary

3 chicken livers (quartered)
¼ lb. mushrooms (chopped)
3 Tbsp. butter
½ c. heavy cream
¾ lb. ground beef
¼ lb. ground veal
2 c. beef broth
½ c. sherry

Heat olive oil in a lg. skillet, brown bacon and prosciutto. Add onions, celery, and carrots until tender. Add meat and cook, breaking up the meat with a fork and cook until pink color dissappears (about 15 minutes) mix together ¾ c. broth and sherry and add to the skillet and cook until liquid is almost absorbed. Stir in the balance of the broth, add rosemary, salt and pepper to taste. While sauce is cooking, saute mushrooms and chicken livers in butter. Add to sauce and cook for 5 minutes. Mix in cream and keep warm.

SALSA DI PUTANA

2 Tbsp. olive oil
2 garlic cloves (minced)
1 celery rib (minced)
1 sweet red pepper (minced)
1 can (3 oz.) plum tomatoes
1 tsp. basil

¼ tsp. dried red pepper
6 anchovies (chopped)
8 stuffed green olives (sliced)
8 black olives (sliced)
1 tsp. capers

Heat olive oil in lg. skillet, add garlic, celery, red pepper and saute until tender. Press tomatoes through a food mill and add to skillet, simmer for 10 minutes. Stir in olives, capers and basil and simmer uncovered for 20 minutes. Serve with hot buttered pasta.

GARDEN SAUCE

½ c. parsley (chopped)
2 garlic cloves (minced)
2 onions (minced)
6 slices prosciutto (minced)
4 radishes (minced)
12 carrots (minced)
1 leek (minced)
1 tsp. dry basil

3 Tbsp. butter
3 Tbsp. olive oil
1 c. cabbage (chopped)
4 tomatoes (peeled—diced)
2 sm. zucchinis (diced)
1 c. chicken broth
salt — pepper
Parmesan cheese

Combine parsley, garlic, onions, prosciutto, radishes, carrots, leek and basil (This is called "soffritto", in Italian.) Heat oil and butter in a lg. pot and stir in the vegetables, simmer until onions and carrots are soft. Stir in cabbage, zucchini, tomatoes and chicken broth. Season to taste. Simmer (covered) for 20 minutes. Serve hot on buttered pasta and lavishly sprinkle with parmesan cheese.

CLAM SAUCE

½ stick of butter
½ c. olive oil
3 onions (chopped)
2½ doz. fresh clams or 2 (7 oz.)
   cans minced clams

1 tsp. basil
1 tsp. oregano
2 c. parsley (minced)

Heat butter and oil in a skillet and saute onions, covered until soft. Add basil and oregano and simmer for 5 minutes. Add parsley, cover and simmer 10 min. Add clams to sauce and season to taste.
(If using fresh clams, open and chop. If using canned clams — drain well.

BECHAMEL SAUCE

¾ stick butter
4½ Tbsp. flour
2 c. hot whipping cream
1 c. white wine

¾ tsp. salt
pinch of pepper
pinch of nutmeg
2 parsley sprigs

Melt butter in skillet over med. heat. Add flour and stir 1 minute. Gradually add hot cream, then the wine, stirring constantly. Season with salt, pepper and nutmeg. Add parsley and bring to a boil and simmer for 10 minutes. Remove the parsley.

* FETTUCCHINI *

1 can cream of mushroom soup
¾ c. milk
3 c. cooked hot noodles.

¼ c. Parmesan cheese (grated)
4 Tbsp. butter

In saucepan stir soup until smooth, add milk and blend. then add cheese. Just before serving, toss hot noodles with the butter.
Serve with additional cheese.

Jean Keys.

* CANNELLONI *

1 pkg. cannelloni (prepare as directed)
tomato sauce (prepared)

Filling:

2 Tbsp. olive oil
¼ c. chopped onions
1 garlic clove (crushed)
1 c. spinach (chopped)
   (fresh or frozen)
2 Tbsp. butter

½ tsp. oregano
1 lb. round steak (ground fine)
5 Tbsp. Parmesan cheese (grated)
2 Tbsp. cream
2 eggs (beaten)
salt — pepper

Saute onion and garlic in skillet with oil until golden brown. Add spinach and simmer for 5 minutes. Place in bowl.

Melt 1 Tbsp. butter in skillet and brown slightly. Add meat and cook until browned and all pieces are broken up. Add meat to vegetable mixture, add cheese, cream, eggs and oregano. Season with salt and pepper.

Bechamel Sauce:

3 Tbsp. butter
4 Tbsp. flour
1 c. milk

1 c. heavy cream
1 tsp. salt
1/8 tsp. white pepper

Melt butter over med. heat, remove from heat and add flour, stir, add milk and cream. Simmer until sauce is thick enough to coat a metal spoon.

Fill pasta shells with the meat mixture. Place a thin layer of tomato sauce on bottom of a baking pan (10 x 14 in.). Lay pasta tubes side by side. Pour cream sauce on top. Sprinkle on more tomato sauce.

Sprinkle cheese over all. Bake uncovered in preheated oven (350°) until cheese is melted and sauce is bubbly. Slip pan under broiler for a few minutes, to brown top.

Evelyn staley

* HAY AND STRAW *

½ lb. white linguini
½ lb. green linguini
olive oil
Boiling salted water (2 separate pots)
½ c. butter (soft)
12 med. mushrooms (sliced thin)
½ lb. prosciutto (sliced thin)

¼ c. chicken broth
1 c. whipping cream
¼ lb. Parmesan cheese (freshly grated)
salt — fresh ground pepper

Cook pasta separately, al dente, adding a few drops of oil to each pot. Drain quickly. allowing some water to remain and combine in one pot over low heat. Stir in butter, mushrooms and prosciutto with lg. wooden spoons or forks. Add chicken broth and cream, tossing gently. Sprinkle with Parmesan cheese, salt and pepper.

Serve in heated bowls and pass additional cheese.

Adele Davis.

* LASAGNA BEL MONTE *

Sauce:

1 med. onion (chopped)	1 can (6 oz.) tomato paste
3 Tbsp: olive oil	½ c. red wine
1½ lb. ground beef	1 tsp. oregano
1 garlic clove (mashed	salt — pepper
2 cans (8 Oz.) each) tomato puree	½ c. water
1 tsp. sugar	

Saute onion in oil until soft, add beef and garlic, stir until meat is browned and crumbly. Add tomato sauce, tomato puree wine and water. Simmer for 10 min. Add salt, pepper and oregano and stir until well mixed. Cover and simmer for 30 minutes.

Pasta:

12 oz. lasagna noodles	½ lb. Mozzarella cheese (sliced thin)
1 lb. (2 c.) Ricotta or sm. curd cottage cheese	½ c. Parmesan cheese (shredded)

Cook noodles in boiling water 15 minutes. Drain and rinse in cold water. Drain well. Arrange noodles (about 1/3) in the bottom of a shallow baking dish. (criss — cross to make a firm bottom). Spread 1/3 of tomato sauce on top, add 1/3 of the Ricotta cheese and 1/3 of the Mozzarella cheese. Repeat layers two more times. Top with Parmesan cheese. Use remaining sauce over all.
Bake in preheated oven (375°) for 30 minutes. Cut in squares to serve.
Note: A pkg. of frozen spinach may be added to the layers for variety.

Roberta Chateauneuf

* GREEN NOODLES WITH FENNEL SAUCE *

1/3 c. olive oil	¼ c. parsley (chopped)
¼ c. pine nuts	6 Tbsp. butter (soft)
2 Tbsp. fennel seeds	1½ lb. green noodles
¼ c. Romano cheese (grated)	

Place in a blender the olive oil and the nuts and blend but do not liquify. Add fennel seeds, cheese, parsley, salt and pepper to make a thick paste. Place in a lg. serving bowl.
Cook noodles in 8 qt. pot with rapidly boiling water. When cooked, rinse quickly in a lg. colander under hot water. Drain well and turn into serving bowl, mix thoroughly. Serve hot.

Francis Wright.

* GLORY CACCIATORE *

1 lb. each veal, pork and beef
3 Tbsp. oil
3 onions (chopped)
4 garlic cloves (minced)
2 celery stalks (chopped)
1 green pepper (chopped)
    3 carrots (sliced)
1 can. (2 lbs.) Italian tomatoes
    (chopped)

1 Tbsp. salt
2 tsp. oregano
2 tsp. thyme
2 tsp. marjoram
1 Tbsp. chili powder
1 tsp. dry mustard
1 lb. cooked vermicelli
1 can (4 oz.) pimentos (sliced)

Trim all fat from the meat. Cut into chunks, about 1½ in. in diameter. Heat oil in lg. skillet and brown meat and set aside. Add onions and garlic to pan and saute for 3 to 4 min. Add remaining vegetables and seasonings (except pimentos) and simmer for 20 minutes. Add meat and simmer for another 20 minutes. Serve on cooked (al dente) vermicelli and garnish with pimento slices.

Nancy Ebsen.

* SAUTED CHICKEN LIVERS WITH NOODLES *

1 lb. chicken livers
    (fresh or frozen)
4 Tbsp. butter
1 oz. salt pork (diced)
¼ lb. onions (sliced)
1 garlic clove (minced)
1 lb. cooked noodles
½ c. parsley (chopped)

pinch of allspice
1 bay leaf (crumbled)
1/3 tsp. pepper
1/3 tsp. salt
2/3 c. white wine
juice of 1 lemon
1 c. Parmesan cheese (grated)

Wash chicken livers and dry. Combine butter, salt pork and oil in a skillet and heat. Add onions and garlic and saute until golden brown. Add chicken livers and simmer for 4 minutes. Add wine and stir. Add parsley and lemon juice and simmer for 5 minutes more. Arrange noodles on a platter, cover with livers and top with cheese.

Judy Pieklo.

* CHICKEN TETRAZZINI *

1 lb. thin noodles or fettucini
1 garlic clove (crushed)
2 sprigs of parsley
2 Tbsp. olive oil
½ lb. fresh mushrooms (sliced)
1 bay leaf (crumbled)
½ tsp. salt
¼ tsp. pepper

6 Tbsp. sweet butter
2 Tbsp. flour
1 c. hot chicken broth
½ c. light cream (warmed)
¼ c. white wine
1 c. cooked chicken (diced)
8 thin slices of chicken breasts
¼ c. Parmesan cheese

Place oil in skillet and heat. Add mushrooms, bay leaf, garlic, parsley, salt and pepper. Cook slowly for 4 minutes. Place butter in another pan, melt and add flour and blend. Add chicken broth, stir until thickened. Remove from heat and add cream and wine.

Prepare noodles, drain and place in buttered casserole. Spoon mushroom mixture over noodles. Place chicken on top. Pour cream sauce over all and sprinkle with cheese. Bake in preheated oven (350°) for 15 minutes until cheese is melted.

Adele Davis.

VEAL SCALLOPINI WITH MARSALA *

½ lb. mushrooms (sliced thin)
4 Tbsp. butter
1½ Tbsp. lemon juice
1½ lbs. boneless veal (trimmed)
¼ c. flour

1 tsp. salt
fresh ground pepper
¾ c. Marsala or Sherry
1 bouillon cube
1 Tbsp. parsley (minced)

Melt 1 Tbsp. butter in a lg. skillet and add mushrooms, sprinkle with lemon juice and cook over med. heat just until mushrooms are limp. Pour out of pan and set aside.

Cut veal into 1 in. strips and dust in flour seasoned with salt and pepper, shake off excess. Melt remaining butter and brown meat at high heat, turning as you brown. Set meat aside as it browns. Pour in wine and bouillon cube and cook rapidly until all browned particles are in the sauce. Return mushrooms and meat to the skillet and heat until hot. Serve at once with buttered pasta.

Francis Wright.

* BAGNA CAUDA *

½ c. unsalted butter
¼ c. olive oil
2 garlic cloves (minced)

6 flat anchovies (drained—chopped fine)
1 sm. truffle (optional)

Heat oil, butter and garlic in the top of a double boiler. Stir until well blended. Add anchovies. Place in a hot bowl over hot plate or serve in chafing dish over a low flame. Keep warm.

Serve with a lg. platter of crisp vegetables. Such as strips of celery, carrots, and green pepper. Sliced sweet onions, zucchini and eggplant. Quarter plum tomatoes, florets of cauliflower, etc.

Each guest should dip their own vegetables in the warm sauce.   Evelyn Staley.

* SPAGHETTI PIE *

6 oz. spaghetti
2 Tbsp. butter
1/3 c. Parmesan cheese (grated)
2 well — beaten eggs
1 c. (8 oz.) cottage cheese
1 lb. ground beef
½ c. shredded Mozzarella cheese

½ c. chopped onion
¼ c. chopped green pepper
1 can (8 oz.) tomatoes (cut up)
1 can (6 oz.) tomato paste
1 tsp. sugar
1 tsp. oregano

Cook the spaghetti according to pkg. directions, drain. (should be about 3 c. spaghetti.) Stir butter into hot spaghetti. Stir in Parmesan cheese and eggs. Form spaghetti mixture into a crust in a buttered 10 in. pie pan. Spread cottage cheese over the bottom of spaghetti crust.

In skillet cook ground meat, onion and green pepper until vegetables are tender and meat is browned. Drain off excess fat. Stir in undrained tomatoes, tomato paste, sugar, oregano and garlic salt and heat through. Turn meat mixture into the spaghetti crust. Bake, uncovered in 350°(oven for 20 minutes. Sprinkle the Mozzarella cheese on top. Bake 5 minutes longer or until cheese has melted.

Judy Pieklo.

* BROCCOLI SPAGHETTI *

1 lg. head broccoli
½ c. butter
3 garlic cloves (pressed)
1 lb. pkg. spaghetti or linguine

boiling water
salt — pepper
Parmesan cheese (grated)

Break broccoli into small florets and steam for 3 minutes or al dente and still bright green.

Melt butter in a sauce pan, add garlic and simmer a few minutes. Remove from heat.

Cook spaghetti until al dente.Drain well. Add broccoli and pour butter mixture on top.

Serve on warm platter and top with Parmesan cheese.

Ingrid Nelson.

* PASTA WITH PEAS *

1 pkg. fettucini (12 oz.)
3 to 4 qts. boiling water
3 c. fresh peas (shelled) or frozen
   petite peas
2 Tbsp. butter

1/8 tsp. nutmeg
2 c. whipping cream
1 egg (beaten)
1 c. Parmesan cheese (grated)

Drop noodles in boiling water, do not cover. When water resumes boiling cook pasta for 3 minutes. Then add the peas and cook for 5 minutes longer (if you use the frozen peas, cook only for 2 minutes. Drain peas and pasta.)

Melt butter in a lg. skillet, add nutmeg and 1½ c. cream. Add pasta and peas and bring to a vigorous boil. Remove pan from the heat and stir in the egg evenly, then mix in the Parmesan cheese. If the mixture is too thick, and more of the cream. Serve very hot.   Col. Jean Lyle.

* POMODORI ALLO SICILIANA *
(Baked Stuffed Tomatoes)

4 tomatoes (firm)	4 anchovy fillets (chopped)
2 Tbsp. olive oil	1 can (7 oz.) tuna (drained)
¼ c. chopped onions	3 Tbsp. parsley chopped)
1 garlic clove (crushed)	2 Tbsp. capers
1 c. bread crumbs	6 black olives (chopped)
1 Tbsp. Parmesan cheese (grated)	

Slice ¼ in. off top of tomatoes. Scoop out all the pulp and seeds, leaving shells ¼ in. thick. Salt inside and turn upside down to drain.

Heat oil in skillet and saute onions and garlic until golden brown. Stir in bread crumbs, anchovies and pieces of tuna. Saute 2 minutes. Remove from heat, add parsley, capers and olives. (if mixture is too dry, add tsp, olive oil). Spoon mixture into tomato shells and sprinkle with Parmesan cheese. Arrange in lightly greased baking dish (shallow) and bake in preheated oven 376°) for 20 to 30 minutes, until tender but not limp. Serve hot or cold.   Rebecca Dixon.

* PEPEROMATA *
(Braised Peppers with Tomatoes and Onion).

2 lbs. sweet green — peppers	1 lb. onions (sliced)
(blanched — peeled — seeded —	1 tsp. wine vinegar
(cut)	salt — pepper
2 lbs. tomatoes (coarsley chopped)	
2 Tbsp. butter	
¼ c. olive oil	

Melt butter and oil in a skillet saute onions until golden brown, add peppers and stir fry for 10 minutes. Add tomatoes, vinegar, salt and peppers, simmer until all liquid is cooked away.

Serve as a hot dish or cold as part of antipasto.   Margaret Holmes.

* TORTINO di CARCIOFI *
(Baked Artichoke Omelet)

4 eggs
½ tsp. salt

1 lb. onions (sliced)
1 can artichoke hearts (quartered)

Beat eggs and salt until frothy. Heat olive oil in a skillet, add artichoke hearts and saute until golden brown.

Spread hearts in a bottom of well buttered baking dish, add beaten eggs. Bake in preheated oven (400°) in upper part of the oven for 15 minutes. Omelet should be firm.   Evelyn Staley.

* GNOCCHI VERDI *
(Spinach Dumplings)

4 Tbsp. butter
¾ c. Ricotta cheese
2 eggs (beaten)
6 Tbsp. (flour)
2 pkgs. frozen chopped spinach
   (squeezed dry and chopped fine)

pinch of nutmeg
¾ c. grated Parmesan cheese
½ tsp. salt
½ tsp. pepper

Melt butter in a skillet, add spinach and saute until all the moisture is gone. Add Ricotta cheese and simmer for 3 minutes more. Place in mixing bowl and add eggs, flour, ¼ c. Parmesan cheese, salt, pepper, and nutmeg. Mix well. Refrigerate until gnocchi is firm.

Bring salted water to a simmer in saucepan (about 6 qts. water). Flour hands lightly, pick up about 1 Tbsp. of the dough and shape into a ball, drop into water and cook until they puff slightly. Remove with slotted spoon and place onto a paper towel to drain.

Pour 2 Tbsp. butter in a baking dish — arrange gnocchis, sprinkle with remaining cheese and set under broiler until cheese melts.   Charlene Do.

* CALZONE *
(Stuffed Rolls)

1 can (10 oz.) parkerhouse rolls
   refrigerated kind)
1 can (8 oz.) tomato sauce
1 tsp. basil
1 tsp. oregano

2 Italian sausages (6 oz. each)
3 Tbsp. olive oil
2½ c. Mozzarella cheese (shredded)
1½ c. Parmesan cheese (grated)

Open rolls and let them stand until they reach room temperature. Heat tomato sauce with the basil and oregano and set aside. Simmer sausage in water to cover for 20 minutes. Drain, cool and remove the casings and slice thinly.

110

For each Calzone, compress half the rolls into a flat cake and roll lightly on a floured board to make a 11 in. circle. Brush lightly with oil and spread half the tomato sauce over half of the circle to within ½ in. of the edge. Top sauce with half of the sausage, sprinkle with half of the cheese.

Fold plain half over the filling to within ¼ in. of opposite edge. Roll bottom edge up over top edge and crimp together to seal. Brush with oil. Repeat to make second Calzone. Using wide spatula, transfer to a greased baking sheet, place slightly apart. Bake in preheated oven (500°) for about 6 minutes until golden brown. Serve hot.   Ida Christoph.

* MOZZARELLA IN CARROZZA *
(Deep — fried Cheese Sandwiches)

1 lb. loaf of French or Italian bread (sliced)	3 Tbsp. milk
1 lb. Mozzarella cheese	1 c. milk
4 eggs	1 c. dry bread crumbs
	oil for deep frying

Using cookie cutter or glass, cut bread into 3 in. rounds. Slice cheese ¼ in. thick (slices should be a little smaller than bread slices.) Make sandwiches of bread and cheese. Beat eggs and add 3 Tbsp. of the milk. Pour milk into shallow bowl. Spread bread crumbs on wax paper. Dip each sandwich in milk briefly and press edges together to seal. Then coat both sides with bread crumbs. (To coat and seal more securely, roll sandwiches one at a time like cartwheels in the bread crumbs).

Dip the sandwiches one at a time in the egg mixture. Fry in deep fat until golden brown on both sides. Drain on paper towels and keep warm. Serve with hot anchovy sauce (optional).   Nathalia Richman.

ISLAND · RECIPES

* PUPU CHIPS *

Taro root
garlic salt
oil for frying

Wash and boil unpeeled Taro until barely tender. Cool and peel and chill thoroughly, then slice as thin as possible. Fry in deep fat until crisp and brown. Drain on paper towels. Sprinkle with garlic salt.   Lorna Burger

* MISO SOUP *

No. 1:

5—6 c. water	1 green onion
1 pkg. Katsuo dashimito	Ajinomoto
½ c. Miso (soy bean paste)	

Bring water to a boil. Add Katsuo dashimito and Miso, stir until Miso is dissolved. Serve in small individual bowls and garnish with chopped onions.

No. 2:

½ c. dried shrimp	½ tsp. Ajinomoto
1 c. Miso	dash of salt
2 blocks of Tofu (cubed)	2 green onions (chopped)

Boil shrimp in 6 c. of water for 15 minutes. Scoop out shrimp and add Miso to water. Let soup come to a boil, add Tofu and seasonings. Garnish with chopped onion and serve hot.   Millie Mesaku.

* WINTER MELON SOUP *

1 lg. stewing chicken (cut up)	1 Tbsp. shoyu
1 fresh pork hock	1 c. water chestnuts (sliced)
1 whole chicken breast	1 c. Bamboo shoots (sliced)
6 dried mushrooms (chopped)	1 tsp. sugar
2 oz. Virginia ham (cubed)	1 Winter melon (10 lbs.)
2 slices of ginger	salt and pepper to taste

Covering chicken and pork with water, bring to a boil and simmer for 1 hour. Add chicken breast and simmer for another 15 minutes. Remove breast from stewing chicken. Continue to simmer for 2 hours. Strain. (Reserve chicken and pork for other dishes.)

Cut top off melon and reserve. Scoop out seeds and stringy portions. Place all ingredients in melon except chicken breast. Set melon in a bowl and make a twine harness. Lower into a cooking pot (steamer) with a rack on the bottom.

Pour chicken broth inside melon ¾ full. Put top on melon. Add enough water to pan to 2 in. up on bottom of the bowl, cover pan and steam over low heat for 3 to 4 hours.

Dice chicken breasts and add to soup just before serving.

Lift melon (still sitting in bowl) and take to the table. Ladle some of the flesh of the melon into each bowl as you serve. (A very spectacular dish).   Adele Davis.

* MANDARIN MUSHROOM SOUP WITH SINGING RICE *

2 cans (13 oz. each) chicken broth
1/3 lb. lean pork (finely diced)
1 garlic clove (crushed)
1 Tbsp. shoyu

¼ c. mushrooms (sliced)
¼ c. water chestnuts (sliced)
1 can green peas (frozen)
* 1 recipe for Singing Rice.

Simmer chicken broth, pork, garlic and shoyu for 10 minutes. Add mushrooms and water chestnuts and peas.

Prepare Singing Rice as directed.

To serve: Pour half of rice in a warm casserole. Pour soup over the rice and serve. Serve remaining rice in a bowl.

Singing Rice:

1 c. long grain rice
4 c. water
2 tsp. salt

Combine rice, water and salt in a 2 qt. saucepan and let stand for 30 minutes. Drain. Spread rice on well greased cookie sheet. Bake for 8 hours at 250°. Turn rice with spatula occasionally. Break rice into bite-size pieces. (may be stored in air-tight containers in the refrigerator at this stage). Heat salad oil in saucepan (2 in. deep) with a basket. Fry rice until golden brown (about 4 minutes). Drain. Keep hot on a serving platter or in a bowl. Anything poured over the rice must be very hot to make the rice sing.   Adele Davis.

* CUCUMBER RELISH *

4 lg. cucumbers (sliced)

Combine:

1 c. sugar or ¾ c. sugar and
    add Sweet 10
1 tsp. salt
1 tsp. dry mustard

1 tsp. celery seed
1 very lg. onion (thinly sliced)

Add cucumbers. Keep in refrigerator for at least 48 hours before serving.

                              Georgia Beasley.

* CUCUMBER NAMASU *

2 med. cucumbers
3 Tbsp. sugar
½ tsp. salt

¼ c. vinegar
½ tsp. Ajinomoto

Peel skin of cucumber at four different places, discard both ends. Cut in half lengthwise and remove seeds. Slice cucumber into thin pieces diagonally and sprinkle with 1 tsp. salt. Let stand for 15 minutes. Squeeze out the water. Mix remaining ingredients and pour over cucumbers. Mix well and refrigerate. If preferred, add one or more of the following.

2 Tbsp. shredded carrots.
3 Tbsp. celery (sliced diagonally)
1 Tbsp. parsley (chopped fine)

Abalone (canned — cut in strips)
Canned clams, shrimp, crabs.

Millie Mesaku.

* SHRIMP TEMPURA *

1 c. ice cold water
1 tsp. salt
1 egg
½ tsp. Ajinomono
4 Tbsp. cornstarch

2 c. cake flour
2 or 3 drops yellow food color
16 to 20 shrimp (shelled—deveined — butterflied)
oil for deep frying

In a lg. bowl, mix water, salt and egg (water must be ice cold or batter will not become crispy.) Mix well and add cornstarch, flour and color

Mix until well blended. Heat oil to 375°.

Dip a shrimp into the batter and deep fry for 1 to 2 minutes or until golden brown. Remove from oil and drain on paper towel. Repeat with rest of shrimp.

Dipping Sauce:

½ c. dried shrimp (available in pkg. in Oriental section)
2 c. water
2 Tbsp. shoyu sauce

½ tsp. sugar (optional)
½ tsp. Ajinomoto
salt to taste

In saucepan mix shrimp with water, simmer over low heat for 25 minutes to get the flavor of the shrimp. Strain broth and discard shrimp. Add other ingredients and salt to taste.

Billie Do.

* CURRIED SHRIMP *

6 Tbsp. butter
6 Tbsp. flour
1½ tsp. salt
1 c. coconut milk
3—4 tsp. curry powder.

2 tsp. ginger (chopped)
1 med. onion (chopped)
2 c. milk
3 c. cooked shrimp

Melt butter in a skillet, add flour and salt and blend. Add coconut milk, milk and simmer until thick and smooth. Add curry, ginger and onion and mix well. Add shrimp and serve with rice.

Daisy Alexander.

* SHRIMP CHINESE *

1 c. cubed onions   3 c. cubed celery
Cook in 1 c. water until barely tender
Mix all:

1 can cream of shrimp soup   4 jar (4 oz.) pimentos (cubed)
1 can evaporated milk   1 lb. cooked shrimp
1 can water chestnuts (sliced)   ½ c. Sherry (optional)
1 can mushroom halves

In the bottom of a shallow casserole sprinkle 1 can (3 oz.) Chow Mein noodles.
Add all shrimp mixture. Top with another can of noodles.
Bake for 1 hour at 350°.
May be made the day before but do not add the top noodles.   Dorothy Tuttle.

* SHABU — SHABU *

¾ lb. lg. shrimp (peeled — cleaned)   1 c. eggplant (sliced)
2 med. chicken breasts (skinned —   1½ c. fresh mushrooms (cut in half)
   deboned — cut thin across grain)   4 c. fresh spinach (stems removed)
½ head Chinese cabbage   10 c. chicken broth
   (coarsely cubed)   1 Tbsp. ginger (grated)

Arrange all meat, shrimp and vegetables on lg. serving platter. Provide chopsticks,
bamboo sticks, fondue forks or wire ladle. Heat chicken broth in Shabu — Shabu
(Chinese hotpot) or fondue cooker. Keep broth bubbling. Pick up desired food
and drop into broth. Lift out when cooked and dip into sauce.
Dipping Sauces.

Chinces hot mustard sauce — Ginger shoyu sauce — peanut sauce.
Serve with individual bowls of rice.
                                                               Adele Davis.

*BAKED PAPAYA AND SHRIMP *

6 firm papayas   2 c. sour cream
2 lbs. bay shrimp (peeled — deveined)   juice of 3 limes
2 cans (8 oz. each) water chestnuts   1 Tbsp. shoyu
   (sliced)

Preheat oven to 350°. Split papayas in half lenghtwise and cut off stems. With
melon baller scoop out flesh, being careful not to tear skin. Place balls in a med.
bowl and set halves aside. Add remaining ingredients to the balls and mix very
gently but thoroughly. Spoon into shells. Place on a baking sheet and bake for
15 to 20 minutes until filling is heated through.   Lucille Grimes.

* SASHIMI *

Fresh aku (bonita) orako (tuna)
Slice fish into very thin slices. Arrange on a layer of shredded daikon (white radish). Top with parsley.
*Sauce:

Combine 1 Tbsp. mustard, 1 Tbsp. water and let stand for a few minutes to "hotten". Add ¼ c. shoyu and blend well.   Jean Keys.

* LOMI LOMI *

1 lb. Aku (skinned — sliced)   2 med. tomatoes (cubed)
   (other fish may be used)   1 Tbsp. sesame seeds (toasted)
1 lg. onion (sliced)   1 Tbsp. sesame oil
1 stalk green onion (chopped)   ½ tsp. ginger (minced)
salt to taste

Place all ingredients in a lg. bowl. Let stand for 3 hours before serving.
                                              Lorna Burger.

* LAULAU *

1/3 lb. butter fish or salmon   16 luau leaves or 1 lb. spinach
1 lb. pork butt   Ti leaves

Cut fish into 4 pieces and soak in water for 60 minutes. Cut pork butt into pieces. Prepare luau leaves (or spinach) by stripping off stem vien. Wash and remove any tough ribs from leaves. Place 2 leaves on a board, place 4 luau leaves in center and add 1 piece of fish and 1 piece of pork on top. Fold leaves over filling to make a bundle. Tie ends. Steam for 3—4 hours   Lorna Burger.

* LOMI SALMON *

1 lb. salted salmon   1 med. onion (finely chopped)
5 tomatoes (pared—diced)   1 c. crushed ice.
10 green onions (sliced thin)

Soak salmon in water for 3 hours. Remove skin and bones. Shred. Combine salmon, tomatoes, green onion and onion. Lomi or knead, be sure it is well mixed. Chill thoroughly. Add ice before serving.   Jean Keys.

* FRIED MAHI MAHI *

1 lb. Mahi Mahi (fish)   1 Tbsp. Sake
1 Tbsp. sugar   1 tsp. curry powder
1 tsp. salt   2 Tbsp. cornstarch
½ tsp. Ajinomoto   1 Tbsp. shoyu
2 eggs (beaten)   Corn Flake Crumbs

116

Combine sugar, salt, Ajinomoto, Sake, curry powder, and shoyu. Marinate Mahi Mahi in sauce for 30 minutes. Dip into beaten eggs and roll in corn flake crumbs. Fry until golden brown. (Other fish may be used).   Lorna Burger.

* FISH TERIYAKI *

1 c. shoyu
½ c. sugar
¼ c. salad
2—3 lbs. fillet of rock cod — seabass —
    red snapper — or ocean perch

2 tsp. ginger (grated)
1 garlic clove (minced)
1 tsp. sesame seeds

Combine shoyu, sugar, oil, ginger, garlic, and marinate fish for serveral hours. Line shallow baking pan with foil. Arrange fillets on foil. Broil for 5—7 minutes. Brush with marinade several times during broiling. Turn fillets and brush again and sprinkle with sesame seeds. Broil 3 minutes longer.   Millie Mesaku.

* HAM HAWAIIAN *

1 can (5 lbs.) ham
1 can (13¼ oz.) pineapple chunks
1 can (12 oz.) coconut syrup
¼ tsp. allspice
whole cloves

1 Tbsp. cornstarch
1½ Tbsp. lemon juice
1 tsp. rum extract
½ c. raisins
¼ c. flaked coconut

Bake ham at 325° for 30 minutes. Drain pineapple, reserving syrup. Combine 1 Tbsp. of the syrup. ½ c. of the coconut syrup and the allspice. Score ham, stud with cloves and baste with coconut mixture. Bake 30 minutes more, basting frequently with remaining coconut syrup mixture.
Mix cornstarch with 1 more Tbsp. of the pineapple juice. In a saucepan combine remaining pineapple syrup, remaining coconut syrup and cornstarch mixture. Cook over med, heat, stirring constantly, until mixture thickens and begins to boil. Cook stirring for one more minute. Remove from heat, stir in lemon juice, rum extract, drained pineapple, raisins and coconut. Serve with the ham.

Jean Ariyoshi.

*MANDARIN TERIYAKI STEAK *
* May be cooked in a Wok.

½ c. shoyu
¼ c. Sherry
2 Tbsp. oil
1 garlic clove (minced)
1 sm. onion (sliced)
2 lbs. flank steak (cut into ½. in. strips)

2 thin slices of fresh ginger
1 green pepper (½ in. slices)
¾ c. pineapple juice
2 tsp. cornstarch
2 c. mandarin orange slices

Combine shoyu, Sherry, oil and ginger in a mixing bowl, add beef and marinate for 1 to 2 hours, turning several times. Remove meat and pat dry with paper towels. Reserve marinade.

Heat Wok with the oil and brown half of the meat at a time. Place in heated dish and pour ½ c. marinade on meat.

Place onions, green pepper and pineapple juice in the Wok, simmer for 5—7 min. Meanwhile, in a saucepan combine remaining marinade with the cornstarch and simmer until thick and glossy. Do not boil. Stir into vegetables. Spoon in mandarin orange slices, meat with the marinade. Stir — fry until oranges are heated through. Serve over rice.

Note: A skillet may be used in place of the Wok. Melon balls may be used in place of the mandarin oranges. A delectable variation.   Adele Davis.

* HEKKA *
(Beef Stew)

* May be cooked in a Wok.

2 lbs. tenderloin beef	3 Tbsp. Sake
1 can bamboo shoots	½ c. sugar
½ lb. dried mushrooms	3 Tbsp. shoyu
2 bunches of green onions	oil
(cut in 1 in. lengths)	

Cut beef into 2 in. strips. Thinly slice bamboo shoots. Soak mushrooms in water for 10 minutes. Drain and slice.

Heat Wok or skillet with the oil, add meat and stir fry for 2 minutes. Add Sake, sugar and shoyu. When liquid boils. Add vegetables and stir — fry until vegetables are on the crispy side. Serve with rice.   Lorna Burger.

*CHINESE MEAT BALLS *

2 med. green peppers	2 Tbsp. cornstarch
1 sm. red pepper (sweet)	1 tsp. shoyu
1 Tbsp. butter or oleo	½ c. vinegar
1 can (14 oz.) pineapple chunks	½ c. light brown sugar
1 lb. ground beef	

Cut peppers in slices. Heat butter in saucepan, add peppers and pineapple in the syrup. Combine shoyu, cornstarch, vinegar and sugar, stir into meat mixture. Cook over med. heat until thickened. Place in rounded meat balls and simmer until done.   Lillian Kann.

118

* SHREDDED BEEF *

Note: Serves 2 to 3 if served along. Serves 4 to 6 with other dishes.

¾ lb. flank steak (shredded)
2 tsp. shoyu
1 Tbsp. water chestnut powder
1 Tbsp. Sherry
1 egg white (beaten)
3 Tbsp. peanut oil
4 scallions — white parts (shredded)

2 tsp. ginger (minced)
½ c. carrots (shredded)
1 c. snowpeas (shredded)
½ c. sweet red pepper (cut-up)
1 whole hot red pepper (shredded)
1 garlic clove (sliced)

* Seasoning Sauce:

1 Tbsp. hoisin sauce
1 Tbsp. bean sauce
2 Tbsp. plum sauce
1 Tbsp. Sherry

1 Tbsp. Chinese red vinegar
2 tsp. hot sauce
1 tsp. water chestnut powder

Mix all seasoning ingredients in a bowl and let stand.

Marinate meat in shoyu, water chestnut powder, Sherry and egg white. Cover and refrigerate for 30 minutes up to 12 hours.

Arrange remaining ingredients on a tray in preparation for the stir-frying. Place Wok over med. heat and heat until oil is hot but not smoking.

Add garlic and stir-fry for 1 minute, add carrots and fry for another minute. Add sweet and hot peppers, snowpeas and scallions, stir-fry for 2 minutes. Transfer to a heated serving dish. Add more oil to the Wok and turn to high heat, add beef and fry until meat losses the redness (about 2 minutes). Add seasoning sauce. Add vegetables and stir-fry rapidly until just mixed. Place on heated dish and serve at once.   Millie Mesaku.

* IRISH — HAWAIIAN BEEF STEW *

2 lbs. pipi ku (stew beef)
½ c. chopped onion
¼ c. chopped green pepper
¼ c. sliced celery
1 sliced carrot

1 can bouillon
potatoes
onions
carrots
cut up as desired

Cut meat into cubes, brown in 3 Tbsp. fat, add chopped onion, green pepper, celery and carrot with a bay leaf, pinch of parsley, salt and pepper to taste. Add can of bouillon and water to cover. Simmer for one hour, add cut-up vegetables and cook until they are done. (Throw in one pinch Makapuu Rock Salt in pot).
                          Betty Guy.

* PEKING ROAST *

3—6 lbs. roast (rump bottom round) 1½ c. dark coffee
garlic or onion chopped 1½ c. water
½ c. vinegar ½ c. Gin (optional)
salt — pepper

Cut slits in roast, insert slices of garlic or onion. Pour vinegar over roast and leave in pan over nite or up to 2 days. Cover and refrigerate, turn occasionally.
Brown in pan with a little oil until almost burnt. Pour on coffee, water and Gin (if used). Bring to a boil and simmer for 2—3 hours. Until fork done. Thicken broth to make gravy. Irma Meyers.

* SWEET AND PUNGENT PORK *

1 lb. spareribs (in long pieces).
Wash them and dry them with a cloth, dip them into bean flour or wheat flour will do. Fry them in deep fat. Drain. Place in pan and add 1 Tbsp. vinegar, a pinch of ginger, ½ c. sugar, tsp. flour, a wine glass of Sherry, a wine glass of shoyu and 1 c. water. Cook with lid off until they candy. Mary Upchurch.

* KAL BI KOREAN RIBS *

½ c. sugar 1½ c. chopped green onions
1 Tbsp. sesame seeds
Spread sugar on meat with sesame seeds and onions.
Mix:
½ c. shoyu
1 Tbsp. sesame oil
1 Tbsp. ginger powder
Marinate for 6 hours or overnite. Bake on BBQ. Jean Keys.

* GINGER RIBS *

6 lbs. pork spareribs or loin back ribs (Preboiled)
Ginger sauce:
½ c. shoyu 3 Tbsp. brown sugar
½ c. catsup 2 Tbsp. ginger (grated)
¼ c. chicken stock or water
Barbecue Sauce:
2 Tbsp. sugar ¼ tsp. tumeric
½ tsp. salt ¼ tsp. celery seed
¼ tsp. paprika

Place ribs in pan large enough to hold them in one layer. Combine ingredients. Remove ribs from marinade and pat dry with paper towel. (Reserve marinade for grilling).

Combine ingredients for barbacue sauce and pat on ribs. Grill or lace on spit accordian — style and roast for 30 to 45 minutes, basting often.

Separate ribs into serving sizes and serve with Chinese dipping sauces.

Adele Davis.

* SWEET — SOUR SPARERIBS *

3 lbs. spareribs, cut into 2 in. pieces.

Marinade:

3 Tbsp. cream sherry
5 Tbsp. soy sauce
¾ c. cornstarch
½ c. salad oil.

Sweet Sour Sauce:

2 Tbsp. cornstarch
¾ c. brown sugar (packed)
¾ c. cider vinegar

¾ c. pineapple juice
4 Tbsp. soy sauce

2 round onions (wedged) — 2 c. pineapple chunks — 1 green pepper (wedged). Marinate spareribs in marinade for 20 minutes. Slowly brown spareribs in the salad oil heated to 350°. Cover and simmer for 25 minutes at 200°. Combine Sweet Sour Sauce ingredients and add to pork. Simmer covered 20 minutes longer, stirring occasionally.

Add onions, pineapple and green pepper. Cover and simmer until vegetables are tender, about 3 minutes.

Jean Ariyoshi.

* SPARE RIBS CANTONESE *

4 lbs. pork ribs
1 jar (12 oz.) orange marmalade
¼ c. water
¼ c. shoyu

½ tsp. garlic powder
½ tsp. ground ginger
dash of pepper

Mix all ingredients (except ribs), blend well.

Cut ribs in serving size pcs. Arrange in 12 in. square pan and bake at 350° for 45 to 60 minutes. Drain off fat. Rearrange pcs. and pour on sauce. Cook uncovered, basting occasionally, about 30 minutes.

Jean Keys.

* CIRIO'S PORK ADOBO *
(Spiced Pork)

2 lbs. pork (cut in 1 in. cubes)	salt
1/3 c. vinegar	¼ tsp. monosodium glutamate
1 Tbsp. minced garlic	¼ tsp. blach pepper
1 Tbsp. minced ginger	(coarsely ground)
4 bay leaves (crumbled)	

Combine all ingredients and marinade overnight in refrigerator. Place in skillet. Cover and cook over med. flame, stirring occasionally, until pork is browned and tender, about 1 hour. Meat will be crispy on outside and all the liquid in the pan will be absorbed. Serve hot with rice. Eloise Tungpalan.

* CHINESE PORK GINGER BALLS *

1 lb. ground pork	1 Tbsp shoyu sauce
1 can (5 oz.) water chestnuts	1 egg
(drained — finely chopped)	peanut or vegetable oil
1 Tbsp. fresh ginger (finely chopped)	

Combine pork, chestnuts, ginger, shoyu sauce and egg in med. bowl, blend thoroughly. Shape mixture with wet hands into 1 in. balls.

Cover the bottom of a lg. skillet with oil and heat over med. heat. Place as many meat balls in the skillet as will fit without crowding. Cook for 5 to 8 minutes, turning often until crisp, and no trace of pink remains on the inside. Transfer to a serving platter with slotted spoon. Serve while hot.

Note: Can be frozen and reheated for 30 minutes in oven 350°. Irma Meyers.

* RIO GRANDE PORK ROAST *

4—6 boneless rolled pork loin roast	½ c. apple jelly
½ tsp. salt	½ c. catsup
½ tsp. garlic salt	1 Tbsp. vinegar
1 tsp. chili powder	1 c. corn chips (crushed)

Place roast (fat side up) on rack in a shallow roasting pan. Combine salt, garlic salt and ½ tsp. chili powder, rub into roast. Bake in preheated oven (325°) for 2 to 2½ hours or until tender.

In a small saucepan combine jelly, catsup, vinegar and the remaining chili powder and bring to a boil. Reduce heat and simmer (uncovered) for 2 minutes. Brush roast with the glaze and sprinkle top with corn chips. Continue baking 10 to 15 minutes more.

Remove roast from pan. Keep warm. Measure pan drippings (including corn chips) add enough water to make 1 c. Heat to boiling and pour onto sliced meat.

Roberta Chateauneuf.

* KALUA PORK *

¾ lb. pork butt (slashed)
1 Tbsp. Hawaiian salt
3 Tbsp. shoyu
1 tsp. M.S.G.
1 garlic clove (minced)

1 Tbsp. fresh ginger (grated)
few drops of liquid smoke
6—8 Ti leaves
1 banana leaf

Combine salt, M.S.G., garlic, ginger, shoyu and liquid smoke and rub sauce mixture over pork butt.

Wash and remove ribs from Ti leaves and banana leaf. Line 9 x 9 in. pan with Ti leaves, extending over pan edge. Place banana leaf on top. Place pork on banana leaf and fold over pork. Secure with string. Cover with foil. Bake (325°) for 4 hours. To serve, open leaf and shred pork. Lorna Burger.

* CHICKEN WAIKIKI *

1 lb. chicken cutlets (boned —
   skinned)
¼ c. dry sherry
¼ c. lemon juice
3 Tbsp. Worcestershire sauce
½ c. flour

1 egg (beaten)
½ c. Macadamia nuts (diced)
½ c. dry unseasoned bread crimbs
* Chutney sauce.

Cut chicken into 1 in. cubes. Place in a bowl. Combine sherry, lemon juice, and Worcestershire sauce. Pour over chicken, toss to coat completely. Marinate for 30 minutes.

Place flour in one bowl and egg in another bowl and combine macadamia nuts and bread crumbs in the third bowl.

Remove chicken from the marinade. Dip chicken first in flour. then in egg, coat with macadamia mixture.

Place chicken in a single layer on a greased shallow baking pan. Bake (uncovered) in a preheated oven 350° until chicken is cooked through and browned, about 20 minutes. Skewer on toothpicks with pineapple chunks and parsley.

Serve with Chutney Sauce.

Chutney Sauce:

¾ c. mayonnaise — ¼ c. prepared mustard — 3 Tbsp. chutney chopped. Combine mayonnaise, mustard and chutney, refrigerate until ready to serve.

Adele Davis.

* ORIENTAL BAKED CHICKEN *

5 lbs. chicken thighs
¾ c. shoyu
¼ c. oyster sauce
¾ c. raw sugar
1 Tbsp. sesame oil
* Sesame seeds

1 Tbsp. grated ginger
2 stalks green onions (chopped)
2 cans button mushrooms
2 Tbsp. cornstarch

Combine all ingredients (except mushrooms and cornstarch). Soak chicken in the sauce several hours or overnight. Place chicken in a shallow pan (skin up) and pour the marinade over chicken. Bake at 350° for 1 hour. Pour juice from pan, skin off any fat, pour sauce into a saucepan and bring to a boil. Combine cornstarch with the liquid from the mushrooms and add to the sauce, stir gently until thickened. Add mushrooms, arrange chicken on a serving platter, pour gravy over and garnish with parsley.   Jean Keys.

* CHICKEN TOFU *

* May be cooked in a Wok, or skillet.
4 pcs. chicken (cut in 1 in. cubes)
2½ Tbsp. sugar
1 tsp. salt
2 c. water
1 Tbsp. oil

¼ c. shoyu
1 bunch green onions (cut 1½ in. long)
1 block tofu (cut in 1 in. squares)

Brown chicken in oil in Wok or skillet. Add sugar, salt, water and shoyu and simmer until chicken is tender. Add green onions and tofu. Do not stir, flip pan in upward motion to mix, stirring will break up the tofu.   Billie Do.

* MAHOGANY CHICKEN WINGS *

6 to 7 lbs. chicken wings
1½ c. dry Sherry
1-1/8 c. Hoisin sauce
¾ c. Chinese plum sauce

18 green onions (chopped)
6 garlic cloves (minced)
¾ c. cider vinegar
½ c. honey

Combine all ingredients (except chicken wings) in a saucepan, bring to a boil and simmer for 5 minutes. Cool. Cut off chicken tips, disjoint wings and place in a lg. container. Pour cooled sauce over and refrigerate overnite. Place oven racks in upper and lower third of the oven and preheat to 375°. Oil two shallow baking pans. Drain wings. Divide between pans and bake uncovered for 1 to 1½ hours, basting every 20 minutes, with remaining sauce and turning to brown evenly. Switch pans halfway through the baking. Remove the wings from the pan and let cool on lg. sheet of foil. When cooled, wrap and store up to 3 days. Serve at room temperature.   Charlene Do.

* LEMON — ORANGE CHICKEN *

4 chicken breasts
1 can (12 oz.) frozen orange juice (thawed)
1 lemon

Skin breasts and remove all visible fat. Pierce flesh of each piece with pointed knife 5—6 times on each side. Place in shallow casserole with a tight lid.
Combine juice of lemon with 2/3 can of undiluted orange juice. Pour over chicken (should cover chicken — if not, add rest of orange juice). Marinate in refrigerator at least 4 hours, turning chicken over several times. Cook covered at 350° for 1½ hours. Serve marinade on the side.　　　　　Joyce Heftel.

* CHICKEN CASHEW *

* May be cooked in a Wok or skillet.

3 chicken breasts
2 pkgs. pod peas (frozen)
½ lb. mushrooms (sliced)
4 green onions (sliced 1 in. long)
1 can bamboo shoots (sliced)
¼ c. salad oil

1 c. chicken stock
¼ c. shoyu
2 Tbsp. cornstarch
½ tsp. sugar
½ tsp. salt
1 pkg. (4 oz.) cashew nuts

Bone chicken and remove skin. Slice into ½ in. strips, then cut in 1 in. long strips. Cook nuts until toasted in 1 Tbsp. oil in Wok. Remove from pan. Add remaining oil and stir-fry chicken until lightly brown, add snow peas and mushrooms, pour in stock and simmer for 2 minutes. Add bamboo shoots.
Mix cornstarch, shoyu, sugar and salt and add to Wok, stir until thickened. Mix in green onions. Sprinkle with the cashew nuts. Serve with rice, noodles or Won Ton.　　　　　Adele Davis.

* ONO CHICKEN CASSEROLE *

1 can (6 oz.) boned chicken
1 can cream of chicken soup
1 c. diced celery
2 Tbsp. diced Maui onion
½ c. chopped walnuts

½ tsp. salt
¼ tsp. pepper
1 Tbsp. lemon juice
¾ c. mayonnaise
3 hard cooked eggs (sliced)

* Top with 2 c. crushed potato chips.

Mix the ingredients and place in a casserole, top with the potato chips and bake in preheated oven 450°. for 15 minutes.　　　　　Dorothy Morrison.

125

* CHICKEN GIBLETS WITH CLOUDS EARS *

3 sets of raw giblets (sliced thin)
½ lb. chinese peas
½ c. water chestnuts (peeled —
    sliced thin)
1 pc. crushed fresh ginger
1 tsp. gourmet powder
1 oz. dried clouds ears (wan yee)

1 c. water
1 c. shoyu sauce
2 tsp. cornstarch
1 clove garlic (crushed)
a pinch of pepper

Soak ears for 15 minutes, wash clean and divide into small pieces. Cook peas in a well greased skillet for 3 minutes. Remove from skillet and add water. Put giblets into hot skillet and cook for 4 minutes, add the other ingredients, except cornstarch and peas. Cook for 5 minutes, add cornstarch and peas and cook a few minutes longer. Serve.   Jean Keys

* SESAME CHICKEN WINGS *

3 lbs. chicken wings
4 Tbsp. flour
8 Tbsp. cornstarch
4 Tbsp. sugar
1½ tsp. salt
½ tsp. Ajinomoto

2 Tbsp. sesame seeds
6 Tbsp. shoyu
2 eggs
2 stalks green onions (chopped)
2 garlic cloves (diced)

Cut chicken wings at joint. Combine salt, Ajinomoto, green onions and garlic and marinate chicken in the mixture for 2 hours. Mix flour and cornstarch. Beat eggs lightly. Dip chicken in eggs and then into flour and then deep fry until golden brown.   Billie Do.

* CHICKEN CHOW MEIN *

2 Tbsp. oil
1 c. onions (sliced)
1½ c. celery (sliced)
1 c. mushrooms (sliced)
2 c. chicken broth
* Chow Mein Noodles.

3 Tbsp. shoyu
3 c. cooked chicken (cut in strips)
1½ Tbsp. cornstarch
½ c. scallions (minced)

Heat oil in Wok or a skillet, add onions, celery and mushrooms and stir-fry until crisp. Add 1 c. of stock, shoyu and chicken. Warm through. Add cornstarch and remaining stock and stir-fry until thickened. Add scallions. Serve hot over Chow Mein Noodles.   Lucille Grimes.

* ADOBO MANOOK *

1 frying chicken, soaked for 3 hours in the following:
1 c. shoyu
1 c. vinegar
2 c. water

Drain. Cook lightly, add ½ of the liquid, garlic, ginger and some red pepper according to your taste. Cook in skillet until tender. (About ½ hour.)

Betty Guy.

* CHICKEN AND LUAU *

4 lbs. stewing chicken
1 Tbsp. salt

4 lbs. luau
3 c. coconut milk

Cut chicken into small pieces. Put in a lg. pot and add salt, cover with water. Simmer until tender.
Wash luau thoroughly, remove stems and fibrous part of veins. Place in saucepan and add 1 c. water, cover, cook for 15 minutes. Drain. Add water and repeat this process 2 more times. Add coconut milk, but do not boil. Put chicken in serving dish with 1 c. of broth. Add luau sauce.

Jean Keys.

* CHICKEN AND VEGETABLES *

peanut oil
1 garlic clove (sliced)
½ tsp. dried chili peppers (crushed)
3 chicken breasts (skinned — boned — cut in 1 in. cubes)
2 Tbsp. black bean paste
6 c. cauliflower (diced)
4 broccoli stalks (florets removed — quartered lengthwise — cut in 2 in. strips)

4—5 carrots (sliced)
1 med. sweet red pepper (cut in 1 in. pieces)
1 c. green onion (cut in ½ in. pieces)
1 can (13½ oz.) chicken broth
1 Tbsp. cornstarch mixed with ¼ c. water

Add 2 Tbsp. oil to Wok or skillet and heat to med. hot, swirling oil to coat sides. Add garlic and red pepper and stir-fry for 1 minute and remove.
Add chicken to the Wok and toss for 1 minute, add 1 tsp. black bean paste and stir-fry for 2 minutes. Remove from Wok and keep warm.
Add 2 Tbsp. oil to Wok, add cauliflower, broccoli and carrots and toss. Add remaining tsp. black bean paste and stir-fry for 3 minutes. Return chicken to Wok and add onions and mix. Add chicken broth and bring to a rolling boil. lower beat and simmer for 15 minutes. Serve on heated platter.   Adele Davis.

* PRESSED DUCK with SWEET — SOUR PLUM SAUCE *

1 four or five lb. duck (cleaned)
1 Tbsp. five — spice powder
1 tsp. salt

1 c. water chestnut powder
oil for frying
toasted almonds — garnish

* Sweet — Sour Sauce:

Place duck in a lg. kettle with enough water to cover. Add spice and salt and simmer, covered for 1 to 1½ hours. Remove duck from liquid and let cool. Remove meat from bones and discard skin.

Pour chestnut powder in a shallow baking pan (powder should be ½ to ¾ in. deep). Press meat into powder, cover and steam for 30 minutes, until has gelatinized into thick, heavy crust. Remove from steamer and let cool and chill until ready to complete.

About 30 minutes before serving time prepare the Sweet-Sour Plum sauce.

* Sweet — Sour Plum Sauce:

1 c. plum preserves or jam
1 c. water
2 Tbsp. catsup

2 Tbsp. vinegar
1 tsp. cornstarch (dissolved in sm.
    amount water)

Combine jam, water, catsup and vinegar and bring to a boil. Add cornstarch and water and stir constantly until thickened. Reduce heat and keep warm until ready to serve. Note: If sauce is too thick, add a little water. To serve: Place duck on a serving platter with the sauce on the side.   Millie Mesaku.

* TOFU AND CHINESE PEAS *

½ block tofu
1 lb. Chinese peas

½ cube butter
dash of curry powder

Saute peas in the butter, add curry. Add drained tofu (cut as desired). Cover. Cook for 10 minutes. Salt or shoyu to taste.   Doris Beyer.

* NAGO YUK CHOW WONG KOR *

½ lb. beef (sliced into thin strips)
3 Tbsp. oil
1 garlic clove (crushed)
1 green pepper (cut in 1 in. squares)
1 sm. onion (cut in 1 in. cubes)

1 stalk celery (cut in 1 in. lengths)
2 med. tomatoes (wedged)
2 stalks of green onions (cut in 1 in.
    lengths)

Seasonings for beef:

1 Tbsp. cornstarch
3 Tbsp. shoyu
1 tsp. sugar

¼ tsp. ginger juice
dash of pepper
pinch of baking soda

Gravy:

¾ c. water

1 tsp. cornstarch

¼ tsp salt

¼ tsp. monosodium glutamate

Combine seasoning ingredients and marinate beef for 10 minutes. Heat 2 Tbsp. oil in Wok or skillet. Saute garlic until light brown. Remove. Add beef and stir-fry for 1 minute or until med. rare. Remove. Add 1 Tbsp. oil to Wok, stir-fry peppers, onions and celery for 1 min. Add beef, tomato and gravy ingredients cook until liquid comes to a boil and is thickened.   Irma Meyers.

* EGGPLANT WITH GARLIC SAUCE *

2 lbs. long eggplant, peeled — cut into 1 in. pieces — 2 Tbsp. oil.

1 Tbsp. oil

1 tsp. minced garlic

¼ lb. ground pork or beef

½ tsp. salt

2 Tbsp. shoyu

2 tsp. red wine vinegar

1 c. chicken broth

2 Tbsp. chopped scallions or
    green onions

(Heat 2 Tbsp. oil in Wok or skillet and stir-fry eggplant for 3 minutes. Add ¼ c. water, cover and simmer until almost tender. Remove. Heat 1 Tbsp. oil, add garlic and meat and stir-fry, add salt, sugar, shoyu and broth. Bring to a boil. Add eggplant and cook for 1 minute. Stir in vinegar and scallions. Serve hot.

Daisy Alexander.

* MIXED ORIENTAL VEGETABLES *

1 head Chinese cabbage (bok choy)
    (chopped)

½ c. carrots (julienned)

2 c. fresh Chinese peas

3 Tbsp. butter

1 basket cherry tomatoes

4 oz. can minitature corn

1 Tbsp. peanut oil

1 c. fresh mushrooms (sliced)

3 c. fresh bean sprouts

* Dressing

Heat oil and butter in a Wok or skillet and stir-fry cabbage, carrots and pod peas until crispy. Add mushrooms, bean sprouts, tomatoes, corn and dressing to taste. Stir-fry for 2 minutes (do not over cook vegetables) Serve hot.

Dressing:

1 c. oyster sauce — 1 c. sugar — 2 c. shoyu.
Blend all ingredients well.

Adele Davis.

* PICKLES SNOW PEAS *

4 lbs. snow or sugar pea pods
boiling water
2½ qts. white vinegar
2½ c. water

¾ c. sugar
¼ c. pickling spices
¼ c. pickling salt

Place peas in colander or steamer and steam for 5 minutes over boiling water. Rinse immediately in cold water. Combine remaining ingredients in kettle and bring to a boil, reduce heat and simmer for 10 minutes. Strain. Pack peas in hot sterilized jars and cover with the liquid, leaving ½ in. space on top. Seal and process 5 minutes in boiling water. Serve as relish or wrap around water chestnuts as a canape.   Adele Davis.

* WATERCRESS AND BEAN SROUTS WITH GOMA SHOYU *

2 bunches of watercress
1 pkg. bean sprouts
salt to taste

Bring salt water to a boil and add watercress, boil 1 minute. Drain and cut into 2 in. lengths. Repeat for bean sprouts.
Goma Sauce:

½ c. shoyu
2 Tbsp. sugar
1 tsp. M.S.G.

1 Tbsp. sesame seeds (Goma)
bonita flakes

Heat goma in skillet (no oil) until golden brown. Grind. Add remaining ingredients and mix. Toss vegetables in sauce and top with bonita flakes.   Billie Do.

* BITSU BITSU *

2 c. raw sweet potatoes (grated)

¼ c. sugar
¼ c. flour

To grated potatoes, add flour and sugar and mix. Shape into patties into 2 in. shapes about ¼ in. thick. Pan fry until golden brown. Serve with meat course. (A Filipino dish)

* SANJUCK *
(Skewered beef and Mushrooms)

½ lb. top round beef
    (3/8 in. thick)
1 can (4 oz.) mushrooms
    (drained — sliced)
2 Tbsp. sesame oil
2 Tbsp. shoyu

1 garlic clove (minced)
½ tsp. sugar
3 eggs (well beaten)
2 bunches of green onions
flour
1 Tbsp. sesame seeds

Cut meat across the grain in strips ¼ in. thick. Then in 2 in. lengths. Toss meat in bowl with mushrooms, oil, shoyu, sesame seeds, garlic and sugar. Cut onions into 2 in. lengths (only to where tops separated).

On short skewers, thread 2 pieces meat (fold in half if too long), then mushrooms then 2 pieces onions. Repeat once.

Roll skewers in flour, then in beaten egg. Let stand for 5 minutes. Cover bottom of skillet with oil, heat to med. hot. Place skewers in pan and cook until all sides are golden brown. Serve hot or cold.   From a Korean Friend.

* HAWAIIAN CURRY *

¼ c. butter
2 med. onions (chopped)
2 apples (cored — peeled — diced)
6 Tbsp. flour
1½ Tbsp. curry
1½ tsp. brown sugar

2 cloves garlic (minced)
1 tsp. ginger (minced)
2 c. chicken stock
1 can frozen coconut milk
1½ tsp. salt
2 c. cooked chicken, beef, lamb or shrimp

Melt butter, brown onion, garlic, apple, add curry powder and ginger. Cook for a few minutes. Add stock, then coconut milk, cook slowly for an hour. Add flour to thicken. Add chicken, slowly cook until heated through. Serve with hot rice and condiments.

Condiments:

Chopped green peppers — chopped green onions — chopped cooked eggs — chopped cooked bacon — chopped macadamia nuts — chopped peanuts — chopped preserved ginger, raisins, currents and grated fresh coconut, and Mango Chutney.   Jean Keys.

* GHEE (INDIA) *

2 c. (4 sticks) unsalted butter

Melt butter in skillet over low heat and allow to simmer gently about 1 hour. Strain, through double thickness of cheesecloth. Strain into a glass jar. Cover and refrigerate.

Note: Many India recipes call for Ghee, use as you would use oil or melt butter.

* JAVANESE CURRY SAUCE (INDIA) *

1 med. onion (chopped)
½ c. cooked ham (finely sliced)
2 slices bacon (finely chopped)
¼ c. curry powder
1 Tbsp. flour
2 c. chicken stock
1 unpeeled apple (chopped)

¼ c. preserved mango or kumquat
1 Tbsp. tomato paste
1 Tbsp. lemon juice
1 Tbsp. honey
1 Tbsp. salt
1 Tbsp. Ghee

Place Ghee in skillet, add ham, onion and bacon and saute until onion is golden. Stir in curry powder and simmer for 1 minute. Blend in flour, then add apples, preserved fruit, tomato paste, lemon juice, honey and salt. Pour in chicken stock and blend well. Allow to simmer for 25 minutes, stirring occasionally. Cool. Note: This pungent mixture makes a good base for chicken, lamb and fish curries. May be stored in refrigerator up to 1 week or can be frozen.

* HAM FRIED RICE *

6 Tbsp. peanut oil
eggs (beaten)
½ c. ham
2 Tbsp. green peas

2 tsp. salt
4 c. cooked rice (cold)
1 Tbsp. onion (chopped)

Heat 2 Tbsp. oil in Wok or skillet and heat to med. Pour eggs in Wok and stir-fry until eggs are in tiny pieces. Remove from pan.
Heat another 2 Tbsps. oil and add rice and onion and stir-fry 1 minutes, add salt. Reduce heat and add eggs and ham and stir until heated through.

Lucille Goderre.

* KABUNI (ALBANIA) *
(Sweet Raisin Pilau)

¼ c. butter
1 c. long grain rice
1 c. chicken stock (hot)

2/3 c. raisins
½ tsp. cinnamon
¼ c. sugar

Melt butter in a skillet and fry rice until transparent. Add stock and cook for 10 minutes. Add raisins and simmer (covered) until liquid is absorbed and rice is tender.
Combine sugar and cinnamon, stir into rice just before serving. Serve Pilau as a dessert with brown sugar or as a dinner course. Adele Davis.

* CHEIN DOI (CHINESE) *
(Doughnuts)

1½ c. Chinese brown sugar
1¼ c. hot water
1 tsp. sherry

3¾ c. (1 lb.) no mei fun (mochi flour)
* Filling

Dissolve sugar in water. Cool. Stir enough liquid into flour to make a stiff dough (do not knead). Add sherry. Shape into a roll 1½ in. in diameter, cut into ½ in. slices. Flatten.
Combine filling ingredients and place 1 Tbsp. filling in center of dough. Pinch edges together and seal and roll into a ball. Deep fry in oil until golden brown. Press balls against side of pan while frying, balls will expand more.

Filling:

½ c. grated coconut
½ c. roasted peanuts (Crushed)

¼ c. sesame seeds (toasted)
3 Tbsp. sugar

Mix all ingredients well.

Charlene Do.

* MALASADAS *

10 lbs. flour
2 c. white sugar
2 c. raw potato buds (cooked in
   3 c. water)
2 lg. cans evaporated milk to 2 cans
   warm water (use same can)
2 Tbsp. salt

1 lb. Nucoa oleo (melted)
2 doz. large eggs (beaten)
6 pkgs. dry yeast mixt mixed with
   1 Tbsp. sugar and 1 c. warm water.

Cook potato buds in boiling water. Beat eggs and set aside. Be sure to cool pota-to buds. Mix yeast with warm water and sugar and set aside. Place flour into a lg. mixing bowl and make a well in center. Pour cooled potato buds into well, add yeast, beaten eggs and sugar. Gradually add melted butter to mixture. When done, rub top of dough with a little oil, then cover with a cloth. Set aside to rise for about 1½ hours. (If dough is too hard add water as needed to make a softer dough. Heat 2 gal. oil in a lg. pan to 400°. Drop dough balls by lg. spoon-fuls into the hot oil and turn when one side is brown. Test with BBQ stick for doneness. Drain on rack. Cool. Dip in syrup and roll in sugar.

Syrup:

4 c. sugar — 1 lg. bottle of Log Cabin syrup — 4 c. water. Bring to a boil for 5 minutes. Let cool.

Flora Azevedo.

* BANDIAY BANDIAY (Filipino) *
(Banana Fritters)

1 c. flour
2 Tbsp. baking powder
1 Tbsp. sugar

¾ c. milk
4—5 whole bananas
oll for frying

Sift dry ingredients and add milk and mix. Peel bananas and slice in half length-wise. Dip bananas in batter. Heat oil in skillet to med. heat, and fry bananas until browned on both sides. Serve hot or cold as part of main dinner meal.

* GINGER YOGURT (INDIA) *

2 c. plain vogurt
6 Tbsp. ginger marmalade or
   crystalized ginger (chopped)

4 tsp. brown sugar
1 tsp. lemon juice

Combine all ingredients in a bowl and beat well. Place in wine glasses or dessert dishes. Serve with lady fingers.

Adele Davis.

* COCONUT MOCHI *

2 pkgs. (11 oz.) mochiko
1 box light brown sugar
1 Tbsp. baking powder

1 can (12 oz.) coconut milk
(plus water to make 4 c.)
sesame seeds

* Kinako (a flavored yellowish brown flour — Japanese).

Mix all ingredients (except sesame seeds and Kinako). And pour into a buttered baking pan, sprinkle with the sesame seeds. Bake in preheated oven 350° for 45 to 60 minutes. Cool. When cooled cut and roll in Kinako and sugar.   Mille Mesaku.

* PEKING GLAZED APPLES *

1 tart apple (peeled—cored—cut
   in 6 wedges)
1 egg (beaten)
3 Tbsp. cornstarch

1 Tbsp. sesame seeds (roasted)
¼ c. sugar
1 Tbsp. oil
oil for deep frying

Heat oil for deep frying, dip apple wedges in beaten egg and then sprinkle with cornstarch. Fry apples (a few at a time) until golden brown (about 5—8 minutes). Remove with slotted spoon to a lightly oiled platter. Combine sugar with 1 Tbsp. oil in saucepan. Melt sugar slowly over very low heat, stirring constantly, then cook without stirring to soft ball stage (275° on candy thermometer). This takes a very short time.

Dip apples into hot syrup, coating thoroughly and sprinkle with sesame seeds. Place bowl of ice water at table and immediately bring in candied apples. Dip fruit in water and hold briefly until syrup forms a crackling glaze.   Adele Davis.

* HAUPIA (HAWAIIAN) *
(Coconut Dessert)

Haupia 1.

1 qt. coconut milk
3 coconuts (meat grated)
1 Tbsp. cornstarch

4 Tbsp. sugar
pinch of salt

Grate coconut and let stand in the milk for 1 hour in a warm place. Squeeze out liquid through a cloth. Put in top of a double boiler, add salt. When warm add starch (mixed with a little milk). Cook until thick (about 15 minutes), stirring constantly. Pour into a shallow pan (9 x 13 in.) and refrigerate. When cooled cut into squares. Note: If Hawaiian starch (called pia) can be obtained, it makes a more delicate dessert than using cornstarch).

Haupia 2.

Pour 1 qt milk over grated coconut and let stand overnite. Strain and put juice in a double boiler and proceed as in Haupia 1.   Lorna Burger.

* MACADAMIA NUT BARS *

1 c. sugar	1 tsp. vanilla
1 egg	1½ c. Macadamia nuts (chopped)
1 c. butter (2 blocks)	2 c. flour

Cream butter and sugar, beat in egg and vanilla. Blend in flour. Stir in half of the nuts. Spread batter evenly in greased 9 x 13 in. pan. Sprinkle remaining nuts on top. Bake in preheated oven (350°) for 20 to 25 minutes. Cut into bars while still warm and remove from pan and cool on rack.   Eillen Weberg

* ALMOND COOKIES *

1 c. sugar	1 c. shortening
1 egg	3 c. flour
2 tsp. almond extract	1 tsp. baking powder
¼ tsp. salt	* almonds

Cut shortening into flour, baking powder, sugar and salt. Beat egg with almond extract and add to dry ingredients. Mix and knead until soft. Form into small balls, flatten to the size of a quarter. Make a dent in center of each cookie and place almond on it. Bake in preheated oven (350°) for 10 to 15 minutes.

Billie Do.

* MANGO BAR COOKIES *

Crust:

2 blocks butter or margarine	2 c. flour
	½ c. sugar

Cut dough as pie crust to pea size and pat in 13 x 13 in. pan.

Filling:

4 c. mangoes (chopped)	1/3 c. water
¾ c. sugar	3 Tbsp. cornstarch

Cook mangoes and sugar over low heat until soft. Dissolve cornstarch in water and add to mango mixture. Simmer until clear. Cool slightly and spread over crust.

Topping:

2 c. oatmeal	¼ c. flour
½ c. sugar	1 block butter

Mix all ingredients, like pea size pieces. Sprinkle evenly over the filling. Bake in preheated oven (350°) for 50 minutes. Cool and cut into squares.

Lorna Burger.

* SESAME COOKIES *

1 c. butter or oleo
1 c. sugar
1 egg (beaten)
1 tsp. vanilla
2 c. flour

½ tsp. soda
¼ tsp. salt
¾ or 1 c. sesame seeds (toasted)

Cream butter and sugar, add egg and vanilla. Sift dry ingredients and add to creamed mixture. Chill for 1 hour. Form into small balls and roll in sesame seeds. Place on a greased cookie sheet and flatten with the bottom of a water glass. Bake in preheated oven (375°) for 10 to 12 minutes.   Billie Do.

* ETHNIC COOKING *

Most of the ingredients used in these recipes may be obtained at most markets, in their special department.
Chinese Five Spice (Ng Heung Fun) is a blend of spices. Bottled spice may be purchased at markets.

Chinese Five Spice Powder.

2 Tbsp. cracked black peppercorns
13 sticks whole cinnamon
12 whole star anise

30 whole cloves
2 Tbsp. fennel seeds

Pulverize all ingredients in blender, electric grinder or mortar. Place in sealed jars, it will keep for over a year. Use sparingly with meat and chicken, never more then ½ tsp. per lb. of meat.

* GLOSSARY *

Ajinomoto: Used in recipes can be replaced by same amount of M.S.G.
Hawaiian salt: Coarse rock salt.
Hekka: Sukiyaki — sliced meat fried in a sauce with vegetables.
M.S.G.: Japanese soybean paste.
Mochi: Japanese rice cake.
Mamasu: Vinegared vegetables.
Oyster Sauce: Chinese oyster flavored sauce.
Pupu: Appetizers.
Shoyu: Soy sauce.
Ti: Ti Plant Leaf.
Won Bok: White Cabbage.

P·O·U·L·T·R·Y

* PATIO CHICKEN DINNER *

4 – 18 x 12″ – aluminum foil
(double thickness)
3 c. cooked rice
1 pkg. dried onion soup
1 cut up chicken or parts
(2 in each pkg.)

½ c. Pet milk
4 Tbsp. butter
Liptons Dry Soup Mix

Put rice in middle of foil, sprinkle on 1 Tbsp. Lipton dry soup. Put chicken on rice on each foil. Pour on 2 Tbsp. Pet milk, 1 Tbsp. dry soup and 1 tsp. butter. Bring together the two short sides of the foil, fold under twice and then fold ends to seal tightly.
Place on cookie sheet and bake in 350° oven for 75 minutes.
Serve in foil packages.

Madeline Ryan.

* OYSTER SAUCE CHICKEN *

1 clove garlic (minced)
3 Tbsp. shoyu
3 Tbsp. sugar
2 Tbsp. oyster sauce
1 piece ginger (minced)

4–5 lbs. chicken (drumettes or
deboned thighs)
1 tsp. salt
2 Tbsp. sherry

Mix together and marinate chicken for 12 hours.

Batter for frying:

1 c. Bisquick
1 c. water

1/3 c. cooking oil
1/3 c. cornstarch

Mix ingredients together and deep fry at 350°. A little water can be added if batter is too thick.

Kate Stanley.

* CHICKEN ADOBO *

1 chicken fryer
½ c. soy sauce
1 bay leaf
6 pepper corns

½ c. rice vinegar
2 c. water
2 garlic cloves
cooking oil

Cut chicken into pieces and put in a pot. Mix vinegar, soy sauce, minced garlic, pepper corns and bay leaf. Add water. Pour mixture on chicken and marinate for 20–30 minutes. Bring to a boil and simmer until chicken is tender and mixture is almost dry. Add cooking oil and brown chicken.
Serve hot or cold.

Patsy Mink.

* INDIAN CHICKEN *

1/3 c. butter
4 lbs. boneless chicken breasts
  (skinned — cut in lg. bite size pcs.)
1 c. chopped onions
1 clove garlic (minced)
2 tsp. salt
1 Tbsp. ground ginger
¼ tsp. chili powder

½ — 1 c. canned tomatoes (drained)
1 c. plain yogurt
½ c. cashews
½ c. flaked coconut
½ c. raisins
2 Tbsp. cornstarch
1 c. whipping cream

Melt butter and brown chicken in a dutch oven. Remove chicken and set aside. Saute onion and garlic in the remaining butter for 5 minutes. Add salt, ginger, chili, tomatoes, yogurt and chicken. Cover and cook for 15 minutes. Stir in coconut, cover and cook for 10 minutes until chicken is tender.

Dissolve cornstarch in cream and add to chicken, stir constantly, heating sauce thoroughly for 5 minutes.

Serve over noodles and top with cashews and raisins.   Liz Howard.

* PARTY CHICKEN *

6 chicken breasts (boned — skinned)
8 slices of bacon
1 jar (4 oz.) chipped beef

1 can cream of mushroom soup
  (undiluted)
½ pt. sour cream

Cover bottom of 9 x 13" baking pan with slices of chipped beef. Wrap the chicken breasts with the slices of bacon and place them in rows on top of the chipped beef.

Mix the soup and sour cream and spoon over the chicken breasts. Bake 3 hours at 175°.   Gladys L. Fox.

* BAKED CHICKEN SUPREME *

Chicken breasts (split — skinned)
2 c. sour cream
¼ c. lemon juice
4 Tbsp. Worcestershire sauce
4 tsp. celery salt

2 tsp. paprika
4 garlic cloves (chopped)
4 tsp. salt

Combine all ingredients, add chicken, covering all pieces and let stand over night in the refrigerator.

1¾ c. packed dry bread crumbs
½ c. shortening (I use all butter)

¼ c. butter

Roll chicken in the crumbs. Place in baking dish in a single layer. Melt butter. Pour one half over chicken and bake for 45 minutes. Pour other half over chicken and bake for 20 minutes longer.   Rebecca Dixon.

* CHICKEN DIVAN *

6 chicken breasts (boned)
Italian herb seasoning
2 bay leaves
4 c. chicken stock
6 slices white bread
Parmesan cheese (grated)
½ soup can milk

8 oz. whipping cream
2 pkgs. frozen broccoli
1 can (10 oz.) cream of chicken soup
1 can (10 oz.) cheddar cheese soup

Poach chicken breasts in stock with the seasoning and herbs (about 20 minutes) While chicken is cooking, cook broccoli for just slightly less time then pkg. directs. Lightly toast bread, heat the soup together, adding the milk (no water). Place toast slices on the bottom of a baking dish, place chicken breasts on top and drained broccoli on top of chicken and pour combined soup over all. Sprinkle with Parmesan cheese. Bake in preheated oven (350°) for 20 minutes. Whip cream until peaks form. When chicken is done, spread cream over chicken and sprinkle more Parmesan cheese. Place under broiler for 5 minutes.

Adele Davis.

* OVEN SAUTED CHICKEN *

Thinly slice 1 lg. onion and scatter over bottom of shallow baking pan.
Coat 2 whole chicken breasts with melted butter, then 3—4 thighs, and 3—4 drumsticks. Place a single layer over the onions. Sprinkle with paprika, 2 tsp. salt. Tuck in 6 whole cloves of garlic. Blend ¼ c. catsup with ¼ c. Sauterne wine and pour over all. Bake in 350° oven for 1 hour. Remove the cover the last 15 minutes, discard garlic, serve with pan juices.   Jean Keys.

* MAYONNAISE BAKE CHICKEN *

1 whole chicken (cut up)
1/3 c. mayonnaise
½ c. bread crumbs

Rinse chicken and pat dry. Brush all sides with mayonnaise, coat with crumbs. Place skin side up in shallow baking dish. Bake at 400° for 45 minutes or until fork tender.   Jean Keys.

* MARINATED FRIED CHICKEN *

2 – 2½ lbs. chicken breasts (skinned)
3 tsp. salt
½ tsp. freshly ground pepper
¼ tsp. garlic powder
½ c. dry vermouth
¼ lb. butter

2 Tbsp. olive oil
1/8 tsp. thyme
2 Tbsp. parsley (minced)
½ c. flour
2 eggs (beaten)
¾ c. dry bread crumbs
2 Tbsp. lemon juice

Wash and dry chicken. Season with a mixture of 2 tsp. salt, pepper and garlic powder. Mix together the vermouth, lemon juice, olive oil, thyme add parsley; marinate the chicken in the mixture for 1 hour. Drain chicken well. Roll in the flour mixed with the remaining salt, then the eggs and finally the bread crumbs. Melt the butter in a lg. skillet and cook the chicken until browned and tender. Turn the pieces frequently.   Rebecca Dixon.

* BARBEQUE FRIED CHICKEN *

2 pkgs. (22 oz.) frozen
   chicken drumettes
4 Tbsp. flour
8 tsp. cornstarch
¼ c. brown sugar
3 garlic cloves (minced)

1 Tbsp. salt
2 eggs
1 Tbsp. oyster sauce
2 Tbsp. ketsup
½ c. chopped green onions.

Combine all ingredients with chicken. Soak for 3 hours or overnite. Mix periodically. Deep fry in oil.
(Makes a great pupu. Tastes better cooled.)   Patsy K. Young.

* BARBEQUED CHICKEN *

2 chickens (cut in half)
1½ tsp. salt
Freshly ground pepper
¼ lb. butter
Juice of 2 limes
¼ c. catsup

few drops of Worcestershire
few drops of Tabasco sauce
1 tsp. savory
1 tsp. thyme
1 garlic clove (crushed)

Wash and dry the chickens, sprinkle on all sides with ½ tsp. salt and pepper. Melt the butter in a sauce pan, add all remaining ingredients, stirring to combine thoroughly. Brush the chicken with the sauce and place on boiled rack, skin side up, over charcoal fire. Grill 20 minutes on each side basting with the sauce. (May need a few minutes longer, depending on heat of fire.)   Jean Keys.

140

* STUFFED CHICKEN IN A HURRY *

3 whole chicken breasts
  (boned — split)
½ pkg. stuffing mix

1 bottle "1890" salad dressing
salt — pepper

Prepare stuffing as per instructions on pkg. Fold each chicken piece in half and stuff with about 1 Tbsp. dressing. Secure with a tooth-pick. Place in shallow baking dish, season with salt and pepper. Pour salad dressing over chicken. Bake in preheated oven at 350° for 50 minutes. (Can be made in advance and chilled)

Charlene Do.

* ONE — POT CURRIED CHICKEN *

2 chickens (quartered)
2 Tbsp. butter
1 Tbsp. oil
1½ c. water
1 c. canned tomatoes (drained)
1 bay leaf

3 Tbsp. curry powder
2 c. tart apples (cored — peeled — cut
  in lg. chunks)
2 bananas (cut in chunks)
1 c. yogurt

Heat a lg. skillet and brown chicken in the butter and oil. Sprinkle with curry powder and make sure the chicken is well coated. Add all the remaining ingredients, cover and simmer for 45 to 60 minutes until chicken is tender. (May be made in advance and reheated). Serve with steamed rice.

Nancy Ebsen.

* CHICKEN MARENGO *

2 frying chickens (quartered)
1 sm. onion (sliced)
½ c. olive oil
½ c. white wine
2 garlic cloves (crushed)
½ tsp. thyme
1 bay leaf
1 c. pitted black olives

sprigs of parsley
1 c. chicken stock
2 c. Italian style tomatoes (canned)
16 — 20 sm. white onions
1 lb. mushrooms (sliced)
¼ lb. butter
juice of 1 lemon

Saute onion in olive oil until golden brown. Remove. Add chicken to skillet and brown on all sides. Season with salt and pepper. Add the following sauce. To make sauce: Combine wine, garlic, thyme, parsley, chicken stock and tomatoes. Season to taste. Cover pot and simmer for 1 hour. Remove chicken, strain sauce and reduce for about 5 minutes. Saute onions and mushrooms in ¼ c. butter with the lemon juice. Until tender.

Arrange chicken, onions, mushrooms and black olives in a deep casserole sprin= kle with Cognac. Add the sauce. Reheat in oven (350°).

Garnish with parsley and serve with rice.

Adele Davis.

141

* STICKY CHICKEN *

¾ c. vinegar
¾ c. sugar
¾ c. soy sauce

5 lbs. chicken thighs or pieces
3 garlic cloves (minced)
1½ Tbsp. fresh ginger (minced)

Combine, vinegar, sugar, soy sauce in a shallow baking dish. Arrange chicken in dish in a single layer, turning to coat well. Cover and marinate overnite in refrigerator.

Transfer chicken and marinade to a lg. skillet. Add garlic and ginger and bring to a boil, cover, med. heat. Reduce heat and simmer 15 minutes, turn occasionally. Uncover and continue simmering until chicken is tender. Remove from pan. Discard ginger and garlic. Increase heat to medium and cook until sauce is reduced and carmelized. (Watch carefully to prevent burning). Return chicken to the skillet and coat with the sauce.

Garnish with cherry tomatoes and watercress.   Judy Pieklo.

* CHICKEN STROGANOFF *

4 chicken breasts (skinned — boned)
6 Tbsp. safflower oil
1 onion (diced)
½ flour
pinch of nutmeg
pinch of thyme
½ tsp. salt

¼ tsp. white pepper
2 tsp. lemon juice
1 c. chicken broth
1 c. sour cream
hot butter spinach noodles
minced parsley for garnish

Cut chicken into bite size pieces. Heat 2 Tbsp. oil in a skillet and saute onion until transparent. Remove onion and set aside. Combine flour, thyme, nutmeg, salt and pepper in a paper bag and dredge chicken pieces.

Add remaining oil to skillet, add chicken pieces and brown over medium heat. Mix in lemon juice and broth and simmer for 10 minutes more. Reduce heat to low. Stir 2 Tbsp. hot chicken sauce into the sour cream, add to pan, stirring constantly and heat to serving temperature. (Do not boil or sauce will curdle). Serve over hot buttered noodles and garnish with parsley.   Francis Wright.

* HOT — HOT CHICKEN *

2 lg. whole chicken breasts (skinned
  — boned — cut in 1 in. cubes)
2 c. peanut oil
1 egg white
½ c. peanuts (roasted)
10 whole dried chili peppers
  (sweet — stems removed)

1 Tbsp. cornstarch
½ tsp. salt
2 garlic cloves (minced)
2 green onions (sliced)

Sauce:

¼ c. chicken stock

2 Tbsp. shoyu

1 Tbsp. Sherry

1 tsp. Chinese five spice

1 tsp. sesame oil

1 tsp. wine vinegar

1 tsp. sugar

1 tsp. cornstarch

Blend all ingredients in a sm. bowl.

Place oil in Wok or skillet and heat to medium heat.

Mix egg white, cornstarch and salt and add chicken pieces and coat evenly. Place small amounts of chicken pieces in Wok and stir fry until golden brown. Remove with slotted spoon and drain on paper towel.

Pour off all but 2 Tbsp. oil. Add chili peppers and stir fry for 1 minute. Return chicken to Wok and heat through. Add sauce and stir until glazed. Quickly mix in peanuts and serve hot. Millie Mesaku.

* CHICKEN PILLOWS *

1 whole chicken breast
   (skinned — boned — pounded)

1 garlic clove (minced)

1 oz. prosciutto

1 oz. Mozzarella cheese (thinly sliced)

2 Tbsp. seasoned bread crumbs

2 Tbsp. Sherry

2 Tbsp. butter

salt — pepper

1 Tbsp. chopped parsley

Preheat oven to 350°. Lightly grease a shallow baking pan. Rub chicken with the garlic. Place prosciutto and cheese on each piece and roll, starting at broader end and secure with a toothpick. Place in baking pan.

Combine Sherry and butter and heat briefly, pour over the chicken, season with salt and pepper. Bake 20 to 30 minutes until chicken is done. Sprinkle with chopped parsley. Note: This recipe is for 2 servings. May be increased if you wish. Billie Do.

* BUSY DAY CHICKEN *

1 frying chicken
   (cut into serving pieces)

1 c. long grain rice

1 can mushroom soup

1½ c. water

1 pkg. onion soup mix (1 envelope)

Scatter rice in the bottom of a buttered baking pan (9 x 13"). Lay chicken pieces on top of rice (skin side up).

Combine mushroom soup, water and onion soup mix, pour over the chicken. Cover pan with foil and bake (325°) for 2 hours. Remove the foil the last ½ hour to help brown. Francis Wright.

* TANDOORI MURG *
(India Curried Chicken)

4 lbs. chicken breasts and
   tights mixed
2 lemons (quartered)
4 c. plain yogurt
1 Tbsp. coriander seed
8 cardamon pods
½ tsp. cinnamon
½ tsp. cloves

½ c. almonds (ground — roasted)
3 med. onions (chopped)
2 garlic cloves (chopped)
1 Tbsp. poppy seed (toasted)
1 Tbsp. ginger (grated)
2 Tsp. tumeric (ground)

Place small amount of yogurt in a blender, add coriander and cardamon and blend well. Mix in cinnamon and cloves. Combine mix with the replace in a lg. bowl. Add tumeric ½ tsp. at a time, until mixture is well colored. Add chicken to marinate, turning to coat evenly. Cover and refrigerate over nite. Turn chicken a few times. Three hours before cooking remove chicken from refrigerator and allow to stand at room temperature. Preheat oven to 350°. Butter lg. baking pan, place chicken (skin side down), leaving space in between if possible. Cover with marinade. Bake uncovered for 30 minutes. Turn and baste often and continue baking for another 30 minutes or until chicken is tender. Arrange on hot platter, serve with rice and condiments. Note: May be kept warm in a low oven for 30 minutes or prepared in advance and reheated.   Adele Davis.

* CHICKEN ZUCCHINI *

3 chicken breasts (skinned — boned)
2—3 medium zucchini
1 sm. eggplant
Batter:
3 eggs (well beaten)
1½ c. light beer
1½ c. flour

12 medium mushrooms
12 artichoke hearts (drained)
oil

1 Tbsp. paprika
2 tsp. salt

Mix together eggs and beer. Sift together flour, paprika and salt and add to egg mixture. Beat until batter is smooth. Chill. Cut chicken into 1 in. cubes. Slice zucchini diagonally ½ in. thick. Peel and cut eggplant in sticks about 3/8 in. thick. Trim mushroom stems. Dry artichokes thoroughly. Arrange on tray for frying. Heat oil in a lg. skillet to medium hot. Dip vegetables and chicken in batter and drop into skillet. Stir fry until crisp and browned. Place browned pieces on a baking sheet lined with paper towels and keep warm in low oven until all pieces are cooked.
Squeeze juice of lemon over each portion when serving.
    Roberta Chateauneuf.

* MUSHROOMS AND RICE STUFFED CHICKEN LEGS *

6 whole chicken thighs and legs
  (not disjointed)
1 Tbsp. butter
½ lb. mushrooms (sliced)
1 onion (chopped)
1 green pepper (chopped)
1 Tbsp. paprika
2 c. wild rice or brown rice (cooked)

½ c. toasted almonds (chopped)
1 tsp. Worcestershire sauce
1/8 tsp. sage
1 c. melted butter
2 Tbsp. lime juice
Watercress for garnish

Using index finger, carefully loosen skin from chicken where thigh and drumstick meet, trying to make as deep an opening as possible.
Preheat oven to 350°. Melt 1 Tbsp. butter in a skillet and add mushrooms, onions and green pepper and saute until tender. Stir in rice, nuts, Worcestershire sauce, sage, salt and pepper and mix. Divide evenly among legs, stuffing tightly between skin and meat and place in a shallow baking pan.
Combine melted butter, lime juice and paprika and brush over chicken. Bake (basting often) about 1 hour until chicken is tender and golden brown.
Arrange chicken over a bed of watercress on serving platter.   Margaret Holmes.

* LEMON — ORANGE CHICKEN *

4 chicken breasts
1 can (12 oz.) can frozen orange juice
1 lemon

Skin breasts and remove all fat. Pierce flesh of each piece with the point of a knife 5—6 times on each side. Place in shallow casserole with a tight lid.
Combine juice of lemon with 2/3 can of undiluted orange juice. Marinade in refrigerator at least 4 hours, turning chicken over several times.
Cook covered at 350° for 1½ hours.
Serve marinade on the side.   Joyce Heftel.

* CITRUS CHICKEN *

3 chicken breasts (skinned — halved)
¼ c. melted butter
1 Tbsp. Orange Liqueur
6 thin slices cooked ham
flour
2 eggs (beaten)
1/3 c. dry bread crumbs

1 stick butter (cut in bits)
2 c. fresh orange juice
1 tsp. grated orange peel
½ tsp. salt
Grated orange peel — Garnish
chopped parsley — Garnish

Preheat oven to 400°. Place chicken halves on a flat surface, smooth side down. Brush with melted butter mixed with Liqueur. Place one piece of ham on each breast and roll up, secure with toothpick. Roll in flour. Shake off excess. Dip in beaten egg and then roll in the bread crumbs.

Arrange chicken in a shallow baking dish. Dot with butter bits. Bake for 15 minutes, turning once.

Mix orange juice, orange peel and salt and pour over chicken. Reduce heat to 350°. Cover and bake 35 minutes longer, basting and turning occasionally. Remove toothpicks from chicken. Place each chicken roll on an orange slice on a heated platter and spoon sauce over all. Garnish with additional orange peel and chopped parsley.   Ida Christoph.

* FRESH PINEAPPLE AND LICHEE CHICKEN *

1 fresh pineapple
2 lbs. chicken breasts
   (skinned — boned — cubed)
¼ c. chestnut flour
1½ c. oil
½ c. white vinegar
½ c. pineapple juice
1 can (8 oz.) lichee nuts

½ c. orange juice
½ c. tomato juice
½ c. sugar
1 tsp. salt
½ lemon
1 Tbsp. cornstarch
   (dissolved in 2 Tbsp. water)

Cut pineapple in half, leaving leaves intact. Remove fruit from shell and dice. Set aside. Dip chicken in the flour. Deep fry in very hot oil until golden brown. Drain on paper towel.

Combine vinegar and juices, sugar and salt in a saucepan. Squeeze lemon juice into the sauce and place lemon half in pan. Bring to a boil, remove lemon shell. Stir in cornstarch and simmer until sauce is thick and clear. Blend in pineapple and lichee fruit and heat through. Spoon into pineapple shell and place chicken on top.   Nancy Ebsen.

* BAKED GUAVA CHICKEN *

12 sm. chicken breasts or 5 lbs.
   chicken parts
1 jar (10 oz.) guava jelly
1 Tbsp. cornstarch
1 c. water
½ c. lemon juice

1½ tsp. Worcestershire
¼ c. shoyu
1 tsp. allspice
½ tsp. Hawaiian salt
½ tsp. white pepper

Place chicken in baking pan. Mix all other ingredients in a saucepan and simmer for 5 minutes. Pour over the chicken. Bake in preheated oven (350° for 40 min. to 1 hour.) Baste frequently. Add water if necessary.   Elizabeth Betty Guy.

* APRICOT CHICKEN *

4 lbs. chicken parts   1 bottle Wishbone Russian dressing
1 pkg. Liptons onion soup mix.   10 oz. bottle apricot preserves

Mix ingredients together and pour over the chicken.
Bake (300° – 325°) for approximately one hour.   Millie Akaka.

* CHICKEN KIEV – MACADAMIA *

½ c. butter (softened)   1 c. flour
¼ c. minced parsley   3 eggs (beaten)
½ jar (3½ oz.) Macadamia bits   oil for deep frying
8 chicken breasts (skinned – boned)

Combine the butter and the parsley, stir in the macadamia nuts. Divide the butter mixture into eight parts and freeze.

Place the chicken breasts between layers of plastic bags and pound with rolling pin. Place one of the frozen butter pats on the side of the chicken that the skin was not on before boning. Roll chicken, making sure the sides are folded in and that the butter is not sticking out. Refrigerate for 1 hour.

Roll each breast in the flour, dip in the eggs and coat with bread crumbs.

Heat oil to 375° and cook chicken for 10 – 12 minutes. Drain on paper towels.
Nathalia Richman.

* CRISPY CHICKEN SKINS *

Note: These are similar to pork cracklings, these crisp appetizers can be served by themselves or with an eggplant dip. Save the skins from other chicken dishes and freeze until ready to use.

Skins from 4 chickens   ½ tsp. peppercorns (crushed)
1 c. white vinegar   salt
4 garlic cloves (ground)   vegetable oil for deep frying

Cut chicken skins into 4 in. squares. Combine remaining ingredients in medium bowl. Mix in chicken skins. Cover and refrigerate overnite, turning occasionally. Drain skins and pat dry. Heat oil in heavy lg. skillet to 375°. Carefully add chicken skins in batches (do not crowd) and cook until crisp, turning several times, about 5 minutes. Drain on paper towels and serve.   Billie Do.

* CHICKEN ROQUEFORT *

1 chicken (cut up)

Season chicken with salt and pepper and brown in butter. In skillet in which chicken browned, add 4 oz. Roquefort cheese (crumbled), 1 garlic clove (chopped) and 1 c. sour cream. Heat this mixture and pour over chicken. Bake in a covered casserole in 350° oven for 1 hour or until tender.   Marian Loo.

147

* CHICKEN IMPERIAL *

Breasts of chicken (boned and soaked in Sherry for 2 hours).

Combine:

2 c. bread crumbs
1 c. Parmesan Cheese
    (freshly grated)
½ c. parsley (chopped)
1/8 tsp. pepper

1 tsp. salt
2 garlic cloves (minced)
½ c. Macadamia nuts (chopped)
½ c. almonds (chopped)

Roll chicken in melted butter and then into the dry batter. Bake in casserole for 30 minutes at 350°. (Save remaining batter, freeze for later use.)

Allison Holland.

* ROAST TURKEY *
(Chinese Style)

1 turkey (12 to 14 lbs.)
3 c. shoyu sauce
1½ c. Sherry
2 Tbsp. sugar
4 slices of fresh ginger

3 scallions
1½ tsp. salt
9 c. water

Boil the water with the seasonings in a roasting pan on top of the stove. Add the turkey and continue to boil for 45 to 50 minutes, turning over from time to time, because the juice does not cover the turkey.

Remove the juice from the roaster. Bake turkey uncovered in a preheated oven (500°) for 45 to 50 minutes.

Baste with sauce every 20 minutes, turning over until well browned. Let stand 15 minutes before carving.

Adele Davis.

* KALUA TURKEY *
(Hawaiian Style)

11 to 12 lbs. turkey
Hawaiian salt

3 to 5 Ti leaves
liquid smoke

Place turkey in a roasting pan. Rub handful of salt inside and out.
Sprinkle with liquid smoke.

Place Ti leaves on top of turkey and seal with foil. Roast in a preheated oven (350°) for 3 hours. Turn off heat and leave in oven for another 2 hours.

To serve: Shred the turkey.

Adele Davis.

* TURKEY VERDE *

3 lbs.; fresh broccoli
1 pkg. (12 oz.) egg noodles
2 Tbsp. butter
1 can (5 oz.) water chestnuts
   (drained — sliced)
1 stick butter
6 c. cooked turkey (bite size pieces).

1 c. almonds (toasted-slivered)
½ c. flour
2 c. heated cream
¼ c. Sherry
salt — pepper
Parmesan cheese

Trim broccoli and blanch in boiling water for 5 minutes and rinse in cold water and drain again.

Remove some of the broccoli florets for garnish. Chop remaining broccoli very coarsely.

Cook and drain noodles, toss with 2 Tbsp. butter in saucepan over low heat and water chestnuts.

In another saucepan, melt remaining butter over low heat, mix in flour and continue stirring for 2 to 3 minutes. Whisk in cream and stir until sauce is thick. Add Sherry and season to taste with salt and pepper. Preheat oven to 350°. Place noodles and water chestnuts in bottom of 2 baking sheets (9 x 13"). Spread broccoli on top, add layer of turkey and spoon half of sauce over each dish.

Decorate edges of pans with broccoli florets and sprinkle with almonds and cheese. Bake for 30 minutes.

Note: Recipe may be cut in half or can be frozen.

Ruth Tufte.

* TURKEY HASH *

¼ c. butter
3 c. raw potatoes (chopped fine)
3 c. cooked turkey (chopped fine)
¼ tsp. salt
green pepper rings — garnish.

fresh ground pepper
¼ c. chopped onion
¼ c. green pepper (chopped)
1 can (10 oz.) chicken gravy
1 c. water
½ tsp. rosemary

Melt butter in a skillet and add all ingredients. Fry over medium heat until vegetables are tender, turning the hash occasionally. Add small amount of water if needed.

Place on warm platter and garnish with green pepper rings.

Note: Makes good use of left over turkey.

Evelyn Staley.

149

* CURRIED TURKEY PIE *

¼ c. light raisins
1½ c. stuffing mix (herb seasoned)
¼ c. butter (melted)
1 can cream of celery soup
   (condensed)
1 tsp. curry powder

1½ c. cooked turkey (cubed)
1 c. cooked peas
1 can (3 oz.) chopped mushrooms
   (drained)
1 Tbsp. onion (chopped)
1 c. milk

Cover raisins with boiling water and let stand for 5 minutes. Drain. Combine stuffing mix, butter and 2 Tbsp. water. Remove ¼ c. of the crumbs, wrap and chill. Press remaining crumbs in a 9 in. pie pan. Blend milk with soup, add remaining ingredients and raisins. Turn into pie shell. Cover and chill at least 4 hours or overnight. Before baking, sprinkle with the reserved bread crumbs. Bake in preheated oven (375°) till heated through (25 to 30 minutes).
Let cool slightly before cutting.

Lucille Grimes.

* TURKEY AMANDINE ON TOAST *

2 cans (10 oz. each) chicken gravy
2 c. cooked turkey (cubed)
2 Tbsp. pimientos (drained —
   chopped)
½ tsp. poultry seasoning

1 c. sour cream
2 Tbsp. flour
½ c. toasted almonds (slivered)
toast points

Combine gravy, turkey, pimientos and poultry seasoning in a sauce-pan. Heat, stirring occasionally. Combine sour cream and flour and stir into turkey mix and heat to just boiling. Remove from heat, add almonds and serve over toast points. Garnish with parsley.

Daisy Alexander.

* TURKEY — POTATO PANCAKES *

3 eggs (beaten)
3 c. uncooked potatoes
   (peeled — shredded)
1½ c. turkey (chopped fine)

1½ Tbsp. onion (grated)
dash of pepper
1½ tsp salt
Cranberry sauce

In mixing bowl, combine eggs, potatoes, turkey, onion, salt and pepper. Mix well. Add flour. Using about ¼ c. of batter to make each pancake, drop batter on a well greased griddle or a skillet. With a spatula spread pancake to about 4 in. in diameter. Cook over medium heat until pancake is done (about 3 to 4 minutes on each side).
Serve warm with cranberry sauce.

Francis Wright.

* TURKEY IN ASPIC *

6 slices cooked turkey
1 can (2½ oz.) deviled ham
1 Tbsp. chopped parsley
2 Tbsp. chopped onion
1 tsp. horseradish (cream style)
2 eggs whites (slightly beaten)

1 Tbsp. lemon juice
2 hard-cooked eggs
2 pkgs. gelatin
1 can (13 oz.) chicken broth
½ c. water

Trim turkey slices (¼ in. thick) to uniform size. Blend together deviled ham, parsley, onion and horseradish. Spread turkey with ham mixture. Slice cooked eggs and arrange 2 slices on top of the ham mixture.

In sauce pan, soften the gelatin in the chicken broth and the water. Add beaten egg white and lemon juice, bring to a boil, stirring constantly, remove from heat and strain through cheesecloth.

Pour a layer of aspic into a 9" x 9" pan. Chill till almost set. Arrange turkey slices on aspic and carefully pour aspic over slices. Cover and chill until firm. Before serving, trim aspic closely around each slice of turkey, serve on lettuce.

Adele Davis.

* CORNISH GAME HENS *

3 Cornish hens
juice of 3 limes
1½ tsp. Brandy
½ c. chicken broth

1½ tsp. olive oil
oregano
1 tsp. butter

Stuffing:

1 tsp. butter
½ c. chopped onions
salt — pepper

1 lb. fresh spinach (chopped)
3 hen livers (minced)

Wash hens and dry with paper towels. Sprinkle cavity with lime juice. Mix Brandy, oil and oregano and season cavities. Lightly stuff birds, truss and secure wings to the body. Brown in butter in a skillet. Place in a warmed casserole. Deglaze skillet with broth and add to casserole. Cover with foil, make a small hole in top to release the steam.

Bake in preheated oven (350°) for 1 hour, basting every 10 minutes. Remove foil the last 10 minutes of baking.

Halve birds and place on warm platter.

Lorna Burger.

151

* GRILLED GAME BIRDS *

6 Cornish Hens
1 lemon wedge
Walnut sausage dressing:
2 Tbsp. butter
½ c. chopped onions
1/3 c. chopped green peppers
½ lb. pork sausage
¼ tsp. garlic salt
¼ c. Cognac

salt — pepper
2 Tbsp. cooking oil

½ c. chopped walnuts
3 c. cooked brown rice
½ tsp. coarse black pepper
1 tsp. salt
1 tsp. onion salt

Melt butter in a skillet, add onions and green pepper and saute until soft. Add sausage and saute until juices are clear. Add walnuts and drain off any fat. Add rice, salt, pepper and cognac and mix well. Cool before stuffing hens.

Raise grill to position farthest from flame. Cover grill with foil, place hens on foil and cover with more foil. Grill for 1 hour or until legs move easily.

Note: as an alternative to grilling, hens may be baked in preheated oven (350°) for 1 hour. Lucille Goderre.

* SQUAB A L'ORANGE *

8 squabs (1½ lb. ea.) or Cornish hens
2 Tbsp. coarse salt
2 tsp. pepper
4 oranges
½ c. sugar
4 c. basic brown sauce

¾ c. dry red wine
¼ c. orange liqueur
1¼ c. orange marmalade (bitter type)
2 tsp. corn starch
watercress — garnish
½ c. red wine vinegar

Preheat oven to 350°. Wash and dry squabs, remove necks, wing tips and giblets. Truss birds, then rub with salt and pepper, place in a roasting pan on a rack. Add giblets and trimmings and roast for 2 hours, until juices run clear when pricked with a fork.

With vegetable peeler, thinly peel 2 oranges, cut into julienned slivers. Place in saucepan and cover with cold water. Remove white pith from both oranges. In a lg. skillet, dissolve sugar in vinegar and stir. When sugar is dissolved increase heat to high and tip pan back and forth, without stirring, until liquid is carmelized. Slowly add brown sauce, ½ c. of wine and orange liqueur. Add orange peel and ¼ c. marmalade. Thicken sauce with the cornstarch and simmer until sauce has thickened.

15 minutes before birds are done, brush with 1 c. marmalade, return to oven and let glaze. Remove birds to serving platter and keep warm. Pour off all fat from roasting pan and deglaze with remaining wine, bring to a boil, loosening brown bits. Strain into sauce.

Section the two oranges and add to sauce.

Decorate platter with watercress.

With lemon stripper, cut lengthwise grooves into skin of remaining oranges, then slice crosswise, arrange on platter. Place birds on watercress and spoon a little sauce over each bird and serve additional sauce in bowl. Very festive recipe.

Adele Davis.

* STUFFED SQUABS *

8 squabs
salt — pepper
½ c. butter (softened)
Stuffing:

1½ c. cracked wheat
2 eggs (beaten)

3 c. chicken broth
1 c. whole almonds (blanched)

Sauce:

1½ c. white wine
½ c. chicken broth
2 c. seedless green grapes

2 tsp. cornstarch
2 tsp. water

Place cracked wheat in a heavy skillet (oven proof) and mix in beaten eggs and cook over high heat, stirring constantly 8 to 10 minutes until grains are dry and separated. Add broth and stir to combine. Cover and bake 25 to 30 minutes at 350°. Remove from oven and cool slightly and fluff with fork. Place almonds on baking sheet and toast until golden brown. Mix with wheat and toss with fork. For sauce: In saucepan, reduce wine to ¾ c. and add chicken broth. Mix cornstarch with water and gradually add to sauce and simmer until sauce thickens. Add grapes and heat for 1 minute, keep warm. Preheat oven to 400°. Stuff and truss birds. Place on rack in shallow pan, sprinkle with salt and pepper and rub over top of each. Bake 35 minutes. Reduce heat to 375° and bake 20 minutes longer, basting several times. Place birds on warm serving platter, pour sauce on top and garnish with watercress.

Ida Christoph.

* ENTE MIT APRIKOSEN (GERMAN) *
(Duck with Apricots)

1 — 4 lb. duck
juice of 1 lemon
1 tsp. salt
2 garlic cloves

¾ c. apricot nectar
1 c. dried apricots
2 Tbsp. parsley (chopped)
fresh ground pepper

Split duck in half, remove skin and as much fat as possible. Rub duck with lemon juice, salt and pepper. Bake in preheated oven (400°) for 10 minutes. Drain off all fat. Reduce heat to 325° and bake for ¾ hour. Mix crushed garlic, apricot nectar, diced apricots and parsley and spread on duck. Bake another 30 minutes or until tender.

Nancy Ebsen.

* FRIED DUCK *

1 duck (3—4 lbs.)
¼ tsp. cinnamon
¼ tsp. pepper
½ tsp. salt
½ tsp. liquor

1 Tbsp. shoyu
1 Tbsp. sugar
4 Tbsp. Chinese parsley (chopped)
3 pieces fresh ginger (minced)
1 — 16 lbs. goose

Prepare sauce and rub on duck. Steam for 45 minutes. When duck has cooled, chop into pieces. Sprinkle with some cornstarch and deep fry until golden brown. Serve on shredded lettuce with hot Won Tons.   Billie Do.

* OIE FARCIE AUX MARRONS (FRENCH) *
(Roost Goose with Chestnut Dressing)

2 lbs. chestnuts (shelled-inner
     skin removed)
chicken stock
1 lb. bulk sausage meat

1 tsp. poultry seasoning
¼ c. Cognac
salt and pepper to taste

Cook chestnuts in stock until barely tender. Drain and chop fine. Brown sausage, drain off fat and add chestnuts. Add poultry seasoning, Cognac, salt and pepper. Mix well. Stuff goose and close openings, rub outside of goose with salt and pepper. Place on rack in roasting pan (breast side up). Bake in preheated oven (325°) 4 to 5 hours, until goose is tender and browned. Remove from pan and siphon off all grease. Blend pan drippings, cornstarch and hot water to make gravy. Serve garnished with watercress and parsley.   Roberta Chateauneuf.

* GOOSE WITH SAUERKRAUT (GERMAN) *

one 12 or 14 lbs. goose
Dressing:
½ c. salt pork (diced)
2 med. onions (chopped)
2 med. apples (chopped)
½ tsp. thyme
Basting sauce:
2 tsp. lamon juice
1 c. red wine

2 tsp. caraway seeds
6 c. sauerkraut (drained)
1 — 10 lb. goose

To prepare dressing: Fry pork in skillet, add onions and apples. Simmer until mixture begins to color. Add thyme, caraway seeds and sauerkraut. Salt and pepper to taste. Rub inside of goose with lemon juice, salt and pepper. Stuff goose with dressing, close openings. Rub outside of goose with lemon juice and salt. Place goose on rack (breast side up) in roasting pan. Roast in preheated oven (350°) 3 to 4 hours. Baste with wine sauce. When done, skim off fat and pour sauce over goose for serving.   Adele Davis.

154

M·E·A·T

* SPECIAL SAUCES FOR MEATS *

Sour Cream Mint Sauce:

1 c. sour cream
½ c. mint jelly (melted)
Blend and serve with lamb

Peachy Ham Glaze:

1 jar peach preserves (16 oz.)
¼ c. orange flavored Liqueur or orange juice

Combine ingredients. Use to baste ham during the last 30 minutes of baking. Serve remaining glaze with the sliced ham.

Bourbon Marinade:

2 onions (sliced)   2 whole cloves
1 carrot (sliced)   1 c. Bourbon
2 shallots (sliced)   ½ c. olive oil
12 peppercorns

Mix all ingredients together. Use for steak marinade or for basting pot roast. Also good for basting chicken. Note: May be made and stored in refrigerator.

Shallot Sauce:

2 Tbsp. butter   ½ c. white wine
3 shallots (chopped)   4 c. chicken stock
1 celery stalk (chopped)   1 bay leaf
1 carrot (chopped)   2 sprigs parsley
¼ lb. mushrooms (chopped)   ½ tsp thyme
2 Tbsp. flour   salt — pepper

Melt butter in skillet, add shallots, carrots and mushrooms. Simmer over medium heat until liquid has evaporated and vegetables are lightly brown. Stir in flour and continue to cook until flour turns a light coffee color. Add wine, stock, bay leaf, parsley and thyme. Simmer over low heat for 1 hour. Strain (or puree if you want a thicker sauce). Add salt and pepper to taste. Note: Can be made several days in advance and refrigerated. Use as a gravy or for leftover meats.

Meerrettich Sauce (German) (Horseradish Sauce)

2 Tbsp. butter   1/8 tsp. cayenne pepper
2 Tbsp. flour   1 c. light cream
½ tsp. salt   2 Tbsp. bottled horseradish
½ tsp. sugar

Melt butter in saucepan, remove from heat and add flour and seasonings and stir. Gradually stir in cream and cook until smooth and thick. Add horseradish and sugar. Serve hot. Excellent served with boiled beef.

Jiffy Barbecue Sauce:

¼ c. vegetable oil
¾ c. onions (chopped)
¾ c. catsup
¾ c. chicken broth
2 tsp. salt

fresh ground pepper
1/3 c. lemon juice
3 Tbsp. brown sugar
3 Tbsp. Worcestershire sauce
2 Tbsp. prepared mustard

Heat oil in skillet, add onion and cook until soft. Add all other ingredients and simmer for 15 minutes, stirring constantly. Cool and refrigerate until ready to use.

Rib Tickling Barbecue Sauce:

½ c. Karo syrup
¼ c. catsup
½ c. finely chopped onion

¼ c. cider vinegar
¼ c. prepared mustard
¼ c. Worcestershire sauce

In saucepan, stir all ingredients. Bring to a boil, simmer for 15 minutes. Brush on meat and barbecue. Makes 2 cups.   Jean Keys.

Spaghetti Wine Sauce:

Cook slightly in a little oil — 1 onion chopped and 2 garlic cloves minced. Add beef cubes — 1 lb. Italian sausage (take off casing). Brown all together. Add: 1 can water, 4 cans (8 oz. each) tomato sauce, 2 cups red wine, 1 medium can tomatoes, 1 c. sliced mushrooms, 1 tsp. Italian seasoning and salt and pepper to taste. Simmer until sauce is thickened and meats are cooked.   Valerie Wilson.

Sweet German Style Mustard:

¼ c. whole mustard seeds
5 Tbsp. dry mustard (preferably
    imported)
½ c. hot tap water
1 c. cider vinegar
¼ c. cold water
2 lg. slices onion
3 Tbsp. dark brown sugar

1½ tsp. salt
2 garlic cloves (mashed)
¼ tsp. each cinnamon, clove, dill weed,
    tarragon, allspice
3 Tbsp. light corn syrup

Soak together mustard seeds, dry mustard, hot water and ½ c. vinegar for at least 3 hours.

One hour before completing mustard, combine in a saucepan remaining ½ c. vinegar, cold water, onion, brown sugar, salt, garlic, cinnamon, allspice, dill, tarragon and cloves. Bring to a boil and cook for 1 minute. Cover and let stand for 1 hour. Place soaked mustard mixture into a blender and process until mustard is the consistency of course puree. Pour mustard into top of a double boiler, set over simmering water and cook for 10 minutes, stirring often. Remove from heat, add corn syrup and pour into storage jar. Leave uncovered until mustard is cool, then store in refrigerator.   Ruth Nelson.

* BARBEQUED MEAT BALLS *

Meat balls:

1 lb. ground beef — ¼ c. cold water — 1 tsp. salt

Barbecue Sauce:

2 Tbsp. catsup   1 Tbsp. Worcestershire
2 Tbsp. sugar   2 Tbsp. vinegar
1 tsp. prepared mustard

Mix ground meat with the other ingredients and roll into 12 or 15 balls and saute until browned. Mix ingredients for the sauce. Place meat balls in a fairly deep pan. Pour sauce over, cover and cook gently for 1 hour.
Freezes well.   Dorothy Tuttle.

* MUSHROOM MEATBALLS *

Blend 1 can of cream of mushroom soup with ½ c. water. Measure 1/3 c. of this with 1 lb. ground beef, ½ c. bread crumbs (fine), 2 Tbsp. minced onion, 1 Tbsp. minced parsley, 1 egg (slightly beaten), ¼ tsp. salt.

Shape into small meatballs, brown in shortening. Put in casserole, add remaining soup mixture and bake for 1 hour at 350°.
Very good served with mashed potatoes and a green salad.   Jean Keys.

* GERMAN MEAT BALLS *

1½ lbs. ground beef   ¼ tsp. pepper
½ lb. ground pork   2 tsp. brown sugar
¼ c. finely chopped onion   ½ tsp. allspice
½ c. fine dry bread crumbs   ¼ tsp. nutmeg
1 c. canned milk   ¼ c. flour (more if needed)
1 tsp salt   ¼ c. (4 Tbsp.) butter or oleo
paprika   1 c. light cream or canned milk
1 egg

Combine the ground beef, ground pork and onion. Beat the egg lightly and mix into the meat mixture with bread crumbs, milk, salt, pepper, brown sugar, allspice and nutmeg. Shape into small balls 1¼ in. in diameter and roll into flour. Brown on all sides in melted butter, in moderately hot frying pan. Brown on all sides. (about 10 minutes). Pour cream or milk over meat balls, cover and simmer slowly for 10 to 15 minutes. (makes 48 meatballs and serves 6 — 8).
Marilyn Bornhorst.

* SPECIAL HAMBURGER *

3 slices of soft bread
1/3 c. milk
¼ c. catsup
2 lbs. ground beef
2 tsp. salt
¼ tsp. pepper

1 egg — slightly beaten
1 Tbsp. butter
2 lg. onions (sliced thin)
9 thin slices of tomatoes
18 slices bacon

Crumble bread in a bowl, add milk and catsup. Mix with a fork. Add beef, salt, pepper and egg. Saute onions in butter until golden brown. Shape meat into 18 thin patties. Place onion and tomato on half of the patties. Top with remaining patties, press together.

Lay 2 strips of bacon crisscross on waxed paper and place patties where strips cross. Fold bacon over and press firmly to secure. Fry at 360°.

Heat 1 Tbsp. butter, add 1 Tbsp. lemon juice, 2 Tbsp. finely chopped parsley, if sauce is desired.   Ann Kobayashi.

* SPICY BURGERBALLS *

1½ lbs. ground beef
1 egg (beaten)
8 lg. stuffed green olives
8 cherry tomatoes
8 sm. onions (parboiled)
½ tsp. onion Juice

1 c. catsup
1 Tbsp. horseradish
½ tsp. Worcestershire sauce
½ tsp. prepared mustard

Mix meat with egg and season with salt and pepper and shape into 24 meatballs. Thread each of four skewers with olives, tomatoes, onions and meatballs, dividing equally among the skewers. Mix all remaining ingredients together. Brush meat and vegetables liberally with the sauce. Broil 2 in. from heat, rotating skewers and brushing with sauce several times, until meat is cooked to desired doneness. Serve with shoestring potatoes, and avocado salad.   Adele Davis.

* HAMBURGER CASSEROLE *

1 Tbsp. oil
1½ lbs. ground beef
½ lb. salt pork (diced)
1 or two onions (chopped)
1 can (4 oz.) pimientos (chopped)
salt and pepper to taste

1 can (1—lb.) peas
1 can (1—lb.) tomatoes
12 oz. spaghetti, (broken — cooked)
½ lb. Cheddar cheese (shredded)
paprika

Heat oil in a skillet, add meats and stir until meats are browned. Add onions, pimientos, peas, tomatoes, spaghetti and cheese and mix well. Season to taste. Turn into 3 qt. casserole and bake at 350° for 45 minutes.   Irma Myers

* MEAT LOAF IN A LOAF *

1 round loaf of French bread
1 lg. can evaporated milk
1 sm. onion (chopped)
1 sm. green pepper (chopped)
Accent

1 lb. ground beef
1 egg
1¼ tsp. salt
½ tsp. pepper

Cut a thin slice from top of the bread. Scoop out inside of loaf. Measure 2 c. of bread crumbs and soak in the milk 10 minutes. Mix all other ingredients, add bread crumbs. Fill bread shell and bake for 1 hour and 10 minutes at 350°.

Betty Guy.

* MEAT LOAF WELLINGTON *

1 med. onion (chopped)
butter
1 egg
1 lb. ground beef
½ c. seasoned bread stuffing mix
3 Tbsp. parmesan cheese (grated)

2 Tbsp. parsley (chopped)
salt — pepper
1 egg
1 Tbsp. water
1 pkg. refrigerated cresent rolls
* Easy gravy

Preheat oven to 350°. Saute onions in butter until soft. Lightly beat 1 egg in med. bowl, add beef, stuffing mix, cheese, parsley and salt and pepper to taste. Add onions, beat thoroughly. Form into a loaf shape (8 x 4 in.) and place on a baking sheet. Beat other egg with water. Separate rolls and lay over top and sides of loaf, patchwork fashion, sealing edges of rolls with egg-water mixture and bake about 1 hour. (If desired, additional rolls may be cut into shapes with cookie cutter and used to decorate the top. Slice and serve with the Easy gravy.

Easy gravy:
1 Pkg. instant brown gravy mix, ½ c. port or red wine, ½ c. water. Combine ingredients, in saucepan and cook over low heat for 5 minutes.   Ida Christoph.

* MEAT LOAF WITH PIQUANT SAUCE *

2/3 c. bread crumbs
1 c. milk
1½ lbs. ground beef
2 beaten eggs
¼ c. grated onions

1 tsp. salt
1/8 tsp. pepper
½ tsp. sage

Soak crumbs in milk. Add meat, eggs and seasonings and mix well. Pour into a loaf pan and cover with the following sauce.

Piquant Sause:

¼ c. catsup
3 Tbsp. brown sugar
  (more if you want it sweeter)

¼ tsp. nutmeg
1 tsp. powdered mustard

Bake at 350° for 45 minutes (This is an old family recipe).   Jean Keys.

* MUSHROOM — FILLED MEAT LOAF *

2 c. fresh mushrooms (sliced)
1 c. onion (chopped)
2 Tbsp. butter
½ c. sour cream
2 eggs
1½ lbs. ground beef

¾ c. bread crumbs
2 tsp. salt
1 Tbsp. Worcestershire sauce
* Sour Cream Sauce

Saute 1 c. mushrooms and onions in butter. Remove from heat and stir in sour cream. Combine remaining ingredients (except sour cream sauce and reserved mushrooms) and put half of the mixture into loaf pan (9 x 5 x 3 in.). Make shallow trough down the center of the meat for filling.

Spoon sour cream-mushroom mixture into this indentation. Shape the rest of meat over the filling, making sure that all the filling is covered.

Bake for 1 hour in a preheated oven (350°). Let stand 15 minutes before slicing. Garnish with remaining mushrooms.

* Sour Cream Sauce:

1 c. sour cream
1 tsp. Dijon mustard
1 tsp. prepared mustard

½ tsp. salt
pinch of nutmeg
pinch of white pepper

Stir together over low heat. Serve hot with the meat loaf.   Nathalia Richman.

* VEGETABLE MEAT LOAF *

1 c. oats
1 sm. onion (minced)
½ tsp. salt and pepper
½ tsp. favorite herb (optional)

½ c. hot low-sodium beef broth (or water)
2 egg whites or 1 whole egg
1 lb. lean ground beef
½ c. chopped or shredded vegetable, such as zucchini, carrots, broccoli, cooked greens.

In lg. bowl stir oats, onion, salt, pepper, herbs and broth, let stand 5 minutes or until oats swell slightly. Add egg, beef and vegetables, mix well. In greased shallow baking dish, shape in loaf. Bake in preheated oven 350° for 1 hour. Note: (This is a good recipe for meat and potato person).   Virginia Black Doyle.

160

* DELUXE MEAT LOAF *

1½ lbs. ground round steak
½ lb. ground pork
2 tsp. salt
½ tsp. pepper

1½ c. cracker crumbs
1 can peeled tomatoes (canned)
2 eggs (beaten)
* Dressing

Mix and fit into greased casserole. Bake 45 minutes at 350°.

Dressing:

½ c. brown sugar
½ c. crushed pineapple

½ tsp. ginger
2 Tbsp. melted butter.

Mix and spread on loaf — bake 15 minutes longer.   Betty Barry.

* SWISS STEAK WITH RICE *

3 lbs. round steak (¾ in. thick)
1 tsp. salt
dash pepper
4 onions (sliced)
3 Tbsp. shortening
¾ c. rice (uncooked)

1 bay leaf
1 can tomato soup
1 c. water
1 No. 2 can green beans

Cut meat into 6 pieces, season with salt and pepper. Brown onions in shortening, remove and brown meat.

Add onions, rice and bay leaf. Combine water, soup and liquid from the beans. Pour over the rice, cover and steam for 1 hour. Add beans and simmer for 30 minutes longer.   Elizabeth Betty Guy.

* MARINATED FLANK STEAK *

2 lbs. flank steak (scored)
1½ c. oil
3/4 shoyu
½ c. wine vinegar
¼ c. Worcestershire sauce

1/3 c. lemon juice
2 Tbsp. Dijon mustard
1 parsley sprig
1 garlic clove (minced)
fresh ground pepper

Place steak in a flat dish. Combine remaining ingredients in a blender and whirl briefly.

Pour over meat. Cover and refrigerate for 12 to 24 hours, turning occasionally. Remove meat from marinade (reserve marinade for other uses). Cook steak until well browned on outside and pink inside.

Cut meat into diagonally thin slices and arrange on serving platter.

                    Francis Wright.

* FLANK STEAK WITH BROCCOLI *

2 lbs. flank steak
1 Tbsp. cornstarch
2 Tbsp. shoyu
3 Tbsp. peanut oil
3 Tbsp. Sherry

1 bunch green onions (chopped)
1 head broccoli (use just florets)
1 lb. fresh mushrooms (sliced)

Slice meat on bias into 1/8 in. slices. Mix cornstarch and shoyu together and pour over meat and marinate for at least 5 hours. Heat oil in skillet and add meat and stir-fry until browned. Add remaining ingredients and stir-fry until vegetables are cripsy. Serve with steamed rice.   Charlene Do.

* POT ROAST (WISCONSIN) *

3½ lbs. rolled rump roast
2 Tbsp. beef suet
¼ c. cider vinegar
2 Tbsp. maple syrup
2 onions (chopped)
16 peppercorns

2 bay leaves
12 allspice berries
3 anchovy fillets
1 pt. beef stock
1 tsp. cornstarch

Brown all sides of roast in melted suet in a lg. skillet. Add all other ingredients and bring to a boil. Reduce heat and simmer for 1½ to 3 hours, until meat is tender. Thicken sauce with the cornstarch, pour over roast for serving.

                                                                        Nancy Ebsen.

* CHUCK ROAST IN FOIL *

1 chuck roast — 1 pkg. dry onion mix.

Place roast on heavy foil and sprinkle on onion mix. Seal well, and place in roasting pan, uncovered. Bake for 5 to 7 hours at 250° - 300°.   Evelyn Staley.

* BARBECUED BRISKET *

5—7 lbs. Brisket of beef — Brown in oven (450°) for 30 minutes.
Barbeque Sauce:
2 c. catsup
2 tsp. chili powder
2—3 Tbsp. liquid smoke
2 c. water

½ c. lemon juice
2 tsp. celery seed
2 tsp. salt

Mix ingredients and bring to a boil — pour over meat and bake at 300° for 2 to 3 hours. Baste frequently. Note: Omit browning and put in a cooking bag. Bastes itself. Another method.   Dorothy Tuttle.

* BEEF STEW *

2 lbs. chuck or round steak
2 Tbsp. oil
3 sm. onions (quartered)
3 carrots (quartered)
4 stalks celery (cut in 2 in. lengths)

1 Tbsp. flour
2–3 c. beef stock
1 tsp. tomato paste
Bouquet Garni
salt — pepper

Cut beef into 2 in. cubes. Heat oil over high heat and brown meat on all sides. Remove beef and add onion, carrots, celery and lower heat and simmer for 10 minutes. Pour off any access fat, stir in flour and cook 2–3 minutes longer. Pour in stock, bring mixture to a boil. Replace meat in pot, add tomato paste, bouquet garni, salt and pepper. (The stock should cover the beef). Cover and simmer, in oven at 350° until beef is tender. Stir occasionally, add more stock if needed. Serve with mashed potatoes. Jean Keys.

* CARAWAY BEEF STEW *

½ c. butter
3 lbs. chuck — sirloin (cubed)
1 doz. sm. onions (sliced)
2 Tbsp. paprika
1 Tbsp. caraway seeds
1 Tbsp. marjoram
* chopped parsley for garnish.

2 tsp. salt
1 Tbsp. lemon juice
1 garlic clove (crushed)
½ c. red wine
1 Tbsp. flour
1 Tbsp. tomato paste

In a lg, stew pot or Dutch oven, melt butter, add meat all at once, turning until cooked on all sides Mix in onion, half of the paprika, caraway, marjoram and salt and pepper. Add lemon juice, garlic and wine. Simmer uncovered, stirring occasionally, for 2 hours, until meat is tender. Blend remaining paprika, flour and tomato paste and mix into stew, simmer for 15 minutes longer. May be made in advance and refrigerated or frozen. Garnish with parsley. Lorna Burger.

* MY FAVORITE BEEF STEW *

1½ to 2 lbs. boneless beef
  (cut into 2 in. cubes)
4 potatoes (peeled)
4 carrots
3 celery stalks
2 medium onions

5 Tbsp. minute tapioca
2 Tbsp. sugar
2 Tbsp. salt
1 pt. canned tomatoes
pepper — salt
3 Tbsp. butter

Sear meat in bottom of a roasting pan over medium heat, but do not brown. Cut all vegetables into rather lg. pieces (diagonally). Add vegetables to the meat. Mix in tapicoa, sugar, salt and pepper. Bake covered in preheated oven (275°) for 4 hrs. Stir once or twice with wooden spoon during baking. Francis Wright.

* ALL DAY BEEF STEW *

3 lbs. beef stew (trimmed — cut into 1 in cubes)
½ c. flour
4 tsp. salt
1 can (10½ oz.) beef broth
2 c. dry red wine
4 med. carrots (cut in 1 in. pieces)
4 med. potatoes (quartered)
1 bag (20 oz.) frozen green beans
1½ lbs. sm. white onions
1 Tbsp. brown sugar
1 bay leaf

Preheat oven to 250°. In Dutch oven, toss meat with the flour and salt until meat Is evenly covered. Stir in diluted beef broth and remaining ingredients. Cover and bake for 4—6 hours. Stir occasionally.   Jean Keys.

* BEEF STROGANOFF *

1½ lbs. sirloin tip steak (cut into ¼ x 1½" pieces)
2 Tbsp. butter
1½ c. beef bouillion
1 c. sour cream
dash of pepper
6 oz. mushrooms (sliced)
½ c. chopped onions
2½ Tbsp flour
½ tsp. salt
2 Tbsp. Sherry wine

Brown meat in the butter, push aside and brown onions and mushrooms. Add broth and bring to a boil. Add flour, blended with the Sherry and cook until slightly thick and smooth. Add sour cream last. (Do not boil). Season with salt and pepper. Serve over hot noodles.   Jean Keys.

* DEVILED BEEF RIBS *

2 racks beef ribs (roasted)
2/3 c. spicy brown mustard
2 Tbsp. brown sugar
2/3 c. bread crumbs

Cut ribs into serving pieces. Combine mustard and brown sugar, using a brush, coat each rib and then roll into bread crumbs. Arrange ribs (rounded side up) on 2 cookie sheets and bake in preheated oven (425°) until ribs are nicely browned. May also be roasted on a barbecue, with hot coals.   Billie Do.

*BEER STEAK *

1—3 lbs. round steak (about 1 in. thick)
flour
1 lg. onion (chopped)
½ tsp. thyme
celery — parsley
1 can (12 oz.) beer (room temperature)
¼ c. oil

With the back of a lg. spoon, work flour into the steak. Pour oil into a lg. frying pan or a Dutch oven and simmer onions until soft. Push aside and brown meat on both sides. Make bouquet garni of parsley and celery and put on steak. Add the thyme and beer and bake at 250 — 275° for 2 to 3 hours. Add a little water if it needs more liquid. (This is delicious and the meat is tender).   Jean Keys.

* BARBECUED BEEF *

5—6 lbs. beef 7 bone roast
1 lg. onion
3—4 bay leaves

Boil until meat is tender. Cool and keep stock.

Barbecue sauce:

1 lg. onion (chopped)	2 c. catsup
5 stalks celery (cut-up)	½ tsp. salt
1 green pepper (cut-up)	pepper to taste
1 Tbsp. vinegar	

Saute onions, celery and green pepper, until soft. Add salt — pepper, vinegar and catsup and simmer, keep warm. Shred the meat and add to the sauce. Toast hamburger buns and serve beef on open bun.   Elinor Edmondson.

* STEAK AND KIDNEY PIE *

4 lbs. top round steak	oil
1 lb. beef or lamb kidneys	butter
2 Tbsp. butter	4 c. canned consomme
1¼ c. flour	2 c. beer
2 Tbsp. paprika	2 c. mushrooms (diced)
2 tsp. salt	1 single — crust pastry
1 egg yolk	
2 Tbsp. milk	

Preheat oven to 350°. Remove fat from steak and cut into 1 in. cubes and set aside. Remove fat from kidneys. Blanch kidneys, removing any fat or membrane and slice thinly. Saute in butter for 4—5 minutes. Shake beef cubes in a mixture of flour — salt — pepper and paprika. Brown meat in a skillet, a few batches at a time. (Add butter or oil if needed). Place beef cubes and kidneys in a lg. casserole. Deglaze skillet with 2 c. stock, add to casserole with the remaining stock and beer. Bake covered for 1½ to 2 hours until meat is tender.
Increase oven to 400°. Add mushrooms and mix. Cover with single layer pastry crust. Brush with mixture of egg yolk and milk. Bake for 15 to 20 minutes or until crust is golden brown.   Adele Davis.

* DRIED BEEF AND CORN COMBINATION *

1 c. dried beef (rinsed —drained)
2 Tbsp. onion (minced)
2 Tbsp. butter
1 Tbsp. flour
¾ c. milk

1 can (17 oz.) cream corn
½ c. Cheddar cheese (shredded)
2 Tbsp. green onions (chopped)
2 Tbsp. pimientos (sliced)

Lightly fry beef and onions in butter until beef begins to curl. Stir in flour, add milk, cooking until thickened. Add corn and cheese and simmer until cheese is melted. Serve in buttered toast cups.

Toast Cups:

Butter muffin tins. Remove crusts from 8—10 thin slices of sandwich bread. Brush with butter and press into muffin tins. Bake in medium oven until toasted. May be made in advance, but toast the cups last.   Roberta Chateauneuf.

* CORNED BEEF BAKED IN POTATOES *

6 medium baking potatoes
2 Tbsp. butter
1 med. onion (minced)
1 garlic clove (minced)
3 c. corned beef cooked — ground)

2 eggs (beaten)
3 Tbsp. cream
1 Tbsp. dijon mustard
¼ c. parsley (minced)
dash of tabasco
salt — pepper

Preheat oven to 400°. Scrub potatoes, dry thoroughly and rub skins with cooking oil. Bake 1 hour until potatoes are soft. Melt butter in a skillet and add onion and garlic and saute until soft and transparent. Cut potatoes in half and scoop insides from each shell. Mash lightly with fork. Combine remaining ingredients with the potatoes and spoon lightly into shells. Place on baking sheet and bake for 30 minutes until tops are browned.   Daisy Alexander.

* CHIPPED BEEF IN SOUR CREAM *

½ lb. chipped beef
2 Tbsp. butter (melted)
1 pt. sour cream
1 jar (6 oz.) artichoke hearts
   (thinly sliced)

½ tsp. paprika
½ c. dry white wine
1 Tbsp. Parmesan cheese (grated)

Cover chipped beef with water and parboil for 2 minutes. Drain. In skillet melt butter and add chipped beef, sour cream and artichoke hearts. Mix all other ingredients (except the Parmesan cheese) and add to the chipped beef. (Add a little flour if needed). Serve over hot buttered toast and sprinkle with the Parmesan cheese.   Dorothy Tuttle.

* SALAMI *

4 lbs. ground beef
¼ c. curing salt
1½ tsp. garlic powder
1¼ tsp. cracked pepper
1 Tbsp. liquid smoke
* Nylon netting

Mix ingredients well, cover and chill for 24 hours.

Divide mixture into 4ths. Shape each into a compact 8 in. log. Place each on a 12 x 18 in. piece of Nylon netting. Roll up tightly, tie ends with string. Place logs on broiler pan with rack. Bake in 225° oven for 4 hours.

Remove from oven, take off netting. Pat logs well with paper towels, to absorb excess fat. Cool slightly then wrap in foil and refrigerate or freeze. (Can add mustard seed to mix if desired).

(Keeps in refrigerator up to 3 weeks or frozen up to 2 months.   Georgia Beasley.

* PORK CHOPS IN THE HAY *

4 thick pork chops (trimmed)
salt — pepper
1 Tbsp. butter
2 Tbsp. olive oil
1 Tbsp. parsley (chopped)
¼ tsp. thyme
1 c. chicken bouillon
¾ c. long grain rice
1 c. onions (sliverd)
½ c. each julienne-cut celery, green
     pepper, mushrooms, ham.
½ c. white wine

Season chops with salt and pepper. Brown in heated butter and oil. Remove. Add rice to skillet and simmer for 2 minutes. Return chops to pan, add herbs, wine and chicken broth, cover and simmer for 5 minutes. Add vegetables and simmer until they are slightly crunchy.   Ruth Tufte.

* CHERRIED PORK CHOPS (GERMAN) *

4 pork loin chops (1½ in. thick)
2 Tbsp. oil
1 oz. Kirsch (heated)
¼ c. beef stock
1 can (1 lb.) pitted dark sweet
   cherries
salt — pepper
½ tsp. each of nutmeg, cloves and
     marjoram
1 tsp. grated lemon rind
2 Tbsp. lemon juice
2 Tbsp. cornstarch
½ c. toasted walnuts (chopped)

Trim excess fat from chops. Salt and pepper chops generously. Heat oil in skillet over medium heat, add chops and cook until browned on all sides. Drain off fat and flambe chops with the heated Kirsch. Pour in stock, cover and simmer for 1 hour over low heat. Drain the cherries. Add seasonings and lemon rind to the syrup. Add lemon juice to the cornstarch and slowly add to syrup mixture. Simmer over low heat until mixture is thick and glossy. When chops have cooked 45 minutes, pour syrup into pan with the chops. Just before serving, add reserved cherries and walnuts and simmer until heated through. Excellent served with creamed spinach and potato pancakes.   Adele Davis.

* PORK CHOPS AND SAUERKRAUT *

½ lb. bacon
1 can (19 oz.) sauerkraut
1 can (15 oz.) applesauce
1 Tbsp. brown sugar
salt — pepper

½ tsp. dry mustard
¼ tsp. paprika
¼ c. dry white wine
6 shoulder pork chops

Cut bacon in pieces and fry crisp. Mix sauerkraut, applesauce, mustard, paprika, wine and salt and pepper to taste. Place all in shallow casserole. Top with pork chops (that have been sauted in the bacon fat). Cover and bake for 1 hour at 350°.   Dorothy Tuttle.

* PORK CHOPS — AURORA *

6—1 in. thick pork chops
1 clove garlic
4 Tbsp. oleo
1 c. sour cream
1 Tbsp. vinegar
Parsley (minced)

1 Tbsp. Worcestershire sauce
½ tsp. salt
¼ tsp. pepper
½ tsp. paprika
3 bay leaves

Rub chops with garlic, brown in the oleo. Place in shallow casserole. Mix other ingredients and pour over chops. Place a bay leaf on each. Sprinkle with chopped parsley. Bake 40 minutes at 350°. Note: Flavor in enhanced if baked in the morning and reheated at dinner-time.   Dorothy Tuttle.

* SPARERIBS WITH SAUERKRAUT *

3 lbs. spareribs
1 qt. sauerkraut
2 c. flour
1 tsp. baking powder

1 c. milk
1 egg (beaten)
salt — pepper

Cut spareribs into portions and place in the bottom of a roasting pan. Season to taste. Add the sauerkraut and bake for 1½ hours at 350°.
Make dumplings by combining the flour, milk, baking powder and egg. Drop by spoonfuls on the sauerkraut. Cover the pan tightly and finish by baking for 30 minutes longer. Note: This recipe was made famous by the Dutch Settlers in Pennsylvania.   Mrs. Ben Box.

* SWEET AND SOUR RIBS *

3 lbs. meaty Spareribs
Sauce:

¼ c. brown	1½ tsp. dark corn syrup
3 Tbsp. lemon juice	½ tsp. ground ginger
1 sm. jar apricots (strained type)	dash of pepper sauce
1½ tsp. molasses	¼ c. chili sauce
½ tsp. dry mustard	1 garlic clove (pressed)
	1 Tbsp. shoyu

Sprinkle ribs with salt and pepper and broil 3 minutes per side. Place in an oblong baking dish. Mix all sauce ingredients in a saucepan and heat briefly until combined. Pour half of sauce over ribs and bake in oven (350°) for 30 minutes. Pour remaining sauce over ribs and bake for another 30 minutes. Place on heated platter to serve.

Lorna Burger.

* SPICY RIBS *

8 lbs. (8 racks) spareribs (parboiled)	1 Tbsp. lemon juice
3 cans (8 oz. each) tomato sauce	1 garlic clove (minced)
½ c. chicken stock	2 tsp. dry mustard
½ c. onion (minced)	3 tsp. chili powder
3 Tbsp. Worcestershire sauce	1 tsp. salt
3 Tbsp. brown sugar	
2 Tbsp. honey	

Combine all ingredients (except ribs) in saucepan and bring to a boil. Reduce heat and simmer for 30 minutes uncovered. Brush ribs with sauce and grill or broil over hot heat for 45 minutes or until tender, basting and turning frequently. Separate ribs into serving portions. Pass remaining sauce.

Charlene Do.

* PEACH GLAZED SPARERIBS *

1 can (16 oz.) sliced peaches	1 clove garlic
½ c. brown sugar	1 tsp. salt
¼ c. catsup	1 tsp. powdered ginger
¼ c. vinegar	dash of pepper
2 Tbsp. Soy sauce	4 lbs. ribs

Sieve peaches (do not use the juice). Puree in blender or by hand. Add remaining ingredients (except ribs). Cut ribs into serving pieces, bake or broil (about 1 hour), remove fat. Pour on glaze and bake 45 minutes longer in a 350° oven. Glaze again before removing from the oven.

Jean Keys.

* BARBECUED SPARERIBS *

4 lbs. spareribs
1 c. sliced onions
1 c. catsup
1 c. water
2 tsp. salt

2 Tbsp. Worcestershire sauce
¼ c. vinegar
¼ c. brown sugar
2 tsp. dry mustard
1 tsp. paprika

Cut spareribs into serving pieces. Brown them in a baking pan over surface heat. Combine the other ingredients and pour over ribs. Cover. Bake in a moderate oven (350°) for 3—4 hours. Spoon the sauce over the ribs several times during baking. Bake uncovered for 15 minutes.   Mae Gomes.

* SIZZLING COUNTRY RIBS *

4 lbs. pork loin ribs
    (cut into serving pieces)
¼ c. brown sugar (packed)
2 Tbsp. cider vinegar

1 tsp. salt
1 tsp. chili powder
¾ c. catsup

Cover pork with water and cook, bring to a boil, simmer for 1 hour. Prepare outdoor grill. In a sm. bowl, combine remaining ingredients. Put ribs on grill, brush sauce on several times and cook 20 minutes. Turn over, brush with sauce and cook a few minutes longer.   Jean Keys.

* TENDERLOIN OF PORK *

6 to 8 lbs. tenderloin pork roast

salt — pepper
Sauce:

½ stick butter
6 shallots (sliced)
½ c. flour
2 c. dry white wine
1 Tbsp. fresh mushrooms (sliced)
1 Tbsp. chives (chopped)

1 tsp. marjoram
2 bay leaves

salt — pepper
2 spanish onions (peeled — sliced)
1 c. sauerkraut and juice
2 c. sour cream
4 bouillon cubes

Preheat oven to 500°. Rub roast with salt and pepper and ½ tsp. Marjoram. Place roast in a baking pan with bay leaves and roast uncovered for 20 to 30 minutes. Remove roast from oven and reduce heat to 350°. In a saucepan, melt butter until it sizzles, brown shallots lightly. Add mushrooms, onions, bouillon cubes, sauerkraut and juice, sour cream, salt, pepper, chives and remaining marjoram. Blend well. Pour sauce over meat, cover and return to oven. Roast 2½ hours. (To test for doneness, pierce with a fork. Juices should run clear, not pink). Slice and serve immediately.   Billie Do.

* PICKLED PORK *

4 lbs. pork butts
4 tsp. salt
9 good sized garlics
3 hot Hawaiian peppers

1 c. vinegar
¼ c. water
5 Tbsp. Wesson oil

Have butcher cut pork butt into small pieces, about 2 x 2 in. Wash pork and trim excess fat, leaving a little fat on each piece. Peel the garlic and mince. Crush or mash peppers. In a lg. bowl place garlic, salt, hot pepper and mix well. Add vinegar and water, stir, and add pork pieces. Mix all ingredients well, cover and place in refrigerator for 36 to 40 hours, stirring the bottom to the top about twice daily.

Place pork in a pot and bring to a boil, lower heat to a steady boiling point. Cook 1 hour or until tender. Remove pork, add oil to a skillet and brown meat on all sides. Serve with sweet bread and scramble eggs.   Mae Gomes.

* SHISH — KEBAB COMBINATIONS *

* Beef cubes with small onions, red and green pepper, and mushrooms.
* Thin slices of veal wrapped around precooked pork sausage with Gerkins and pickled onions.
* Beef chunks with parboiled leek cubes and yellow turnip wedges.
* Small pieces of calves liver, chicken, beef and seasonings.
* Cocktail sausages with parboiled onions and cheese cubes, brushed with currant jelly spiked with horseradish.
* Bacon wrapped oysters alternated with stuffed olives.
* Eggplant cubes, tomato wedges, celery chunks and onion slices.

* SHISH — KEBABS (ARMENIAN) *

3 lbs. leg of lamb
½ lb. onions (sliced)
½ tsp. salt
½ tsp. cracked black pepper

½ c. Sherry
2 Tbsp. olive oil
1 tsp. oregano
1 garlic clove (minced)

Bone the lamb and remove all fat and gristle, cut into 1 in. cubes. Mix all the ingredients and add lamb and marinate at least 4 hours or preferably overnite. Broil on all sides (do not overcook).

Lamb should have a pink tinge in center. Serve with rice or pilaf.

Adele Davis.

* MUSTARD SHISH — KEBABS *

2 lbs. boned leg lamb (cut into 1 in. cubes)
3 Tbsp. Dijon mustard
2 Tbsp. wine vinegar
2 Tbsp. olive oil
¼ tsp. rosemary

¼ tsp. sage
3 garlic cloves (minced)
salt — pepper
1 lg. green pepper (cut in ¾ in. squares)
butter (room temperature)

Combine mustard, vinegar, olive oil, rosemary, sage and garlic in a medium bowl. Add lamb and sprinkle with salt and pepper. Marinate in refrigerator for at least 3 hours. Remove meat ½ hour before cooking. Preheat broiler or barbecue. Alternate meat and peppers on skewers and cook until meat is browned. Brush with butter while cooking.   Francis Wright.

* TURKISH KEBABS *

1½ lbs. lean lamb
(cut into 1 in. cubes)
¼ c. olive oil
¼ c. vinegar
½ c. dry white wine
3 medium onions (quartered)
1 sm. eggplant (unpeeled — cut in 1 in. cubes)

1 onion (chopped)
1 tsp. pepper
1 garlic clove (minced)
¼ tsp. cloves
4 bay leaves
* garnish — chopped mint

Marinate lamb cubes for at least 4 hours in mixture of oil, vinegar, wine, chopped onions, garlic, cloves. Drain and pat dry. Spear onion quarters, lamb, eggplant and bay leaves on four 14 in. skewers. First start with the lamb cube, next the bay leaf, an onion quarter, a lamb cube, eggplant cube, etc., until skewer is filled. Brush liberally with olive oil and broil close to heat source, rotating skewers and brushing frequently with oil, until lamb is cooked to desired doneness.   Roberta Chateauneuf.

*STUFFED LEG OF LAMB *

3 garlic cloves
3 lg. shallots
¼ lb. mushrooms
2 Tbsp. butter
1 slice white bread (torn into pcs.)
½ lb. lamb (cubed)
1/3 c. oil
½ c. dry white wine
1 Tbsp. lemon juice

1 leg of lamb (4 lbs. after boning)
½ c. parsley (chopped)
¼ c. pistachio nuts (blanched — skinned)
1 lg. egg (beaten)
salt — pepper
1 tsp. each thyme, oregano, and savory
Garnish: parsley, lemon wedges, cherry tomatoes

Mince garlic, shallots and mushrooms. Heat 2 Tbsp. butter and 2 Tbsp. oil in skillet and saute mushroom mixture for 3 to 5 minutes. Mince bread and parsley together and combine with the mushrooms. Chop the ½ lb. lamb coarsely and add to bread mixture, season with salt and pepper.

Sprinkle inside of lamb with salt and pepper. Spread with stuffing. Roll up lengthwise neatly and tie with string. Season with herbs. Salt and pepper. (Lamb may be prepared the day before at this stage). Combine 1/3 c. oil, wine, lemon juice, and salt. Place meat on a rack in baking pan and sear in preheated oven (450°) for 15 minutes, reduce heat to (350°) and roast about 1—1½ hours, basting frequently during cooking. Allow meat to rest 10 to 15 minutes before slicing. Place on warmed platter and garnish with parsley, lemon wedges and cherry tomatoes.   Ida Christoph

* LAMB CURRY (INDIA) *

1/3 butter
3 medium onions
2 garlic cloves
1 carrot (chopped)
1 celery stalk (chopped)
½ green pepper (chopped)
2 Tbsp. parsley (minced)
1 Tbsp. flour
1½ c. beef stock
½ c. Sherry
½ c. tomato (diced)
3 c. cooked lamb (trimmed of all
    fat and cut into 1 in. cubes)
½ c. coconut milk

¼ c. lime juice
3 Tbsp. chutney
2½ Tbsp. brown sugar
2 Tbsp. golden raisins
1/3 tsp. curry powder (moistened
    with water)
½ tsp. cinnamon
½ tsp. cumin
1/8 tsp. nutmeg
salt — black pepper
2 tart apples (peeled — quartered —
    cubed)
¼ c. yogurt or sour cream

Melt butter in a sauce pan and add onion, garlic, carrot, celery, green pepper and parsley and saute until onion is golden brown. Combine flour with a little stock in a small bowl. Add to sauteed vegetables and blend thoroughly. Stir remaining stock, wine and tomato and simmer for 5 minutes. Add coconut milk. Lime juice, chutney, brown sugar, spices, salt and pepper to taste and simmer for 20 to 30 minutes. Gently stir in lamb, apple and yogurt and heat through. Serve in center of a rice ring on a platter, surround platter with bowls of condiments. Condiments:

Chopped hard cooked eggs, minced green onions, chopped peanuts, chutney, sliced black olives, raisins, shredded coconut and a few mint leaves.

Adele Davis.

* LAMB STEW (MOROCCAN) *

5 lbs. boneless lamb
  (cut in 1 in. cubes)
2 Tbsp. cooking oil
2¾ c. onions (chopped)
2 garlic cloves (chopped)
1/3 parsley (snipped)
2 whole cloves
1 tsp. ginger
¾ c. golden raisins
2/3 c. blanched almonds
5 hard-cooked eggs (halved)
¼ tsp. saffron
1½ tsp salt
1 tsp. pepper
2 cans (16 oz. each) tomatoes
2 bay leaves
2 lg. sweet onions (cut in quarters)
3 Tbsp. butter

Brown lamb in skillet with the cooking oil. Saute onions and garlic until browned. Stir in parsley, cloves, ginger and saffron and cook for 2 minutes. Stir in salt, pepper, tomatoes and lamb. Add bay leaves. Bring to a boil and simmer until meat is tender. Simmer uncovered until slightly thickened. Remove bay leaves. Saute onion quarters in butter until golden, remove and keep warm. Saute almonds in skillet until golden, stir in raisins and keep warm.

To serve: Turn stew onto a lg. serving platter.

Arrange onions and eggs around the edges. Sprinkle with almonds and raisins.

Francis Wright.

* LAMB CHOPS WITH CAULIFLOWER *

2 (5 oz.) lamb chops (trimmed of fat)
3 Tbsp. nonfat milk
2 tsp. butter
1 tsp. flour
1 c. cooked cauliflower
salt
fresh ground pepper
2 egg yolks
1 Tbsp. Parmesan cheese (grated)

Puree enough cauliflower in a blender to make 1 c. Set aside. Preheat broiler. Combine 2 Tbsp. butter and flour in sm. saucepan over low heat and simmer for 3 minutes, stirring constantly, as mixture thickens. Add pureed cauliflower, salt and pepper and mix well. Beat egg yolk with remaining 2 Tbsp. milk and stir into cauliflower mixture. Add Parmesan, remove from heat.

Broil lamb chops 4 in. from broiler for 5 minutes on each side and then cover with cauliflower mixture and return to the broiler and broil until puffed and golden brown. Serve at once.

Note: This recipe is for 2 servings. For more servings, increase the recipe for portions you wish to serve.

Nathalia Richman.

* GRILLED LAMB RIBLETS *

3 lbs. lamb riblets (parboiled) 1 Tbsp. lemon juice
1 can (16 oz.) applesauce 1 Tbsp. honey
2 garlic cloves (minced) 1 Tbsp. Worcestershire sauce
2 Tbsp. brown sugar ½ tsp. salt

Combine all ingredients (except lamb). Brush generously on riblets. Grill or broil over very hot heat for 25 to 30 minutes, turning and basting frequently until desired doneness.   Lucille Grimes.

* LAMB WITH COLD PEANUT SAUCE (INDONESIAN) *

2 racks lamb (fat trimmed) 3 Tbsp. honey
¾ c. oil 2 bay leaves
1/3 c. celery (diced) 2 tsp. A—1 sauce
1/3 c. onion (diced) 1 tsp. oregano
1 garlic clove (minced) 2 dashes hot pepper sauce
½ c. prepared mustard 1 lg. lemon (juice — peel)
¼ cider vinegar * Cold peanut sauce
3 Tbsp. curry powder

Heat oil in medium skillet over medium heat. Add onions, celery and garlic and simmer until onion is transparent. Reduce heat, stir in all the remaining ingredients (except lamb) and simmer briefly until heated through. Pour into a bowl and cool slightly. Cover and refrigerate for 2 hours. to allow flavors to blend. Transfer marinade to a lg. shallow baking dish or pan. Add lamb turning several times to coat. Place baking rack in center of oven and preheat oven to 550°. Grease baking pan. Drain marinade from meat and set aside. Wrap lamb in foil, leaving meaty portions exposed. Place in pan and brush with marinade. For rare meat, bake 15 minutes, turning once and basting. For more done meat, bake additional time.

Place on warm platter and serve with the Cold Peanut Sauce.

* Cold Peanut sauce:

½ c. creamy peanut butter ¼ tsp. salt
   (room temperature) dash hot pepper sauce
½ c. coconut milk 2 Tbsp. lemon juice
2 Tbsp. shoyu
1 Tbsp. Worcestershire sauce

Combine all ingredients in sm. mixing bowl and blend thoroughly. Cover and chill and serve cold.   Francis Wright.

* BAKED SPICED HAM *
(Thomas Jellerson Favorite)

1 smoked ham (12 to 15 lbs.). Not precooked.
Soak ham in water overnite. Drain. Cover with water and simmer for 3 hours.
Let cool in water cooked in. Drain and trim.
Place in baking dish, stick with cloves and cover with brown sugar. Bake in oven
350° for 2 hours. Baste with white wine.   From a very old cookbook.

* PLUM — GLAZED HAM *

Precooked ham
whole cloves
* Glaze:

¼ c. chutney (chopped)   1 Tbsp. Dijon mustard
¼ c. plum jam   1 garlic clove (minced)
1 tsp. wine vinegar   ½ c. brown sugar
1/8 tsp. Tabasco

Preheat oven to 325°. With sharp knife remove any rind and excess fat from
ham. Score any remaining fat in diamond pattern and stud with cloves at each
intersection. Place ham on rack in roasting pan. (If ham weighs under 8 lbs. plan
on cooking for 19 to 20 minutes per lb. If larger, cook it 10 to 15 minutes per
lb.). Place ham in oven and bake required time. Before ham is ready, spread
chutney mixture evenly over the top and sides, cover surface with brown sugar
and continue baking until ready. Let stand 10 minutes before slicing.

To make glaze:

In a saucepan combine chutney, plum jam, vinegar, Tabasco, mustard and garlic
and heat mixture until syrupy.   Roberta Chateauneuf.

* HAM IN FRUIT WINE SAUCE *

1 slice ham (2 in. thick)   ¼ c. brown sugar
1 Tbsp. Dijon or plain mustard   ¼ tsp. cinnamon
1 can fruit cocktail   ¼ tsp. cloves
½ c. port wine   1 Tbsp. cornstarch

Place ham in shallow baking pan. Spread with mustard. Drain fruit cocktail.
Use the liquid to mix with the rest of the ingredients. Cook mixture, stirring
constantly until sauce bubbles and is transparent. Pour over ham, cover and bake
(350°) for 20 minutes. Put fruit on top and bake for 10 minutes longer.
(Also good served cool as a leftover).   Opal Harper.

* HAM LOAF *

¼ lb. brown sugar
2 slices pineapple
1 lb. ham (grounded)
½ lb. pork (ground)
1 c. soft bread crumbs
¼ c. tsp. pepper

1 egg
1 c. milk
¼ c. onion (minced)
¼ c. celery (minced)
½ tsp. salt

Spread brown sugar on the bottom of greased loaf pan, top with the pineapple. Combine remaining ingredients. Pack meat mixture into loaf pan over pineapple. Bake at 350° for 1 hour and 30 minutes.   **Jean Ariyoshi.**

* HAM LOAVES WITH CHERRY SAUCE *

1½ lbs. ground ham
1½ c. soft bread crumbs
1 egg (beaten)
* Cherry Sauce.

½ tsp. dry mustard
¼ c. brown sugar
1 tsp. prepared mustard

Combine ham, bread crumbs, beaten egg, and dry mustard and mix well. Fill greased muffin tins with mixture and round tops. Mix brown sugar and prepared mustard and spread over tops. Bake at 350° for 45 minutes.
Serve with cherry sauce.

Cherry Sauce:

1 No. 2 can red pie cherries
2 Tbsp. cornstarch
½ c. sugar

Dissolve cornstarch in cherry juice, add sugar and cherries. Cook over low heat until thickened. To serve: place ham loaves on platter and pour sauce on top. Sprinkle with a little nutmeg.   **Francis Wright.**

* HAM MOUSSE *

1 Tbsp. gelatin
¼ c. cold water
2 c. cooked ham (ground)
½ c. celery (finely chopped)

1 Tbsp. parsley (minced)
2 Tbsp. prepared horseradish
1 c. heavy cream (whipped)

Stir gelatin into cold water to dissolve. Set over boiling water to completely dissolve. Cool. Stir in ham, parsley, and celery. Whip cream and fold into mixture. Pack in ring mold and chill. To serve: unmold on round plate and fill center with Waldorf salad. Surround with lettuce. Overlap half slices of oranges and artichoke halves and dot with black olives.   **Judy Pieklo.**

* VEAL ROLLATINE WITH POLENTA *

2 lbs. veal (cut from leg or shoulder)
6 Tbsp. butter
1 garlic clove (crushed)
6 parsley sprigs (leaves only
    chopped)
salt — pepper
Flour

3 slices Proscuitto (minced)
6 Tbsp. parmesan cheese (grated)
2 Tbsp. olive oil
1 medium tomato (chopped)
* Polenta

Cut veal into 8 slices. Place between waxed paper and pound thin. Sprinkle lightly with flour, brush one side with butter. Mix garlic, parsley, salt, pepper, Proscuitto and half of the cheese. Add 2 Tbsp. butter and mix well. Spread 1 tsp. mixture down center of meat, roll up and secure with toothpick.
Heat remaining butter and oil in a skillet, add meat and brown on all sides. Add tomato and simmer for 25 minutes.

Polento:

1 c. cornmeal
1 c. cold water
1 tsp. salt
4 c. boiling water.

2 Tbsp. butter
½ to ¾ c. melted butter
½ to ¾ c. Parmesan cheese (grated)

Combine cornmeal, cold water and salt. Stir into boiling water, stir constantly, over low heat. Add butter and stir. Place in greased shallow pan and chill. Cut into ½ in. slices and slowly saute in ½ olive oil and ½ butter. To serve: Place serving of Polento on each plate and add two veal rolls and sprinkle with remaining cheese.

Evelyn Staley.

* WIENER SCHNITZEL (GERMAN) *

4 veal chops
bread crumbs
2 Tbsp. fat
lemon slices
fried or poached egg

salt — pepper
1 egg (beaten)
lemon juice
capers

Cut veal into serving pieces. Dip in egg, then bread crumbs and brown in hot fat in a skillet. Sprinkle with lemon juice.
 Serve on platter and garnish with lemon slices and top with fried or poached egg, and capers.
(May top with sour cream in place of egg).

Adele Davis.

* APPLE STUFFED VEAL ROLLS *

6 Tbsp. butter
1 onion (chopped)
1 garlic clove (minced)
1 c. soft bread crumbs
2 c. apples (peeled — chopped)
1 tsp. salt

½ tsp. poultry seasoning
12 veal scallops (thin)
flour
¼ c. apple cider or juice
2 Tbsp. Calvados or Apple Jack
Garnish: Cooked crabapples or cooked
apple slices

Melt 4 Tbsp. butter in a skillet and saute onion until golden. Add garlic, bread crumbs, apple, salt and poultry seasoning. Stir over low heat until well mixed. Pound veal until very thin. Divide stuffing among veal slices, roll up and secure with toothpicks. Coat veal rolls with flour. Heat remaining butter in a skillet. Brown rolls well on all sides. Add Calvados. Simmer covered for 25 minutes until tender. Remove toothpicks and place on a heated platter. Spoon sauce over veal. Garnish with crabapples or apple slices. **Jean Lyle.**

* ROAST VEAL NORMANDE *

1½ lbs. veal roast (boned — rolled)
sage
celery salt
pepper
½ stick butter
2 medium onions (sliced)
1 Tbsp. vegetable oil
2 medium carrots (sliced)
2 celery stalks (diced)
1 garlic clove (minced)

1 Bay leaf
5 medium green apples
water
2 Tbsp. lemon juice
4 Tbsp. lemon juice
1½ c. heavy cream
t tsp. tarragon
1 c. Swiss cheese (grated)
1/3 c. Cognac
1 tsp. thyme

Preheat oven to 350°. Rub roast with sage and sprinkle with celery salt and pepper. Heat 2 Tbsp. butter and 1 Tbsp. oil in roasting pan, add roast and brown lightly on all sides. Remove pan from heat. Scatter onions around meat, add carrots, celery, garlic, and thyme. Roast for 30 minutes. Turn meat, cover loosely with foil and continue to roast for 45 minutes. Turn roast and bake for an additional 30 minutes.

Peel and core apples, cover with lemon juice. Melt remaining butter and saute apples until just soft, but not limp. Heat Cognac over medium heat in sm. pan, ignite. Pour over meat. Remove roast from pan and place on a heated platter. Keep warm Add cream to roasting pan and place over medium heat. Bring to a gentle boil stirring and scraping bottom to get all browned parts. Add tarragon and simmer for a few minutes, strain and reserve.

Increase oven heat to 450°. Slice roast and put apples between slices, keep roast and apples as compact as possible. Pour 2 to 3 Tbsp. pan liquid over roast, sprinkle with grated cheese. Place all in oven for about 7 minutes.

Place roast on a serving platter. Transfer remaining gravy to a bowl and serve with roast.   Nancy Ebsen.

* DILLED VEAL ROAST *

1½ c. sour cream   ¼ c. fresh dill (snipped)
1 pkg. onion soup mix   salt — pepper
3 to 4 lbs. veal roast

Preheat oven to 325°. Combine sour cream, soup mix, dill, salt and pepper, in sm. baking dish or roasting pan. Mix well. Add veal, cover and bake until almost tender (about 2½ hours). Uncover and bake until veal is browned and tender (about 30 minutes longer).

To serve, slice across grain and arrange on serving platter. Pour sauce over slices.
                                                             Billie Do.

* MEXICAN CHILI *

¼ c. salad oil   2 Tbsp. chili powder
1 c. chopped onion   1 Tbsp. sugar
1 c. chopped green peppers   3 tsp. salt
1 clove garlic, crushed   ¼ tsp. pepper
2 lbs. beef   2 bay leaves
2 cans (1 lb. size) tomatoes   1 tsp. cumin
   (drained)   1 tsp. basil leaves
1 can (6 oz.) tomato paste   dash Cayenne
2 cans (1 lb. size) kidney beans
½ c. grated Cheddar cheese

In hot oil saute onion, pepper and garlic. Stir 5 minutes then drain off fat. In a 5 qt. Dutch oven, brown meat, drain off fat. Add vegetables mixture, then all remaining ingredients (except beans and cheese). Simmer ½ hour till very thick. Add beans, heat several minutes sprinkle with cheese and place under broiler for a few minutes.

(If you like a thinner sauce, save the canned juices from tomatoes and add to this).   Jean Keys.

* EGGPLANT CHILI *

2 c. kidney beans (cooked)

2 onions (quartered)

1 garlic clove (sliced)

1 tsp. oregano

3 lbs. stewing beef (cubed)

flour

oil

1 egg plant (unpeeled — cut in 1 in. cubes)

1 green pepper (chopped)

1 pkg. dry onion soup mix

3 Tbsp. chili powder

4 cloves

1 tsp. basil

1 can (2 lbs.) tomatoes

2 Tbsp. vinegar

¼ c. tomato paste

Dust beef cubes with flour and brown in a skillet with oil. Add spices and onion soup mix, add small amount of water and bring to a boil. Reduce heat and simmer until meat is tender. Brown eggplant in another skillet and add eggplant and beans to meat. Heat together thoroughly.   Rebecca Dixon.

 F·I·S·H

* MOILUA PERNO *
(Red Snapper)

Marinate 1 lb. Moilua in juice of 1 lemon, 2 oz. Perno and dash of Soy sauce for 1 hour or more. Flour fillets and saute in hot oil for 2 minutes on each side. Remove from pan.

To marinade, add 2 oz. unsalted butter, ½ c. sliced mushrooms, 1 c. artichoke hearts and ¼ c. chopped parsley.

Place in over (400°) for 7 minutes.

Serve on bed of mushrooms and artichokes.   Carol Burnett.

* SWEET AND SOUR FISH *

(¾ lb. rock fish, sea bass, red snapper (including head and tail)
cornstarch

oil for frying
* Sweet and Sour sauce

Sweet and Sour sauce:

¼ c. sugar
½ c. cider vinegar
½ c. catsup
½ c. water

juice of 1 lemon
1 tsp. soyu sauce
½ c. baby peas (fozen)
¼ c. cornstarch

To make sauce: Combine sugar, water, catsup and lemon juice in saucepan, cook over medium heat 3—4 minutes. Stir in soyu and dissolve cornstarch, bring to a boil, then simmer until thickened and clear. Stir in peas.

To prepare fish: Scale and clean fish. With sharp knife make 5—6 slashes (diagonally) on each side. For ease in frying, cut fish in half crosswise using diagonal slice. (Fit together after frying). Shake fish so it opens up like a flower (this will allow the skin to become crisp).

Sprinkle both sides of fish with cornstarch (excluding head). Heat enough oil for frying in Wok or skillet. Fry 7—10 minutes on each side, until deep golden brown, turning gently so as not to break the skin.

Place on warmed platter and serve with the sweet, sour sauce.

Millie Mesaku.

* STEAMED FISH *

Cut a few slices of fresh ginger, garlic, mushrooms, onions and pork. Place on whole fish, add soyu sauce, salt to taste. Place a little water in the pan and steam until well done.   Mary Upchurch.

* LOBSTER THERMIDOR *

Recipe for two:

1 lobster (2 lbs.)
4 Tbsp. butter
2 Tbsp. flour
1 c. cream or milk
1 c. mushrooms (quartered)

½ tsp. white pepper
¼ tsp. salt
½ tsp. dry mustard
4 Tbsp. Sherry
½ c. Parmesan cheese (grated)

Boil lobster and split in half lengthwise. Remove meat and cut into 1 in. cubes. Melt 2 Tbsp. butter in a skillet, add flour and cook until bubbly, then add cream, salt, pepper and mustard. Cook until thick. Add Sherry and egg yolk. Stir thoroughly. Keep warm over hot water. Saute mushrooms in the remaining butter, add lobster meat and the sauce. Sprinkle part of the cheese in the bottom of the shell, add mixture and add remaining cheese. Brown in a preheated oven to 375°. Note: May be made ahead, frozen and then browned when ready to serve.

Ruth Tufte.

* LOBSTER NEWBURG *

1 can (5 oz.) lobster (drained — cubed)
6 Tbsp. butter
2 Tbsp. flour
1½ c. light cream
3 egg yolks (beaten)

2 tsp. lemon juice
3 Tbsp. white wine
¼ tsp. paprika
¼ tsp. salt

In chafing dish, melt the butter, blend in the flour, stirring constantly until thickened. Place over water bath that is hot. Stir a small amount of mixture into the beaten egg yolks and return to hot mixture. Cook until thickened. Add lobster, wine, lemon juice and salt to taste. Sprinkle with paprika and serve on toast or in patty shells.

Francis Wright.

* LOBSTER CANTONESE *

1 lg. lobster cut in half
4 ozs. chopped lean pork
3 eggs (beaten)
2 scallions (chopped fine)
½ tsp. salt
1 tsp. black beans

½ tsp. sugar
1 tsp. gourmet seasoning
2 tsp. cornstarch
a dash of pepper
1 c. stock

Boil lobster and cut into ½ in. cubes. Wash and soak black beans. Crush beans and garlic together. Put unshelled pieces of lobster, pork and beans in a well greased skillet, saute for 2 minutes. Add stock, pepper, gourmet seasoning, sugar and salt and cook for 5 minutes. Add scallions, eggs and mix thoroughly, then add cornstarch and cook for 2 minutes longer.

Mary Upchurch.

* LOBSTERS WITH VERMICELLI *

3 lobsters (1 lb. each)
6 Tbsp. flour
1 tsp. basil
3 garlic cloves (mashed)
½ c. sweet butter
2 eggs (beaten)
¼ c. olive oil

¼ c. diced onions
pinch of salt
½ tsp. pepper
½ c. Sherry
8 oz. vermicelli
¼ c. Parmesan cheese (grated)

Cook lobsters in salted boiling water for 10 minutes. Allow to cool in water for another 10 minutes, remove from pot, tear off claws (crack and save the meat). Split lobsters in half and clean. Remove meat and cut in lg. pieces, flour slightly. Mix basil, garlic and butter and let stand. Dip floured lobster in beaten eggs. Place oil in skillet, saute onion until golden brown, add lobster meat and cook for 10 minutes.
Prepare vermicelli. Drain and put in pot to keep warm. Add remaining butter, a little of the sauce and some cheese.
To serve: Place vermicelli on hot platter. Spoon lobster and sauce on top, sprinkle with more cheese.   Judy Pieklo.

* SUSU CURRIED SHRIMP (INDIA) *

1½ c. medium shrimp (shelled —
   deveined)
2 garlic cloves (minced)
½ tsp. caraway seeds (grounded)
pinch of cayenne
½ tsp. tumeric
1 Tbsp. butter
½ c. whipped cream

1½ Tbsp. fresh coconut (finely chopped)
1 Tbsp. horseradish
1 Tbsp. lemon juice
2 dashes hot pepper sauce
1 tsp. salt
* Javanese Curry sauce.

Place shrimp in bowl and add garlic, caraway seeds, tumeric, cayenne and salt. Toss well and let stand for 1 hour. Melt butter in a skillet over medium heat, add shrimp and cook briefly, just until they begin to turn pink. Remove from heat.
Combine Javanese curry sauce with whipped cream and heat over low heat and simmer for 5 minutes. Stir frequently. Remove from heat and mix in coconut, horseradish, lemon juice, hot pepper sauce and salt. Add shrimp and return to the heat and cook gently until shrimp are warmed through. Serve with a rice ring.
* Javanese Curry sauce may be obtained at a specialty food market.
                                    Adele Davis.

* SHRIMP CURRY *

Blend and set aside:

¾ c. flour
7—8 tsp. curry powder
4 tsp. salt

½ tsp. ginger
2 tsp. sugar

For sauce:

1 c. minced onions
1 c. diced green apples (pared)
¾ c. oleo
1 qt. chicken broth
2 c. milk
1 Tbsp. butter or oleo

1½ c. mushrooms (fresh or canned)
3 lbs. shrimp
2 Tbsp. lemon juice

Saute onions and apples in the ¾ c. butter and cook until tender. Add dry ingredients and slowly add the chicken broth, stirring until thickened. Remove from heat and add drained mushrooms. If fresh shrimp is used clean and saute in oleo for 5 minutes. If canned shrimp is used, drain well and then stir into the mixture, add lemon juice. Serve with rice and the following condiments: Coconut (grated). chopped nuts, sliced black olives, chopped egg and chutney.

Irma Meyers.

* SHRIMP ROSEMARY *

¼ c. green pepper (chopped)
2 Tbsp. olive oil
1/3 c. onions (minced)
2 garlic cloves (minced)
½ tsp. sweet basil
½ tsp. rosemary

½ tsp. black pepper (coarse)
½ c. Sherry
½ c. tomatoes (minced)
½ c. parsley (minced)
garlic salt
20 lg. shrimp

Shell — clean — devein — butter fry the shrimp. Pour olive oil in a lg. Add the basil, rosemary, pepper, and shrimp and stir-fry for 5 minutes. Sherry, tomatoes and garlic salt to taste. Stir-fry until shrimps are curled. Serve on warm platter with rice and garnish with parsley. Charlene Do.

* SHRIMP A LA KING *

¼ c. chopped green pepper
1 Tbsp. butter
1 can cream of shrimp soup
½ c. milk

½ c. cooked shrimp
1 Tbsp. pimientos (chopped)
patty shells or toast.

Simmer pepper in butter until tender, add remaining ingredients, stir and heat thoroughly. Serve in patty shells or on hot toast. Ida Christoph.

* SHRIMP VEGETABLE SCAMPI *

2 lbs. lg. raw shrimp
  (shelled — deveined)
1 pinch each of salt, pepper
  and garlic powder
1 Tbsp. peanut oil
1 Tbsp. lemon juice
1 Tbsp. chopped chives
1 Tbsp. chopped parsley

1 c. beef bouillon
1 tsp. dry onion flakes
1 tsp. shoyu
2 c. mushrooms (sliced)
1 c. green beans (sliced)
2 c. bean sprouts
1 green pepper (chopped)

Preheat oven to 350°. Place shrimp in a shallow pan and marinate in shoyu, salt, pepper and garlic powder for 10 minutes, turning occasionally. Bake shrimp for 10 minutes. Place remaining ingredients in a skillet and add vegetables and stir-fry until vegetables are just crisp. Place vegetables on a warmed platter and serve shrimp over the vegetables. Nancy Ebsen.

* SHRIMP CASSEROLE *

3 lbs. lg shrimp (shelled —
  cleaned — deveined)
½ c. lemon juice
½ c. butter
1 garlic clove (minced)
1 lb. Feta cheese

¾ c. Cream Sherry
1 c. green onion tops (chopped)
3 lg. tomatoes (peeled — cut in wedges)
1 tsp. oregano
salt — pepper

Sprinkle shrimp with lemon juice and set aside. Melt butter in a skillet and saute garlic, onion tops, and tomato wedges. Add shrimp and season with oregano, salt and pepper. Turn the shrimp frequently and saute until pink. Add Feta cheese and Sherry, bring to a boil and cook 3 to 4 minutes.
Remove shrimp carefully to a casserole and spoon in sauce. Bake in preheated oven (350°) for 25 to 30 minutes until sauce is bubbly. Roberta Chateauneuf.

* SHRIMP MELANGE *

3 Tbsp. oleo
3 Tbsp. flour
½ tsp. salt
½ tsp. paprika
dash of white pepper
1-1/3 c. milk
¾ c. Swiss cheese (grated)
3 Tbsp. fine bread crumbs

1 Tbsp. catsup
2¼ c. cooked rice
1/8 tsp. basil
1/8 tsp. oregano
1 lb. shrimp (shelled — cleaned)
1 pkg. (9 oz.) frozen artichoke hearts
1 Tbsp. oleo

Melt oleo in saucepan over low heat, blend in flour, salt, pepper and paprika. Cook and stir until mixture is thickened and bubbling. Stir in wine. Heat thru. Stir in cheese and catsup and stir until cheese is melted.

In a small bowl combine rice, basil and oregano. Place in casserole. Drop shrimp into salted boiling water and boil until they turn pink. Drain and set aside. Prepare articokes as per instruction. Combine artichokes and shrimp and add to cheese mixture and then pour over rice. Combine the 1 Tbsp. oleo with the bread crumbs, sprinkle on top. Bake preheated oven (350°) for 25 minutes.

Adele Davis.

* SHRIMP AND ASPARAGUS HOT DISH *

1-2/3 c. cooked rice	1 can cream of chicken soup
1 can mushroom pieces.	1 can cream of celery soup
1 can (15 oz.) asparagus (drained)	2 or 3 cans (7 Oz.) shrimp
	grated cheddar cheese

Mix soups, rice and mushrooms, in buttered casserole, add a layer of rice mixture, then the shrimp and asparagus, ending with a layer of the rice. Sprinkle with grated cheese. Bake at 350° until bubbly. Madeline Ryan.

* GINGER SHRIMP *

1 lb. med. shrimp (shelled) — deveined)	¼ c. chopped green onions
1½ tsp. cornstarch	1 Tbsp. ginger (minced)
½ tsp. salt	¼ c. catsup
2 c. peanut oil	¼ c. chicken stock
¼ c. chopped onions	1 Tbsp. sugar
2 Tbsp. Chinese five spices	1 Tbsp. Sherry

Halve shrimp lengthwise. Combine cornstarch and salt and sprinkle over shrimp. Add oil to lg. skillet and heat to medium heat and deep fry the shrimp for 1 minute. Remove and drain on paper towels. Pour off all but 2 Tbsp. oil from skillet. Add onions and ginger and stir-fry 1 minute increase heat to high, add catsup, stock and sugar and bring to a boil. Add shrimp and remaining ingredients and stir-fry for 2 minutes.

Serve with hot rice. Francis Wright.

* PINEAPPLE SHRIMP *

1 lb. shrimp
1 can (303) pineapple tibits
2 Tbsp. toasted sesame seeds

Batter:

1 c. flour
1 egg (beaten)
½ tsp. salt
1/8 tsp. Accent

Sauce:

3 Tbsp. brown sugar
1 Tbsp. cornstarch
2 Tbsp. vinegar
½ c. pineapple juice
¼ c. water

Clean shrimp. Combine ingredients for the batter. Dip shrimp in batter and deep fry until browned. Combine ingredients for the sauce and bring to a boil. Place shrimp on a warmed platter, place drained tibits on top and pour sauce over all.   Elizabeth Betty Guy.

* PINEAPPLE SHRIMP KABOBS *

1 lb. shrimp (shelled)
¼ c. margarine or butter

20—25 cocktail onions
20—25 pineapple chunks (fresh or
        canned)

Dip shrimp in melted butter, push cocktail onions, pineapple chunks and shrimp on skewers. Broil. Time: 4—5 minutes on first side, 3—4 minutes on second side. Stick kabobs into whole pineapple and serve with curried Sour Cream Dip. (If desired).   Jean Ariyoshi.

* SHRIMP AND ALMONDS *

2 eggs
2 c. milk
2½ lbs. jumbo shrimp
    (peeled — deveined)

salt — pepper
4 c. almonds (sliced)
* Orange mustard sauce.

Orange mustard sauce:

¾ c. marmalade
¼ c. chicken stock
few drops of pepper sauce

2 Tbsp. lemon juice
1 tsp. dry mustard

Beat eggs until light and fluffy in a medium bowl. Stir in milk and gradually mix in flour, blending well. Add salt and pepper to taste. Holding shrimp by the tail, dip into the batter, allowing excess to drip back in the bowl. (Do not cover the tails). Sprinkle all sides of shrimp with the almonds, place on cookie sheet and refrigerate for at least 2 hours before frying.

Heat oil for deep frying to medium hot. Fry shrimp a few at a time until they turn pink, about 2 minutes (do not overcook). Drain on paper towels and keep warm until all are cooked. Serve immediately with Orange Mustard Sauce. To prepare sauce: Thoroughly combine all ingredients and warm over low heat. Place in bowl to serve with the shrimp.   Rebecca Dixon.

* SWISS AND CRAB SUPPER PIE *

1 unbaked pie shell (9 in.)
1 c. Swiss cheese (shredded)
1 can crabmeat (7½ oz.)
    (drained — flaked)
2 green onions (diced)
3 eggs (beaten)
1 c. light cream

½ tsp. lemon peel (grated)
½ tsp. salt
¼ tsp. dry mustard
¼ tsp. mace
¼ c. sliced almonds

Arrange cheese over bottom of the pie shell and top with crabmeat. Sprinkle with green onions. Combine other ingredients (except almonds) pour over crab and top with almonds. Bake in preheated oven (325°) for 45 minutes. Remove from oven and wait 10 minutes before serving.   Jean Lyle.

* CRAB RANGOON *

½ lb. fresh crabmeat (drained —
    chopped)
½ lb. cream cheese
½ tsp. A—1 sauce

¼ tsp. garlic powder
1 egg yolk (well beaten)
2½ to 3 doz. Won Ton wrappers

Combine crabmeat with cheese, add seasonings and blend well. Place heaping tsp. of mixture on each Won Ton and gather up the four corners on top. Moisten edges with egg yolk, pinch tight and twist. Heat some oil in a skillet. Add Won Tons in small batches and stir-fry until golden brown. Drain on paper towels. Serve hot or cold with Chinese mustard sauce.   Millie Mesaku.

* CRAB FRITTER WITH GINGER SAUCE *

½ lb. crabmeat
1 tsp. cumin
1 tsp. ground ginger
½ tsp. nutmeg
¼ tsp. mace
1 tsp. salt
oil for deep fry

¼ c. parsley (chopped)
1 Tbsp. fresh dill weed
¼ c. grated coconut
1 c. soft bread crumbs
3 egg whites (slightly beaten)
bread crumbs for frying
* Ginger sauce

189

Ginger sauce:

3 sm. slices fresh ginger (grated)
2 garlic cloves (minced)
1½ c. shoyu

2 Tbsp. sugar
1 tsp. hot mustard
2 Tbsp. chopped green pepper

Mix all ingredients for the sauce, cover and let mellow. Combine crabmeat, cumin, ginger, nutmeg, mace, salt, parsley and dill and blend. Add coconut and bread crumbs and mix thoroughly. Shape into cylinders 1½ in. long by ½ in. wide. Chill for 2 hours. Roll fritters in egg white then in the bread crumbs. Pre-heat oil to medium hot and fry fritters until golden brown on all sides. Remove with slotted spoon and drain on paper towels. Serve with the Ginger sauce.

Adele Davis.

* CURRIED SEAFOOD CREPES WITH CHUTNEY *

½ stick butter
4 shallots (chopped)
1 lb. cooked crabmeat
6 mushrooms (sliced)
3 c. Bechamel sauce
2 Tbsp. curry powder.

salt — pepper
Gruyere cheese (grated)
Parmesan cheese (grated)
chutney for garnish

* Note: Recipe for the Bechamel sauce is listed under the Pasta Chapter.

Melt butter in a saucepan and gently saute the shallots until soft. Add seafood, mushrooms, salt and pepper to taste. Simmer, covered for 5 to 10 minutes until completely heated through. Add curry powder to sauce and taste for seasoning. Reserve 1 c. Bechamel sauce. Mix remainder into seafood mixture and gently heat. Spread crepes with seafood mix and roll up. Place in lg. shallow greased baking dish, seam side down. Gently spoon remaining sauce over the center of crepes, sprinkle with grated cheese and brown under broiler. Serve with the chutney.

Daisy Alexander.

* CRAB RING *

1 pkg. lemon jello
3 sm. pkgs. cream cheese
1 can tomato soup (undiluted)
½ c. each of chopped celery, onions, green pepper

1 c. Best Foods mayonnaise
3 hard boiled eggs
1 can or shrimp
½ c. boiling water

While jello sets in ½ c. water, dissolve cream cheese in heated soup and pour into jello. Add other other ingredients and pour into lg. ring mold. Let stand over-night. Note: Makes two lg. ring molds. Can also be made without the crabmeat.

Betty Barry.

* CURRIED CRABMEAT AU GRATIN *

1 c. hot med. cream sauce
1 tsp. curry powder
2 c. crabmeat (diced)

¼ c. Swiss cheese (grated)
1 tsp. butter

Combine cream sauce, curry powder and crabmeat. Pour into buttered casserole and cover with Swiss cheese and dot with butter.
Place under broiler until golden brown.   Lucille Goderre.

* CRAB — EGGPLANT BASKET *

1 lg. eggplant (round)
4 Tbsp. melted butter
1 tsp. minced onion
dash of cayenne
½ lb. crabmeat (flaked)

fine bread crumbs (topping)
grated Parmesan cheese (topping)
paprika (topping)

Cut eggplant in half from stem and slash flesh in crisscross pattern (be careful not to cut through the skin). Bake in preheated oven (350°) flesh side down until tender (about 25 minutes).
Scoop out pulp and leave skin ¼ in. thick. Puree in blender, add remaining ingredients (except crabmeat) and blend well. Fold in crabmeat and season to taste. Fill shells, sprinkle lightly with cheese and the paprika. Return to oven and bake for 20 minutes.   Eileen Weberg.

* LOUISIANA SEAFOOD GUMBO *

¼ lb. bacon (diced)
¼ c. onion (chopped
¼ c. green pepper (chopped)
1 c. celery (diced)
3 sprigs parsley (chopped)
1 c. cooked rice

salt — pepper
2 c. fresh or canned tomatoes
4 c. stock
1 c. fresh shrimp
1 c. fresh or frozen crabmeat
2 c. frozen okra or fresh

Saute until yellow. Add parsley, tomatoes and stock and simmer until vegetables are tender. Add shrimp, crabmeat, okra, rice and season to taste. Simmer for 30 minutes and serve hot.   Annie Ebsen.

* ARTICHOKES WITH SEAFOOD *

2 lbs. shrimp or scallops (cleaned —
    cut in ½ in. pieces)
¼ c. butter
8 green onions (chopped)
1 lb. mushrooms (sliced)
1½ c. croutons
8 lg. artichokes (cooked — trimmed)

salt — pepper
1 tsp. tarragon
½ tsp. dill
½ tsp. celery seed
½ tsp. paprika
1½ c. Hollandaise sauce
¼ c. Sherry

191

Melt butter in a saucepan and saute onions, garlic and mushrooms. Add seafood, croutons, tarragon, dill, celery seed, and paprika, heat stirring constantly, just until seafood is cooked. Add Sherry and simmer for 2 minutes. Season with salt and pepper. Stir in Hollandaise sauce (½ c.). Spread artichoke leaves apart. Fill cavities with seafood mixture, spoon any extra between leaves. Top with Hollandaise sauce. Place on greased cookie sheet and tent with foil. Bake in preheated oven (350°) for 10 to 15 minutes. Remove foil and place under broiler until tops are lightly browned. Note: May be made in advance and refrigerated. Bring to room temperature before baking.   Judy Pieklo.

* OYSTERS ROCKEFELLER *

16 lg. fresh oysters (in shell)   2 Tbsp. Pernod
2 sticks butter   3 Tbsp. bacon (cooked-crumbled)
1 c. spinach (freshly cooked)   ½ tsp. salt
1 c. celery (chopped)   3 dashes tabasco sauce
½ c. parsley (chopped)   1/3 c. Parmesan cheese (grated)
1 c. onion (chopped)   rock salt
1 c. dry bread crumbs   lemon wedges

Shuck oysters, reserving the liquid and bottom shell and scrub bottoms until clean. Melt butter in a saucepan on low heat, add spinach, celery, parsley, onions, bread crumbs. Pernod, bacon, salt and tabasco. Simmer until heated through. Grind in meat grinder or food processor. (This mixture may be made ahead and refrigerated overnite). Place one oyster on each of the shells, moisten with reserved oyster liquid. Preheat oven to 425°. Spread the spinach mixture over oysters, completely covering oysters and shells. Sprinkle with Parmesan cheese. Arrange oysters on a bed of rock salt on a oven proof platter and bake for 15 minutes or until top of vegetable mixture has a light crust. Serve with lemon wedges.   Adele Davis.

* ANGELS ON HORSEBACK *

4 doz. medium oysters   12 slices bacon (uncooked)
1 c. chili sauce   ¾ c. Parmesan cheese (ungrated)
2 Tbsp. chopped green pepper
2 Tbsp. Worcestershire sauce

Place oysters (well drained) in a skillet, cover with chili sauce, green pepper and Worcestershire sauce. (Skillet should be ovenproof). Place in preheated oven (350°) and bake until oysters begin to puff. Remove from oven and sprinkle with bacon (cut in fine dice) and cheese. Return to oven and bake for 10 min. more. Keep hot until ready to serve. Serve with rye bread squares.

                                        Lorna Burger.

* ESCARGOTS *

1 c. butter (softened)
1 Tbsp. shallots (chopped)
2 garlic cloves (chopped)
2 Tbsp. white wine
1 Tbsp. Worcestershire sauce
1 Tbsp. parsley (chopped)

1 tsp. Brandy
1 tsp. lemon juice
½ tsp. salt
pinch of pepper
36 snails and shells

Mix, but do not whip all ingredients (except snails). Heat mixture in a lg. skillet. Add snails and simmer for 10 to 15 minutes, allowing liquid to cook into snails. Preheat oven to 350°. Put small amount of butter mixture into bottom of each shell, insert snail by using a fork, continue until all shells are filled. Place in shallow baking dish. Pour remaining mixture over snails and bake until bubbling (about 10 minutes).   Francis Wright.

* SALMON LOAF *

2 Tbsp. onion (minced)
½ c. celery (chopped)
1 Tbsp. butter
2 eggs
½ c. milk
1 can (1 lb.) salmon

¼ tsp. salt
¼ tsp.
½ can celery soup (condensed)
2 Tbsp. mayonnaise
1 c. cooked rice.

Simmer onion and celery in butter until soft. Beat eggs, add all ingredients, including salmon liquid and mix. Bake in buttered bread pan in preheated oven (350°) for 55 minutes. Invert on platter.
Serve with a cream sauce and buttered peas.   Evelyn Staley.

* CREAMED SALMON WITH MUSHROOMS *

1 Tbsp. butter
1 Tbsp. onion (minced)
1½ tsp. shallots (chopped)
¼ lb. fresh mushrooms (finely sliced)
1 Tbsp. flour
¼ c. liquid from salmon or ¼ c.
    clam juice

¼ c. white wine
¼ c. whipping cream
1 Tbsp. parsley (chopped)
1 can (1 lb.) salmon (drained — broken
    into bite size pieces)
Toast triangles or patty shells

Heat butter in a skillet, add onion and shallots, stirring until onion wilts. Mix in mushrooms. Sprinkle evenly with flour. Add wine and salmon liquid, stirring rapidly with a whisk until thickened and smooth. Simmer for 5 minutes. Add cream, parsley and salt and pepper to taste. Fold in salmon and heat through. Serve over toast or in patty shells.   Roberta Chateauneuf.

193

* BAKED SEAFOOD SALAD *

1 Tbsp. minced onions
1 c. celery (chopped)
1 green pepper (chopped)
¾ c. mayonnaise

1 tsp. salt
1 c. shrimp (cooked)
1 c. crabmeat (cooked)
1 tsp. Worcestershire sauce

Mix all ingredients and place in baking shells. Top with buttered bread crumbs. Bake in preheated oven (350°) for 30 minutes. Dorothy Tuttle.

* TUNA — CHEESE FONDUE *

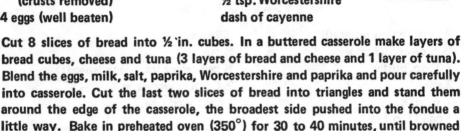

1 can (7 oz.) tuna (drained — flaked)
1 c. Swiss cheese (grated)
10 slices white bread
   (crusts removed)
4 eggs (well beaten)

2 c. milk
1 tsp. salt
¼ tsp. paprika
½ tsp. Worcestershire
dash of cayenne

Cut 8 slices of bread into ½ in. cubes. In a buttered casserole make layers of bread cubes, cheese and tuna (3 layers of bread and cheese and 1 layer of tuna). Blend the eggs, milk, salt, paprika, Worcestershire and paprika and pour carefully into casserole. Cut the last two slices of bread into triangles and stand them around the edge of the casserole, the broadest side pushed into the fondue a little way. Bake in preheated oven (350°) for 30 to 40 minutes, until browned on top and bubbly. Nancy Ebsen.

* CRAB — CHEESE SANDWICHES *

6 sour dough English muffins
butter
2 c. crabmeat (cooked — drained)
1½ c. Swiss cheese (shredded)
½ c. sour cream

½ tsp. horseradish
2 tsp. lemon juice
½ tsp. Worcestershire sauce
dash of hot pepper sauce paprika

Spread the muffin halves with butter, then toast on the outside until crisp and browned. Combine all the other ingredients and mix well. Spread on toasted muffin halves, sprinkle with cheese. Bake in oven (400°) for 10 minutes.
Lillian Kann.

B·R·E·A·D·S

* CHRISTMAS STOLLEN *
(My Mother's Recipe)

6 to 8 c. flour (sifted)
2 cakes compressed yeast
1½ c. milk (scalded — cooled)
¾ c. sugar
1½ c. butter
3 eggs

¾ tsp. lemon juice
½ lb. raisins
½ c. almonds (chopped)
1 c. candied fruit (chopped)
1 c. almond paste

Crumble yeast in cooled milk, add 1 c. flour. Let rise in warm place until double in bulk. Sprinkle a little flour over raisins, fruit and nuts.
Beat butter until very soft, gradually add sugar. Beat in eggs, (one at a time), add lemon juice and salt. Add fruit and nuts. Add yeast sponge and remaining flour. Knead dough until smooth. Let rise in buttered bowl (in warm place) until double in bulk. Toss on floured board and divide in two loaves, roll out into circles. Spread almond paste on top and roll (more candied fruit and nuts may be added on top of the paste). Place on greased pans, brush tops with melted butter. Let rise again until double in bulk. Bake in preheated oven (350°) for 45 minutes. When cool glaze with Lemon Glaze.

Lemon Glaze:

1¼ c. confectioners sugar
¼ tsp. vanilla

¼ tsp. almond extract
¼ c. lemon juice

Mix until smooth.

Adele Davis.

* CHOREKI (BRAIDED GREEK BREAD) *

1½ c. flour
1 Tbsp. yeast
½ c. hot tap water
3 Tbsp. nonfat dry milk
½ tsp. anise seed (ground)

¼ c. butter
¼ c. salt
2 eggs (room temperature)

Topping:

1 egg mixed with 1 Tbsp. milk
2 Tbsp. sesame seeds

2 Tbsp. sugar
2 Tbsp. almonds (chopped)

For bread: In a lg. mixing bowl combine flour and yeast. In separate bowl thoroughly blend water, milk, anise, butter, sugar and salt. Slowly pour into dry ingredients and beat for 1 minute. Add eggs and beat 2 minutes longer. Add remaining flour and beat until dough comes clean from bowl. If needed, add more flour, 1 Tbsp. at a time.

Turn dough onto a floured board and knead until smooth. Place dough in greased bowl and turn to coat sides. Cover with plastic and a hot towel. Allow to rise in a warm place until double in bulk (about 1 hour). Punch dough down and turn onto a floured surface and let stand for 10 minutes. Divide into 3 parts. Using palms of hands, roll each piece into a long rope like strip. Place lengths side by side. Start in the middle and braid loosely toward each end and pinching ends to prevent braid from breaking loose during rising. Place on lightly oiled baking sheet, cover with waxed paper and allow to rise in a warm place for 1 hour or until doubled.

Preheat oven to 350°. Brush dough with egg and milk, sprinkle with sesame seeds and almonds.

Dust with sugar. Bake 30 minutes or until well browned and wooden pick inserted in the center comes out clean and dry. Cool lightly on wire racks and serve warm.   Francis Wright.

* EASTER BREAD (FINNISH) *

2 pkgs. dry yeast
½ c. lukewarm water
1½ c. evaporated milk (scalded)
5 eggs yolks
1 c. sugar
1 c. sugar
1 c. butter (melted — cooled)
1½ tsp. salt
2 tsp. cardamon seed (freshly crushed)

2 tsp lemon peel (grated)
2 Tbsp. orange peel (grated)
1 c. golden raisins
1½ c. almonds (chopped)
1 c. fruit cake mix
1 c. rye flour
1 c. milk (scalded — cooled)
4 to 4½ c. unsifted flour

Dissolve yeast in warm water, stir in evaporated milk and 2 c. flour and beat until smooth. Cover and let rise until doubled (½ to 1 hour). Stir in eggs, sugar, butter, salt. cardamon seeds, grated peels, fruit cake mix., raisins and nuts. Beat well. Stir in scalded milk and rye flour until combined, then the rest of the flour (except 1 c.) to make a stiff dough. Sprinkle the rest of the flour on a board and turn dough onto it, knead until smooth (about 10 minutes).

Butter a lg. bowl and place dough into it, turning so all sides are well greased. Cover lightly and let rise in a warm place until double in bulk. Punch down and form into a round ball.

Place dough, rounded side up in a buttered 4 qt. pail and let rise until doubled or divide dough and use 2 lb. coffee cans buttered. Bake in preheated oven (350°) for 1½ hours for the 4 qt. pail or 1 hour for the coffee cans.

Test with wooden skewer for doneness. Cool in pans 20 minutes before turning out.   Eileen Weberg.

* WALNUT HEARTH BREAD (FRENCH) *

4 c. unbleached flour
½ c. whole wheat flour
1 pkg. dry yeast
1 Tbsp. salt
2 Tbsp. corn meal

1/3 c. warm water
1 c. walnuts (chopped)
3/4 c. onions (chopped)
½ c. unsalted butter (softened)

Lightly grease a lg. bowl and set aside.

Combine 1¾ c. flour, whole wheat flour, yeast and salt in mixing bowl. Add milk and water and beat about 2 minutes. Stir in walnuts, onion and butter and mix well. Blend or knead in remaining flour to make a stiff dough. Place in a greased bowl. Turning dough to grease all sides. Cover with plastic and hot damp towel and let rise in a warm place until doubled. Sprinkle baking pan with cornmeal. Punch dough down and place on a lightly floured board, knead for 3 to 4 minutes. Shape into a ball and place on baking pan. Let rise uncovered in a warm place for 15 minutes.

Preheat oven to 425°. Place pan of water on the lowest rack in oven. Make slashes on top of dough with a knife. Place dough on middle rack and bake for 30 minutes. Remove pan of water and reduce heat to 300°. and bake until bread sounds hollow when tapped. Cool on rack.

(Bread may be made in 2 loaves if desired). Ida Christoph.

* SWEDISH RYE BREAD *

1¾ c. boiling water
1/3 c. brown sugar
¼ c. quick cooking oatmeal
¼ c. butter
¼ c. molasses
1 Tbsp. salt
2 tsp. caraway seeds

1 tsp. anise seeds
¼ c. warm water
1 pkg. dry yeast
3 c. unbleached flour
3 c. rye flour
1 egg white
Caraway seeds (optional)

Lightly grease lg. bowl and two 9 x 5 in. loaf pans. Combine boiling water, brown sugar, oatmeal, butter, molasses, salt, caraway seeds and anise seeds and let stand until lukewarm. Mix warm water and yeast and place in lg. bowl. Add 2 c. white flour and beat until smooth. Blend in rye flour and add additional flour to make a soft dough. Turn dough on a lightly floured board and cover with bowl and let rest for 10 minutes. Knead dough until smooth and elastic. Place in greased bowl and turn to coat all sides. Cover with plastic and a hot damp towel and let rise in a warm place until double in volume. Punch down and let rise for another 30 minutes. Form dough into loaves. Bake in preheated oven (375°) until well browned and when tapped loaves should sound hollow. 10 minutes before bread has finish baking, brush tops with beaten egg whites and add caraway seeds. Cool on racks. Margaret Holmes.

* BRAN BREAD *

1 egg
1½ c. Bran (Kelloggs all-bran)
1 tsp salt
1 c. flour
½ tsp. baking powder

¼ c. molasses and sugar (mixed)
1 c. warm water
2 Tbsp. margarine (melted)

Mix all ingredients together. Place in buttered 9 in. pie pan. Bake at (350°). (You can tell when done by touch).   Dorothy Tuttle.

* 6 WEEK BRAN MUFFINS *

1 box (15½ oz.) raisin bran flakes
1 c. Crisco oil
3 c. sugar
4 eggs (beaten)

1 qt. buttermilk
5 tsp. baking soda
2 tsp. salt
5 c. flour

Mix dry ingredients well. Add oil, eggs and buttermilk. Mix. Store covered in refrigerator up to 6 weeks. Bake in greased muffin tins 2/3 full at 400° for 15 to 18 minutes. (Optional additions; chopped nuts, coconut, maraschino cherries or chocolate bits.   Lynne Waihee.

* HERB BREAD *

6 c. flour
2½ tsp. salt
2 Tbsp. butter
½ c. honey
1 c. rolled oats
2 c. boiling water

2 pkgs. active yeast
1/3 c. lukewarm water
2 tsp. sage
1 tsp. nutmeg
4 tsp. celery seed

Pour boiling water over oats and let stand for ½ hour. Soak yeast in warm water for 5 minutes. Add salt, honey, butter, sage, nutmeg and celery seed to oats. Add 2 c. flour, then 2 more c. flour. Knead in the last 2 c. flour, until smooth and elastic. Set in greased bowl to rise until double (approximately 2 hours). Punch down, divide and place in 2 well greased bread pans. Let rise until even with top of pans. Bake in a preheated oven 325° for 50 minutes.

Ingrid Nelson

* BEER BREAD *

3 c. self-rising flour
3 Tbsp. sugar
1 can (12 oz.) beer

Mix well and place in greased bread pan. Bake 1 hour in preheated oven at 350°.
Lucille Goderre.

198

* FLOWER POT CHEESE BREAD *
(A Prize Winning Recipe)

4 red clay flower pots (5 x 5 in. deep and 4 in. base)
Preheat oven to 375°. Wash and generously grease pots with shortening. Bake 5 to 10 minutes until pots are well heated and shortening has been absorbed. Regrease and bake for another 10 minutes. Cool. When cooled, butter pots well and line sides with buttered wax paper. (Do not cover the bottom). Lightly grease lg. bowl and set aside.

1¾ c. warm water
3 Tbsp. butter
2 Tbsp. honey
4 lg. eggs
1 egg white
7 c. unbleached flour
2 pkgs. dry yeast

1 Tbsp. sugar
2 tsp. salt
1 tsp. baking powder
2 c. sharp Cheddar cheese (grated)
1 egg yolk (beaten)
poppy seeds

Combine warm water, butter, honey in a mixing bowl. Beat 4 eggs and egg white, 3½ c. flour, yeast, sugar and salt. Mix thoroughly until well combined. Continue to beat for 2 minutes. Then add baking powder and additional flour, ½ c. at a time, beating constantly until soft dough is formed. Quickly mix in cheese. Turn dough onto a lightly floured board and knead until smooth and elastic (about 10 minutes). Place in prepared bowl and turn to coat all sides. Cover with plastic wrap and let rise in a warm place until doubled in bulk. Punch dough down and turn onto a floured board and knead for 3 minutes. Divide dough into balls. Layer balls in pots, placing last ball in center.
Preheat oven to 425°. Brush each bread with egg yolk and sprinkle with poppy seeds. Place double thickness of foil on oven rack. Bake for 10 minutes. Reduce heat to 375° and bake until golden brown and sounds hollow when tapped (about 25 to 30 minutes). If top browns too fast, cover with foil. Cool pots on rack for 15 minutes then carefully remove loaves. Let cool before slicing.
Note: For added attraction, bread (in the pots) may be sliced at the table.
Adele Davis.

* CORN BREAD *

3 c. Bisquick
1 c. sugar
½ c. cornmeal
1 tsp. baking powder

1 c. melted butter
1½ c. milk
3 eggs (beaten)

Mix first 4 ingredients in a bowl. Melt butter and add to milk, beaten eggs, then add liquid all at once to the dry ingredients. Stir only to moisten. Bake at 350° for 35 minutes.
Jean Keys.

* EXTRA SPECIAL CORN BREAD *

3 c. pancake mix
¼ c. yellow cornmeal
3 eggs (well beaten)
2 cubes Margarine (½ lb.) (melted)

2½ tsp. baking powder
1 c. sugar
1½ c. milk

Mix dry ingredients and add milk, eggs and margarine, stir thoroughly. Pour into a 9 x 13 in. pan and bake for 30 minutes in a preheated oven at 350°. Note: (This recipe sounds odd but it is the best, most delicate cornbread I have ever eaten. It is not a spoon bread — you do cut it in squares).   Dorothy Tuttle.

* SKILLET CORN BREAD *

½ c. yellow cornmeal
   (stone ground if possible)
1¼ tsp. baking powder
¼ tsp. salt
¼ c. plus 1 Tbsp. oil
½ c. sour cream

¼ c. fresh corn
1 can (4 oz.) chopped green chilies
   (drained)
1 egg (slightly beaten)
¼ c. Monterey cheese (grated)

Heat over to 400°. Combine cornmeal, baking powder, salt in a medium bowl. Add the ¼ c. oil, sour cream, corn, chiles, egg and cheese. Stir ingredients with a wooden spoon until just blended. Heat the Tbsp. oil in a 9 in. skillet over med. heat till rippling. Pour oil into mixture, stirring to combine. Pour mixture back into skillet, place in center of the oven and bake until bread puffs up and top is golden brown, about 25 to 30 minutes. Serve cut in wedges.   Jean Keys.

* CREAMY CORN SPOON BREAD *

1-1/3 c. canned whole kernel corn
1-1/3 c. canned (cream style)
½ c. (1 stick) margarine (melted)
1 c. sour cream

2 eggs (beaten)
1 pkg. (8½ oz.) corn muffin mix
¾ c. Cheddar cheese (grated)

Preheat oven to 375°. Stir corns and margarine in a deep 2 qt. round baking dish. Fold in sour cream and eggs. Add corn muffin mix and blend well. Bake until center of spoon bread is just set (about 1 hour). Sprinkle cheese over the top and continue baking until melted. 1 to 2 minutes. Serve hot.   Arlene Wright.

* CRANBERRY NUT BREAD *

2 c. flour
1 c. sugar
¾ c. orange juice
1½ tsp. baking powder
½ tsp. baking soda
½ c. chopped nuts

1 tsp. salt
1 Tbsp. grated orange peel
2 Tbsp. shortening
1 well beaten egg
1 c. Ocean Spray fresh cranberries

In a bowl mix together flour, sugar, soda, baking powder and salt. Stir in orange juice, orange peel and shortening, then egg. Mix well. (I use electric beaters). Stir in cranberries and nuts. Bake at 350° for 55 to 60 minutes in a 9 x 5" pan. Smaller pans 35 to 40 minutes.   Jean Keys.

* NUT BREAD *

2 eggs well beaten
½ c. sugar
½ c. brown sugar
3 tsp. baking powder

3 c. flour
1 tsp. salt
1 c. milk
½ c. walnuts

Mix all ingredients and place in a greased loaf pan. Let stand for 30 minutes. Bake 45 minutes for 30 minutes in a preheated oven at 325°. Do not slice for 24 hours. Makes one regular loaf.   Dorothy Tuttle.

* ARABIAN NUT LOAF *

¾ c. hot coffee
1/3 c. shortening
1 c. brown sugar
2 eggs
1¾ c. flour
1 c. chopped dates

½ c. chopped nuts
1½ tsp. baking powder
½ tsp. salt
½ tsp soda
½ tsp. vanilla

Pour hot coffee over the dates. Cream shortening, sugar and eggs. Sift dry ingredients together, add alternating with coffee and date mixture, add vanilla and nuts. Pour into a greased loaf pan. Bake at 350° for 1 hour or until knife comes out clean.   Rosella Reiner.

* PINEAPPLE NUT BREAD *

2 eggs (unbeaten)
1¾ c. flour
2 tsp. baking powder
½ tsp. salt
¾ c. sugar
¼ tsp. soda

½ c. raisins
¾ c. chopped nuts
3 Tbsp. soft oleo
1 c. crushed pineapple (not drained — an
     3½ oz. flat can)

Topping: 2 Tbsp. white sugar — ½ tsp. cinnamon (a few chopped Maraschino cherries may be added for color).

Rinse raisins in boiling water to plump them. Grease a 9 x 5 x 8 in. pan or glass loaf pan. Gradually beat sugar and oleo, beat in eggs, one at a time, add raisins and nuts. Sift dry ingredients together. Sift in half on the flour mixture into the sugar, stir until just moist and fairly smooth. Add pineapple and syrup, stir in remaining flour, gently spoon into pan. Add topping. Bake for 60 to 70 minutes at 350. Turn out on rack to cool.   Rosella Reiner.

* POI NUT BREAD *

No. 1:

1 lb. poi — ¾ c. water

Mix together and let stand in bowl.

No. 2:

2 c. flour	2 tsp. baking powder
¾ c. sugar	1 tsp. salt
2 tsp. cinnamon	

Mix all in another bowl

No. 3:

3 eggs (slightly beaten)	2 tsp. vanilla
1 c. oil	1.2 c. nuts

Combine mixtures together and place in greased loaf pans. Bake at 350° for 45 minutes. Optional: I added ½ can frozen coconut and ½ c. raisins — Delicious.

Elizabeth Betty Guy.

* DELICIOUS PRUNE NUT LOAF *

1/3 c. butter or margarine (6 Tbsp.)	2 tsp. lemon rind (grated — or 1 Tbsp.
2/3 c. sugar	lemon juice)
2 eggs	2 c. all — purpose flour
½ c. prune juice	1 tsp. baking powder
½ tsp. salt	½ tsp. soda
	1 c. pitted prunes (chopped)

Cream together butter or margarine and sugar. Add eggs, one at a time, lemon rind and prune juice. Sift together all dry ingredients and add to creamed mixture. Mix well. Stir in prunes. Pour into 2 sm. greased bread pans or 1 lg. loaf pan. Bake at 350°, small pans about 40 minutes. The larger pan bake a little longer. Lightly shake granulated sugar over loaf and a few chopped nuts.

Note: Prunes were soaked in cold water overnite and juice was used in the recipe.

Madeline Ryan.

* CRANBERRY NUT BREAD *

2 c. sifted flour
1 c. sugar
1½ tsp. baking powder
1 tsp. salt
¼ c. shortening

¾ c. orange juice
1 Tbsp. grated orange rind
1 egg (beaten)
½ c. chopped nuts
1 c. fresh cranberries (coarsely chopped)

Sift together the first 5 ingredients. Cut in shortening until mixture resembles coarse cornmeal. Combine juice, grated rind and beaten egg. Pour all at once into dry ingredients, mix just enough to moisten. Fold in nuts and cranberries. Spoon into 9 x 5 x 3 in. loaf pan greased and lined with wax paper. Bake at 350°. for 1 hour until crust is golden brown. Cool completely before serving.

Kate Stanley.

* DATE BREAD *

2 c. sifted flour
1½ tsp. baking powder
2 lg. eggs
2½ to 3 bananas (1 c. mashed)
½ c. margarine
1 c. chopped nuts

1 c. sugar
1½ Tbsp. butter or sour milk
1 tsp. lemon juice
1 pkg. (8 oz.) chopped dates
½ tsp soda

In a lg. bowl sift flour, baking powder and soda.
Puree eggs, bananas, margarine, sugar and lemon juice. Mix in dry ingredients, blend in dates and nuts. Bake 1 hour and 15 minutes in 350° preheated oven. Do not let it get too brown. It is done when it breaks away from the edges. Note: There are many date bread recipes, not as good as this. I call this recipe "My Own".

Ebba Kirschbaum.

* BEST MANGO BREAD *

2 c. flour
2 tsp. cinnoman
2 tsp. baking soda
¼ tsp. salt
3 well beaten eggs

1½ c. sugar
¾ c. oil
2 c. diced mangoes
½ c. chopped nuts or raisins

Sift flour, form a well in center of bowl and mix in the rest of the ingredients, except mango and nuts. Add that last. Pour into two loaf pans and bake at 350° for 40 to 50 minutes. Test to sure it is done. Very moist and tasty bread.

Jean Keys.

* MANGO BREAD *

2 c. flour
2 tsp. baking soda
2 tsp. cinnamon
½ tsp. salt
1¼ c. sugar
¾ c. oil

3 eggs
1 tsp. vanilla
2 c. chopped mangoes
½ c. nuts
¾ c. raisins

Sift dry ingredients in a mixing bowl. Make a well in center. Add oil, eggs, vanilla and mangoes. Beat until well blended, fold in nuts and raisins. Pour into 2 greased loaf pans and bake at 400° for 20 minutes, then 350° for 25 minutes. Cool completely before serving. Note: Easy, delicious and a wonderful way to use those extra mangoes.   Nancy Young.

* FAMOUS HUNKY BUNCH MANGO BREAD *

2 c. flour
2 tsp. cinnamon
2 tsp. baking soda
1½ c. sugar
½ tsp. salt

2 c. mangoes (diced)
1 c. grated coconut
¾ c. salad oil
3 eggs (lightly beaten)
½ c. raisins

Mix flour, cinnamon, baking soda, sugar and salt together. After mixing well, add remaining ingredients and stir well.

Lightly butter 4 loaf pans, (2½ in. by 5 in. or 2 larger loaf pans). Pour in batter, until 2/3 full and bake for 55 minutes. (1 hour for larger pans) at 350°. Cool and serve or wrap in foil and freeze.   Connie Chun.

* PINEAPPLE — APRICOT BREAD *

6 Tbsp. butter or margarine
¾ c. sugar
2 eggs
1 No. 1 flat can crushed pineapple

3 c. biscuit mix
1/3 c. dried apricots (chopped)
½ c. walnuts (chopped)

Cream butter and sugar. Add eggs, one at a time, beating well after each addition. Stir in pineapple and juice. Combine biscuit mix and apricots. Stir biscuit mix, apricots and nuts into batter just until moistened. Pour into a greased 9" by 5" loaf pan. Bake at 350° for 1 hour or until done.   Jean Ariyoshi.

* BLANCHE'S BANANA BREAD *

½ c. butter or oleo
1 c. sugar
2 eggs
1 c. mashed bananas

1 tsp. soda
½ tsp. salt
1 tsp. soda

204

Mix all together well. Use standard loaf pan. Grease pan and bake at 300° for 1 hour and 15 minutes. Note: My recipe, the bread is very dark. I am told if margarine is used instead of oil, the bread will be much lighter.   Dorothy Tuttle.

* WHEAT GERM ZUCCHINI BREAD *

3 eggs
1 c. salad oil
1 c. white sugar
1 c. brown sugar
3 tsp. maple flavoring
2 c. Zucchini (coarsley-shredded)

2½ c. flour
½ tsp. wheat germ
2 tsp. soda
½ tsp. baking powder
1 c. walnuts (finely chopped)
1/3 c. sesame seeds

With mixer, beat eggs, add oil, sugars, flavoring and continue to beat. (Mixture should be thick and foamy). Using a spoon stir in zucchini and blend gently. Combine flour, wheat germ, soda, salt, baking powder and nuts. Stir gently into mixture. Pour into 2 greased and floured 5 x 9 in. pans, then lightly press the sesame seeds on top. Bake at 350° for 1 hour.   Jean Keys.

* ZUCCHINI BREAD *

2½ c. sugar or 1 c. sugar,
   1¼ c. honey
3 eggs
1 c. Wesson oil
3 tsp. vanilla
1¼ tsp. baking powder
3 c. flour

3 tsp. cinnamon
1 tsp. salt
1 tsp. baking soda
2 c grated zucchini (medium grate)
1 c. chopped walnuts

Beat eggs, (add honey if used), Wesson oil and vanilla. In another bowl mix baking powder, flour, cinnamon, salt and baking soda. Add the dry ingredients to the egg mixture. Add zucchini and nuts. Fill loaf pans ¾ full and bake for 45 minutes at 350°.   Marie Wong.

* CARROT BREAD *

½ c. oil
1 c. sugar
3 eggs
2 tsp. vanilla
2 c. grated carrots
1 c. chopped walnuts

2 c. flour
2 tsp. soda
2 tsp. cinnamon
½ tsp. salt

Beat eggs, add sugar, oil, flour, soda, cinnamon, salt and vanilla. Mix well. Fold in carrots and walnuts. Pour into greased loaf pan and bake at 300° for 1 hour and 15 minutes.   Dorothy Tuttle.

* CARROT— PINEAPPLE BREAD *

In a lg. bowl combine:
2 c. sugar
1½ c. oil
3 eggs (beaten)
1½ tsp. Vanilla
Sift:
2½ c. flour and 1 Tbsp. more
1½ tsp. salt
1½ tsp. cinnamon
2 tsp. baking soda
Combine both mixtures, then add
2 c. grated carrots
1 can (8 oz.) crushed pineapple (with juice)
1 c. chopped walnuts.
Bake in buttered pan (9 x 13 in.) in preheated oven 350° for 40 to 45 minutes.

Adele Davis.

* PUMPKIN BREAD *

Note: Makes 4 — 1 lb. loaves.

4 c. sugar
1 can (29 oz.) pumpkin
3 eggs
1 c. oil
5 c. flour
1 Tbsp. baking soda

2 tsp. cinnamon
1½ tsp. cloves
1 tsp. salt
2 c. dates (chopped)
2 c. toasted walnuts (chopped)
* whipped cream cheese (optional)

Preheat oven to 350°. Grease 4 — 1 lb. coffee cans or 8 x 4 in. loaf pans. Combine sugar, pumpkin and eggs in a mixing bowl and beat until well blended. Add oil and continue to beat. Thoroughly blend in flour, soda, cinnamon, cloves and salt. Stir in dates and nuts. Fill prepared pans ¾ full to allow for rising during baking. Bake for 1 hour or until toothpick inserted in center comes out clean and bread has pulled away from the sides. Serve with whipped cream cheese.

Nancy Ebsen.

* MANDEL BROT (GERMAN) *
(Almond Bread)

6 eggs (well beaten)
1½ c. sugar
½ lb. butter
2 tsp. baking powder
½ tsp. salt

1 tsp. vanilla
1 c. almonds (blanched — chopped)
4 c. shifted flour

206

Cream butter and sugar. Sift flour, salt and baking powder, add to butter mixture, alternately with the eggs. Add almonds and vanilla. Refrigerate dough until firm enough to handle. Form into rolls and place on greased baking sheet. Bake in preheated oven (350°) for ½ hour. Remove from oven, slice ½ in. thick while still warm, place on baking sheet and toast under broiler until brown on both sides. Serve hot.   Ida Christoph.

* BLITZ KUCHEN (GERMAN) *

¾ c. shortening
1 c. sugar
4 eggs (separated)
1½ c. cake flour (sifted)
2 tsp. baking powder
¼ tsp. salt
1/3 c. milk
½ tsp. vanilla
* cinnamon — chopped nuts.

Cream shortening and sugar, add beaten egg yolks. Sift flour, baking powder and salt. Add to shortening mixture, alternately with the milk. Add vanilla. Fold in beaten egg whites. Bake in buttered pan 12 x 8 x 2 in. preheated oven 350° for 30 to 35 minutes. Before baking sprinkle top with cinnamon and chopped nuts.
                                                Francis Wright.

* SOUR CREAM COFFEE CAKE *

2 sticks oleo (1 cup)
2 c. sugar
2 eggs
3 c. flour
2 tsp. baking powder
2 tsp. baking soda
16 oz. sour cream
2 tsp. vanilla
* topping: ½ c. sugar, 1 tsp. cinnamon,
    1 c. chopped nuts.

Cream oleo and sugar and add eggs and mix well. Sift flour baking powder and baking soda, add to the egg mixture. Add sour cream and vanilla. Pour into buttered pans and top with topping mix.

Bake: 1 hour in angel food pan at 350°.
       ½ hour in 9 x 12" pan at 350°.
       45 minutes in 3 small loaf pans at 350°.   Georgia Beasley.

* BIG PARKER HOUSE ROLL *

1 pkg. dry yeast
¼ c. warm water
1 Tbsp. sugar
1 Tbsp. salad oil
1 egg
1 c. flour

In a small bowl mix yeast and water. Let stand for 5 minutes. Stir in oil, eggs and sugar (that have been lightly beaten with a fork). Add flour and mix. Turn out onto a floured board and knead for 2 minutes. Roll into a 7 in. round and fold in half just off center. Place on greased pan or sheet and let rise for 25 min. (It will puff up). Bake at 350° for 25 minutes. Easy and delicious.   Jean Keys.

* CORNMEAL PARKER HOUSE ROLLS *
(My Mother's Recipe)

1 c. rye or barley flour
¾ c. cornmeal
¼ tsp. salt
1 Tbsp. sugar

3 tsp. baking powder
1 tsp. fat
1 egg
½ c. milk

Sift dry ingredients and cut in fat. Add milk and egg and stir to make a soft dough. Roll out on lightly floured board to 1/8 thickness. Cut with biscuit cutter and fold over (like parkerhouse rolls). Place on greased cookie sheet and bake in preheated oven (350°) until slightly browned. Serve hot.
Note: My Mother made a notation on this recipe that the cost for making rolls was 13 cents for a dozen rolls. How times have changed!!!   Adele Davis.

* BLUEBERRY LEMON MUFFINS *

1¾ c. flour
2/3 c. sugar
2½ tsp. baking powder
1 tsp. shredded lemon peel
1 beaten egg

¾ c. milk
1/3 c. cooking oil
¾ c. fresh or frozen blueberries (thawed)

In a lg. bowl stir together flour, 1/3 c. sugar, baking powder, lemon rind ¾ tsp. salt. Make a well in center. Combine egg, milk and oil. Add egg mixture all at once to flour mixture. Stir until just moist, batter should be lumpy. Drain berries, carefully fold them into batter. Spoon into greased or paper lined muffin cups. Fill 2/3 full. Bake in 400° oven for 20 to 25 minutes, remove from oven, dip tops in ¼ c. melted butter and then in remaining sugar.   Jean Keys.

* CRUNCHY ORANGE MUFFINS *

1½ c. whole wheat flour
½ c. soy flour
1 tsp. sea salt
2 tsp. baking soda
½ c. peanut butter
½ c. plain yogurt

1 egg (beaten)
¼ c. orange juice
grated peel of 1 orange
1 c. honey
¼ c. roasted peanuts (chopped)
¼ c. butter

Preheat oven to 375°. Sift flours, salt and baking soda and set aside. Cream peanut butter, honey and butter until smooth. Add yogurt, egg, orange juice, orange peel and roasted peanuts. Mix well. Add dry ingredients and stir until barely moistened. Spoon into well greased muffin tins. Bake at 15 to 20 minutes or until tested done. Serve muffins with honey and butter.   Arlene Wright.

* REFRIGERATOR MUFFINS *

Mix and set aside:

1 c. shredded wheat	1 c. chopped dates
2 c. All bran	1 c. boiling water

Cream:

1½ c. sugar	½ c. margarine
2 eggs (beaten)	2 c. buttermilk
2½ c. flour	2½ tsp. soda

Mix everything together. Bake at 375° for 20 to 25 minutes, (it is better to use paper liners for the muffin cups). Keep unused part in covered bowl, up to 10 weeks, using when you want only a few. Do not freeze.

Dorothy Tuttle.

* REAL BRAN MUFFINS *

2 c. boiling water	5 c. flour
1 heaping c. Crisco	5 tsp. soda
2 c. Nabisco bran 100%	4 c. Kellog All bran
2½ c. sugar	
4 eggs (beaten)	
1 qt. buttermilk	

Add water to Nabisco bran and let stand. When slightly cooled, add Crisco, sugar, flour, soda, eggs, buttermilk and kellog's all bran. Mix all well. Bake at 350° for 20 to 30 minutes in greased muffin pans.
Note: Keeps well in refrigerator for 6 weeks (put in fruit jars). Take out as many as needed at a time. Elinor Edmondson.

* FOREVER MUFFINS *

In extra lg. bowl put:
4 c. Kellogs All bran
2 c. Nabisco 100% enriched bran
Pour over this 2 c. boiling

In another bowl mix:

1 c. Crisco oil (any oil)	5 c. flour
3 c. sugar	5 tsp. soda
4 eggs (beaten)	2 Tbsp. salt

Add 1 qt. buttermilk to the second mixture. Pour all into the first mixture and stir. Bake as needed in a 400° oven for 25 minutes. Virginia Doyle.

* MIX AND MATCH MUFFINS *

½ c. milk
2 c. prepared biscuit mix

1 pt. chocolate ice cream (softened, but thick)

Mix all ingredients until biscuit mix is dampened. Bake in greased muffin tins in a preheated oven (350°) for 25 to 30 minutes, (test with toothpick).
Note: Variations; Any ice cream may be used as butter pecan, etc. Raspberry and lemon sherbert are also good.   Adele Davis.

* QUICK GINGERBREAD *

¼ c. sugar
½ tsp. soda
1 tsp. cinnamon
1 egg
¼ c. milk

¼ c. shortening
1 tsp. ginger
1 c. flour
¼ c. molasses
1 tsp. baking powder

Beat egg in a lg. bowl and then add all the other ingredients in order given and beat well. Bake 25 minutes in 350° oven.   Zana Luis.

* WHEATLESS GINGERBREAD *

Preheat oven to 325°.
Sift together:

1¼ c. rye or rice flour
1½ c. cornstarch
2 tsp. soda
Mix:
½ c. sugar
1 c. molasses

1 tsp. cinnamon
¼ tsp. cloves
¼ tsp. ginger

½ c. butter —— with the flour mixture. Add 1 c. boiling water. Add 2 well — beaten eggs. Bake in 9 in. round pan for 30 minutes. Note: Unusual, yet perhaps the best of all.   Adele Davis.

* FIST BISCUITS *

2 c. flour
1 Tbsp. baking powder
½ tsp. salt

2 Tbsp. shortening
¾ c. buttermilk

Sift dry ingredients, cut in shortening and slowly add buttermilk. Stir with a fork until dough is soft and fairly moist. Knead lightly (if desired), pat or roll to ½ in. thick. Cut into desired shapes. Bake in preheated oven (450°) for about 15 minutes until browned. (Dough may also be used for the top crust of a casserole dish. Note: Southern cooks often melt the fat to add to the milk and do not roll the dough. They pinch off bits, shape into balls between their palms. Holding the balls of dough in one palm, they flatten it with a swift stroke with the other hand. That is why they are called "fist biscuits".   Adele Davis.

* SESAME BISCUITS *

¼ c. soft butter
¼ lb. Cheddar cheese (grated)
½ c. flour

½ tsp. salt
dash of cayenne
toasted sesame seeds

Combine all ingredients (except sesame seeds) and shape into rolls, 1½ in. in diameter, slice 3/8 in. thick and roll in sesame seeds. Place on cookie sheet. Bake in preheated oven (375°) for 12 to 15 minutes. Serve while warm. Note: You may prepare in advance, wrap and freeze for future use.   Millie Mesaku.

* BUBBLE BISCUITS *

1 pkg. refrigerated biscuits
½ c. walnuts (chopped)
1/3 c. sugar

½ tsp. cinnamon
1/3 c. mayonnaise

Grease 10 muffin tin cups. Combine walnuts, sugar and cinnamon. Separate biscuits. Cut them into quarters and shape into balls. Coat each ball with mayonnaise, then roll in walnut mixture. Place 4 balls into each muffin cup. Bake in preheated oven (400°) for 25 to 30 minutes until browned. Serve warm.

Roberta Chateauneuf.

* POPOVERS *

1 c. flour
¼ tsp. salt
1 c. liquid nonfat milk

3 lg. eggs
4 Tbsp. shortening

Preheat oven to 375°. Combine flour and salt in a mixing bowl, stir in milk. Then add eggs, one at a time and beat until batter is completely blended. Place 1½ tsp. shortening in bottom of each 12 custard cups or lg. muffin tins. Place in oven and heat for 5 minutes or until shortening has melted and cups are hot. Fill each cup 2/3 full and bake for 45 minutes. Note: Curb any desire you have to peek at the popovers while they are baking. They need privacy.

Nancy Ebsen.

* PARMESAN POPOVERS *

¼ c. Parmesan cheese
    (Fresh grated)
1 c. milk
1 c. flour

1 Tbsp. butter (melted)
¼ tsp. salt
2 lg. eggs

Place oven rack on next to lowest shelf. Preheat oven to 450°. Grease 6 deep muffin tins or custard cups and sprinkle with the cheese. Set aside.

Combine milk, flour, butter and salt in a mixing bowl, mix in eggs just enough to blend (overbeating will reduce the volume). Fill cups ¾ full and bake 15 min. Reduce heat to 350° and bake for another 20 minutes longer. (Do not open the oven) Carefully remove popovers with a spatula and serve immediately.

Francis Wright.

* CINNAMON POPOVERS *

3 eggs
1 c. milk
1 c. flour

3 Tbsp. butter or oleo (melted)
1 tsp. cinnamon
¼ tsp. salt

In blender combine eggs, milk, flour, butter, cinnamon and salt. Cover and blend for 3 minutes. Fill 6 to 8 well greased muffin tins or custard cups half full. Bake in a 400° oven 40 minutes. Immediately prick with a fork to let the steam out. Serve with apple jelly.

Jean Keys.

* LAVASH *

2¾ c. flour
¼ c. sugar
½ tsp. salt
½ tsp. baking soda

½ c. butter
1 c. buttermilk

Mix flour, sugar, baking soda and salt. Cut in the butter then add the buttermilk and mix well. Roll the dough directly on an ungreased cookie sheet, about ¼ in. thin. Sprinkle on sesame seeds or poppy seeds. Bake at 400°. for 10 minutes or until golden brown.

Millie Mesaku.

* LAVASH *

2 pkgs. yeast dissolved in 2 c. warm water

Add ¼ lb. margarine (melted — cooled) and 1½ c. flour. Beat 2–3 minutes in electric mixer.

Add 2½ c. whole wheat flour, 1 tsp. salt and beat well. (Add enough white flour to be able to knead. Knead until smooth (about 4 to 5 minutes). Let rise, punch down and let rise again. Divide into 12 balls and let rest a few minutes. Roll thin, then place on ungreased cookie sheet. Paint with 1 beaten egg mixed with ¼ c. cold water. Sprinkle with sesame seeds. Bake at 400° for 8 to 10 minutes (watch carefully). If some bake a light brown faster than others — remove and continue baking the remainer. Keeps well frozen.

Valerie Wilson.

* OLIEBOLLEN *
(Dutch Doughnuts)

1 pkg. dry yeast
¼ c. warm water
1 Tbsp. sugar
3 Tbsp. butter
1 c. milk (scalded)
1 tsp. nutmeg
2 tsp. salt

2 eggs (beaten)
5 c. flour
raisins
diced citron
1 apple (peeled — diced)
oil for deep fry

Soften yeast in warm water with 1 Tbsp. sugar. Add butter to hot milk, cool to lukewarm and then add the yeast mixture, stir in ¾ c. sugar, nutmeg, salt and eggs. Gradually add enough flour to make a soft dough. Mix well.

Knead dough on a lightly floured board about 6 minutes until dough is smooth and satiny. Place in a greased bowl and turn so greased side is up. Cover and let rise in warm place for 1 hour. Punch dough down, shape into a ball and let rest for 10 minutes. Pinch off 1¼ in. ball of dough. Put 2 raisins, 2 pieces citron and a few pieces of apple in center of each. Shape into a ball and put on lightly greased cookie sheet, cover and let rise for 40 minutes

Lift carefully with floured spatula and drop into preheated oil. Fry until golden brown and drain on paper towels. (Do not fry too many at one time). Roll in mixture of sugar and cinnamon.   Francis Wright.

* BERLIMER PFANN KUCHEN (GERMAN) *
(Plum Doughnuts)

1½ cake compressed yeast
1½ c. lukewarm milk
6 c. flour
2 eggs
1 egg yolk
grated rind 1 lemon
½ c. sugar

¼ c. butter (melted)
2/3 c. plum jam
pinch of salt
few drops of vanilla
oil for deep frying

Dissolve yeast in half of lukewarm milk. Sift flour in a bowl, make well in center. Pour in yeast mixture, sprinkle a little sugar on top. Place dish towel on top and let rise in warm place for 15 minutes. Add eggs, egg yolk, sugar, lemon rind, salt, vanilla and melted butter and remaining milk. Beat well. Place on floured board and roll out to finger thickness, cut into 3 in. circles. Put spoonful of plum jam in center of each circle. Place another circle on top. Press edges firmly down with dampened fingers. Put dough in warm place to rise for 10 minutes. Heat oil in deep fryer, and test with cube of bread for proper heat. Fry doughnuts until golden brown (do not pierce). Drain on paper towel and sprinkle with sugar.

Adele Davis.

* ANISE TOAST *

2 eggs
2/3 c. sugar

1 tsp. anise seeds
1 c. flour

Beat eggs and sugar thoroughly, add flour and anise seeds. (A stiff dough). (Do this with a spoon).

Butter and flour a pan (9 x 5 x 3 in.). Spread stiff batter in pan. Bake at 375° until toothpick inserted comes out clean (about 30 minutes). Remove from pan and slice. Place slices on buttered cookie sheet. Bake about 5 minutes until browned on bottom. Turn and repeat. (Discarded ice cube trays make excellent pans.)

Dorothy Tuttle.

* HOT HERB BREAD *

(Italian Style)

1 loaf French or Italian (about 4")
½ c. soft butter or margarine
½ tsp. oregano (crumbled)
¼ tsp. dry dill

bread
1 clove garlic (minced)
grated Parmesan cheese
1 tsp. parsley flakes

Cut bread diagonally into 1 in. slices. Blend butter, parsley, oregano, dill and garlic. Put bread slices together with the butter mixing top open. Sprinkle top with parsley and cheese. Heat in oven for 10 minutes.

Note: If I am taking to a pot luck party, I wrap it completely to heat.

Valerie Wilson.

* DOUBLE CORN BREAD *

½ c. cornmeal
½ c. flour
½ tsp. baking soda

½ tsp. baking powder
½ tsp. salt
2 tsp. sugar

Mix above ingredients with a fork.

¾ c. milk
¼ c. oil

2 eggs
1 can (8 oz.) creamed corn

Mix above ingredients and add to the dry ingredients. Heat oven to 400°.
Heat 6" or 7" skillet with ½ Tbsp. bacon fat. Pour batter into hot skillet. Bake 40 minutes.

Ruth Nelson.

 C·O·O·K·I·E·S

* MUSHROOM MERINGUES *
(My Prize Winning Recipe)

These charming petits fours are a work of art. They call for patience and talent with the pastry bag and must have a dry atmosphere.

½ c. egg whites about 3 or 4
   if eggs are lg.
1 c. sugar
cocoa

¼ tsp. cream of tartar
1 tsp. vanilla
chocolate

Adjust two racks to divide oven into thirds. Preheat oven to 225°. Cut aluminum foil to fit two cookie sheets, at least 12 x 15".

In a small bowl, beat egg whites at low speed until they become foamy. Add the salt and cream of tartar, increase the speed to moderate and beat until whites hold a soft shape. Continue to beat and start adding the sugar, one rounded Tbsp. at a time. When half of the sugar has been added, increase the speed to high and add vanilla. Beat until meringue is very stiff and sugar is melted.

To hold the foil in place, put a small amount of the meringue in each corner of the sheets and press firmly.

Do not let meringue stand. Fit a round tube in the pastry bag (tube ½ or ¾ in.). Fold down the top of the bag to form a deep cuff on the outside. Support the bag by holding it under the cuff with one hand. Using a rubber spatula, transfer the meringue into the bag. Lift the top up and twist the top closed.

On one prepared cookie sheet make the stems first. Hold the bag at a right angle and close to the foil. Press out gently while slowly raising the bag straight up. Keep the stems as straight as possible. (Don't worry if there are points on top, it can be snipped off with scissors after baking). They should be placed on the cookie sheet ½ to 1 in. apart.

Strain some cocoa through a strainer and sprinkle on tops to resemble soil and natural mushroom color. Place in oven on the top rack.

On the other cookie sheet shape the caps. Holding the bag straight up and close to the foil, press out even rounds of the meringue. The caps should be about ½ in. apart. Strain cocoa over tops and bake in the bottom rack.

Bake one hour until mushrooms can be removed from the foil. Turn the heat off and prop open the oven door a little and let dry until cooled. When cooled snip off any points.

Melt two squares of semi-sweet chocolate in top of double boiler. Hold mushroom cap upside down, spread layer of chocolate to the edge. It should be thin but not too thin. Place stem on the cap and place upside down, until chocolate hardens.

Do not freeze or cover mushrooms air-tight. They will keep for weeks in an open straw basket.

Adele Davis.

* CHRISTMAS BARS *

1 c. butter — ¼ c. sugar — 2 c. flour. Sift and cut in butter (like cornmeal). Press into a 9 x 13 in. pan.

Filling:

½ c. flour
1 c. sugar
½ tsp. baking powder
½ tsp. salt

1 c. chopped nuts
1 c. chopped candied fruits
4 eggs

Beat eggs, add sugar and beat, add flour, baking powder and salt and mix well. Add chopped nuts and candied fruit, pour over crust. Bake at 400° for 5 minutes reduce heat and bake at 350° for 30 minutes. Cut while warm and sprinkle with powdered sugar.

Jean Keys.

* SPRITZ COOKIES (GERMAN) *

1 c. butter
½ tsp. baking powder
2/3 c. sugar

2¼ c. flour
1 egg (beaten)
1 tsp. almond extract

Cream butter, add sugar and beaten egg. Sift dry ingredients, add to butter mixture. Stir in almond extract. Using cookie press, press into desired shapes. Bake on ungreased cookie sheet at 375° for 8 to 10 minutes.   Francis Wright.

* ALMOND SPRITZ XMAS COOKIES *

1 c, unsalted butter
½ tsp. baking powder
3 oz. almond paste (imported)
   kind)
1 lg. egg (beaten)

2 c. flour
1 tsp. vanilla
1 tsp. almond extract
dash of salt

* Sliced candy cherries, chopped nuts sugar sprinkles for decoration. Preheat oven to 375°. Cream butter and sugar until light and fluffy. Add almond paste and egg, beat thoroughly. Add flour gradually, then flavorings and salt. Blend. Put dough through a cookie press or pastry bag using No. 5 star tube. Squeeze into S-shapes or desired shapes onto an ungreased cookie sheet. Decorate as desired. Bake for 8 to 10 minutes until edges are slightly brown. Remove to rack to cool.

Note: Domestic almond paste may be used but imported paste has less sugar and makes a better cookie. When working with dough, keep remainder in refrigerator between batches.

Adele Davis.

* LEBKUCHEN (GERMAN) *
(Honey Cakes)

1 c. honey
¾ c. light brown sugar
juice and rind 1 lemon
2 eggs (beaten)
2½ c. flour (sifted)
1 tsp. baking soda

½ tsp. nutmeg
½ tsp. cloves
1 tsp. cinnamon
¼ c. almonds (shredded)
¼ c. citron (chopped)

Combine honey, sugar, lemon juice and rind. Beat in egg. Sift dry ingredients and add to egg mixture. Add citron and nuts and let stand one day (covered). Roll out dough ½ in. thick and cut into fancy shapes. Bake on buttered cookie sheet in oven (400°) until browned.   Francis Wright.

* SHORT BREAD *

1 c. sugar
2 c. butter
4 c. flour

* Remove 4 Tbsp. flour and replace
with 4 Tbsp. rice flour

Mix butter and sugar with your hands, then add flour and mix well. To roll out, use powdered sugar instead of flour. Roll to desired thickness. Bake on a cookie sheet or cut as cookies. Prick with a fork. Bake in slow oven 300 — 350° about 20 minutes until they are golden brown.   Gladys Box.

* SCOTCH SHORT BREAD *

1½ c. superfine sugar
5 c. flour
1 lb. butter (cannot use margarine)

With your fingers, break the butter into small pieces. Work in flour and sugar with your hands until mixture has the consistency of cornmeal, and can be pressed together.
Turn dough out on floured cloth or board and knead it well until you have a smooth dough.
Roll dough to desired thickness (I like it ¼ to 3/8 in. thick) and cut into shapes. Prick each with a fork (dip in flour if it sticks).
Place on lined (heavy brown paper) cookie sheets. Bake at 325° for about 15 minutes until lightly brown and golden. Cool on lined sheets. Store in airtight container but do not put in refrigerator. They will keep crisp for weeks.
                    Irene Pimentel.

* PENNSYLVANIA DUTCH COOKIES *

4 eggs (beaten)
2 c. brown sugar
1¾ c. flour
1 tsp. baking powder
¼ tsp. cloves
1 tsp. cinnamon
1 c. nuts
1 c. raisins

Mix all together. Bake on paper lined — greased jelly roll pan (10 x 15") at 375° for 25 minutes. Remove from oven — and frost at once with: 2 c. powder sugar and 2 Tbsp. butter. Cut into squares while in pan.   Dorothy Tuttle.

* GINGER SNAPS *

2¼ c. flour (sifted)
2 tsp. baking soda
½ tsp. salt
1 tsp. ginger
1 tsp. cinnamon
½ tsp. cloves
¾ c. shortening
1 c. sugar
¼ c. molasses
1 egg
3 Tbsp. sugar
3 Tbsp. water

Sift flour with soda, salt and spices. Cream shortening, add sugar gradually and cream until fluffy. Add molasses and egg and mix. Add sifted ingredients and mix well. Allow 1 Tbsp. of dough for each cookie. Shape into a ball, dip tip of cookie in remaining sugar, then in water. Place on ungreased cookie sheet. Bake in preheated oven (375°) for 10 minutes. Cool.   Ida Christoph.

* GINGER COOKIES *

1 c. brown sugar
1 c. molasses
1 c. shortening
   (lard or and butter)
1 tsp. soda
½ tsp. salt
½ tsp. ginger (grated)

Place in saucepan, molasses, and shortening and slowly bring to a boil. Cool. Add enough flour to make a very stiff dough. Roll thin as paper on floured board. (If desired, sprinkle with sugar and roll once with rolling pin). Bake in hot oven (375°) on greased cookie sheets. Do not let them get too brown.

Judy Pieklo.

* CRISPY DELICIOUS COOKIES *

1 c. sugar
1 c. brown sugar
1 c. oleo
1 c. Mazola oil
1 egg
1 tsp. vanilla
½ c. nuts
1 tsp. salt
1 tsp. cream of tartar
1 tsp. soda
1 c. Rice Krispies
1 c. flake coconut
1 c. dry oatmeal
3½ c. sifted flour

Cream sugars and oleo, add beaten egg, then vanilla and oil. Add sifted dry ingredients. Rice Krispies, coconut, nuts and oatmeal. Roll into balls and place on greased pan and press with fork. Bake in moderate oven till lightly brown around edges. Leave on cookie sheet for a few minutes to complete baking. Cool.

Madeline Ryan.

* SWEDISH HONEY COOKIES *

½ c. butter or margarine (softened)
2/3 c. brown sugar (packed)
1/3 c. honey
1 egg
2 c. flour

1 tsp. ground coriander
½ tsp. baking soda
½ tsp. salt
¼ tsp. cinnamon

Cream butter, sugar, honey and beat in egg. Sift flour with remaining ingredients. Stir into creamed mixture, working to make a soft dough. Divide in half, wrap in wax paper and chill. On well floured surface, roll each portion to 1/8 in thickness. Cut into desired shapes with cookie cutters, place on ungreased cookie sheet and bake at 375° till golden — 5 to 7 minutes. Jean Keys.

* MARSHMALLOW MOSAIC COOKIES *

6 sq. semi — sweet chocolate
2 eggs
1 bag (10 oz.) colored
    miniture marshmallows

1½ c. toasted nuts (chopped)
2 c. graham cracker crumbs
1 tsp. vanilla

Melt chocolate in top of double boiler. Remove from heat, beat in eggs and vanilla, fold in marshmallows and 1 c. nuts. Combine graham crackers crumbs and remaining nuts. Cut 6 pieces of waxed paper 12 in. long. Spread crumb mixture evenly over half of each piece of paper, keeping crumb side closest to you. Place spoonfuls of the marshmallow mixture along edges of wax paper on top of the crumbs, divide the mixture between the 6 pieces. Twist ends of paper and refrigerate until chocolate is set. Cut on diagonal into ¼ in. slices with serrated knife. Note: Rolls may be wrapped in foil and frozen. Adele Davis.

* BROWNIES *

½ c. butter (melted)
2 c. sugar
2 Tbsp. instant coffee
4 eggs
1 tsp. vanilla
¾ c. unsifted flour

4 sq. unsweetened chocolate (melted)
¼ tsp. salt
1 c. macadamia bits (if salted omit
    the salt)
1 c. chocolate bits.

Butter a 11 x 13 in pan. In a lg. bowl, blend sugar, instant coffee and butter. Add eggs, one at a time and beat well after each addition. Add vanilla, flour, chocolate and salt. Pour into pan. Sprinkle nuts over mixture and bake at 250° for 25 minutes. Spread chocolate bits over cookies while still warm. Cool before cutting.   Maggie Inouye.

* CHOCOLATE CHIP BARS *

½ c. sugar
½ c. brown sugar
½ c. oleo or butter (softened)
1 tsp. vanilla
1 egg

1¼ c. flour
½ tsp. baking soda
½ tsp. salt
½ c. chopped nuts
6 oz. semi-sweet chocolate bits.

Mix the sugars and butter until creamy. Add egg, vanilla and mix well. Add flour, baking soda, salt and mix. Add nuts and chocolate bits. Spread dough in a greased 12 x 9 in. pan. Bake at 375° for 12 to 15 minutes. Cool and cut into bars.   Jean Keys.

* ROCKY ROAD FUDGE BARS *

Base:

½ c. butter or oleo
1 oz. (1 square) unsweetened
   chocolate
1 c. flour
1 c. sugar

¾ c. chopped nuts
1 tsp. baking powder
1 tsp. vanilla
2 eggs

Filling:

1 pkg. (8 oz.) cream cheese
   (softened)
¼ c. butter (softened)
½ c. sugar

2 Tbsp. flour
½ tsp. vanilla
1 egg
1 pkg. (6 oz.) (1 cup) semi-sweet
   chocolate chips

Frosting:

2 c. minature marshmallows
¼ c. butter
¼ c. milk
1 tsp. vanilla

1 oz. (1 square) unsweetened chocolate
3 c. powdered sugar

Heat oven to 350°. Grease and flour 13 x 9 in. pan. In lg. saucepan, over low heat, melt butter and chocolate. Add flour and remaining base ingredients, mix well. Spread in prepared pan.

In small bowl, combine all filling ingredients (except nuts and chocolate chips). Beat 1 minute at medium speed until light and fluffy, stir in nuts. Spread over chocolate mixture, sprinkle evenly with the chocolate chips.

Bake at 350° for 25 to 30 minutes or until toothpick inserted in center comes out clean. Immediately sprinkle marshmallows over top, return to oven and bake for 2 minutes longer.

In lg. saucepan, over low heat, melt ¼ c. butter, 1 oz. chocolate. Reserved 2 oz. cream cheese and milk. Remove from heat, stir in remaining frosting ingredients and stir until smooth. Immediately pour frosting over marshmallows and lightly swirl with knife. Chill.   Adele Davis.

* TOLL HOUSE COOKIES *

Sift together and set aside:
2½ unsifted flour
1 tsp. baking soda
½ tsp. salt
Cream:

1 c. butter (softened)   ¾ c. sugar
1 c. peanut butter   ¾ c. brown sugar (packed)
1 tsp. vanilla

Add 2 eggs, sifted dry ingredients and stir. Add 1 bag (12 oz.) chocolate bits, 1½ c. raisins and 2 c. rice krispies. Stir well. Bake at 375° for 8 minutes. Cool for 5 minutes before removing from pan.   Maggie Inouye.

* CHOCOLATE MINT SURPRISE COOKIES *

3 c. flour (sifted)   3 eggs (beaten)
1 tsp. soda   2 Tbsp. water
½ tsp. salt   2 tsp. vanilla
1 c. butter or oleo   1 pkg. (9 oz.) thin chocolate mint wafers
1 c. sugar
½ c. brown sugar

Cream butter and gradually add sugars, blend in eggs, beat well and add water and vanilla. Sift dry ingredients and add to mixture. Cover and chill for 2 hours. To bake: Take about 1 Tbsp. of dough and enclose one mint wafer. Place on greased baking sheet about 2 in. apart. Top cookie with walnut half if desired. Bake in preheated oven (375°) for 10 to 15 minutes.

Lucille Grimes.

* CHERRY CHOCOLATE KISSES *

1 c. butter or oleo
(softened)
1 c. powdered sugar
2 tsp. maraschino cherry juice
½ tsp. almond extract

few drops of red food coloring
2¼ c. flour
½ tsp. salt
½ c. maraschino cherries (drained —
chopped)
48 chocolate kisses

Heat oven to 350°. In large bowl. Combine butter, powdered sugar, cherry juice, almond extract and food coloring. Blend well. Stir in flour and salt. Add cherries and mix well. Form dough into 1 in. balls and place 2 in. apart on ungreased cookies sheets. Bake at 350° for 8 to 10 minutes or until lightly browned on edges. Immediately top each cookie with a chocolate kiss. Cool.

Adele Davis.

* MOCHA BALLS *

Mix together:
2 eggs
1 c. sugar

1½ c. flour
2 tsp. baking powder

Bring ½ c. milk to a boil and add 3 tsp. butter. Add this to the dry ingredients and beat well. Pour into a greased 9 x 12 in. pan and bake at 350° for about 25 minutes. Cool. Cut into squares and frost with your favorite frosting (when you add mocha flavoring or strong coffee). Roll in chopped peanuts. Note: A pound cake mix may be used in place of the above cake.

Ruth Tufte.

* MEXICAN MOCHA BALLS *

1 c. butter or margarine (softened)
½ c. sugar
1 tsp. vanilla
2 c. flour
¼ c. sweetened cocoa powder

1 tsp. instant coffee crystals
¼ tsp. salt
1 c. finely chopped walnuts
½ c. finely chopped maraschino cherries
extra fine granulated sugar

Cream first three ingredients, stir flour with cocoa, coffee and salt. Gradually beat into creamed mixture. Stir in nuts and cherries. Chill 1 hour. Form into 1 in. balls, place on ungreased baking sheet. Bake at 325° for 20 minutes. Cool. While warm dust with sugar.

Jean Keys.

* FAVORITE LEMON BARS *

Part 1.
1 c. flour
½ c. butter
¼ c. powder sugar

222

Mix above with pastry blender (like pie crust) and press into a baking pan 9 x 13 in. Bake for 15 minutes at 350°.

Part 2.

2 c. sugar
4 Tbsp. flour
1 tsp. baking powder

4 Tbsp. lemon juice
rind of 2 lemons
4 eggs (beaten)

Sift together flour, baking powder and sugar. Add eggs, lemon juice, and lemon rind and mix well. Pour on top of baked mixture. Bake 25 minutes. Sprinkle sugar on top while still warm. Cut into squares and loosen around the edges as they might stick.   Francis Wright.

* LEMON CRISPS *

1 c. unsalted butter (softened)
1½ c. sugar
4 egg yolks
juice of 1 lemon
2 tsp. grated lemon rind

½ tsp. lemon extract
3 c. flour
½ tsp. salt

Cream butter and sugar until fluffy. Add egg yolks, lemon juice, rind and extract. Continue beating until light. Mix in flour and salt and blend. Form dough into 2 cylinders, each 2 in. in diameter. Wrap and chill in refrigerator for several hours. (May also be frozen). Preheat oven to 375° Grease cookie sheets. Slice dough 1/8 in. thick and place slices 1½ in. apart on sheets. Bake for 8 to 10 min. until lightly brown on edges. Remove to rack to cool. Store in tightly sealed container.   Sarah Hemings.

* PUMPKIN COOKIES *

2 c. shortening
2 c. sugar
1 can (16 oz) pumpkin
2 eggs
2 tsp. vanilla
4 c. flour
2 tsp. baking powder

2 tsp. cinnamon
1 tsp. soda
1 tsp. nutmeg
½ tsp. allspice
2 c. raisins
1 c. chopped nuts
1 tsp. salt

Cream shortening and sugar. Add pumpkin, eggs, vanilla, beat well. Stir together flour spices and salt, add to batter. Mix well. Stir in nuts and raisins. Drop by tsp. 2 in. apart on greased cookies sheet. Bake at 350° for 12 to 15 minutes. Cool on rack.   Jean Keys.

* PUMPKIN PISTACHIO MACAROONS *

2/3 c. raw honey (unfiltered)
¼ c. pumpkin seeds
¼ c. undyed pistachios
   (unsalted — chopped fine)

2 c. unsweetened coconut (shredded)
¼ tsp. anise seeds (crushed)
3 egg whites (stiffly beaten)

Preheat oven to 300°. Blend honey, pumpkin seeds, pistachio, coconut and anise. Fold into stifly beaten egg whites (add more coconut if batter is too thin). Drop by tsp. onto lightly greased cookie sheet and bake for 25 to 30 minutes until golden brown. Let cookies stand for about 10 to 15 minutes before removing from the pan. Place in single layer on clean cookie sheet. When cookies are all baked, cool oven to 100°. Return cookies to oven to dry for at least 1 hour or overnite.   Adele Davis.

* HAWAIIAN DELIGHT COOKIES *

Crust:

1 pkg. (8 oz.) cream cheese
2 blocks margarine

2½ c. flour
½ c. Macadamia nuts (chopped)

Cream margarine and cheese, add flour gradually. Roll dough into 1 in. balls. Spread out dough like pie crust in greased muffin tins. Sprinkle nuts on top of dough.

Fillings:

3 eggs
1½ c. brown sugar
½ c. Macadamia nuts (chopped)

2 Tbsp. flour
½ c. shredded coconut
1 tsp. baking powder

Beat eggs and add brown sugar and beat very well. Add remaining ingredients and mix again. Place mixture on crust. Bake in preheated oven 350° for 15 to 17 minutes reduce heat to 250° and bake for another 10 minutes.   Lorna Burger.

* LILIKOI RAISIN BARS *
(Passion Fruit)

Crumb Crust:

¾ c. soft butter
1 c. brown sugar
1¾ c. flour

½ tsp. salt
½ tsp. soda
1½ c. rolled oats

Cream butter and sugar until soft and fluffy. Sift dry ingredients together and mix in rolled oats. Mix all together and spread ½ of crumb mixture into greased 9 x 13 in. pan. Press down thoroughly.

224

Filling:
2½ c. raisins
1–2 c. sugar
2 Tbsp. cornstarch

¾ c. water
3 Tbsp. Lilikoi juice

Combine filling ingredients and cook over low flame, stirring constantly until thickened. Cool. Spread filling evenly over crust and top with remaining crumbs. Bake in preheated oven (375°) for 25 to 30 minutes. Cut while warm.

Daisy Alexander.

* WEST POINT DATE BARS *

Filling
1 lb. dates
½ c. brown sugar

½ c. water
1 tsp. flour

Cook until thick —flavor with vanilla
Dry ingredients:
½ c. flour
2 c. rolled oats
½ tsp. soda (in flour)

¾ c. melted butter
1½ c. brown sugar

Mix all together and spread ½ of the mixture in bottom of pan. Spread filling over it. Put other half of mixture to top. Bake for 20 minutes in a moderate oven. Note: This is my Mothers tried and true recipe. It is very good.

Elizabeth Betty Guy.

* FAVORITE DATE BARS *

Crust:
½ c. butter
¼ c. sugar
1 c. flour

Mix all and press firmly into a 9 x 9 x 1 in. pan. Bake for 10 to 12 minutes in 400° oven. Do not brown.

Filling:
½ c. flour
½ tsp. baking powder
¼ tsp. salt
1 c. brown sugar
2 eggs (beaten)

¼ c. chopped nuts
1 tsp. vanilla
½ c. chopped dates

Mix flour with baking powder and salt and set aside. Beat eggs, add sugar and dates and beat well. All flour mixture, vanilla, nuts. Spread over baked crust and bake for 30 minutes in 350° oven. Cut into bars when cool.
Note: A favorite Family recipe.

Jean Keys.

* PINEAPPLE BARS *

Blend: 2 c. sugar — ½ c. butter
Add and mix well:

1 can (No. 2) crushed pineapple (drained)	½ tsp. salt
	½ tsp. baking soda
1 c. walnuts (chopped	6 eggs

Bake in greased pan 10 x 15 c 2 in. at 350°. about 30 to 35 minutes.

Dottie Morrison.

* ALMOND ROCA COOKIES *

1 c. butter	2 c. sifted flour
½ c. brown sugar	10 oz. milk chocolate or chocolate chips
½ c. white sugar	1 c. finely chopped nuts
1 egg yolk	
1 tsp. vanilla	

Cream butter and sugar, add egg yolk and vanilla. Stir in flour. Spread mixture thinly on greased cookie sheet. Bake at 350° for 15 to 20 minutes.
Melt chocolate over hot water and spread over warm baked cookies. Sprinkle on nuts and press them firmly. Cut in bars while still warm. Let stand until chocolate is dry.

Maude Daughters.

* BUTTER PECAN CRUNCHERS *

2 Tbsp. plus ½ c. butter (softened)	½ tsp. baking powder
1¾ c. brown sugar (firmly packed)	1 egg
1 c. chopped pecans	1 tsp. rum flavoring
2 c. flour	½ tsp. vanilla

Combine 2 Tbsp. butter, ½ c. brown sugar and pecans. Mix until just blended. Set aside. In large mixing bowl combine ½ c. butter, 1¼ c. brown sugar and remaining ingredients. Blend well. Stir into pecan mixture until well distributed. Shape into balls using a rounded tsp. Place on ungreased cookie sheet and flatten slightly with bottom of a glass greased and dipped in flour. Bake at 375° for 10 to 12 minutes. Cool.

Jean Keys.

* PATSY'S OATMEAL COOKIES *

1 c. sugar	½ tsp. salt
2 blocks butter	2 c. rolled oats
1 egg	¾ c. each raisins —chocolate chips
2 c. flour	½ c. walnuts
1 tsp. baking powder	

Cream butter and sugar. Add egg, add flour baking soda and salt. Add remaining ingredients. Spoon teaspoons on lightly greased baking sheet. Bake at 350° for 15 minutes. Cool.

Patsy Young.

* PEANUT BUTTER BALLS *

1 lb. margarine
2 c. peanut butter
2½ lbs. powdered sugar

1 tsp. vanilla
2 pkgs. (12 oz. each) chocolate chips
1 bar parafin wax

In top of double boiler, melt margarine, peanut butter sugar and vanilla. Mix thoroughly. Cool. Roll into small balls.

Dipping sauce:

Melt chocolate and wax over very slow heat. Using toothpick, dip each ball into chocolate mixture. Cool on wax paper. (Keeps indefinately in refrigerator).

Adele Davis.

* CHERRY CEREAL FLAKE KISSES *

3 egg whites
1 tsp. salt
1½ c. sugar

1½ c. shredded coconut
3 c. cereal flakes
½ c. Maraschino cherries

Beat egg whites and salt until stiff, slowly add sugar. Fold in remaining ingredients. Drop by tsp. on greased cookie sheet and bake in preheated oven at 350° for 15 to 20 minutes.

Judy Pieklo.

* CORN FLAKE COOKIES *

Cream together ½ c. butter — ¾ c. white sugar.

Add: 1 egg, 2 Tbsp. milk — 2 tsp. baking powder — 2 c. corn flakes (slightly crushed). Mix well. Drop by tsp. on a greased baking sheet and bake at 350° for 8 minutes until brown. Note: These spread while baking, so do not put them too close together.

Dorothy Tuttle.

* JEAN'S GRANOLA *

2½ c. oats
1 c. shredded coconut
½ c. chopped or slivered almonds
½ c. sesame seeds
½ c. sunflower seeds

¼ c. wheat germ
¼ c. oil
½ c. honey
½ c. dried apricots (chopped)
¼ c. raisins

Combine oats, coconut, almonds, sesame seeds, sunflower seeds, with wheat germ. Combine honey and oil. Add to the first mixture and blend well. Spread out in a 13 x 9 in. pan and bake in a 300° oven for 45 minutes. Stir every 15 minutes. Remove, stir in apricots and raisins, then cool. Put into plastic jars or plastic bags and seal. Delicious.

Jean Keys.

* PINK CLOUD COOKIES *

Crust:
1½ c. flour — ¾ c. margarine — ½ c. brown sugar. Mix and pack in an 8 x 12 in. pan (greased). Bake for 25 minutes at 325°.

Filling: Make a syrup of 2 c. sugar and ½ c. water. Boil for 2 minutes. Meanwhile, dissolve 2 pkgs. unflavored gelatin in ½ c. cold water. Add to hot syrup and beat for 10 minutes with electric beater. Add 1 tsp. vanilla, ½ c. chopped nuts and 2—3 drops of pink food coloring. Pour over thoroughly cooled crust. Sprinkle with grated coconut. Refrigerate until ready to use.

Note: Beautiful for a special dessert or tea.   Jean Keys.

* CHINESE NOODLE COOKIES *

1 pkg. (12 oz.) peanut   1/3 chopped pecans
   butter chips   1/3 c. miniature marshmallows
1 can (5 oz.) chow mein noodles

Heat peanut butter in top of double boiler until melted. Gently stir in noodles. Divide mixture into thirds. Stir pecans into one portion. Blend marshmallows into another (remainder is plain). Drop all 3 mixtures by rounded tsp. onto waxed paper. Let cookies set until cool.   Ruth Tufte.

* ANISE TOAST *
(Italian Cookie good with Fruit or Cheese)

2 eggs   1 tsp. anise seed
2/3 c. sugar   1 c. flour

Heat oven to 375°. Grease and flour a loaf pan (9 x 5 x 3 in.). Beat eggs and sugar thoroughly. Add anise seed, gradually mix in flour. Spread this stiff dough in prepared pan. Bake 30 to 40 minutes or until toothpick stuck in center of loaf comes out clean. Remove from pan and cut loaf into 16½ in. slices. Place slices on buttered baking sheet. Bake 5 minutes more, until all sides are browned. Cool. Serve with ice cream, fruit or cheese.   Zana Luis.

* ROCKY ROADS *

15 lg. marshmallows
1 c. crunchy peanut butter
2 c. semi-sweet chocolate pieces.

Cut marshmallows into quarters using wet scissors. Arrange on the bottom of buttered 8 in. square pan. Melt peanut butter and chocolate in small saucepan. Stir to blend as it melts. When completely melted, drizzle over marshmallows, spread evenly. Chill, cut into squares.   Jean Keys.

* UNBAKED COOKIES *

Boil 3 minutes exactly — 2 c. sugar — ½ c. milk — ½ c. butter. Add: 3 c. oatmeal — 1 c. coconut, 6 tsp. cocoa and 1 tsp. vanilla. Mix well and then drop by teaspoonful on waxed paper. Cool and serve.   Jean Keys.

* DIABETIC HEALTH COOKIES *

2 c. flour
1 tsp. soda
½ tsp. salt
1 c. shortening — cholesterol
    free oil or oleo
½ c. Sweet and Low
2 eggs
1 c. raisins

1 tsp. vanilla
½ c. Quaker oats
½ c. wheat germ
½ c. shredded coconut
½ c. bran
½ c. peanut butter
1 c. walnuts

Mix together — pat into cookies and place on waxed paper. Place on cookie sheet and bake in 400° oven for 8 to 10 minutes.   Roberta Chateauneuf.

* HEALTHFUL SNACKS *
(Special Recipes by Renee Coscina)

PEANUT BUTTER BALLS OR BARS.

2/3 peanut butter (crunchy)
1 c. toasted Hi-Pro Granola or
1 c. toasted wheat germ
½ c. honey
¼ tsp. salt

½ c. chopped raisins
1 c. toasted, unsweetened coconut or
1 c. toasted sesame seeds

Combine ingredients, adding enough peanut butter to make a stiff dough. Roll mixture into balls or press on a flat surface with hands or rolling pin to about ½ in. thick. (Cut into 1½ in squares. Cover balls or squares with coconut or sesame seeds. Store in covered container in refrigerator.

LOVE CANDIES:

1½ c. pitted dates (chopped)
1¼ c. almond meal
coconut (grated)

Combine first two ingredients, making a stiff consistency. Form into balls and roll in coconut. Refrigerate.

POPPED PUMPKIN SEEDS:

1 c. pumpkin seeds (raw)
1 Tbsp. oil, cold pressed

Heat oil in skillet with seeds. Shake pan to circular motion across the burner to prevent burning. Pops like popcorn.

CAROB DELIGHT:

1 c. sunflower seeds   ¼ c. honey
1 c. almond or sesame butter   ½ c. rolled oats
½ c. carob powder

Mix all ingredients well. Roll into balls then roll in shredded coconut or ground almonds.   Renee Coscina.

* OATMEAL COOKIES *

1 c. butter   1 tsp. soda
1 c. white sugar   ½ tsp. salt
1 c. brown sugar   1 tsp. vanilla
2 beaten eggs   2 cups oatmeal
2 c. sifted all purpose flour   1 c. wheat germ

Mix in order given. Drop by tsp. on cookie sheet and flatten. Bake in 350° oven for 10 to 12 minutes on ungreased baking sheet.

Amy Matsuda.

CAKES & PIES

* STRAWBERRY MERINGUE PIE *

1 baked pie shell (10 in.) or lady fingers
9 egg whites   1 Tbsp. cornstarch
2½ c. sugar   1 qt. strawberries (washed — hulled)
powdered sugar

Preheat oven to 375°. If lady fingers are used, place in bottom of pie pan, and trim to fit neatly. Beat egg whites until soft peaks form. Very gradually add sugar and cornstarch, beating constantly. Transfer half into another bowl. (Reserve 4 of the largest berries for garnish). Coarsely chop remaining berries and gently fold into half of the meringue. Transfer to the pie shell and smooth surface. Use remaining meringue for topping. Swirl into designs. Sprinkle lightly with powdered sugar. Bake until golden (about 15 minutes). Cool before serving. Garnish with halved strawberries.   Adele Davis.

* PINEAPPLE MERINGUE PIE *

1 baked 9 in. pie shell   2 egg yolks
2 c. crushed pineapple (drained)   3 egg whites
¼ c. Galliano (optional)   1/8 tsp. salt
3 Tbsp. sugar   6 Tbsp. super fine sugar
1 Tbsp cornstarch   1/8 tsp. cream of tartar
1 Tbsp. butter
1 tsp. lemon juice

Place pineapple, Gallino, sugar, cornstarch, butter and lemon juice in pan and cook over medium heat, stirring constantly until thick. Beat egg yolks lightly and stir into the pineapple mixture. Cook over very low heat until thick. Cool slightly and pour into pie shell. Preheat oven to 350°. Beat egg whites until foamy. Add cream of tartar and salt. Beat in the super fine sugar, 1 Tbsp. at a time. Continue beating until stiff and glossy. Spread meringue over filled pie, swirling into peaks. Make sure that all the edges are covered.
Bake about 15 minutes until meringue is slightly browned on the tips.
    Ruth Tufte.

* PINEAPPLE GLAZED APPLE PIE *

1 can (12 oz.) pineapple juice   ½ tsp. salt
¾ c. sugar   1 (9 in.) baked pie shell
3 Tbsp. cornstarch   1 tsp. vanilla
1 Tbsp. butter
7 medium tart apples (7 c.) (peeled —
    cored — cut in wedges)

In large saucepan combine 1¼ c. pineapple juice and sugar and bring to a boil. Add apples, turn down heat and simmer (covered) until apples are tender but not soft. Lift apples from sauce and set aside to drain. Combine cornstarch and remaining pineapple juice, add to syrup in saucepan. Cook until mixture thickens and bubbles. Remove from heat and stir in butter, vanilla and salt. Cool for 10 minutes without stirring. Pour half of syrup into shell, arrange apple slices on top. Spoon remaining mixture over apples. Cover and refrigerate until chilled. Before serving, garnish pie with whipped cream and chopped nuts.

Roberta Chateauneuf.

* TWO — CRUST LEMON PIE *

2 unbaked (9 in.) pie shells
  (top and bottom)
3 lemons (peeled — seeded —
  cut thin)
2 Tbsp. lemon rind (grated)
1 egg white
sugar

½ c. cold water
1/3 c. butter (soft)
1½ c. sugar
3 Tbsp. flour
3 eggs (well beaten)

Put lemon slices in cold water and set aside. Preheat oven to 450°. Cream butter and sugar together. Add flour and salt and blend well. Add eggs and beat for 2 minutes. Add ingredients to the lemon and water and mix well.
Fill unbaked pie shell with the lemon mixture. Top with the other shell and crimp edges tightly. Brush beaten egg white on top. Bake for 10 minutes. Reduce heat to 350°. and bake for 45 minutes more. Remove from oven and cool. Serve at room temperature.

Francis Wright.

* MILE — HIGH CHIFFON PIE *

2 lemons (juice —grated rind)
5 eggs (separated)

1 c. sugar
1 baked pie shell

Beat egg yolks until light and fluffy, add sugar, lemon juice and rind. Place in top of a double boiler and cook until thick and smooth. Cool. Beat egg white until stiff (save ¼ of the egg whites for the meringue) and fold into egg mixture, pour into pie shell. Add 3 Tbsp. sugar to remaining egg whites, spread on top for meringue. Bake in preheated oven (350°) for 20 minutes or until nicely brown. Cool.

Nancy Ebsen.

* LEMON CHIFFON PIE *

9 in. baked graham cracker crust

Filling:

½ envelope gelatin
2 Tbsp. cold water
2 eggs (separated)
juice of 1 lemon and grated rind
    of ½ lemon

½ c. sugar
pinch of salt
½ c. heavy cream (whipped to soft peaks)

In sm. bowl sprinkle gelatin over cold water and let stand 5 minutes. Beat egg yolks with half of the sugar, salt, lemon juice and rind. Pour into top of double boiler and cook, stirring over gentle heat till consistency of heavy cream. Take from heat. Dissolve gelatin over pan of hot water and then stir into lemon mixture. Cool. Beat whites till stiff and beat in remaining sugar. When lemon mixture begins to set, beat until smooth and fold in meringue, with the whipped cream. Pour into pie shell, chill until set.   Jean Keys.

* ANY PORT IN A STORM CHERRY PIE *

Crust:

1 unbaked pie crust (10 in.)
1/3 c. brown sugar

2 Tbsp. butter
½ c. pecans (chopped)

Custard:

4 eggs
½ c. sugar
½ tsp. salt

dash of cinnamon
2 c. milk (scalded)
¾ tsp. nutmeg

Topping:

2 cans (16 oz.) each) pitted dark
    sweet cherries
½ c. port wine
2 Tbsp. currant jelly

grated rind of 1 orange
2 tsp. cornstarch (dissolved
    in 1 Tbsp. water)

For crust: Preheat oven to 425°. Bake pie crust for 5 minutes. Combine sugar and butter in a saucepan and simmer until sugar melts and bubbles. Remove from heat, stir in pecans and spread over bottom of the crust. Return to oven and bake for 5 minutes more. Allow to cool.

For custard: Combine eggs, sugar, nutmeg and salt and whisk together. Slowly pour milk into mixture and stir well. Carefully pour custard into pie crust and bake for 25 to 30 minutes until knife inserted in center comes out clean.

Topping: Thoroughly drain cherries. Cook port wine to reduce to ¼ c. stir in jelly and orange rind. Stir in cornstarch and simmer until thickened and glossy. Blend in cherries. Cool before spooning over custard. Chill before serving.

Adele Davis.

* RASPBERRY BAVARIAN PIE *

Pastry:

1/3 c. butter	1 egg yolk
1½ Tbsp. sugar	1 c. flour
1/3 tsp. salt	1/3 c. almonds (chopped)

Filling:

1 pkg. (10 oz.) frozen raspberries (thawed — drained)	¼ tsp. vanilla
2 egg whites	¼ tsp. almond extract
1 c. sugar	1/8 tsp. salt
1 Tbsp. lemon juice	1 c. whipping cream

For pastry: Grease a 10 in. pie pan. Cream butter, sugar and salt until fluffy. Add egg yolk and beat well. Mix in flour and almonds. Press into prepared pie pan. Bake in preheated oven (400°) for 12 minutes. Cool.

Filling: Combine all filling ingredients (except cream) in a bowl and beat until mixture thickens and expands in volume. (Electric mixer is easier to use). Whip cream and fold into raspberry mixture. Pile into pie shell and freeze for at least 8 hours. Additional whipped cream may be served with the pie.

Sarah Hemings.

* LILIKOI CHIFFON PIE *

4 egg yolks	1 envelope gelatin
pinch of salt	¼ c. water
1 c. sugar	4 egg whites
½ c. lilikoi juice	baked pie shell

Beat egg yolks, add salt and half of the sugar and juice. Cook over low heat until thick. Dissolve gelatin in water. Add to egg mixture, and cool. (It will thicken slightly). Beat egg whites until stiff, gradually add remaining sugar (½ c.) Fold into first mixture. Pour into baked shell and top with whipped-cream.

Jean Keys.

* MANDARIN ORANGE PIE *

1 pkg. gelatin
2 Tbsp. cold water
1 c. boiling water
1 c. sugar
½ c. lemon juice

1 c. whipping cream
1 can (11 oz.) mandarin oranges (drained)
1 baked (9 in.) pie shell
Garnish — fresh sliced oranges

Soften gelatin in cold water. Stir in boiling water. Add sugar and stir until dissolved. Add lemon juice. Refrigerate until slightly thickened but not set.
Whip cream until thick and fold into gelatin mixture. Add mandarin oranges and stir very gently. Pour into pie shell. Cool. Garnish with orange slices. Refrigerate for at least 3—4 hours.
Francis Wright.

* QUICK LIME RUM PIE *

2 cans (14 oz.) sweetened
 condensed milk
4 egg yolks
juice and grated rind of 2 fresh
 limes

1 baked (9 in.) pie shell or graham
 cracker crust
lightly sweetened whipped cream
1/3 c. light rum

Pour milk into deep bowl. Add egg yolks and stir well with a fork, hand beater or blender. Add lime juice, rind and rum, stir well. Pour into shell and refrigerate until ready to use. Just before serving, spread pie with thin later of whipped cream.
Lucille Grimes.

* GLAZED MANGO PIE *

Fill baked — cooled pie shell with sliced mangoes.

Make a glaze:

1 c. crushed mangoes
½ c. sugar
½ c. water
1 Tbsp. cornstarch

Cook for a few minutes till thick and clear. Remove from heat and add 1 Tbsp. butter and 1 tsp. brandy flavor. Pour glaze over pie filling, chill and serve with whipped cream.
Jean Keys.

235

* GUAVA MERINGUE PIE *

1 — nine in. baked pie shell

Filling:

¾ c. sugar
4 Tbsp. cornstarch
¼ tsp. salt
1 c. boiling water
2/3 c. guava concentrate

2/3 c. water
2 egg yolks (beaten)
2 Tbsp. butter
2 Tbsp. lemon juice

Combine sugar, salt and cornstarch in saucepan and add boiling water, stirring slowly. Add guava concentrate and 2/3 c. water and cook stirring slowly. Add beaten egg yolks slowly to the mixture. Continue cooking for 3 minutes. Remove from heat, add lemon juice and butter. Pour into baked shell and top with the meringue.

Meringue:

2 egg whites
¼ tsp. cream of tartar
6 Tbsp. sugar

Combine egg whites and cream of tartar and beat until soft peaks form. Gradually add sugar and heat until stiff peaks form and sugar is dissolved. Cover filling with the meringue, seal to edge of pastry. Bake in preheated oven (350°) for 12 to 15 minutes. Meringue should be golden brown.   Judy Pieklo.

* RUM WALNUT PIE WITH PUMPKIN *

Pastry for one crust 9 in. pie. Prepare pastry and roll out, line pan, trim and flute.

1½ c. pumpkin
¾ c. brown sugar (packed)
1 tsp. cinnamon
½ tsp. ginger
½ tsp. nutmeg

¾ c. chopped walnuts
3 eggs
1 can evaporated milk
½ c. whipping cream
2 tsp. sugar
3 Tbsp. dark rum

In a bowl, combine pumpkin, brown sugar, spices. Lightly beat eggs into mixture, stir in milk, rum and mix well. Stir in nuts. Place filling into pie shell and bake at 375° for 25 minutes. (Foil the edge of crust to prevent over browning). Remove foil and bake another 20 minutes. Beat whipping cream with sugar and spoon on cooled pie.   Jean Keys.

* PRALINE PUMPKIN PIE *

Praline shell:

1/3 c. pecans (chopped)
1/3 c. brown sugar

1 unbaked pie shell (chilled)
2 Tbsp. sweet butter (soft)

Blend pecans, sugar and butter. Gently press (with back of a spoon) into pie shell.

Filling and Meringue:

3 whole eggs
2 eggs (separated)
1 c. canned pumpkin
1½ c. brown sugar
¼ c. rum

½ tsp. salt
1 tsp. cinnamon
¼ tsp. ginger
¼ tsp. mace
¼ tsp. cloves
2 Tbsp. powdered sugar

Blend all ingredients (except egg whites and powdered sugar). Pour into pie shell and bake in preheated oven (400°) for 50 minutes. Meantime, make the meringue and return to oven (425°) to brown. Watch carefully.   Adele Davis.

* RUM PECAN PIE *

½ c. butter
½ c. sugar
¾ c. light corn syrup and ¼ c.
   maple syrup
3 eggs (slightly beaten)
3 Tbsp. light rum

1½ c. whole pecans (divided)
1 pie shell (unbaked)

Cream butter and sugar until light and fluffy. Add syrups, eggs and rum and beat well. Stir in ¾ pecans. Pour filling into pie shell and top with the remaining pecans. Bake (350°) oven for about 55 minutes.   Jean Keys.

* CARROT PIE *

1 c. carrots (cooked — mashed)
¾ c. sugar
1 Tbsp. flour
2 tsp. cinnamon

¾ tsp. cloves
1 tsp. ginger
1 egg (beaten)
1 c. milk

Mix all ingredients and pour into an unbaked pie shell. Bake 400° for about 45 minutes (until knife comes out clean) Note: It is like pumpkin pie.
                                        Dorothy Tuttle.

* SILK PIE (FRENCH) *

1-1/3 c. graham cracker crumbs | ¼ c. sugar
1/3 c. melted butter | 2 eggs (beaten)
1¼ c. softened butter | 1 tsp. vanilla
1½ oz. semi sweet chocolate (melted)

Combine crumbs and melted butter in a 9 in. pie pan and press firmly on bottom and sides. Refrigerate. Cream softened butter, gradually add sugar and beat until very fluffy. Add eggs, vanilla and chocolate and blend well. Pour into pie shell and chill until ready to serve. May be served cold or at room temperature.

Adele Davis.

* CHOCOLATE COFFEE PIE WITH ALMOND CRUST *

Crust:
2 egg whites | 2 pkgs. (8 oz. each) almonds
1/8 tsp. cream of tartar | (blanched — chopped)
½ c. sugar
Filling:
1 c. sugar — 1 egg yolk | 1 Tbsp. instant coffee
1 pkg. gelatin | 1 c. milk (non-fat)
2 eggs (separated) | 1 pkg. (12 oz.) semi-sweet chocolate
1 c. whipping cream | ¼ c. Coffee Liqueur
1 tsp. vanilla | 2 lg. cans evaporated milk

For crust: Combine all crust ingredients and mix well. Press firmly into a 10 in. pie pan and bake in a preheated oven (375°) for 10 to 12 minutes. Cool completely.

For filling: Pour evaporated milk in an ice tray and place in freezer until icy around the edges. Mix gelatin, sugar, coffee and a little salt in a saucepan. Beat egg yolk with non-fat milk and Liqueur and add to the gelatin mixture. Cook, stirring over medium heat until mixture begins to thicken. Remove from heat and cool. Beat egg whites until soft peaks form. Beat icy milk in a bowl until it looks like whipped cream. Fold into egg whites and then fold into gelatin mixture. Turn into pie shell, top with almonds and chill until firm.

Rebecca Dixon.

* CALYPSO PIE *

30 chocolate cookies wafers | 1 qt. coffee ice cream (4 c.)
(crushed — about 1½ c.) | (slightly softened)
1/3 c. butter or margarine | 12 oz. jar (1 c.) fudge ice cream topping
(softened) | or favorite fudge sauce
½ c. coconut (grated) | cashew or macadamia nuts
3 Tbsp. cashew or macadamia nuts (finely chopped)

In medium bowl, combine chocolate wafers, margarine, coconut and nuts. Press mixture over bottom and sides of 9 in. pie pan. Chill for 15 minutes. Carefully spoon softened ice cream into chilled crust. Freeze. Cut into wedges to serve. Top individual servings with spoonful of fudge sauce and sprinkle with some nuts.   Ida Christoph.

* GRASSHOPPER PIE *

18 cream filled chocolate cookies (crush)

3 Tbsp sugar

1 c. sugar

1 pkg. gelatin

4 eggs (separated)

½ c. water

1 tsp. vanilla

¼ c. butter (melted)

For crust: Preheat oven to 350°. Combine crushed cookie crumbs, melted butter and 3 Tbsp. sugar in a 9 in. pie pan and press bottom and sides with the crumbs very firmly. Bake for 10 minutes. Cool.

For filling: Place ½ c. sugar and gelatin in a saucepan. Blend egg yolks with water and the vanilla. Stir into gelatin mixture. Cook over medium heat, stirring constantly until it comes to a boil. Remove from heat, cool and then refrigerate until thickened. Beat egg whites until foamy, add remaining ½ c. sugar, 1 Tbsp. at a time, beating until eggs form very stiff peaks. Fold gelatin mixture into the egg whites and spoon into the shell. Chill before serving.   Sarah Hemings.

* CREME DE MENTHE PIE *

18 chocolate cookies (crushed fine) and 4 Tbsp. butter. Mix well and spread evenly in a 9 in. pie tin lined with wax paper. Put in refrigerator for several hours. Filling: 2/3 c. milk, add 24 lg. marshmallows. Melt together and cool in refrigerator until thick. Add 1 c. cream (whipped stiff), 2 jiggers Creme De Menthe and 1 jigger of Creme De Cacao, pour into pie shell and freeze.   Betty Guy.

* BRANDIED BUTTER PASTRY FOR PIES *

1 c. flour, ¼ tsp. salt, 6 Tbsp. butter, 3 Tbsp. brandy. Combine, chill and shape into pan.   Jean Keys.

* HAPPINESS CAKE *
(From and old cookbook)

1 cup of good thoughts

1 cup of kind deeds

1 cup of consideration of others

2 cups sacrifice

2 cups of well beaten faults

3 cups forgiveness

Mix thoroughly. Add tears of joy, sorrow and sympathy. Flavor with love and kind service. Fold in 4 cups of prayer and faith. Blend well. Fold into daily life. Bake well with warmth of human kindness and serve with a smile anytime. It will satisfy the hunger of starved souls.   Jean Keys.

* CAKE FROSTINGS *

CARMEL FROSTING:

½ c. brown sugar
3 Tbsp. butter
2 c. powdered sugar (sifted)

3 Tbsp. cream or evaporated milk
1 tsp. vanilla

Place sugar, cream and butter in a sauce pan, bring to a boil and cook for 2 min. Remove from heat and add powdered sugar to a spreading consistency. Add vanilla and spread on cake.

CHOCOLATE SOUR CREAM FROSTING:

1½ c. semi-sweet chocolate bits
¾ c. sour cream
dash of salt

Melt chocolate over hot water. Remove from heat and stir in sour cream and dash of salt. Beat until creamy. Spread on cake.

PEANUT BUTTER FROSTING:

1 lb. powdered sugar (sifted)
½ c. peanut butter (cream style)
¼ to 1/3 c. milk

Combine all ingredients and spread.   Ida Christoph.

* LADY FINGERS *

3 egg whites
1/3 c. powdered sugar
2 egg yolks

1/3 c. bread flour (sifted)
1/8 tsp. salt
¼ tsp. vanilla

Beat egg whites until stiff, then add sugar gradually and continue beating. Add egg yolks (beaten to lemon color), then vanilla. Cut and fold in flour and salt. Shape 4½ in. long and 1 in. wide. Place on wax paper on cookie sheet. Bake for 8 minutes (350°). Sprinkle with powdered sugar.
Note: May be filled with whipped cream.   Mary Upchurch.

* BISCUIT CAKE *

1 Tbsp. butter
1¼ c. sugar
1¼ tsp. cinnamon
½ c. raisins
½ c. strawberry, raspberry
    jam or marmalade

1 Tbsp. chopped nuts
2 pkgs (16) butterflake biscuits
½ c. melted butter

Preheat oven to 375°. Butter bottom of a 6 or 6½ cup ring mold. Combine sugar cinnamon and raisins. Place 1 tsp. jam at ½ in. intervals around the mold. Sprinkle with nuts. Dip biscuit in butter and then into cinnamon mixture. Place biscuits in mold (not too crowded). Drizzle rest of butter over top. Place mold on cookie sheet in middle of the oven. Bake for 30 minutes until crusty. Let stand for 5 minutes before inverting on a serving plate. Do not remove the mold for 5 minutes.   Francis Wright.

* FROSTED GRAHAM CRACKER CAKE *

1½ pts. heavy cream
6 Tbsp. cocoa
dash of salt
2 (1 oz. each) squares semi-
 sweet chocolate.

1 tsp. vanilla
8 Tbsp. sugar
50 graham crackers

Beat cream until stiff and add sugar, cocoa, salt and vanilla, until thick enough for spreading. Refrigerate 1/3 of the frosting mixture. With remaining frosting, spread 25 of the crackers with a layer about ¼ in. thick. Place another cracker on top (sandwich style) and stand on end in a continuous row. Spread some frosting along inside of row. Frost remaining crackers and put together the same way, placing this row up against the first row, in parallel line. With refrigerated frosting, cover top and sides and top with chocolate curls (prepared from semi-sweet chocolate). Refrigerate. To serve: Cut loaf at an angle into ½ in. slices.
                                                                                                Adele Davis.

* MIRACLE WHIP CAKE *

Cream together:
1 c. sugar — 1 c. Miracle Whip Salad Dressing.
Sift together:
2 c. flour — 2 tsp. cake soda — pinch of salt — 4 Tbsp. cocoa.

Mix with creamed mixture. Then add 1 c. cold water and 1 tsp. vanilla. Bake in greased pan, slightly floured pan for 35 to 40 minutes at 350°, or until done.
                                                                                                Elizabeth Betty Guy.

* SPONGE CAKE *

Beat 8 egg yolks, add 2 Tbsp. water. Add 2 tsp. grated orange rind. Sift 3 times, 1-1/3 c. flour and ¾ c. sugar. Beat 8 egg whites, ½ c. sugar and ¼ tsp. salt. Beat until stiff. Fold into flour and pour into greased cake pan. Bake at 350° for 45 minutes.   Mary Upchurch.

* CHOCOLATE ROLL *

5 eggs (separated)   3 Tbsp. cocoa
1 c. powdered sugar   1 Tbsp. flour

Beat egg whites until stiff. Add powdered sugar and beat until fluffy. Fold in beaten egg yolks. Sift flour and cocoa and add. Butter cookie sheet and place wax paper on top. Bake in preheated oven at 450° for 12 minutes.

Frosting:

½ c. powdered sugar   2 Tbsp. cream
1 Tbsp. cocoa   * 1 pt. whipping cream
½ tsp. vanilla

Mix the ingredients (all but whipping cream).

To make roll:

Place cake on wax paper and roll. Unroll and spread with frosting, then re-roll. Spread with whipped cream.   Lillian Kann.

* MAYONNAISE CHOCOLATE CAKE *

3 c. flour   1½ tsp. baking soda
1/3 c. cocoa   1½ c. mayonnaise
1½ c. sugar   1½ c. water
2¼ tsp. baking powder   1½ tsp. vanilla

Sift together dry ingredients, place in large bowl and stir in mayonnaise. Gradually stir in water and vanilla to make a smooth batter. Pour into two 9 in. round cake pans that have been lined on the bottom with waxed paper. Bake at 350° for 30 minutes or until it tests done. Cool then frost.

Frosting:

6 Tbsp. butter   2 c. powdered sugar
2 Tbsp. cocoa   ¼ c. wheat germ
3 Tbsp. milk

Combine butter, cocoa and milk, heat to a boil. Mix in powdered sugar and wheat germ.   Jean Keys.

* ONE — STEP COCOA CAKE *

2½ c. flour   1 c. milk
1¾ c. sugar   2/3 c. butter or margarine (softened)
½ c. cocoa   2 tsp. vanilla
2 tsp. baking soda   ¼ c. sliced almonds
½ tsp. salt
3 eggs

242

Heat oven to 350°. Grease and flour 13 x 9 in. pan. In a large bowl combine all ingredients (except almonds). Beat at low speed for 1 minute in mixer, then beat 3 minutes at highest speed. Pour batter into prepared pan. Sprinkle almonds on top. Bake for 35 to 45 minutes or until tested done. Cool. Cut into squares. May be topped with your favorite frosting.   Billie Do.

* SPICE CAKE WITH OATMEAL TOPPING *

1 c. sugar	½ c. butter
2 c. flour (sifted)	1 egg
1 tsp. baking powder	1 Tbsp. molasses
½ tsp. cinnamon	1 c. sour cream
½ tsp. cloves	1 c. raisins
½ tsp. salt	

Cream butter and sugar. Sift dry ingredients. Beat egg, molasses and sour cream and add to sugar mixture. Gradually add dry ingredients. Pour into a greased baking pan, spread topping on batter. Bake in preheated oven (350°) for 30 to 40 minutes.

Oatmeal topping:

½ c. butter
½ c. brown sugar
1 tsp. vanilla
uncooked oatmeal.

Mix butter, sugar and vanilla well, add enough oatmeal until it becomes crumbly. Spread evenly over cake.   Adele Davis.

* KONA COFFEE SPICE CAKE *

1 c. butter	¼ tsp. allspice
2 c. sugar	¼ tsp. cloves
3 eggs (separated	1/8 tsp. nutmeg
1 c. cold strong Kona coffee	¼ tsp. ginger
4 c. flour	½ c. currants
5 tsp. baking powder	½ c. citron (thinly sliced)
2 Tbsp. molasses	¾ c. raisins (cut-up)
¾ tsp. cinnamon	1 tsp. vanilla

Cream butter and gradually add sugar. Beat eggs yolks into coffee and add to first mixture. Sift spices, baking powder and flour (except ¼ c.) then add molasses and beat well. Fold in stiffly beaten egg whites. Dredge fruit with the remaining flour and add with the vanilla. Bake in deep pan for 45 minutes at 350°. Sprinkle with powdered sugar or make your favorite icing.   Jean Keys.

* SPICE CAKE *
(My Mothers)

1 c. sugar
½ c. shortening
1 c. butter milk or sour milk
1 tsp. soda
1½ c. flour (sifted)
1 tsp. cinnamon

½ tsp. cloves
½ tsp. nutmeg
1 tsp. lemon extract
raisins and nuts if desired
2 eggs

Cream shortening and sugar until light and fluffy. Add egg and milk and stir well. Sift dry ingredients and add to egg mixture. Add lemon extract. (If adding fruit and nuts — flour slightly before adding to mixture). Bake in preheated oven (350°) in 9 x 9 x 2 in. pan. Bake until cake springs back at touch.

Adele Davis.

* FRUIT COCKTAIL CAKE *

1 c. flour
½ tsp. salt
1 c. sugar

1 can (med.) fruit cocktail (drained)
1 egg
1 tsp. baking powder

Sift flour, salt, sugar and baking powder. Add egg and fruit cocktail. Pour into 8 in. square pan.

Topping:

½ c. brown sugar
¾ c. broken walnuts

Mix and sprinkle over batter. Bake in preheated oven (350°) for 45 minutes.

Nancy Ebsen.

* TOMATO SOUP CAKE *

2¼ c. cake flour or all purpose flour
1-1/3 c. sugar
4 tsp. baking powder
1 tsp. soda
1½ tsp. allspice
1 tsp. cinnamon

½ tsp. cloves
1 can condensed tomato soup
½ c. shortening
2 eggs
¼ c. water

Preheat oven to 350°. Generously grease and flour 2—8 in. pans. Measure dry ingredients into a lg. bowl. Add soup and shortening. Beat in mixer at low speed, then on medium speed. Scrape often. Add eggs and water and beat for 2 min. Pour into pans and bake for 35 to 40 minutes. Let stand 10 minutes after baking to cool. Frost with cream cheese topping.

Jean Keys.

* APPLE SWIRL CAKE *

1 pkg. yellow cake mix
1 lb. can apple sauce
3 eggs

¼ c. sugar
2 tsp. cinnamon

Blend first three ingredients and beat for 4 minutes. Mix sugar and cinnamon. Butter a bundt or tube pan. Sprinkle 2 Tbsp. sugar mixture on sides and of pan. Pour in ½ cake mixture, sprinkle with remaining sugar and cinnamon. Pour remaining batter into pan. Bake at 350° for 40 minutes. Let stand for 15 minutes. Let cool on cake rack. Drizzle with lemon or powdered sugar, and sprinkle with chopped nuts.   Caraline Spencer.

* LEMON JELLO CAKE *

1 pkg. Duncan Hines Supreme
   cake mix (lemon)
4 eggs

¾ c. oil
¾ c. boiling water
1 pkg. lemon Jello

Beat all ingredients at once in bowl with electric beaters, 4 to 5 minutes. Bake in butter oblong pan (13 x 9 in.) for 40 minutes in 350° oven.

Frosting:

1 c. powdered sugar and ¼ c. lemon juice mixed together. Pour over cake while cake is still hot. Note: Can also be used with orange cake mix and orange Jello.

Jean Keys.

* APRICOT AND CHERRY — UPSIDE — DOWN CAKE *

¼ c. brown sugar
1 Tbsp. butter (melted)
1 tsp. lemon juice
½ tsp. cinnamon
1 can (8 oz.) apricot halves
   (drained)
½ c. pitted dark bing cherries
   (drained)

1 c. sifted cake flour
1½ tsp. baking powder
dash of salt
2 eggs (separated)
½ c. sugar
5 Tbsp. hot water
1 tsp. vanilla

Preheat oven to 350°. Lightly oil a 8 in. square pan. Combine brown sugar, melted butter, lemon juice and cinnamon, spread evenly in pan. Arrange apricots and cherries in a design. Sift flour baking powder and salt in a bowl. Beat egg yolks in a small bowl, gradually add sugar and continue to beat until yolks are thick and lemon color. Add water then flour and vanilla, beating very well. Whip egg whites until very stiff, fold into batter and carefully spoon over fruit. Bake for 35 minutes or until cake tests done. Cool on rack for 10 minutes. Invert on plate and turn carefully. Cool before cutting.   Roberta Chateauneuf.

* ORANGE CAKE *

1 c. sugar
½ c. shortening
2 eggs
1 c. sour milk or buttermilk
2 c. sifted flour

1 tsp. soda
1 tsp. baking powder
¼ tsp. salt
1 c. raisins ground with rind of 1 orange
Juice of 1 orange

Cream sugar and shortening and add beaten eggs, milk and flour sifted with soda, baking powder and salt. Add raisins and orange rind and some nut meats if desired. Bake at 350° for 30 to 40 minutes.

Topping:

Dissolve ½ c. sugar and the juice of the orange and cook slowly until thickened. Pour carefully over the cake while still hot, so the syrup sinks into the cake.

Zana Luis.

* HAWAIIAN PINEAPPLE CAKE *

1 can (1 lb. 4 oz.) crushed pineapple
2 c. Bisquick
1 c. sifted all purpose flour
1 tsp. sugar
¾ c. dairy sour cream

½ c. butter or margarine
2 tsp. vanilla
2 lg. eggs
2 Tbsp. rum
1 tsp. soda

Drain pineapple well, save syrup for glaze. Stir Bisquick, flour and soda together. Beat sugar, sour cream, butter and vanilla for 2 minutes. Add eggs and beat for 1 minute. Add flour mixture and beat 1 minute longer. Mix in drained pineapple and rum. Bake in moderate oven (350°) about 40 to 45 minutes. Remove from oven and spoon half of glaze over cake. Let stand 10 minutes, turn onto serving plate and spoon remaining glaze on cake. Cool before cutting.

Glaze:

¾ c. sugar
¼ c. butter or margarine
juice from pineapple

Stir over low heat until sugar is dissolved and butter melted. Remove from heat and add 2 Tbsp. rum.

Jean Ariyoshi.

* YUM YUM CAKE *

2 c. flour
1½ c. sugar
1 No. 2 can crushed pineapple

2 eggs (lightly beaten)
2 tsp. soda.

Mix all ingredients together well. Pour into greased (9 x 12") pan and bake at 350° until tested done. Cool then frost. (very moist).

Velma Harmas.

* PINEAPPLE CHIFFON CAKE *

¾ c. egg whites
½ tsp. cream of tartar
1¾ c. cake flour (sifted)
1¼ c. sugar
1 Tbsp. baking powder

½ tsp. salt
1/3 c. oil
4 egg yolks
1 c. pineapple puree
½ c. pineapple syrup

Beat egg whites with cream of tartar until stiff. Sift together cake flour, sugar, baking powder and salt. Make a well in center of the dry ingredients and add oil, egg yolks, pineapple puree and drained pineapple syrup. Stir until dry ingredients are moistened. Fold egg whites into flour mixture. Pour into a 9 in. tube pan. Bake at 325° for 65 minutes. Note: To make pineapple puree, place 1 cup of well grained pineapple into a blender, blend until smooth. Reserve ½ c. of the drained juice to use in the recipe.   Jean Ariyoshi.

* MANDARIN ORANGE CAKE *

1 c. flour
1 c. sugar
1 egg

1½ tsp. baking powder
½ tsp. vanilla
1 can (11 oz.) mandarin oranges (drained)

Place all ingredients in mixing bowl and beat real hard or use mixer. Pour into buttered 8 x 8 in. pan and bake in preheated oven (350°) for 35 minutes.
Topping:
¾ Tbsp. brown sugar
3 Tbsp. butter
3 Tbsp. cream or milk
Mix in saucepan and bring to a boil and pour over hot cake (when taken from the oven.)   Francis Wright.

* ORANGE PEEL CAKE *

3 lg. orange peels (grated)
1 c. raisins (chopped fine)
1 c. sugar
½ c. butter (soft)
½ c. walnuts (chopped)
2 eggs

¾ c. buttermilk
2 c. flour
1 tsp. baking powder
½ tsp. baking soda
½ tsp. salt

Preheat oven to 325°. Cream sugar and butter until light. Add eggs and buttermilk and mix well. Sift together flour, baking powder, baking soda and salt and stir into batter. Mix in raisins, orange peel and nuts. Pour into a well greased 9 or 10 in. spring mold. Bake about 45 to 50 minutes until cake tests done. When cake is done let stand for 10 minutes. Re-invert and do not cut for several hours. Note: Do not use a bundt pan for baking, the cake becomes too dark.
                    Charlene Do.

* ORANGE — CARROT CAKE *

3 c. flour
2 c. sugar
2½ tsp. soda
2½ tsp. cinnamon
1 tsp. salt
1¼ c. oil
2 tsp. vanilla

1 tsp. grated orange peel
1 can (11 oz.) mandarin oranges
   (juice too)
2 c. shredded carrots
3 eggs
1 c. coconut

Measure all ingredients (except coconut and carrots). Beat at high speed for 2 minutes. Add coconut and carrots, beat and blend well. Pour into a greased 13 x 9" pan or tube pan. Bake at 350° for 45 to 50 minutes. Test. Cool.

Jean Keys.

* CARROT CAKE *

Mix together:
2 c. sugar
1½ c. oil
4 eggs
Add:
1 tsp. salt
2 c. flour
1 tsp. soda
2 tsp. cinnamon

3 c. grated raw carrots
¾ c. chopped nuts (walnuts, pecans)

Bake in greased — floured pan at 350° for 30 to 40 minutes.
Frosting:
½ c. powdered sugar, 1/3 stick margarine, 1 tsp. vanilla, ½ pkg. (4 oz.) cream cheese. Cream margarine, cheese and sugar, add vanilla. Spread frosting on cooled cake and sprinkle with chopped nuts.   Lynne Waihee.

* RHUBARB CAKE *

1½ c. brown sugar
½ c. shortening
1 egg
1½—2 c. rhubarb
   (cut up very thin)
1 tsp. vanilla

½ c. sugar
1 c. sour cream or buttermilk
2 c. flour
1 tsp. soda
1 Tbsp. cinnamon

Cream together, brown sugar, shortening, add egg. Add sour cream, flour, soda and vanilla. Mix well. Add rhubarb last. Place in 9 x 13" greased — floured pan. Sprinkle top with sugar and cinnamon mixed together. Bake at 350° for 35 minutes.

Georgia Beasley.

* VI'S GALLIANO CAKE *

Mix in small bowl:

4 eggs	¼ c. Galliano
½ c. oil	¼ c. Vodka
¾ c. orange juice	

Mix in large bowl:
1 box yellow cake mix
1 pkg. Instant vanilla pudding

Add wet mixture to dry ingredients and beat for 4 minutes. Pour into lightly oiled and floured bundt pan. Bake at 350° for 45 minutes. Let stand 20 minutes then remove and glaze with orange juice and powdered sugar.   Jean Keys.

* RUM CAKE *

1 box yellow cake mix	½ c. light rum
1 box vanilla instant pudding (small)	½ c. water
4 lg. eggs	½ c. chopped nuts
½ c. Crisco oil	

Sprinkle nuts on bottom of greased and floured tube or bundt pan. Put all other ingredients into a bowl and stir until all ingredients are moistened. Mix two min. at med. speed. Bake at 350° for 50 to 60 minutes until done.

Elizabeth Betty Guy.

* WINE CAKE *

1 box yellow cake mix	¾ c. Sherry wine
1 sm. box vanilla instant pudding	1 tsp. nutmeg
4 eggs	¾ c. oil

Beat all together for 5 minutes. Pour into greased — floured tube pan, or two loaf pans. Bake in preheated oven 350° for 45 minutes. Cool for 5 minutes and turn out. Frost if desired.   Jean Keys.

* BUSY DAY CHEESECAKE *

1 pkg. (8 oz.) cream cheese	1 pkg. Jello instant lemon pudding
2 c. milk	
1 cooled 8—9 in. graham cracker crust	

Place cheese in bowl and stir with a fork to soften. Add ½ c. of the milk, blend well, add remaining milk and beat. Add pudding mix and beat again. (should be well mixed, about 1 minute). Pour into crust, chill until ready to use.

Jean Keys.

* LEMON – GLAZED CHEESECAKE *

2 c. graham cracker crumbs	3 eggs
5 Tbsp. melted butter	2 tsp. lemon rind (grated)
2 Tbsp. sugar	2 tsp. vanilla
3 pkg. (8 oz. each) cream cheese	2 c. sour cream
¾ c. sugar	2 Tbsp. sugar
¼ c. lemon juice	* Lemon Glaze

Garnish: Curled lemon strips, strawberries, mint leaves. Preheat oven to 350°. Combine graham crumbs, melted butter and 1 Tbsp. sugar. Press into sides and bottom of buttered 9 x 3 in. spring form mold. Bake for 5 minutes. Cool. Beat cream cheese and sugar thoroughly. Add eggs one at a time, beat well after each addition. Mix in lemon juice, rind and vanilla. Turn into pan and bake for 35 minutes. While cake is baking, blend sour cream, sugar and vanilla. Remove cake from oven and gently spread sour cream mixture over top. Return to oven and bake for 12 minutes. Cool on rack for 30 minutes. Spread with lemon glaze. Chill for several hours or overnite before removing sides of pan. Garnish with lemon strips and mint leaves.

Lemon Glaze:

½ c. sugar	1/3 c. lemon juice
1½ Tbsp. cornstarch	1 egg yolk
¼ tsp. salt	1 Tbsp. butter
¾ c. water	1 tsp. lemon rind (grated)

Combine sugar, cornstarch and salt in a saucepan. Combine water, lemon juice and egg yolk, mix and then add to sugar mixture. Cook over low heat, stirring constantly, until mixture comes to a slow boil, and is thickened. Add butter and lemon rind. Allow to cool slightly. Spread on cheese cake before glaze begins to set.

Adele Davis.

* GUAVA CHEESECAKE *

Beat one 8 oz. and one 3 oz. pkgs. cream cheese, (softened) and 2 eggs, slightly beaten, ½ c. sugar. 1 tsp. vanilla. Pour into graham cracker crumb crust and bake for 20 minutes at 350°. Cool.

Topping: Combine ¼ c. sugar, juice of one lemon, 1½ Tbsp. cornstarch, and 1 can frozen guava juice (thawed) and cook until thickened. Spread over cheese cake when cooled.

Graham cracker crust:

1¼ c. graham crumbs
1/3 c. melted butter
3 Tbsp. sugar

Mix thoroughly and shape into a cheesecake pan.

Jean Keys.

* JELLO CHEESECAKE *

Preheat oven to 400°.

Crust:

1 block butter	1 c. sifted flour
¼ c. sugar	½ c. nuts (optional)

Grease bottom of pan 9 x 13 in. Mix in order given and pat evenly in pan. (Chilled dough is much easier to work with, but you don't have to).

Cream cheese filling:

1 pkg. (8 oz.) cream cheese	¼ c. sugar
1 lg. box or 2 oz. box of	1 sm. box lemon Jello
Dream Whip	1 c. boiling water

Melt Jello in boiling water. Cream together cream cheese and sugar. Add cooled Jello slowly. (Adding too fast makes the cream cheese lumpy). Prepare Dream Whip following directions on pkg. Fold into cheese mixture. Pour over crust and chill until completely set.

Jello layer:

Boil 3 c. water, add 3 sm. boxes of lemon Jello and cool. When completely cooled, pour over firm cream cheese and chill until Jello hardens. Note: If you pour Jello over cream cheese before cheese hardens it will mix in the Jello.

Flora Azevedo.

* NO – BAKE PEACH YOGURT CHEESECAKE *

1 graham cracker crust (9 in.) chilled	½ c. almonds (slivered)
3 pkgs. (8 oz.) cream cheese	½ tsp. almond extract
(room temperature)	1 pkg. (10 oz.) frozen sliced peaches
1½ pkg. gelatin	(thawed – drained)
4 cartons (8 oz. each) peach yogurt	* Peach custard sauce.

In mixing bowl, beat the cream cheese. Soften gelatin in a little cold water, stir over low heat until dissolved. When cooled slightly, pour into cheese. Add yogurt, ½ at a time, beat after each addition. Blend in almonds and extract and carefully pour into pan. Refrigerate for at least 12 hours. To serve, remove sides of pan carefully. Garnish top with peach slices and top with the custard sauce.

Peach Custard Sauce:

2 cartons (8 oz. each) peach yogurt
1 pkg. (3¾ oz.) vanilla instant pudding mix.

Place in a bowl and mix well. Chill and spread over cheesecake.

Sarah Hemings.

* CHOCOLATE MARBELIZED CHEESECAKE *

Crust:

4 oz. chocolate wafer cookies — 1 oz. (2 Tbsp.) sweet butter melted. Separate the sides from the bottom of an 8 x 3 in. spring form pan. Butter sides only. (If bottom is not buttered the finished cake can be transfered easily to a cake plate). Replace bottom and set aside. The cookies should be ground very fine, you should have 1 c. of crumbs. Place crumbs in mixing bowl and add melted butter, mix with a spatula. (You will think there is not enough butter, but do not add more, the mixture should be dry and crumbly).

Cheese Mixture:

6 oz. semi-sweet chocolate	2 eggs (lg.)
12 oz. cream cheese	2 c. sour cream
1 tsp. vanilla	pinch of salt
½ c. sugar	

Break up chocolate and place in top of double boiler over hot water on medium heat. Melt and stir until smooth. Cool slightly. In a lg. bowl mix cream cheese with an electric mixer and beat until smooth. Add vanilla and sugar and beat again. Add eggs one at a time.

Beat until smooth after each addition. Add 1½ c. sour cream (reserving ½ c.) and salt. Remove from the bowl and set aside 1½ c. of the mixture. In a sm. bowl mix melted chocolate with the reserved sour cream. Place the two batters alternating colors by spoonfuls over the chilled crust. Use the face of a spatula and knife through to marbelize. (Do not over do it or you will lose the contrast). Bake in preheated oven 350° for 10 minutes. Remove to rack and let cool. Place in refrigerator for at least 6 hours or longer. (This should be cold when served, it will become firm when adequately chilled. When just right it should be slightly soft and custardlike in center.)

Adele Davis.

* BOILED FRUIT CAKE *

Combine and boil for 3 to 5 minutes:

1½ c. water	¾ tsp. nutmeg
1½ c. sugar	½ tsp. cloves
1½ c. raisins	1 tsp salt
¾ c. crisco or oleo	1 c. candied fruit.

When cold add:

3 c. flour and 1½ tsp. soda (sifted). Last add ½ c. chopped nuts.
Bake in greased loaf pans at 350° for 1½ hours.

Dora Beyer.

* GRANDMOTHER'S NUT CAKE *

Cream together, 1½ c. sugar — ½ c. shortening. Cream until fluffy
Add 2 c. flour — 1 tsp. baking powder and ¾ c. milk
Fold in 4 whites (stiffly beaten). Add 1 c. walnuts (slightly chopped). And ½ tsp. almond extract. Bake in greased angel cake pan at 325° for about 1 hour. (No additional liquid is needed).   Dorothy Tuttle.

* GUM DROP FRUIT CAKE *

Cream 2½ c. margarine and 2½ c. brown and white sugar. Add 7 eggs (well beaten). Add dry ingredients alternately with mincemeat mixture.

Dry Ingredients:

5 c. flour (softed)	½ tsp. cloves
3 tsp. baking powder	1 tsp. nutmeg
pinch of salt	1 tsp. cinnamon
1 tsp. allspice	

Mincemeat Mixture:

1 jar (12 oz.) mincemeat	2 tsp. lemon extract
½ c. Brandy	3 tsp. vanilla
1 sm. jar Maraschino cherries and juice	

When batter is thoroughly mixed, fold in gumdrop mixture.

Gum drop mixture:

1½ lbs. gum drops (chopped)	½ lb. walnuts (chopped)
1 lb. glazed fruitcake mix	1 c. flour
1 lb. raisins	

Toss ingredients with flour before adding to batter mix. Place in oiled baking pans and bake in preheated oven (350°) for 1 hour, reduce heat and bake for 1 hour longer.   Nancy Ebsen.

* WHITE SCOTCH FRUIT CAKE *

Cream 1 lb. butter and 2 c. sugar — add 6 eggs one at a time and beat well after each egg.
3 c. flour (add 1 c. to the fruit) — 1 lb. fruit cake mix and ½ box golden raisins. Mix all together thoroughly. Place in 3 foil pans and bake at 275° for 1 hour and 30 minutes or until golden brown.   Elizabeth Betty Guy.

* JAPANESE FRUIT CAKE *

1 c. butter	1 tsp. vanilla
2 c. sugar	1 tsp. cinnamon
1 c. milk	1 tsp. allspice
4 eggs (beaten)	¼ tsp. cloves
1 tsp. baking powder	* Fruit filling — topping

Preheat oven to 350°. Line bottoms of four 8 in. round cake pans with wax paper. Cream butter and sugar until light and fluffy. Combine eggs and milk. Sift flour and baking powder together. Add alternately with egg mixture to the butter — sugar mixture. Blend well after each addition. Add vanilla.

Spoon half of the batter into 2 pans. To the remaining batter, add spices and raisins and blend (mixture will seem solid with raisins). Spoon mixture in the 2 remaining pans. Bake all layers for 30 to 35 minutes, until done. Cool cakes on a rack, removing layers while slightly warm. Remove paper.

Fruit Filling and Topping:

2 whole lemons (seeded — ground in blender)	2 c. sugar
	1 c. boiling water
1 can (4 oz.) coconut (flaked style)	2 Tbsp. cornstarch
	1 can (9 oz.) crushed pineapple (drained)

Combine all ingredients in medium saucepan and cook over medium heat, stirring constantly until mixture comes to a boil. Lower heat and simmer until thick. About 15 to 20 minutes. Cool. To serve: Spread layers of cake and on top, alternating the light and the dark layers. Note: A very special fruitcake.

Adele Davis.

* EGG NOG LOAF *
(Wow!!! Cake)

Split standard angel food cake into 5 layers. Spread filling on all layers. Put together and frost with:

1 pt. cream (whipped) mixed with 2 Tbsp. sugar and 2 Tbsp. Rum or Brandy. Filling:

½ lb. butter (creamed) — add 1 lb. powder sugar — add 5 egg yolks (beaten) — ½ c. Bourbon plus 1 Tbsp. Rum. — 1 doz. sm. macaroons (crumbled) — ¾ c. almonds (toasted — slivered).

For appearance: Sprinkle with a few reserved almonds.

Note: This cake freezes well before frosting. Keeps several days in refrigerator after icing. A good "make ahead". I make mine in a loaf shaped angel food cake pan, makes better servings. Could use two regular loaf pans. Dorothy Tuttle.

D·E·S·S·E·R·T·S

* CHOCOLATE MOUSSE *

1 pkg. (8 oz.) semi-sweet chocolate
½ c. sugar
½ c. water
5 egg yolks (beaten)
½ tsp. cream of tartar

1 Tbsp gelatin
2 Tbsp. dark Rum
5 egg whites
¼ ts. salt
2 c. whipping cream (whipped)

Melt chocolate in a saucepan over very low heat. Cool in a lg. bowl. Mix sugar and water in a sm. saucepan and bring to a boil and boil until transparent and syrupy. Cool slightly. Slowly pour syrup into the egg yolks, beating vigorously with a whisk. Soften gelatin in the Rum and add to warm egg mixture and blend well. Gradually stir in the chocolate (using a whisk). Allow to cool. Whip the egg whites with the cream of tartar and salt until stiff and glossy. Fold into chocolate mixture. Spoon into dessert dishes or a lg. glass bowl. Chill for at least 4 hours.   Adele Davis.

* EASY CHOCOLATE MOUSSE *

2 pkgs. (12 oz. each) semi-sweet
    chocolate chips
1½ ts. vanilla
1½ c. whipping cream
    (heated to boiling point)

6 egg yolks
2 egg whites
* whipped cream — garnish

Combine chocolate, vanilla and a pinch of salt in a blender and mix for 1 min. Add the boiling cream and continue to mix until chocolate has melted. Add yolks and mix again. Beat egg whites until stiff peaks form and gently fold into chocolate mixture. Place in a serving bowl or parfait glasses and cover with plastic and chill. Serve with whipped cream. Note: This recipe may be used for frozen chocolate crepes, but omit the egg whites.   Francis Wright.

* COCONUT — PISTACHIO MOUSSE *

2 c. half and half
1 c. coconut syrup
3 eggs (separated)
2 pkgs. gelatin
pinch of salt
* toasted shredded coconut

1 Tbsp. sugar
6 Tbsp. crushed pistachios
10 slices of pound cake (½ in. thick)
whipped cream flavored with
    coconut syrup

Combine cream, coconut syrup, beaten egg yolks, gelatin and salt in a saucepan. Place over medium heat, stirring constantly until gelatin is dissolved. Pour into a bowl and place in bowl of cold water. Chill until thick, stirring frequently. Beat egg whites until stiff peaks form, gradually add sugar and beat until stiff. Carefully fold into gelatin mixture and then fold in nuts. Pour into 9 or 10 molds (4 oz.) and place a slice of pound cake atop each, trimming to fit. Cover with plastic and chill for 2 hours, unmold onto serving dishes and top with flavored whipped cream and toasted coconut.   Ida Christoph.

* KAHLUA MOUSSE *

1 envelope gelatin
½ c. sugar
1/8 tsp. salt
1 c. milk
1 pkg. (6 oz.) semi-sweet
    chocolate pieces. (1 cup)

¼ c. Kahlua
1 tsp. vanilla
1 c. whipping cream (whipped)

Mix gelatin, sugar and salt in 2½ qt. saucepan. Stir in milk and chocolate pieces. Place over medium heat and stir constantly until gelatin is dissolved and chocolate is melted. Remove from heat and beat with rotary beater until chocolate is blended. Stir in Kahlua and vanilla. Chill, stirring occasionally until mixture mounds slightly. Fold in whipped cream. Turn into a 4 c. mold and chill until firm. Unmold and garnish with chocolate curls.   Jean Keys.

* MAPLE MOUSSE *

2 pkgs. gelatin
½ c. water
4 egg yolks (beaten)
1 c. pure maple syrup

½ c. light brown sugar
4 egg whites
2 c. whipping cream (chilled)

Sprinkle gelatin on the cold water. Let soften for 5 minutes then set in a pan of hot water and stir until gelatin dissolves. Add gelatin to beaten egg yolks. Mix in maple syrup and cook over low heat until mixture thickens and coats a spoon, stirring constantly. Do not let mixture boil. Remove from heat, stir in brown sugar blend well. Place in a lg. bowl and let cool to room temperature. Beat egg whites until stiff peaks form. Whip cream only until stiff enough to hold shape. Fold cream into the syrup mixture, then fold in egg whites. Spoon mixture into a mold (that has been rinsed with cold water), cover with plastic and chill for 4 hours. Unmold on serving dish and slice.   Lorna Burger.

* MANGO MOUSSE *

Grind up enough mangoes to make 4–6 c. Add 1 c. sugar, juice of 1 lemon, jigger of Triple Sec. Mix thoroughly and let stand at room temperature. Mix 3 pkgs. gelatin in ½ cup water, then put over hot water to dissolve. Pour gelatin mixture into mangoes and blend well. Chill. Whip 3 c. heavy cream, chill then fold into mousse. Pour into tubular mold and chill for several hours. To serve, unmold and fill center with chopped mangoes.   Jean Keys

* "WOW" TORTE *

Split standard angel food cake into five layers.

Filling:

½ c. butter - 1 lb. powdered sugar. Beat together. Add 4 egg yolks — 1 doz. small macaroons (crumbled) — ¼ c. whiskey — 1 Tbsp. rum — ¾ c. toasted slivered almonds. Put layers together. Cover cake with 1 pt. whipped cream — 2 Tbsp. powdered sugar — 2 Tbsp. rum, all mixed. Keeps several days in refrigerator. Freezes well before topping with whipped cream.   Dorothy Tuttle.

* LINZER TORTE (GERMAN) *

¾ c. butter

¾ c. sugar

2 eggs

¼ c. almonds (chopped)

¼ c. strawberry or raspberry
     preserves

2 c. flour (scant)

1 tsp. baking powder

2 tsp. vanilla

1 tsp. cinnamon

¼ tsp. cloves

juice and rind of 1 lemon

powdered sugar

Blend sugar and butter until creamy. Add eggs, almonds, vanilla, cinnamon, cloves, lemon juice and rind. Slowly add flour (that has been sifted with baking powder). Butter and flour a baking pan and place 2/3 of the dough in pan. Top with preserves. Roll out remainder of dough and cut into strips. Place strips criss-cross on top. Bake in preheated oven (350°) for 45 minutes. After cake has cooled, brush liberally with powdered sugar.   Adele Davis.

* MOHN TORTE (GERMAN) *

(Poppyseed Torte)

Part 1.

¼ c. butter

1 Tbsp. sugar

1 c. flour

1 egg yolk

Cream butter and sugar, add egg yolk and flour. Pat and shape dough into greased baking dish ¼ in. thick. Refrigerated for several hours.

Part 2.

1 c. poppyseeds

6 eggs (separated)

¾ c. sugar

grated rind 1 lemon

2 Tbsp. chocolate (grated)

2 Tbsp. raisins

¼ c. almonds (ground)

Grind poppyseeds very fine. Beat egg yolks with the sugar. Add other ingredients (except egg whites). Mix well. Beat egg whites until very stiff and fold into batter. Spread poppyseed mixture on cooled dough. Bake in preheated oven (350°) until set.   Ida Christoph.

* CHOCOLATE ANGEL TORTE *

2 Tbsp. gelatin
¼ c. water
4 oz. unsweetened chocolate
1½ c. hot water
1 tsp. vanilla

6 eggs (separated)
¼ tsp. cream of tartar
2/3 c. sugar
1 angel food cake (10 in.)
   (broken into pieces)

Soak gelatin in cold water. Melt chocolate in saucepan, add hot water, egg yolks. Beat egg whites with the cream of tartar until stiff. Add sugar gradually and beat until very stiff. Fold into chocolate mixture. Pour over angel food pieces and toss lightly. Pack lightly in 10 in. spring mold. Chill until firm. Unmold on serving platter and serve with whipped cream and top with shaved chocolate. Nancy Ebsen.

* STRAWBERRY TORTE *

1 angel food cake mix
1 pkg. strawberry Jello
1 c. hot water
2 c. strawberries and juice
   (frozen — thawed)
3 Tbsp. lemon juice

12 reg. size marshmallows
2 c. whipping cream
¼ tsp. salt
½ c. chopped walnuts (optional)

Make cake mix according to pkg. Bake in 13 x 9 x 2 pan. Cool. Remove cake from pan. Cut cake through the center, save ½ for another use. Put other half back in the pan. Melt Jello in c. of hot water. Put on low heat and melt marshmallows. Combine strawberries. Juice and lemon juice and salt. Add to Jello, stir and put in refrigerator to cool until syrupy. Whip cream and add to Jello fruit mixture. (Add nuts if desired). Pour mixture over cake in pan, to form an even thick layer. Let set overnight or until firm in refrigerator. Judy Piehlo.

* JEAN'S DELICIOUS CHOCOLATE PUDDING *

2¼ c. milk
½ c. sugar
2 sq. unsweetened chocolate

1 tsp. vanilla
3 Tbsp. cornstarch
¼ tsp. salt

Melt chocolate, then add milk on medium low burner. Blend well. Mix sugar and cornstarch, add to milk, cook until thick and smooth. Cool Add vanilla. Note: This is a smooth chocolate pudding and delicious. I have had this recipe for years and always enjoy it. Jean Keys.

* CHOCOLATE STEAMED PUDDING *

Pudding:

¼ c. milk

½ c. flour

½ c. brown sugar

¼ c. butter (melted)

2 Tbsp. cocoa

1 tsp. Rum

1 tsp. vanilla

Combine pudding ingredients and place in buttered glass baking dish.

Cake:

½ c. sugar

½ c. flour

3 Tbsp. cocoa

* whipped cream for garnish

¼ tsp. baking powder

½ c. chopped walnuts

1 c. water

Sift together sugar, flour, baking powder and cocoa and lightly spoon over pudding mixture. Slowly and evenly add water (do not mix). Bake in pre-heated oven (350°) for 50 to 60 minutes. Serve warm or chilled with whipped cream. Rebecca Dixon.

* BAKED INDIAN PUDDING *

Boil 1 pint of milk and ½ c. cornmeal until thick. Add 1 c. molasses, pinch of salt, 1 tsp. cinnamon and another pint of milk. Bake in a slow oven for 3 hours. Serve warm with whipped cream. May also be served cold. Note: This is a very old New England Recipe. Evelyn Berg.

* SUET PUDDING *

1 c. raisins (finely chopped)

1 c. suet (chopped)

1 c. milk

2 c. flour

1 c. molasses

1 tsp. cinnamon

1 tsp. cloves

¼ tsp. nutmeg

pinch of salt

1 tsp. soda dissolved in the milk

Mix all ingredients and steam in a double boiler for 3 hours. Very necessary to keep water boiling. Serve with hard sauce. For christmas dinner it may be made more festive by adding a little green food coloring to the hard sauce and top with a red candied cherry. Note: Our Christmas dessert every Christmas dinner in Brocton. Mass. Evelyn Berg.

* BAKED APPLE PUDDING *

Combine and beat in mixer:

1/3 c. butter or margarine

1 c. sugar

1 egg

259

Blend in:

1 c. unsifted flour	¼ tsp. cinnamon
1 tsp. baking powder	1 tsp. vanilla
¼ tsp. salt	2 c. grated unpeeled apples
¼ tsp. nutmeg	½ c. chopped nuts

Mix all well. Pour into ungreased 8 in. square pan and bake at 350° for 35 minutes. Serve warm or cold topped with whipped cream or ice cream.

Roma Carmody.

* SIMPLE FRUIT PUDDING *

1 cube butter

1 pkg. Jiffy cake mix

1 can prepared pie filling, cherry, apple or pineapple. Pour pie filling into a baking dish. Sprinkle the cake mix over the top. Bake in moderate oven about 25 minutes. Serve warm or cold with or without whipped cream.

Gladys Box.

* PERSMMON PUDDING *

2 c. sugar	1 c. light raisins (washed — chopped)
2 c. sifted flour	2 c. persimmon pulp
4 tsp. baking soda	1 c. milk
4 tsp. baking powder	2 Tbsp. butter (melted)
½ tsp. salt	2 tsp. vanilla
1 c. blanched almonds (chopped)	

Garnish: chopped persimmons.

Generously butter a 8 c. mold. Sift together flour, baking soda, baking powder, salt and sugar. Add almonds and raisins and mix to coat. Mix persimmon pulp, milk, butter and vanilla in a lg. bowl. Gradually add flour mixture, blend well after each addition. Pour into greased mold and cover with waxed paper. Place small rack in bottom of a lg. kettle, place pudding on rack. Steam pudding in simmering water for 3 hours. Check water level occasionally, add more hot water if needed. Remove mold from water and unmold on a serving dish. Garnish with chopped persimmons.　　　Millie Mesaku.

* PRUNE AND NOODLE PUDDING *

1 lb. pitted prunes

12 oz. wide noodles

Seasonings to taste — butter, cinnamon, sugar and bread crumbs. Cook pitted prunes and peel. Cook noodles and drain. Put in casserole in layers — sprinkle with seasonings. Sprinkle bread crumbs on top. Add 1 c. of the prune juice. Bake at 350° for 1½ hours, turn heat down to 325° and bake until it begins to bubble.　　　Lillian Kann.

* STEAMED CRANBERRY PUDDING *

1 c. flour
1½ tsp. baking powder
1/3 c. brown sugar
1/3 c. milk

½ c. bread crumbs
2/3 c. suet (chopped)
1 c. cranberries (chopped)
1 egg.

* Foamy Cranberry Sauce.

Mix ingredients in order given. Turn into a well greased mold, cover with wax paper and steam for 2 hours. Serve with foamy cranberry sauce.

Cranberry sauce:

4 Tbsp. butter
1 c. powdered sugar
2 eggs (separated)

¼ c. sweetened cranberry juice
grated rind of 1 orange

Cream butter and sugar together, add beaten egg yolk and cranberry juice and rind. Beat egg whites until stiff and fold into cranberry mixture just before serving.   Arlene Wright.

* RAISIN – RICE AND RUM PUDDING *

6 Tbsp. rice
1 c. cold water
½ c. raisins
½ c. dark rum

6 c. whipping cream
1½ c. sugar
12 egg yolks
1 Tbsp. vanilla

Place rice and water in a sauce pan and bring to a boil, reduce heat and simmer for 12 to 15 minutes. Remove from heat and let stand covered for 1 hour. Drain off any liquid. Add raisins and rum and let stand for 1–3 hours at room temperature.

Mix cream and sugar in a lg. saucepan and heat, stirring constantly until just under boiling point. In another bowl gently beat the egg yolks. Add cream and sugar mixture a little at a time, mixing gently. Blend in vanilla. Preheat oven to 325°. Place 2 level Tbsp. rice in 12 (6 oz.) custard cups. Sprinkle with a little nutmeg. Pour custard over rice in cups. Place in pan of hot water, should come halfway up sides of cups.

Bake for 1½ hours until knife inserted in center comes out clean. Serve warm or chilled.

Lucille Goderre.

* GREAT PLUM PUDDING *

1 jar (4 oz.) candied fruit and peels (assorted)
1 c. seedless raisins (dark)
¾ c. chopped walnuts
½ c. chopped dates
1 c. flour
¾ c. buttermilk
¼ c. brandy or wine
2 eggs

¾ c. molasses
¼ c. very fine suet (chopped)
23 vanilla wafers (rolled fine)
¾ tsp. baking soda
¾ tsp. salt
¼ tsp. cloves
¼ tsp. cinnamon
¼ tsp. nutmeg

* Hard Sauce Recipe follows:

Toss fruits and peels with dates and ½ c. flour. Combine eggs molasses, buttermilk, suet and wine. Combine remaining flour with vanilla wafers, soda, salt, spices and stir into egg mixture. Add floured mixture and mix well.

Pour into a 1½ qt. well greased mold, cover and set on rack in a deep kettle. Add enough boiling water to come to 1 in. of the top. Steam for 3½ to 4 hours. Add water if necessary.

Hard Sauce:

½ c. butter (softened)
1 c. powdered sugar

½ tsp. vanilla
½ tsp. orange flavoring

Cream butter and gradually add sugar, add flavorings and refrigerate before serving.   Jean Keys.

* PISTACHIO DESSERT *

Crust:

1 c. flour
½ c. eleo
½ c. chopped nuts

Mix ingredients well. Place in 9 x 13 in. pan. Bake for 15 minutes at 350°.

Second Layer:

1 pkg. (8 oz.) cream cheese
1 c. powdered sugar
lg. Cool Whip (reserved for top)

Mix and spread over crust.

Third Layer:

1 pkg. instant Pisachio pudding
2½ c. milk

Beat until thick and spread over second layer. Spread Cool Whip on top. chill. May be garnished with chopped nuts.   Madeline Ryan.

* PASKA (RUSSIAN) *
(Easter Dessert)

1 lb. unsalted cottage cheese
  (drained)
1/8 tsp. salt
¼ c. raisins
1/3 c. candied fruit (mixed)
½ c. almonds (blanched — chopped)

3 egg yolks and 1 egg
½ c. unsalted butter
¾ c. sugar
1 tsp. vanilla
¼ c. whipping cream

Rub the cheese through a strainer. Add salt, raisins, candied fruit, and almonds. Mix well. Cream butter and sugar, add eggs and vanilla, beat well. Fold in the whipped cream. Heat mixture in the top of a double boiler over simmering heat. Stir constantly until bubbles emerge around the edge and is thick enough to coat a spoon. If you do not have a Paska mold, use a clean flower pot. Line it with damp cheesecloth. Pour in mixture, cover top with cheesecloth, place a small plate on top to keep mixture down. Chill for 3 to 4 hours. To serve: Drain off surplus moisture and unmold on a plate. remove the cheesecloth and serve cold.   Adele Davis.

* FLOATING ISLAND *

2 eggs
2 egg yolks
¼ c. sugar

¼ tsp. salt
2 c. milk (hot)
1 tsp. vanilla

Combine slightly beaten eggs and egg yolks with sugar and salt in a saucepan and add hot milk gradually and stir until sugar is dissolved. Simmer until custard coats a metal spoon. Add vanilla and turn into sherbert dishes and top with meringue.

Meringue:

¼ tsp. cream of tartar
¼ tsp. salt
2 egg whites
¼ c. sugar

Add cream of tartar and salt to the egg whites and beat until peaks form. Add sugar gradually and beat until stiff. Divide in equal portions and drop them in boiling water in a shallow pan. Bake in preheated oven (325°) for 15 minutes. Remove from pan with skimmer. Place on custard and chill. Add a spoonful of currant Jelly on the meringue before serving.   Ida Christoph.

* CREME BRULEE *

1 c. milk
6 egg yolks
½ c. sugar
½ c. flour

1 tsp. vanilla
¼ c. whipping cream
powdered sugar

Pour milk into top of a double boiler and bring to a boiling point. Combine eggs and sugar and beat. Add milk slowly to the sugar mixture, beating continuously. Whisk in flour and vanilla. Place over hot water in the double boiler and cook until mixture is thick, stirring constantly. Remove from heat, allow to cool, then chill. Whip cream and fold into custard. Serve in dessert dishes or parfait glasses.

Nathalia Richman.

* OLD FASHIONED PRUNE WHIP *

2 jars strained prunes
   (baby food jars)
½ c. prune juice
½ c. brown sugar
¼ tsp. cinnamon
2 Tbsp. cornstarch

1 c. boiling water
¼ c. cold water
1 Tbsp. lemon juice
2 egg whites (stiffly beaten)
½ c. heavy cream (whipped)

Mix prunes, prune juice, boiling water, sugar, cinnamon and salt. Mix cornstarch in cold water until smooth, add to prune mixture. Cook over low heat (stir constantly) for 5 minutes. Cool. Stir in lemon juice and fold in egg whites and whipped cream. Place in individual dishes and chill.   Sarah Hemings.

* BAKED COMPOTE *

½ lb. pitted prunes
½ lb. pitted apricots (dried kind)
½ lb. dried peaches
½ lb. raisins
½ lb. dried pears
½ fresh papaya (sliced)

2 bananas (sliced)
2 c. apple cider
1½ c. orange juice
1 Tbsp. grated orange rind
1 Tbsp. honey

Cut fruit (except papaya and bananas) in small pieces. Place in a jar or bowl. Add the cider, cover and let stand overnite at room temperature. Preheat oven to 350°. Pour fruit into buttered casserole. Top with the bananas and papaya, add orange juice, grated rind and honey. Bake covered for 30 minutes. Serve hot.

Rebecca Dixon.

* PEACH DUMPLINGS *

2 c. flour
¼ tsp. salt
4 tsp. baking powder
2 Tbsp. shortening
½ c. milk

1 lg. can sliced peaches (drained)
1 Tbsp. cornstarch
½ tsp. almond extract

Cream shortening and add milk. Sift dry ingredients and add to milk mixture. Roll out batter on lightly floured board to ½ in. thickness. Cut into 4 in. circles. Sprinkle with some sugar. Place 3—4 slices of peaches on top and fold over and seal well. Bake in shallow greased pan in preheated oven (350°) until tops are browned (about 30 minutes). Mix cornstarch and extract in peach juice and heat slowly until it becomes thick. Dumplings may be served hot or cold.

Francis Wright.

* GLAZED APPLES WITH SESAME SEEDS *

1 egg white (beaten)
1/3 c. water
¼ c. flour
1 Tbsp. cornstarch
3 tart apples (peeled — cored — quartered)

¾ c. sugar
1/3 c. water
1 Tbsp. oil
1 tsp. vinegar
1 Tbsp. sesame seeds
oil for frying.

Generously oil a serving platter. Combine egg white and 1/3 c. water, flour and cornstarch in a mixing bowl and beat until smooth. Heat oil in a skillet, dip apples in the batter and fry in batches until golden brown. Drain on paper towels. When apples are all cooked. Wash, dry and oil a slotted spoon, keep additional oil handy. Combine the remaining water and sugar in a saucepan and bring to a boil over medium heat, stirring constantly. Reduce heat to low and stir in 1 Tbsp oil. Continue cooking until a small amount dropped in cold water spins a thread and is golden brown. Carefully stir in vinegar. Add apples 2 or 3 at a time to syrup and mix gently, remove with a slotted spoon. Serve on a platter and sprinkle with toasted sesame seed.

Adele Davis.

* BAKED PAPAYA *

4 firm papayas (unpeeled)
¼ c. butter (melted)
3 Tbsp. brown sugar

cinnamon
nutmeg
1 lime or lemon

Slice papayas into 1 in. thick circular pieces, remove the seeds. Arrange the papayas in a shallow, buttered baking dish. Sprinkle with brown sugar, cinnamon and nutmeg. Squeeze a few drops of lemon or lime over each piece. Bake for 30 minutes in a preheated oven (350°). Serve warm.

Daisy Alexander.

* CHERRY DESSERT *

1 can pie cherries (sweet kind)
1 can (No. 2) crushed pineapple
1 c. coconut (fine)
1 pkg. yellow cake mix

1 c. pecans or walnuts (chopped)
1 c. butter (melted)

Use one ungreased 9 x 12 in baking pan (preferably a pyrex pan). Pour in layers (do not mix). First the cherries, then pineapple, coconut, dry cake mix, chopped nuts and top with the melted butter. Bake in preheated oven (350°) for 1 hour. Cool. To serve, cut into squares and top with whipped cream.

Francis Wright.

* QUICK FRUIT DESSERT *

1 stick of butter
1 c. sugar
1 tsp. baking powder
1 c. sifted flour

1 lg. can fruit or berries
pinch of salt
¾ c. milk
lemon juice and spices (desired)

Cut butter into pieces and place in baking dish. Mix sugar, flour, fruit (using fruit liquid) and heat to boiling. Pour batter into buttered baking dish and pour hot fruit on top. Bake in medium oven until done. Opal Harper.

* MANGO COBBLER *

7 c. ripe firm mangoes (sliced)
¾ c. brown sugar
3 Tbsp. cornstarch
¼ tsp. salt
½ tsp. cinnamon

½ tsp. nutmeg
pie crust
1 Tbsp. lemon juice
1 Tbsp. butter

Preheat oven to 400°. Grease a 9 in. square pan. In lg. bowl, combine mangoes with sugar, cornstarch, spices and salt. Prepare crust and roll into a square. Cut into ½ in. strips to make lattice top. Put mango mixture into pan, top with juice and dot with butter. Put lattice work on, bake at 400° for 45 to 50 minutes. Should be golden brown. Delicious served with ice cream. Jean Keys.

* UNCOOKED APPLESAUCE *

6 to 9 apples (peeled) cored —
    chopped)
¾ c. apple cider
2 Tbsp. lemon juice

1 tsp. cinnamon
½ tsp. allspice
honey

Pour the cider into a blender add a few handfulls of apples and blend well. Continue blending until all batches are smooth. Pour into a serving bowl and add lemon juice spices and honey to taste. Note: For variations, add ½ c. raisins or sunflower seeds or both. Ruth Tufte.

* BAKED APPLESAUCE *

juice of 1 lemon   1/3 c. sugar
2 lbs. tart apples   1 tsp. cinnamon

Preheat oven to 350°. Pour lemon juice into a casserole with a tight fitting lid. Peel and core apples and quarter. Put in casserole and toss with the lemon juice. Bake about 45 minutes, until apples have turned to sauce. Remove from oven and flavor with sugar and cinnamon. Serve hot or cold.   Billie Do.

* MANGO DELIGHT *

2 pkgs. (2 oz. each) lemon gelatin   1 pkg. (8 oz.) cream cheese
1¾ c. boiling water   2 c. chopped mangoes

Dissolve gelatin in hot water. Let cool until thickened. Mix mangoes and cheese in a blender until smooth. Add gelatin and blend. Pour into mold and chill until firm.   Jean Keys.

* APRICOT CHEESE DELIGHT *

1 can (29 oz.) apricots (drained —   2 c. hot water
   cut up)   1 c. of combined fruit juices
1 can (29 oz.) crushed pineapple   1 c. miniature marshmallows
   (drained)
2 pkgs. orange Jello

Mix Jello with hot water then add fruit juice. Cool. Fold in fruit and marsh-mallows. Chill until firm.
Topping:
½ c. sugar   1 egg (slightly beaten)
3 tsp. flour   1 c. fruit juice
2 Tbsp. butter   1 c. whipping cream

Combine sugar, flour and beaten egg, gradually add fruit juice. Cook until thick, stirring constantly. Remove from heat and add butter. Cool thoroughly. Whip the cream and fold into custard mixture. Spread evenly over Jello. Grated Cheddar cheese to sprinkle over the top. Refrigerate before serving.

                                           Annon Swope.

* CARMEL APPLE BLOCKS *

4 pkgs. gelatin   ½ c. butterscotch or carmel topping
¼ c. sugar   1½ c. apples (peeled — chopped)
2 c. apple juice (heated to boiling)

In a lg. bowl mix gelatin and sugar, add hot apple juice and stir until gelatin is dissolved. Stir in apples and ice cream topping. Pour into a 8 or 9 in. square pan and chill until firm. Cut into squares.   Adele Davis.

267

* RAINBOW JELLO *

Part 1:

½ c. water

2 pkgs. gelatin

1 can sweetened condensed milk

1½ c. hot water

Dissolve gelatin in cold water. Mix milk with hot water and combine both. Set aside to cool.

Part 2:

1 pkg. each orange, lime, lemon, strawberry

4 pkgs. gelatin

Mix one pkg. of Jello at a time using ¼ c. water and 1 pkg. gelatin (dissolved) 1 box of Jello in ¾ c. hot water, mix both of these together. Pour one Jello mixture in layers. Have each layer set before adding next. Cut into squares to serve. Other Jello flavors may be used. Millie Mesaku.

* PASSION FRUIT PARTY DESSERT *

1 Tbsp. unflavored gelatin

¼ c. cold water

6 eggs (separated)

¾ c. passion fruit juice

1 large angel food cake

1½ c. sugar

1 c. heavy cream (whipped — sweetened)

Soften gelatin in water. Combine egg yolks, juice and ¾ c. of sugar. Stir well. Cook over low heat stirring until it coats a spoon, about 20 minutes. Remove from heat, add softened gelatin and stir till dissolved. Beat egg whites till stiff. Adding remaining sugar gradually, beating constantly then fold into cooked mixture. Tear cake into small pieces and arrange a layer on bottom of a large oiled tube mold. Pour a layer of the mixture over this. Arrange another layer of cake, a layer of mixture and so on till finished. Chill until firm. Unmold and frost with whipped cream. Jean Keys.

* MANGO JELLO *

3 pkgs. (3 oz.) orange Jello

4 c. boiling water

1½ c. sugar

4 pkgs. unflavored gelatin

1 c. cold water

2 c. firm ripe mangoes (diced)

¼ c. lemon juice

Dissolve Jello in boiling water, add sugar. Dissolve gelatin in cold water. Combine Jello and gelatin. Add diced mangoes and lemon juice. Pour into pan and chill. Cut into desired shapes. Billie Do.

* DATE LOAF *

30 marshmallows (cut up). Soak 30 minutes in ½ c. cream or ½ c. orange juice. Then add 1-1/3 c. sliced dates, 1 c. graham cracker crumbs, (fine), ½ c. chopped walnuts. Mix all together and roll in waxed paper and chill. Slice and serve with whipped cream topping. Velma Harmas.

* PINEAPPLE — BERRY DELIGHT *

1 can crushed pineapple
1 can blueberry pie filling
1 can Eagle Brand milk

1/3 c. Macadamia nuts (chopped)
1 carton of Cool Whip

Mix all ingredients well. Pour into pie tins and put in freezer. Serve when firm. Dorothy Morrison.

* CREAMY AMBROSIA *

1 container (8 oz.) plain or vanilla
    yogurt
½ c. Best Foods Mayonnaise
1 can (30 oz.) fruit cocktail
    (well drained)

1 can (20 oz.) pineapple chucks (well grained)
1 can (3 oz.) shredded coconut
½ c. raisins

In large bowl fold together yogurt and mayonnaise. Fold in remaining ingredients. Cover and chill several hours or overnite. (I add a small can of drained grapes and a small can of drained mandarin oranges). Jean Keys.

* PINEAPPLE PARFAIT *

1 (3 oz.) pkg. orange — pineapple
    gelatin
1½ c. hot water
1 pt. vanilla ice cream (softened)

1 c. crushed pineapple (drained)

Dissolve gelatin in hot water. Add ice cream and stir until dissolved. Add pineapple and chill, stirring occasionally until mixture mounds. Pour into parfait glasses and chill until firm. Jean Ariyoshi.

* MANGO ICE CREAM *

½ gallon vanilla ice cream — softened
    slightly
1 c. cold mango puree
1 c. cold mango pieces.

Mix all together and place in a bowl, cover — put in freezer. Serve in chilled glasses. Dorothy Tuttle.

* MANGO ICE CREAM PIE *

1 Graham cracker pie crust (baked)
2 c. vanilla ice cream
1 c. mangoes (ripe)
1 pkg. lemon Jello
1 pkg. gelatin

½ c. boiling water
1 Tbsp. water
mango slices
whipped cream

Grate 1 c. mangoes. Dissolve gelatin in water. Dissolve Jello in boiling water and add gelatin. Add ice cream to Jello mixture and blend well. Add grated mangoes and pour into pie shell. Chill for 4 hours. Garnish with whipped cream and mango slices.

Eileen Weberg.

* PASSION FRUIT ICE CREAM *

2 eggs (separated)
1/3 c. sugar
1 c. light cream
¼ tsp. salt

2 Tbsp. sugar
1 Tbsp. lemon or lime juice
1 c. frozen passion fruit juice

Beat egg yolks slightly, add sugar and salt. Cook over low heat until spoon is coated, remove from heat and add juice. Chill. When mixture is cooled, add passion fruit juice. Beat egg whites until stiff and then add 2 Tbsp. sugar. Fold egg whites in juice mixture and pour into ice cube tray. Stir during freezing.

Lucille Goderre.

* SORBET *

1 large can milk
1 c. water

1 c. sugar
1¼ c. grapefruit juice

Mix thoroughly until sugar is dissolved. Place in freezer in plastic container. Freeze until the mushy stage. Take out and beat with electric beaters until nice and smooth. Return to freeze and freeze until completely solid. Serve in parfait glasses. Note: Other juices may be used, if they are sweetened, cut down on the sugar.

Millie Mesaku.

* ORANGE ALASKA SUPREME *

8 oranges
¼ c. Grenadine
1 pt. vanilla ice cream

3 egg whites
½ c. sugar

Cut off tops of oranges and remove pulp and membrane. Cut pulp into bits. Soak in Grenadine and chill. Beat egg whites until stiff and gradually add sugar. Fill orange cups (about half full) with orange bits. Place ice cream on top and cover with the meringue (seal all edges well). Bake in preheated oven (425°) until meringue is browned. Serve at once.

Nancy Ebsen.

* FLOWER POT DESSERT *

1. Choose small flower pots, sterilize in hot water and cool.
2. Place a piece of cake in the bottom of each pot to cover the hole. Fill each pot ¾ full with ice cream or sherbert of your choice. In middle of the pots, force a large soda straw into cream and cut even with the top.
3. Pile meringue (of your choice) around inside of pot (leave space over straw open.
4. Bake in preheated oven (400°) until meringue is golden brown.
5. Place fresh or artificial flowers in the straw when serving.
6. May be made in advance and stored in the freezer and baked just before serving.

Note: This is a delicious and eye catching dessert.   Adele Davis.

* PORCUPINE MOLD *

3 qt. melon mold   1 lb. toasted almonds (slivered)
1 qt. coffee ice cream   1 c. cream (whipped)
1 qt. chocolate fudge ice cream   * fresh or frozen raspberries for garnish.
1 qt. raspberry sherbert

Note: When filling mold with the ice cream, put in freezer between each addition, so layers will harden separately. Spread coffee ice cream around inside of the mold, for first layer. Spread chocolate fudge ice cream for 2nd. layer on top of the coffee ice cream. (Leaving a hollow in the middle). For inner layer. Fill hole with the sherbert. Freeze thoroughly. When ready to serve, unmold on serving platter and stud with the almonds (to look like a porcupine). Use pastry tube to make a whipped cream border.   Adele Davis.

* CREAM PUFFS *

¼ c. butter   ¼ tsp. salt
½ c. boiling water   2 eggs
½ c. sifted all purpose flour

Melt butter in boiling water in a medium saucepan over high heat. Turn heat low. Add salt and flour all at once, stirring vigorously with a spoon until mixture leaves the sides of the pan in a smooth compact mass, and a metal spoon pressed into it leaves a clear impression.
Immediately remove from heat, beat in eggs one at a time, beating until each is blended and mixture is smooth. Continue beating until mixture forms a stiff dough. Drop by heaping Tbsp., 2 in. apart on cookie sheets, shape with wet spoon into rounds which point up in center. Bake in hot oven (450°) for 10 minutes then lower heat to 400°. for 20 to 25 minutes.

To serve, split cream puffs in half and fill with any cream filling. A simple filling such as instant Jello vanilla pudding is an excellent one. Sprinkle top of cream puffs with powdered sugar.

Amy Matsuda.

* COFFEE ICE BOX PUDDING *

32 lg. marshmallows — 1 pt. whipping cream — 1 c. strong coffee — lady fingers. Melt marshmallows and coffee in the top of a double boiler. Cool slightly. Fold in whipped cream. Pour into a spring form mold, lined with split lady fingers. Let stand for about 4 hours in the refrigerator.　　　　Lillian Kann.

* APPLE SAUCE LOAF *

3 c. flour
1 Tbsp. baking powder
½ tsp. salt
1 tsp. cinnamon
½ c. chopped nuts

½ c. shortening
1 c. sugar
2 eggs
1 c. applesauce

Sift together, flour, baking powder, salt and cinnamon. Cream sugar and shortening until light and fluffy. Add eggs and mix well. Blend in applesauce. Add flour mixture, stirring only enough to mix. Stir in nuts. Bake in greased 5 x 9 in. loaf pan in mod. oven 350° for 1 hour.　　　　Elizabeth Betty Guy.

R·E·L·I·S·H·E·S

* CHUTNEY *

3 lbs. mangoes
3 lbs. sugar and water to cover
4 oz. garlic (finely chopped)
4 oz. ginger (finely chopped)

¼ oz. fine chili pepper
½ lb. dried apricots (cut in strips)
½ lb. raisins
1 pt. cider vinegar
1 Tbsp. salt

Cook mangoes well done in sugar. Add garlic, chili, ginger and salt. Cook until like thick jam. Add raisins and apricots, cook for 7 minutes, stirring constantly. Remove from heat, stir in vinegar thoroughly. Seal jars when cooled.

Carol Burnett.

* MANGO CHUTNEY — NO. I *

12 c. mangoes (half ripe sliced)
7 c. sugar (raw or 3 lb. brown sugar)
3 c. vinegar
2 pkgs. (15 oz.) raisins
4 Hawaiian red peppers

3 Tbsp. chopped garlic
½ c. chopped fresh ginger
½ c. chopped preserved ginger
3 c. slivered almonds

Simmer sugar, vinegar and spices for ½ hour. Add mangoes and cook 1 hour. Add almonds, put in sterilized jars.

Jean Keys.

* MANGO CHUTNEY — NO. II *

2½ c. vinegar
6½ c. sugar
1 tsp. Hawaiian salt
15 c. green mango slices
6 Hawaiian chilis (finely chopped)
1 tsp. pickling spice

5 garlic cloves (chopped)
1 c. seedless raisins
1 c. currants.
6 lg. onions (sliced)
8 cloves
¼ c. lime juice
1 c. almonds (slivered)

Grated orange and lemon rind to taste.

Boil sugar, salt and vinegar for 5 minutes. Add sliced mangoes and simmer until tender. Add all other ingredients (except grated rind). Cook slowly for 35 to 60 minutes or desired consistency. Add grated rinds 10 minutes before canning. Pack in sterilized jars.

Daisy Alexander.

* CHATNI (INDIA) *
(Chutney)

1 lb. (5 c.) apples (chopped
½ lb. dry apricots (chopped)
3 limes or lemons (cut into
   thin wedges)
1½ c. brown sugar

1½ tsp. salt
1 tsp. cinnamon
1 tsp. chili powder
½ tsp. coriander
¼ tsp. cayenne pepper

273

2 tsp. ground ginger
½ tsp. black pepper

Combine all ingredients in a large pot and bring to a boil, reduce heat to simmer and cook about 1½ hours, stirring frequently, until mixture is thick and syrupy. Ladle into sterilized jars and seal.   Adele Davis.

* TOMATO — APPLE CHUTNEY *

12 lg. tomatoes (finely chopped)
12 lg. green apples (chopped)
8 medium onions (chopped)
2 lg. green peppers (seeded — chopped)
1½ qts. white vinegar

4 c. brown sugar
2 c. golden raisins
4 tsp. salt
1/3 c. pickling spices (tied in cheese cloth)

Combine all ingredients in a large pot and bring to a boil. Reduce heat to simmer and cook for 1½ hours, stirring frequently until mixture is thick. Remove bag. Ladle into sterilized jars and seal. Cool. Store in cool, dry place. (Chutney may be stored in refrigerator or frozen.)   Francis Wright.

* GREEN PEAR CHUTNEY *

1 qt. vinegar
5 lbs. sugar
3 medium onions (chopped)
6 garlic cloves (chopped)
3 sm. red peppers (chopped)

¼ lb. ginger root (shaved thin)
2 Tbsp. salt
2 oz. whole cloves

Boil these ingredients for 10 minutes. Add 1 lb. dried apricots (that have been soaked overnite) 1 lb. raisins, ½ lb. preserved ginger, 5 lbs. green pears (that have been peeled and cubed). Boil until clear, about 40 minutes. Add 1 lb. almonds, boil for 5 minutes and put in sterilized jars.   Jean Keys.

* PEAR CHUTNEY *

4 lbs. pears (peeled — chopped)
2½ c. brown sugar
2 c. white vinegar
1½ c. golden raisins
½ c. onions (chopped)
1 Tbsp. salt

3 garlic cloves (minced)
½ tsp. cayenne pepper
½ c. crystalized ginger (chopped)
2 Tbsp. mustard seed (crushed)

Combine all ingredients in lg. saucepan and bring to a boil over medium heat, stirring frequently. Reduce heat to simmer and cook until thick (about 40 — 50 minutes). Pour into sterilized jars and seal well. Can be refrigerated in jars.
                                                                Annie Ebsen.

* PEACH CHUTNEY *

8 c. peaches (peeled-sliced)
1 medium onion (chopped)
1 garlic clove (chopped)
1 c. seedless raisins (chopped)
1 Tbsp. chili powder

2¼ c. brown sugar
1 c. crystalized ginger (chopped)
2 Tbsp. mustard seed
1 Tbsp. salt
1 qt. cider vinegar

Place all ingredients in a lg. saucepan and bring to a boil, stirring constantly until sugar is dissolved. Reduce heat, simmer uncovered until quite thick and a deep brown color, (about 45 to 60 minutes). Seal or refrigerate in jars.

Adele Davis.

* DATE AND LEMON CHUTNEY *

8 oz. pitted dates (chopped)
½ c. fresh coconut (chopped)
¼ c. lemon juice
freshly ground pepper

1 Tbsp. parsley (minced)
½ tsp. fennel seeds (pulverized)
½ tsp. salt

Combine all ingredients in bowl and mix very well. Place in plastic bowl and cover. May be kept in refrigerator for 1 week or can be frozen up to 3 months. No cooking required. **Judy Pieklo.**

* AUNT OCCIES GREEN TOMATO CHUTNEY *

4 lbs. green tomatoes (peeled
    seeded — chopped)
1 lb. tart green apples (peeled
    cored — chopped)
1 Tbsp. dry mustard
1½ in" piece fresh ginger
5 c. malt vinegar

1 lb. onions (chopped)
1 lb. raisins
1 tsp. salt
½ tsp. ground red pepper
1 lb. light brown sugar
½ c. malt vinegar

Combine tomatoes, apples, onions, raisins and pepper in a heavy large saucepan. Tie mustard and ginger in cheesecloth and add to pan. Pour in enough vinegar to cover. Bring to boil over high heat.

Dissolve sugar in ½ c. vinegar and add to pan. Reduce heat and simmer until mixture is thick and spreadable (about 70 minutes). Discard cheesecloth bag and cool.

(Can be made up to 1 week, covered and refrigerated. To preserve for longer storage, process chutney in boiling water bath 10 minutes for half-pint jars.

Aunt Occie.

* GUAVA CATSUP *

3 qts. guava pulp
5 onions (sliced fine)
2 lg. garlic cloves (crushed)
5 sm. red peppers (seeded —
　　chopped fine)
¼ c. water

3 c. vinegar
4 tsp. cinnamon
2 tsp. cloves
6 c. sugar
1 tsp. salt

Cook onion in water until soft. Combine all ingredients and cook for 30 — 40 minutes until thick. Pour into hot sterilized jars and seal.　　　　　Lorna Burger.

* PEPPER RELISH *

12 sweet red peppers (seeded)
12 sweet green peppers (seeded)
3 or 4 medium onions

½ c. sugar
1 tsp. salt
vinegar (about 1 qt.)

Place peppers and onions in a blender (use medium or course blade). Pour boiling water over mixture to cover and let stand 10 minutes. Drain. Add sugar and salt and enough vinegar to cover. Cook slowly for 20 minutes. Pack in hot jars and seal.　　　　　Ida Christoph.

* JEAN'S PICKLED TURNIPS *

2 c. sliced white turnips
　　or white radishes
2 Tbsp. salt

1 c. vinegar
¾ c. sugar

Peel turnips and cut into thin slices. Add salt and let stand 30 minutes. Drain off moisture. Mix vinegar and sugar in a saucepan, bring to a boil, add turnips and boil for 1 minutes. Put in jars and seal. Stand overnite, then refrigerate.

Jean Keys.

* CUCUMBER ONION PICKLES *

7 c. sliced — unpeeled cukes
1 c. thinly sliced onions
1 Tbsp. salt

1 tsp. celery seed
1 tsp. mustard seed

Mix in lg. bowl.
2 c. white vinegar and 2 c. sugar, heat just enough to melt sugar. Pour over cucumbers, cover and let stand overnite (stir several times to mix spices well. Put into jars — no sealing necessary — will keep in refrigerator 6 months or more.

Dorothy Tuttle.

* PORTUGUESE PICKLED ONIONS *

3 lbs. onions
2 green peppers
1½ c. vinegar

1½ c. water
1 Tbsp. Hawaiian salt
3 hot red peppers (optional)

Cut onions and green peppers in wedges and put in lg. jar. Combine vinegar, water salt and red peppers. Add to onions and green peppers. Stand overnite or 24 hours. Then refrigerate. Jean Keys.

* CUCUMBER RELISH *

4 large cucumbers (sliced to pickle width)

Combine:

1 c. sugar
1 tsp. salt
1 tsp. dry mustard

1 tsp. celery seed
1 very lg. onion (thinly sliced)

Mix all until dissolved. Add cucumbers. Keep in refrigerator for at least 48 hours before serving. Georgia Beasley.

* OLD — FASHIONED CORN RELISH *

1½ c. cooked corn kernels or 1 can
   (16 oz.) whole corn kernels —
   drained
½ c. vinegar
1 tsp. salt
½ tsp. celery seed

¼ tsp. mustard seed
¼ tsp. hot pepper sauce
2 Tbsp. green pepper (chopped)
1 Tbsp. pimento (chopped)
1 Tbsp. green onion (minced)

Combine vinegar, sugar, salt celery seed, mustard seed and hot pepper sauce. Place in medium saucepan and bring to a boil. Cook for 2 minutes. Remove from heat and cool. Prepare remaining ingredients in a bowl, mix and add to cooled mixture. Chill. (This relish will keep indefinitely in the refrigerator, the flavor improves with standing.) Ida Christoph.

* COPPER PENNIES *

2 lbs. carrots (thinly sliced)
1 sm. onion (thinly sliced)
1 sm. green pepper (thinly sliced)
3 stalks celery (diced)
1 can tomato soup

1 c. sugar
¼ c. oil
¾ c. cider vinegar
1 Tbsp. mustard
1 Tbsp. Perrin sauce.

Cook carrots until tender (on crispy side). Heat tomato soup, sugar, oil, vinegar and mustard and pour over carrots. Refrigerate. Adele Davis.

* CHOW CHOW *

2½ lbs. green tomatoes (chopped)   3 green peppers (seeded — chopped)
2½ lbs. sm cucumbers (chopped)   1 sm. cabbage (sliced)
4 c. yellow onions (chopped)   ¾ c. pickling spices

Place all ingredients in saucepan and bring to a boil and cook for 3 minutes. Drain and set aside.

Vinegar sauce:

2 c. vinegar   1 tsp. mustard seed
2 c. sugar   1 tsp. hot pepper sauce
1 Tbsp. salt   1 c. water
1 Tbsp. celery seed

Combine all ingredients in saucepan and bring to a boil and cook for 3 minutes. Add vegetables and heat until very hot, but not boiling. Spoon into sterilized jars and seal or store in sealed jars in the refrigerator. Flavor improves.

Franny Wright.

* APFELKREN (AUSTRIAN) *

3 eating apples (peeled —   2 tsp. paprika
   cored grated)   2 Tbsp. dry white wine.
¼ c. sugar
1 Tbsp. prepared horseradish

Combine all ingredients in a bowl and blend well. Serve as relish especially good with pork or roast goose. Roberta Chateauneuf.

* SCACCIATA RELISH *

2 c. celery (diced — including   1 tsp. oregano
   a few leaves)   1 Tbsp. olive oil
2 Tbsp. pimiento olives (crushed) salt and pepper to taste

Combine all ingredients and cover. Marinate for about 4 hours in refrigerator. Serve as a relish. Adele Davis.

* CRANBERRY HARVEST RELISH *

1¾ c. water   1 c. celery (chopped)
1 pkg. (6 oz.) strawberry Jello   1 c. nuts (chopped)
1 c. sugar   1 medium unpeeled orange (quartered)
½ c. lemon juice   1 tart apple (cored — chopped)

In saucepan bring one cup of water to a boil, add Jello and sugar stir until dissolved. Add lemon juice and remaining water. Chill. Place remaining ingredients in a blender and blend to a coarse grind. Add to Jello and pour into mold. To serve: Unmold and garnish with fresh mint. Nancy Ebsen.

* KASTANIAN MIT PFLAUMEN (GERMAN) *

1 onion (minced)
2 Tbsp. butter
1 lb. chestnuts (blanched — diced)

1 lb. dried pitted prunes
2 Tbsp. sugar
1 c. red wine

Cook chestnuts in water until tender. Drain. Cook prunes in water until tender. Drain. Combine all ingredients and place in a buttered casserole. Bake 1 hour in preheated oven (350°).
Serve hot or cold with meat course.

Charlene Do.

* KIM CHEE (KOREAN) *

2 lbs. cabbage or won bok
½ c. Hawaiian salt
4 c. water
½ tsp. paprika
1 Tbsp. sugar

¼ tsp. Ajinomoto
2 tsp. red pepper (minced)
3 Tbsp. garlic (minced)
½ tsp. ginger (minced)

Wash cabbage and cut into 1½ in. lengths. Dissolve salt in water and soak cabbage in brine for 4—5 hours. Rinse and drain. Combine seasonings, add to cabbage mix. Pack in qt. jars. Cover loosely and let stand at room temperature for 2 days.
Chill before serving.

Millie Mesaku.

* PAM'S PEAR CONSERVE *

6 c. sugar
8 c. pears (pared — sliced)
2 c. raisins

juice of 4 oranges
2 lemons (grated rind and juice)
2 c. chopped walnuts

Boil all ingredients (except walnuts) for 5 minutes or until thick. Add nuts, cook for 5 minutes more.
Seal in hot sterilized jars.

Jean Keys.

* PAM'S AMBER *

8 c. ground pears
6 c. sugar
1 jar maraschino cherries
   (cut in half)

1 can crushed pineapple
2 Tbsp. lemon juice

Mix all ingredients, cook until thick. Seal in sterilized jars.

Jean Keys.

* HOT PEPPER JELLY *

2—3 c. red and green peppers
   (diced fine)
   (or use food processor)
2—3 red hot peppers (seeded — diced)

6 c. sugar
1½ c. cider vinegar
2 pkgs. pectin

Bring to a boil the sugar, peppers, vinegar, then simmer 10 minutes. Set aside for 20 minutes. Then bring to a boil. Add pectin and stir for 1 minute. Pour into sterilized jars and seal. Note: Good Pupu - a block of cream cheese with some pepper jelly spooned over the top, good with crackers. Ono, delicious.

                                                            Jean Keys.

* COFFEE JELLY *

½ box gelatin or 2 Tbsp.
   granulated gelatin
½ c. boiling water

1/3 c. sugar
2 c. strong coffee

Soak gelatin for 20 minutes in cold water, dissolve in boiling water, strain and add sugar and coffee. Pour into a mold and chill.   **Elizabeth Betty Guy.**

* LILIKOI JELLY *

3 c. sugar
1 c. water

½ c. lilikoi juice
½ bottle or ½ c. Certo

Boil sugar and water together for 1 minute. Take off stove. Add Certo and stir well. Then add the lilikoi juice. Pour into sterilized jars and cover with paraffin.

                                                  Daisy Alexander.

* ACEROLA JELLY *

3½ c. acerola juice (about 2 lbs. ripe cherries)
7 c. sugar
1 bottle of liquid Pectin
1 prepare juice

Wash fruit. Measure 4 c. fruit, crush lightly and cover with 4 c. water. Bring to a boil and simmer for 15 — 20 minutes. Extract juice.

To make Jelly:

Measure juices and sugar into a lg. kettle. Stir well. Bring to a boil, stirring constantly. At once stir in Pectin. Bring to a full boil, and boil hard for 1 minute, stirring. Remove from heat, skin off foam. Bottle and seal.

                                                  Daisy Alexander.

H·I·N·T·S

THE RECIPE

There is a saying that I recall
That helped me as a child
It seemed to be a recipe
For everything worthwhile.

Only the best is good enough
The wise have found it true
For when you give the best you have
The best returns to you.   *Jean Keys.*

1. To prevent the pot from discoloring when cooking artichokes, add a cut lemon to the water.
2. Roll the fruit and raisins in part of the measured flour in the recipe to keep from sticking together.
3. Mash ripe bananas, add a tiny bit of lemon juice and freeze for later use.
4. Save orange and lemon peels when using juice of same. Grate or put into food processor to chop and use for breads, muffins or cookies.
5. Save an extra apple in the frig. Dice and add to green salads for flavor and crunchiness.
6. Keep extra raisins fresh by putting in a small jar with Sherry wine.
7. To keep garlic fresh and ready for use in cooking and salad dressings, peel and add to jar of olive oil kept in refrigerator.
8. Too many lemons to use immediately? Squeeze juice and put into empty oleo containers and freeze. Great for making lemonade, margaritas and adding to special dishes when thawed.
9. Buy large containers of walnuts and but through food processor to chop, then measure into 1 or 2 c. containers and freeze until ready to use.
10. Try chopped pieces of crystalized ginger over fruit salads. Delicious.
11. Recipes are written for regular or large eggs, jumbo eggs will add too much liquid to the recipe.
12. There are 2 c. brown sugar in a one pound box.
13. It is easier to grate or "zest" citrus rind that has been frozen.
14. Save time and energy by cooking several dishes in the oven at one time.
15. When cooking with herbs use twice as much fresh as the dried counterpart.

16. Make a crunchy and nutritional salad by adding hulled sunflower seeds, also as topping for casseroles.
17. Write the date on everything when stored in the freezer, so older items can be used first.
18. Put onion in freezer for 15 minutes before slicing to eliminate odor.
19. Raisins, dates and prunes are easier to grind if frozen.
20. Keep a package of baking soda near the stove to douse fires on stove or burners in the oven.

Jean Keys.

* HELPFUL HINTS AND TIME SAVERS *

* Baked Potato jackets may be scraped, buttered, seasoned with salt and pepper. Placed in a hot oven to crisp for an appetizer. (Cut in pieces).
* Save tuna, anchovy and sardine oils to use in salads.
* Chill meats in freezer for 30 minutes for easier slicing.
* Cooking ahead is not only wiser but good for the dish, time helps flavors mellow.
* Add a Tbsp. of cold water to simmering stock, more film will rise and decrease the time you need to skim.
* The use of instant flour for pie crusts produces a flakier crust.
* To prevent soggy pie crusts, cover pan with slightly beaten egg white.
* To prevent apples, peaches, etc. from turning brown after peeling, drop them in cold salt water before peeling.
* To make dainty tea sandwiches, use frozen sandwich loaf, spread filling while still frozen. Easier to cut with a sharp knife.
* To make water boil quicker in bottom of a double boiler. Add a pinch of salt.
* To restore lumpy powdered sugar, place in a blender. Seal in airtight container.
* To strain deep fat cooking oils. Place a coffee filter in a funnel used to pour back in the bottle.
* Bake potatoes in muffin tins for easier handling.
* When stuffing fowl, insert a heel of bread to close opening, eliminates trussing.
* When melting chocolate (one or two squares) use a large metal ladle and hold in the hot water to melt. Easier to handle.
* When wooden bowls become dull, rub them with a little mineral oil.
* To prevent curry from curdling, never boil sauce after coconut milk has been added, and salt just before serving.
* Soak Tofu in salted water a few minutes, will keep Tofu from crumbling.
* A little cooking oil added to the water will prevent vegetables, pasta and rice from cooking over.

* For flakier popcorn, sprinkle a little cold water on the kernels before popping.
* If a boiling egg becomes cracked, add a tsp. of salt to the water, that will seal the crack.
* To make onion juice: Cut a slice off the top and squeeze (as you would oranges) on a reamer.
* A slice of green papaya rubbed over roasts, steaks, etc. will help to tenderize the meat.
* When frying small fish, sprinkle a little coarse salt on the oil before frying, will make the fish more crispy.
* When cutting cooked meringue, butter both sides of the knife.
* If cheese becomes dry, soak it in buttermilk to become normal freshness.
* When frosting a cake, dust a little flour on cake, icing will not run.
* Use bay leaves to discourage weevils in staples. Place them on shelves where you keep flour, etc.
* Add a few slices of raw potatoes to soups, stews or vegetables while they are cooking if they are too salty.
* Fine bread crumbs used instead of flour to thickening make a sauce creamed mixture more delicate.
* Butter your measuring cup when recipes call for molasses or karo syrup. Will not lose any.
* Lemons will yield more juice if dropped in hot water a few minutes before squeezing.
* Fresh tomatoes, peeled, chopped fine and seasoned may be frozen in your ice trays. Serve in ice cold glasses or cups, topped with curried mayonnaise.
* Add a few drops of lemon to the butter in the skillet when sauteing mushrooms, vegetables, etc. Will be more glossy.
* Cream mixed with honey, substitute for syrup for pancakes, etc.
* Place crumbled pieces of newspaper in covered plastic containers to remove the odors.

Adele Davis.

* SOME EXTRA SPECIAL IDEAS *

Fruit dipping: (Do's and Don'ts).

* Do not attempt chocolate or glazing on a hot, humid day or rainy day. (Frostings and fondant will work).
* Be sure all fruit is dry on surfaces.
* Do not substitute butter or margarine for vegetable oil in chocolate dip. They have too much moisture.

* To dry very moist fruits (such as orange segments) place them in a sieve in a warm oven for 2—3 minutes.
* For chocolate dip, stir constantly, stirring tempers the dip. Keep water in the bottom of the double boiler just simmering. Too hot, it will turn grayish or dull when hardened.
* For drying, use waxed paper, foil or lightly greased cookie sheets.
* Do not store glazed or chocolate coated fruit in refrigerator, this causes sweating.
* For dipping, hold fruit by stem if possible, hold oranges, tangerines, apples, etc. by fingertips.
* For chocolate — German, sweet, semi-sweet or bitter chocolate are excellent for dipping.
* Packaged chocolate bits come in a wide range of flavors, mint, mocha, bitter sweet, semi-sweet, milk, white, and butterscotch. All may be used for substitute in recipes.

* FRUIT DIPPING SAUCES *

Chocolate coating:
4 oz. semi-sweet chocolate
1 Tbsp. vegetable oil

In top of a double boiler over simmering (not boiling) water, melt and stir chocolate with oil until satiny and smooth. Remove from heat and dip fruit, draining excess back into pot. Place on foil to harden. Note: Only drop fruit about 2/3 of the way up on fruit.

Fondant Coating:
1½ c. granulated sugar
¾ c. water
1 Tbsp. vegetable oil
6½ c. powdered sugar (sifted)

orange, lemon or rose water flavoring (optional)
1½ Tbsp. light corn syrup

Combine sugar, water and syrup in a saucepan and cook over medium heat until clear and syrup (about 10 minutes). Remove from heat and let stand for 3—4 minutes. While syrup is still hot, beat in powdered sugar (gradually) until smooth, shiny and lukewarm. If too thick add a tsp. of hot water. Tint and flavor as desired. Dip fruits into fondant, holding by stems or lightly fastened with a bamboo skewer. Drain excess back into pot. Cool and let harden on wax-paper or foil. Keep fondant workable by re-stirring over simmering water. Note: Fondant may be covered, refrigerated and used later. Simply reheat and stir to dipping consistency over simmering water in top of double boiler.

* FROSTED FRUITS *

1 egg white   1 c. sugar
2 Tbsp. water   2 lbs. grapes (sm. clusters)

Lightly heat egg white in a small bowl. Pour sugar into a shallow bowl. Wash and dry the grape clusters. Dip each cluster in the egg white, covering all surfaces and let excess drip back into dish. Set aside on wax paper until all grapes have been dipped. Surface will be tacky to the touch. Dip grapes in the sugar, shake off excess. Let dry on the cake rack for ½ hour. Repeat frosting process. Allow to dry thoroughly. May be made in advance and stored in the refrigerator for 1 day. Note: Other fruit may be used, frosted in the same way, such as strawberries, cherries, melon and other small whole fruit.

* CHOCOLATE ACORN AND LEAF DECORATIONS *

1 sq. bittersweet chocolate   1 Tbsp. butter
1 sq. semi-sweet chocolate   6 walnut halves (perfectly matched)
* camellia or lime leaves (washed — dried)

Melt both squares of chocolate in the top of a double boiler over medium heat. Let cool. Using chocolate as a filling. Using a small paint brush, coat back of each walnut, press two together and then dip one end in the chocolate to complete the "acorn" look. Dry on wax paper. For leaf decorations, use sm. paint brush and flow chocolate on the backs of the leaves. Place in freezer on waxed paper. When set, carefully pull away the leaf. Return the chocolate leaves to freezer to use when needed.   Adele Davis.

* HINTS FROM ANNETTE BUCHANAN *

1. Do not lift cover on cauliflower while cooking — it will stay white.
2. Add onion salt to lima beans while cooking, for a different flavor.
3. For more moist pork chops. Use knife to cut slashes into the chop, then use edge of a saucer to beat flour into slashes. Very tender after baking or frying.
4. Add a few Tbsp. frozen peas to your salad (defrosted — uncooked). Can use broccoli the same way.
5. Put sliced raw onions into a little beet juice and water. Add honey or sugar and lemon juice to taste.
6. Cut up a raw potato and add to your vegetable salad a few minutes before serving. Crisp and tasty.
7. When making stews, etc. add onion or celery salt, if you do not have the real thing.
8. Add leaf lettuce (pulled into small pieces) just before serving to your peas or green beans.
9. For cabbage slaw: Shred cabbage, add leaf lettuce (small pieces) celery seeds mix, then add frozen Guava juice (if too tart — add some white raisins.

INDEX

* CHAPTER THREE *
(Soups)

* CHAPTER FOUR *
(Salads)

* CHAPTER FIVE *
(Vegetables)

* CHAPTER SIX *
(Casseroles)

* CHAPTER EIGHT *
(Italian Cuisine)

* CHAPTER SEVEN *
(Quiche and Souffles)

* CHAPTER NINE *
(Island Recipes)

* CHAPTER TWELVE *
(Fish)

* CHAPTER THIRTEEN *
(Breads)

* CHAPTER SIXTEEN *
(Desserts)

* CHAPTER SEVENTEEN *
(Relishes and Jelly)

* CHAPTER EIGHTEEN *
(Hints)